ISBN 978-1-333-53938-2
PIBN 10517158

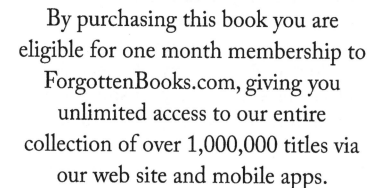

English
Français
Deutsche
Italiano
Español
Português

www.forgottenbooks.com

Mythology Photography **Fiction**
Fishing Christianity **Art** Cooking
Essays Buddhism Freemasonry
Medicine **Biology** Music **Ancient
Egypt** Evolution Carpentry Physics
Dance Geology **Mathematics** Fitness
Shakespeare **Folklore** Yoga Marketing
Confidence Immortality Biographies
Poetry **Psychology** Witchcraft
Electronics Chemistry History **Law**
Accounting **Philosophy** Anthropology
Alchemy Drama Quantum Mechanics
Atheism Sexual Health **Ancient History**
Entrepreneurship Languages Sport
Paleontology Needlework Islam
Metaphysics Investment Archaeology
Parenting Statistics Criminology
Motivational

THE

MESSIAH

TRANSLATED

FROM THE GERMAN OF

MR. KLOPSTOCK.

A NEW EDITION, IN ONE VOLUME.

BUNGAY:

PRINTED AND PUBLISHED BY C. BRIGHTLY.

1808.

TO THE PUBLIC.

MR. KLOPSTOCK has received from his *Messiah* the honour of being esteemed the *Milton of Germany*, and is considered as having completed what that favourite son of the British muse had left unfinished.

Mr. Klopstock's *Messiah* is formed upon an extensive and important plan, and includes the sufferings, death, and resurrection of Christ. It abounds in strength of invention, in grand imagery, and in a great variety of characters, some of which are entirely new, and all of them appear well supported. He particularly shines in his descriptions and speeches, in which there is sometimes an amazing sublimity, that seems impossible to be transfused, with such force and energy, into another language.

CONTENTS.

BOOK I.

The Messiah, withdrawing from the multitude, ascends the mount of Olives ; and, in a solemn prayer, repeats his promise to undertake the redemption of mankind. He sends Gabriel to present his petition to the Most High. The seraph proceeds through a path illuminated by suns, and, reaching heaven, hears a song of praise. Eloa meets Gabriel, and conducts him to the altar of the Messiah ; upon which he offers incense. The omnipotent Father at length opens with his thunders the holy sanctuary. A discourse between Eloa and Urim, on the prophetic visions seen in that sacred place. God speaks. Eloa proclaims his more particular orders. Gabriel is sent to the angels of the earth, and to those of the sun. He descends to the earth and finds the Messiah asleep, addresses him, and then proceeds to the guardian angels of the earth, who reside in its centre ; where he finds the souls of infants, which are there prepared for heaven. Thence he ascends to the sun ; where he sees the souls of the patriarchs, with Uriel, the angel of that orb.   1

BOOK II.

The souls of the patriarchs see the Messiah awake at break of day ; and the parents of the human race alternately salute him with a hymn. Raphael, John's guardian angel, tells Jesus that this disciple is viewing a demoniac among the sepulchres on the mount of Olives. He goes thither, heals the demoniac, and puts Satan to flight ; who, returning to hell, gives an account of what he knows of Jesus, and determines his death ; but is opposed by Abbadona. Adramelech speaking in support of Satan's determination, all hell approves it ; on which Satan and Adramelech return to the earth, to put their design in execution. Abbadona, following them at a distance, sees at the gate of hell, Abdiel, a seraph, once his friend, whom he addresses : but Abdiel taking no notice of him, he proceeds forwards ; bewails the forfeiture of his glory ; despairs of finding grace ; and after vainly endeavouring to destroy himself, descends on the earth. Satan and Adramelech also advance to the earth, and alight on the mount of Olives.   25

BOOK III.

The Messiah still continues among the sepulchres. Eloa descends from heaven, and counts his tears. The souls of the patriarchs send the seraph Zemia from the sun, to observe the words and actions of Jesus, while the darkness of the night prevents their seeing him. The Messiah sleeps for the last time, and while his disciples seek him about the mount of Olives, their guardian angels give Zemia their several characters. Satan appears in a dream to Judas Iscariot in the form of his deceased father. The Messiah, awaking, comes to his disciples, and mentions their approaching flight. Judas, who had concealed himself, overhears the Messiah, and feels his mind distracted by contending passions. 57

BOOK IV.

Caiaphas assembles the Sanhedrim, relates his dream, and proposes the death of Jesus. Philo, a Pharisee, supposes the dream a fiction, but joins, with great vehemence, in recommending the death of Christ. They are warmly opposed by Gamaliel and Nicodemus. Judas has a private conference with Caiaphas. The Messiah sends Peter and John to prepare the passover. Peter sees Mary the mother of Jesus, Lazarus, Mary his sister, Semida, and Cidli, coming in quest of Jesus. The pious love of Semida and Cidli. Mary proceeds in search of Jesus, who stops at the tomb of Joseph of Arimathea, near Golgotha. He proceeds to Jerusalem, and is met by Judas. Ithuriel, no longer able to continue that traitor's guardian angel, is made Peter's second angel. Jesus institutes the memorial of his death. Judas goes out. Jesus prays with his disciples, and returns to the mount of Olives.   83

BOOK V.

God descends toward the earth, and is met by the wise
men of the east, newly released from their bodies, one of
whom addresses the Most High. He is seen by the first
inhabitant of a guiltless world, who relates to his happy
offspring, what he has heard of the fall of man, and the
coming of the Messiah. God rests on Tabor. Jesus
prays ; when Adramelech, coming to insult him, is by a
look put to flight. The Messiah comes to his disciples,
whom he finds asleep. He then returns to pray. Abba-
dona comes, and after mistaking John for the Messiah,
finds him, and gives vent to his thoughts. The Messiah
again returns to his sleeping disciples, and a third time
prostrates himself in prayer, when God sends Eloa to
comfort him by singing a triumphant song on his future
glory. All the angels, except Eloa and Gabriel, with-
draw, and God himself returns to his celestial throne. 129

BOOK VI.

The Messiah is seized and bound. The assembled priests
are filled with consternation at being informed that the
guard were struck dead. Their fears are removed by
the arrival of a second and a third messenger. Jesus
being taken before Annas, Philo goes thither, and brings
him to Caiaphas. John expresses the agitations of his
mind. Portia, Pilate's wife, comes to see Jesus. The
speeches of Philo and Caiaphas, with the evidence
given by the suborned witnesses. Jesus, on declaring
that he is the Son of God, is condemned. Eloa and
Gabriel discourse on his sufferings. Portia, deeply af-
fected, withdraws, and prays to the chief of the gods.
Peter, in deep distress, tells John that he has denied his
Master, then leaves him, and deplores his guilt.   155

BOOK VII.

Eloa welcomes the returning morn with an hymn. The
Messiah is led to Pilate, and accused by Caiaphas and
Philo. The dreadful despair and death of Judas. Mary
comes, sees her divine Son standing before the Roman .

governor, and, filled with grief, applies to Portia, who comforts her, and tells her dream. The Messiah is sent to Herod, who, expecting to see him work a miracle, is disappointed : when Caiaphas, observing his dissatisfaction, accuses Jesus, who, after being treated with derision, is sent back to Pilate. That governor endeavours to save him ; but is prevailed on to release Barabbas, and condemn Jesus. He is scourged, arrayed in a purple robe, and crowned with thorns, and in this condition Pilate shews him to the people to excite their compassion, but finding all in vain, he delivers him to the priests, who cause him to be led to crucifixion.   179

BOOK VIII.

Eloa descends from the throne of God, and proclaims that now the Redeemer is led to death ; on which the angels of the earth form a circle round mount Calvary, also named Golgotha. Then, having consecrated that hill, he worships the Messiah. Gabriel conducts the souls of the fathers from the sun to the mount of Olives, and Adam addresses the earth. Satan and Adramelech, hovering in triumph, are put to flight by Eloa. Jesus is nailed to the cross. The thoughts of Adam. The conversion of one of the malefactors. Uriel places a planet before the sun, and then conducts to the earth the souls of all the future generations of mankind. Eve, seeing them coming, addresses them. Eloa ascends to heaven. Eve is affected at seeing Mary. Two angels of death fly round the cross. Eve addresses the Saviour, and the souls of the children yet unborn.   213

BOOK IX.

Eloa returns from the throne of God, and relates what he has seen. The behaviour of Peter, who joins Samma and a stranger, and afterwards successively meets Lebbeus, his brother Andrew, Joseph, and Nicodemus, and then returns to Golgotha, where he sees John, and the female friends of Jesus. A conversation between Abraham and Moses. They are joined by Isaac. Abraham and Isaac address the Messiah. A cherub conducts the souls of some pious heathens to the cross. Christ speaks to John and Mary. Abaddona, assuming the appearance of an angel of light, comes to the cross; but being known by Abdiel, flies. Obaddon conducts the soul of Judas to the cross, then gives him a distant view of heaven, and at length conveys him to hell. 237

BOOK X.

God looks down from his throne, while the Messiah casts his eyes on the sepulchre, and prays; then with a look fills Satan and Adramelech with terror. Many elevated souls are now given to the earth, one of whom delivers his thoughts of the dying Redeemer. A character of these souls. A conversation between Simeon and John the Baptist. Miriam and Deborah lament the dying Saviour in a hymn. Lazarus comforts Lebbeus. Uriel gives notice that the first of the angels of death is descending to the earth. The impression this makes on Enoch, Abel, Seth, David, Job, and more particularly on our first parents, who descend to the sepulchre of Jesus, and pray. The angel of death descends, addresses the Messiah, and makes known the divine command. The Messiah dies. 263

BOOK XI.

The glory of the Messiah soars from Calvary to the Holy of Holies in the temple. The earth shakes, and the veil of the temple is rent. Gabriel tells the souls of the patriarchs that they must retire to their graves. The Messiah leaves the temple, and raises the bodies of the saints. The resurrection of Adam, Eve, Abel, Seth, Enos, Mehaleel, Jared, Kenan, Lamech, Methuselah, Noah, Japheth, Shem, Abraham, Isaac, Sarah, Rebecca, Jacob, Rachel, Lea, Benjamin, Joseph, Melchisedec, Azariah, Mishael, Hananiah, Habakkuk, Isaiah, Daniel, Jeremiah, Amos, and Job. The converted thief on the cross dies. The resurrection of Moses, David, Asa, Jehoshaphat, Uzziah, Jotham, Josiah, Hezekiah, Jonathan, Gideon, Elisha, Deborah, Miriam, Ezekiel, Asnath, Jephtha's daughter, the mother and her seven martyred sons, Heman, Chalcol, Durda and Ethan, Anna the prophetess, Benoni, Simeon, and John the Baptist.

BOOK XII.

Joseph obtains Pilate's permission to bury the body of Jesus. He and Nicodemus, having wrapped it in spices, perform the interment, which is solemnized by choirs of risen saints and angels. The disciples, many of the seventy, and Mary, with some devout women, meet in John's house, and are joined by Joseph and Nicodemus; the latter bringing the crown of thorns, which he had taken from the body at its interment. The death of Mary the sister of Lazarus, who, with Nathaniel and Martha, sees her die: Lazarus returns to the company of believers at Jerusalem, and endeavours to comfort them. Salem, John's angel, strengthens him with a vision. 333

BOOK XIII.

Gabriel assembles the angels and the risen about the sepulchre, where they wait the Messiah's resurrection. The emotions of Cneus, the Roman officer on guard. The soul of Mary, Lazarus's sister, comes into the assembly of the saints. Obaddon, the angel of death, calls Satan and Adramelech, and orders them to leave the Dead Sea, and either to repair to Hell, or to the sepulchre. Satan determines on the latter, and Adramelech on the former, but after changing his resolution, dares not to put it in execution. The angel of death leaves it to Abbadona either to come to the sepulchre or not, as he pleases. The glory of the Messiah descends from heaven. Adam and Eve pay their adorations. The Messiah rises from the dead. The acclamations of the angels and the risen. The seven martyrs, the sons of Thirza, sing a hymn of triumph. Some of the saints come down to him from the clouds, and at last Abraham and Adam. The soul of a Pagan brought before him, on which he judges the soul and disappears. Gabriel orders Satan to fly to hell. Some of the soldiers of the guard, and also Cneus, enter the assembly of the priests. Philo puts an end to his life, and Obaddon meeting his soul in Gehenna, conducts it to hell. 357

BOOK XIV.

Jesus appears to Mary Magdalene, nine other devout women, and Peter. This they relate to the assembly. Thomas doubts the reality of his appearance. Jesus discovers himself to Matthias and Cleophas at Emmaus. Thomas goes into a sepulchre on the mount of Olives, where he laments his incredulity, and prays. One of the risen, whom he knows not, converses with him. Matthias and Cleophas return. Lebbeus likewise is not yet convinced. Jesus appears to the assembly.   393

BOOK XV.

Several of those who had been raised from the dead appear; particularly to Nepthoa, one of the children whom Christ had placed before the people; to Dilean; to Tabitha, whom Peter restored to life; to Cidli; to Stephen; to Barnabas, the son of Joses; to Portia; to Beor, blind from his birth, and brought to his sight by Jesus. Abraham and Moses would appear to Saul; but it is forbidden by Gabriel. Some of those raised from the dead also appear to Samma, Joel, and Elkanan, Simeon's brother, and to Boaz: to Mary, the mother of Jesus; to Cidli, Jairus's daughter, and to Semida, the young man of Nain   425

THE
MESSIAH.

BOOK I.

THE ARGUMENT.

The Messiah withdrawing from the multitude, ascends the mount of Olives; and, in a solemn prayer, repeats his promise to undertake the redemption of mankind. He sends Gabriel to present his petition to the Most High, The seraph proceeds through a path illuminated by suns; and, reaching heaven, hears a song of praise. Eloa meets Gabriel, and conducts him to the altar of the Messiah; upon which he offers incense. The omnipotent Father at length opens with his thunders the holy sanctuary. A discourse between Eloa and Urim, on the prophetic visions seen in that sacred place. God speaks. Eloa proclaims his more particular orders. Gabriel is sent to the angels of the earth, and to those of the sun. He descends to the earth and finds the Messiah asleep, addresses him, and then proceeds to the guardian angels of the earth, who reside in its centre; where he finds the souls of infants, which are there prepared for heaven. Thence he ascends to the sun; where he sees the souls of the patriarchs, with Uriel, the angel of that orb.

INSPIRED by thine immortality, rise my soul, and sing the honours of thy great Redeemer: honours obtained in hard adversity's rough school— obtained by suffering for the sins and woes of others, himself sinless. Recount, with humble gratitude, those guiltless sufferings, the bitter consequences of love to man's degenerate race. In vain Satan raged against the Lord's Anointed: in vain Judea set

B

herself against him ; he accomplished, in his humanity, the great work of our redemption.

O work divine, compleatly known only to the omnipresent God ! May the muse presume, with awful distance, to penetrate the secret veil that surrounds thee, and feeble man attempt thy praise ! Can a weak mortal explain thy heights, thy depths ? Assist me, O thou divine Spirit, before whom I suppliant bow ! lead and inspire me, that full of rapture—full of thee, I may penetrate the depths profound of heavenly wisdom ; contemplate the glorious plan of man's redemption, through the obscurity of ages past, and enlightened by thy revelations, in exalted strains, display the great Messiah's love to Adam's ruined race.

Rejoice, ye sons of earth, in the honour bestowed on man. He who was before all worlds : he who spake this visible creation into being, came down to earth as your Redeemer ! Hear and join my song, ye noble few, ye favorites of the amiable Mediator ; inspired by his example, with filial love, with devout piety, tread the path of life, and with humble hope, wait for the rich rewards of virtue, when crowned with glory and arrayed in righteousness, he again shall descend, and come to judge the world.

Near Jerusalem, once the city where God displayed his grace : once the nurse of the holy prophets, though she had now thrown away the crown of high election, and was become an altar of blood, shed by murderers ; the divine Messiah withdrew from the multitude, and sought retirement. He concealed himself from a people, who, though they had paid him honours, strewing his path with branches of palm, and shouting forth his praises in loud hosannahs, received him not with the singleness of heart that pleaseth the all-piercing eye of God.

Looking for a temporal king, arrayed in earthly glories, and the vain pageantry of mortals, they set at nought God's great Vicegerent: to see their Saviour under the form of a Carpenter's son, their eye was too dim, their faith too weak. From Heaven God himself had descended. A mighty voice proclaiming, I have glorified my Son, and will again glorify him, anounced the present Deity. But, blinded by their lusts, they despised his mission, and refused to accept him as the Messiah, whose coming was foretold by the holy prophets. From these, slow of heart, Jesus withdrew

On the side where the sun first gilds Jerusalem with his beams, rises a mountain, whose top the holy Mediator had often honoured with his presence, when during the solitary night, he, wakeful, spent his hours in fervent prayer. Thither he now went to offer up his supplications to the eternal Father, and once more to declare his full, his free resolution to sanctify the favoured sons of men. John, his beloved disciple, followed him as far as the sepulchres of the prophets, intending to watch the tedious night with his divine friend; but to the summit of the mountain Jesus ascended alone. Around him glimmered the distant light of sacrifices, flaming to appease the Deity, on high Moria ; where, ignorant of the salvation offered them by the divine Messenger of God, they shed the blood of bulls and of goats, as an atonement for the sins of the people. Vain oblations, without renovation of heart, and amendment of life! Here he rested, where the olive spreads her refreshing shade and gentle breezes hovered round. Gabriel the seraph sent from heaven to the Messiah, to execute his orders on earth, now stood between two perfume-breathing cedars, contemplating on the salvation of man, and the triumphs of eternity. Jesus passed

by. Gabriel knew the time of man's redemption
was at hand, and filled with holy rapture, thus ad-
dressed the Messiah ; wilt thou, O divine Saviour
of men !—wilt thou again spend the lonesome night
in prayer ? Or do thy weary limbs demand repose ?
Here the cedar stretches forth her verdant arms to
shelter thee ; and here the fragrant shrubs breathe
their sweets. Shall I of that soft moss prepare a
couch on which thou mayest rest thy sacred head ?
O thou compassionate Redeemer ! how art thou
spent ! To what sufferings art thou exposed from
thy fervent love to the human race ! Jesus answered
not ; but rewarded him with an expressive look of
divine complacency.

The Messiah now reached the summit of the
mountain. This was the confines of heaven ; for
God was there ; and there Jesus prayed. Earth
resounded, and his voice penetrated the gates of
the deep : but it was not the voice of threatenings
dreadfully uttered in storm and tempest : it was
the voice of the blessed Saviour, speaking peace on
earth, good-will towards man. Earth rejoiced as
at the renewal of her beauty ; her hills, overspread
with an amiable twilight, shouted forth their joy :
but only the eternal Father and himself knew the
whole of the divine petition. This alone the
tongue of man can utter.

Divine Father ! the day of salvation and heaven-
ly grace ;—of suffering for the salvation of man,
draws near. In the solitude of eternity, ere the
cherubim and seraphim were formed, were we to-
gether. Filled with divine love we saw man, ere
I, by thy power, formed him of the dust—We saw
him miserable ; the immortal become polluted dust,
stained with sin. Then saidst thou, frail man will
fall ; but who by suffering will renew the divine
image in his soul, and by dying save him from death

eternal ? I alone offered to perform the arduous task, and cried, lo l will do thy gracious will, O God ! Then was formed the glorious yet awful mystery of redemption. Eternal Father, thou knowest—it is also known to all the host of heaven, with what ardour I have longed to fulfil the divine work. O earth how wast thou, before my humiliation in this human form, my chosen, my beloved object ! and thou O Canaan, sacred land, how oft has my compassionate eye been cast on thee ! At length my heart fluttered with transports of joy at my being man, and that many righteous shall flock to me, and all generations through me be able to obtain salvation. Here I lie, O holy Father ! and still united to mankind, pour out my prayers before thee ; but soon shall I, filled with amazement, be slain by thy justice. Already I hear thee, O thou Judge of the earth—already do I hear thee far dis-

fore me. Already I sink before thee in the lowly dust, covered with the sweat of death. Behold, O my Father ! here am I ready to suffer for man —to die that man may live.—Thine anger, thy justice will I support ! and become a willing sacrifice for the sins of men. Yet still am I free : still might I pray to thee, to send me myriads of celestial spirits to conduct me back in triumph to thy sacred throne : but I will suffer what no seraph can—what no meditative cherub can conceive will I suffer.—This agonizing death, with all its terrors, will I, O Eternal, suffer ! Farther he said : I lift my head to the heavens, and spread mine hands in the clouds, and swear, that I will redeem mankind.

Thus spake the holy Jesus, and arose. In his countenance shone sublimity, filial love, and resignation. The Eternal Father looking with delight and complacency on his divine Son, answered, I

raise my head above the highest heavens, and
stretch my hand through the immensity of space,
and swear to thee, my beloved Son, that I will for-
give the sins of the repentant children of men.

While the Eternal thus spake, all nature shook;
souls just emerging from non-existence, which had
not yet begun to think, trembled, and first caught
sensation. Unusual awe overwhelmed the heart of
the seraph; he was agitated like the earth, when
she expects an approaching tempest. The apostate
spirits, in the fiery deep, shook on their burning
thrones, in fearful expectation of encreasing tor-
ment. They sunk lower in the bottomless pit, and
on each fell an huge mass of flaming sulphur. All
hell resounded with the execrations of these malig-
nants, against God and his anointed, the holy Jesus.

The Messiah still continued standing before the
Eternal Father. At a distance Gabriel lay on his face
in prostrate adoration, filled with new and rapturous
contemplations. During the innumerable ages of
his existence, never had he felt ideas and sensations
so affecting and sublime. The infinite love and
condescension of the almighty Father, the grace and
compassion of the great Redeemer, now opened on
his astonished mind. The seraph arose—he stood
amazed—he prayed.—Joy inexpressible thrilled
through his whole frame. From him issued such
refulgent light and spendor, that the earth melted
under his feet: when the divine Mediator, seeing
the summit of the mountain illuminated by his
brightness, said, O Gabriel, veil thy lustre, and re-
member that thou ministerest to me on earth. Haste
now to lay this my request before my Father, that
the noblest of the human race the blessed patriarchs
and prophets, with all the celestial spirits, may be-
hold that fulness of time for which they had so ar-
dently longed. There thou needest not shrowd thy

glory, since thou wilt not appear as the messenger of the Messiah.

Silent the seraph, with heavenly grace and lustre, ascended. Jesus followed him with his eyes, tracing his rapid course to the confines of heaven. Now the Father and the Son entered on discourses myste-rious and profound : obscure even to the immortals : discourses of things which, in future ages, should display the love of God to man.

The seraph entered the borders of the celestial world, whose whole extent is surrounded with suns, which, as an ethereal curtain of interwoven light, extend their lustre around heaven. No dark planet approaches the refulgent blaze. Clouded nature flies swiftly by, far distant. There the terrestrial orbs seem to roll minute and imperceptible, as the dust, the habitation of worms, is seen to rise from under the foot of the traveller. Around heaven are a thousand paths of extent immeasurable, also bor-dered by suns.

Along the ethereal way that leads from heaven to earth, when first created, constant flowed, from a source celestial, down to Eden's happy groves, a lucid stream, through which God and his angels descended, when they deigned to hold blest inter-course with man. But ah ! too soon the lucid stream rolled back to its source : for man, by sin polluted, had turned a rebel to his God. The im-mortals then no longer visibly appeared in all their radiant lustre : they withdrew from a land defaced by guilt, and made a prey to death. They left the silent hill where yet remained the vestiges of the Eternal's presence : the whispering groves, honour-ed by the appearance of the Most High : the sacred peaceful vales, once with pleasure frequented by the youth of heaven : the umbrageous bowers, where the human heart first overflowed with sweet sensations and ecstatic, grateful rapture ; and where the first man wept for joy that he was thus to live forever. These, these the blest spirits left. Cursed was the earth ; it became the general tomb of its once immortal inhabitants. But when hereafter, purified by fire, it shall triumphant rise from its ashes, renewed in beauty, and God, by his omnipotent voice, shall unite the terrestrial orbs to the heaven of heavens, the world shall be one Paradise. Then shall the ethereal stream of heavenly light again roll from its celestial source, and with resplendent brightness flow to a new Eden. Then shall assemblies of radiant spirits, coming to the earth, frequent its lucid banks, and seek sweet communion with the new immortals.

2. Up this sacred way Gabriel now ascended, and soon approached heaven, the peculiar residence of the divine glory.

3. In the centre of the assemblage of suns, heaven rises into an immense dome. The Origin of worlds, the Architype of all that is fair and lovely, diffuses beauty, in flowing streams, through the infinite expanse. The harmonic choirs, borne on the wings of the wind, to the borders of the sunny arch, chant his praise, joining the melody of their golden harps, while he who looks with complacency and delight on all his works, smiles benignant, at the effusions of their gratitude and love.

O thou who teachest my tongue to utter celestial strains ! associate of angels ! prophetess of God ! instruct me to rehearse the song then sung by the sons of heaven.

Hail sacred land, where the Most High displays his majesty and grace ! Here our dazzled eyes behold him unveiled and shiding in unclouded light, diffusing joy and rapture through all the blessed. How infinite art thou in all thy perfections, O Jo-hovah! Our songs, poured forth with grateful fervor, and all the powers of harmony, in vain attempt to extol thine excellence. Lost in thine immensity, in feeble strains we strive to express thy glory. Thou alone art perfect—thou alone, from thine essential excellence, wert ever sublimely happy: nor can our homage add to thine underived felicity. Yet, O Most Gracious! prompted by thine overflowing goodness, thou hast created beings to taste thy love, and share thy bliss! Thou heaven wast first created, then us, heaven's inhabitants. Far wast thou then from thy birth, thou young terrestrial globe; thou sun, and thou, O moon, the favoured earth's attendants!

First born of the material creation, what was thine appearance, when, after an eternity of ages, God descended and created thee the mansion of his glory? Thine immense circle called to existence was stretched out and assumed its glorious form. The creative voice went forth, with the first tumult of the crystalline seas. Their banks heard thy voice and rose like terrestrial worlds. Then big with thought, didst thou, Creator omnipotent, sit in solitude on thy new exalted throne! Oh hail—hail in joyful transports the thoughtful Deity!—Then, then were ye created, ye angels, ye cherubim, and seraphim, incorporeal beings, sublime in thought, and quick to perceive, adoring the wonders of your great Creator! Hallelujah, a joyful hallelujah we will incessantly sing to the First of Beings! At thy voice solitude fled : at thy word the angelic spirits arose to life and bliss. Hallelujah.

During the hymn the Mediator's refulgent messenger stood on one of the suns nearest heaven. The Eternal Father rewarded the celestial choir with a look of benignity, and then beheld the seraph. He also attracted the eyes of all the heavenly host,

and bowing low in awful adoration, the first of
the seraphs went to conduct him in solemn state to
the sacred presence. His name with God is the
Chosen; but by the heavenly host he is called Eloa.
This is the fairest spirit of heaven: his thoughts
are more sublime than the enraptured soul of man
can conceive: his looks more lovely than the vernal
morn, brighter than the stars, when with youthful
splendor they flew from the Creator's forming hand
to run their courses. At his creation the Eternal
reduced the resplendent crimson of the morning
into an ethereal body, and the radiant clouds of
heaven instantly gathered round him. God then
with out-stretched arm raised him from them, and
blessing him, said, behold thy Creator! The seraph
stood before him, and seeing the Eternal, viewed
him with rapture, till he sunk overpowered by the
refulgent brightness of the divine countenance. At
length he uttered the new and elevated sensations of
his heavenly mind: but worlds shall perish, a new
system be raised from the dust, and ages be lost in
eternity, before the most axalted Christian shall feel
sensations so sublime.

Eloa, who flew with glowing beams, and in all
his lustre, to conduct Gabriel to the altar of the
Mediator, knew him far distant, and melted into
pleasing rapture at the sight of one with whom he
had before taken a circuit through all the wide
creation of God, visiting each world with its inhabi-
tants, and performing actions not to be imitated by
the most perfect of the race of man. Now to each
other known, they, with cordial looks of love and
open arms, fly swift into each other's embrace, where
they remain tremulous with joy. Thus tremble
two virtuous brothers, who, after braving death for
their country, and performing immortal deeds, meet,
full of heroic ardour, and embrace before their still

greater father. God from afar beheld and blessed them. They moved towards the celestial throne, friendship giving a brighter glow to their heavenly lustre, while they approached the sanctuary of God. Near the seat of the divine splendor, on a celestial mount rests the night of the Most Holy. A brilliant light encompasses the divine mysteries; but the inside is concealed by a sacred gloom from the eyes of angels; except when God himself by his majestic thunder, opens the veil of darkness, and then the celestial spectators behold and adore.

At the entrance of the sanctuary, the altar of the Messiah, like the mount of God, instantly stood unclouded. Thither Gabriel went in festal splendor, carrying two golden censers: then stood wrapt in thought. Eloa, who was with him, called forth from his harp divine harmony to prepare the offering seraph for supplications fervent and sublime. The flowing melody filled Gabriel with an heavenly transport and swelled his labouring thoughts to ecstacy. Thus the ocean rises, when the voice of the Lord moves over it with mighty winds. The messenger of the Messiah then raised his eyes to God, and offered up his petitions. The Eternal heard his prayer, and with him all the celestial host. The Supreme himself caused a descending flame to light the incense. Fumes of fragrance then arising, ascended to God as from the earth resplendent clouds rise towards heaven.

God had fixed his all-seeing eyes on this terrestrial globe, where the Redeemer, transported with love to man, was still engaged in prayer: but now the face of the Almighty, beaming with grace and mercy, filled all heaven with effulgent glory. With silent rapture the exalted spirits adoring, wait the voice of the Lord. The celestial cedars no longer wave: the crystalline ocean lies silent within its

lofty shores : the breathing winds, with expanded
wings, stop within the brazen mountains. While
all listened expecting the words of the Eternal,
thunder suddenly rolling from the sanctuary, pro-
claimed the approaching answer. When it ceased
the veil which covered the Most High opened to
prepare the expecting heavens. Then to the mighty
Eloa, the cherub Urim, wrapt in divine contempla-
tions, said what, O Eloa, dost thou see ! At this
the seraph arose, and advancing with solemn pace,
cried, I see on those golden pillars the mysterious
tables of prescience. There the book of life is
opened by the breath of mighty winds. That of
the general judgment now opens dreadful, like the
waving banners of hostile seraphs, and threatens de-
struction to all the workers of iniquity. The Al-
mighty draws back the veil : I see, Urim, the sacred
candlesticks glimmer through a silver cloud, that
resembles the morning dew descending on the hills.
Thus in prophetic vision shine the Christians, the
future heirs of salvation. I see thousands and ten
thousands of those golden candlesticks, typical of
the churches. O Urim ! count the sacred number.
Urim replied, we can number the worlds, we can
count the radiant seats of the angels, and the man-
sions of the blessed ; but not the effects of the great
redemption, nor the boundless mercies of the Most
High. I now see, returned Eloa, the judgment
seat of Christ. How tremendous art thou, O
Judge of the earth, seated on high, and rising on
tempestuous clouds, amidst the bursts of rolling
thunder ; radiant with mercy, and armed for de-
struction !

Thus conversed Eloa and Urim on these myste-
rious visions. Seven times had the thunder opened
the sacred darkness, when the awful voice of the
Eternal slowly descended.

·   I am love. Such was I before the existence of
my creatures—before I formed the worlds : and
now I am love in my conduct towards man ; in the
accomplishment of the great work of redemption,
by my sending my beloved Son to die for sinners.
Did not my almighty arm support you, ye exalted,
but finite beings, the tremendous sight of his awe-
ful death, would put a period to your existence.

· The Eternal was silent. Struck with deep amaze-
ment, the ethereal spirits with folded hands stood
before him.   Now making a sign to Eloa, that
seraph. with humility in his look, viewed the face
of heaven's gracious King, and instantly reading
                                                    lestial
audience, and said, Behold the Eternal, ye righte-
ous sons of heaven, and know his counsels. Next
to his dear Son, were ye most beloved, for whom he
laid the gracious plan of redemption. That ye have
ardently longed to see the day of salvation, and to
behold the great Messiah triumph over the powers
of hell, God is your witness.   Blessed be ye his
offspring. Shout for joy that ye see the glory of
his face, who is the source of being, the Eternal
and Unchangeable, whose mercy endureth for ever.
He whom no creature can conceive, condescends to
term you his children.   For your sake alone, this
messenger of peace is sent by his beloved Son, to
the celestial altars.   Rejoice ye inhabitants of the
earth, we will join with you in admiring the won-
ders of your redemption, which we shall behold with
clearer light, with purer devotion, and more ecstatic
rapture, while we give our pity to you, ye devout
and humble friends of the Redeemer, who are still
liable to darkness and error.. But while his cruel, his
obdurate persecutors have their names erased from
the book of life, to you, ye faithful, your Saviour
sends a divine light.   Ye shall then no longer, with

weeping eyes, behold his sacred blood; but joyful
shall see it stream for you, flowing into eternal life.
Then, solaced in the bosom of peace, ye triumphant,
shall celebrate the festival of everlasting repose.
Ye souls now escaped from the snares of life, and
raised to glory, begin the eternal jubilee, which
shall last when time shall be no more. The righte-
ous children of the earth shall, generation after
generation, be gathered to you, and join your blessed
assemblies, till at last, at the consummation of all
things, they and you shall at the general judgment,
be clothed with new and immortal bodies, and
enter into more perfect felicity. Meanwhile, ye
exalted angels of the throne, inform the guardians
of God's immense creation, that they prepare to
celebrate the chosen day; and ye saints of the hu-
man race—ye progenitors of the Messiah, to you is
also imparted the joy which God alone feels entire,
mingled with the sensations of the Deity. Ye im-
mortal souls arise and hasten to the sun that illumines
the orb of redemption: there shall ye distant see
the first sufferings of the great Redeemer. Descend
by that luminous path, whence ye shall behold the
whole extent of nature, rising to your view in renew-
ed beauty. Hear it, O heavens! the great Jehovah
will establish a day of sacred rest, a second sab-
bath, more solemn than that when ye spiritual in-
telligences, and ye seraphic spirits, with joyful
acclamations celebrated the completion of the great
work of creation. New born nature then smiled
with ravishing beauty. The morning stars sang
together, and joined with you, ye angels, in paying
homage to the great Creator. Now the Messiah,
the effluence of his glory, will accomplish a work
of grace and mercy still more resplendent. Thus
rapt in astonishment, Eloa spake. Silent the
heavenly host looked up to the santuary: when, at

a sign from God, the messenger of the Messiah ascended to the lofty throne, and there received secret orders to be delivered to Uriel, and the guardians of the earth, concerning the miracles to be performed at the death of Christ.

In the mean time the cherubim had descended from their seats. Gabriel followed, and approaching the altar of the earth, distant heard from the high-bending arch of heaven, sighs and ejaculations in plaintive accents breathed for the salvation of man : above all he distinguished those uttered by the first of the human race.

This is the altar of which the prophet of the new covenant saw the celestial model on the shore of Patmos, where he heard the voices of the mar-tyrs, in mournful sounds, ascend, while, with an-gelic tears, they lamented that the Judge so long delayed the day of vengeance.

The seraph having descended to the altar of the earth, Adam, filled with eager expectation, hasted towards him, not unseen. A lucid ethereal body was the radiant mansion of his blessed spirit, and his form as lovely as the bright image in the Creator's mind, when meditating on the form of man in the blooming fields of Paradise. Adam approached with an amiable smile, that diffused over his face an air of sweetest dignity, and thus uttered his impassioned accents ; Hail happy seraph ! mes-senger of peace ! at the voice of thy blessed em-bassy, which resounded from afar, my soul arose joyful. Thou, dear Messiah, may I too, like this seraph, behold thee in thy sacred manly beauty, in the garb of compassion in which thou hast consent-ed to reconcile my fallen offspring. Lead me, O seraph, to the steps imprinted by the feet of my Redeemer, the friend of all my race. At due distance will I attend him. Shew me where he

pours out his soul in fervent prayer for man. Ah,
may the first of sinners presume to behold him,
through his gushing tears of joy! O earth, my
native land! I was once thy first inhabitant! On
thee I cast a tender look: thy fields, blasted by
the thunder of the curse, would, in the company of
the divine Messiah, now vested in a mortal body,
like that I left in the dust, be more delightful,
than, O Paradise! thy flowery plains, copyed from
the celestial meads.

Thy desire, first of men, answered the seraphs,
with friendly voice, I will mention to the Mediator.
If it be his pleasure, he himself will intimate to
thee, that thou shalt see him as he is, with all his
glories shrouded by his humiliation.

Now the angelic spirits leaving heaven, swiftly
distributed themselves among all the various worlds,
formed by the hand of the Omnipotent. To the
earth Gabriel descended alone; and on his ap-
proach, the neighbouring stars saluting it, began to
shed upon it their first rays. Instantly resounded,
from every quarter, new names given to the terra-
queous globe, which they termed, the favorite of
heaven, the place where God a second time dis-
plays his glory, the lasting witness of the mercy
and compassion of the great Messiah. Thus an-
gelic voices from each orb resounded through the
wide expanse. Gabriel heard them, while with
speedy flight he descended to the earth.

Here the unruffled veil of darkness covered the
mountains; cool and silent repose reigned in the
lowly vales. With eager looks Gabriel entered the
gloom, seeking the Messiah. Him he found in a
lonely valley, winding between the aspiring summits
of Olivet's sacred mount. Overcome with thoughts
profound, the blessed Saviour was fallen asleep,
but his ever-active mind was still employed in great

ideas of love to man. The bare rock was the couch of the mighty Prince of Peace. Placid love, a divine smile, benignity and grace inexpressible, appeared in his face, while a tear of soft compassion gently stole down his cheek ; and though the lineaments of his expressive countenance wanted the glow of life and active spirit, they still spoke his tender friendship for mankind. Gabriel beholding his sweet aërial slumbers, stood gazing on him in fixed attention. Thus a travelling seraph views the blooming earth when clad in vernal beauty, dew drops glittering hang on every flower, and Hesperus lights his evening lamp, to guide the pensive sage to groves where sacred meditation and peaceful rapture dwell.

After long and silent contemplation, Gabriel thus spake ; O thou whose piercing veiw extends to the heavens, thou who hearest me amidst the slumbers of thine earthly frame, with assiduous care have I executed all thy commands. While thus employed, the first of men expressed with longing ardour, his desire to see thy face. Now I obey thy great Father's will, and hasten hence to glorify thy redeeming love. Meanwhile be silent

only in soft and tremulous murmurs rise. Ye hovering clouds shed from your bosoms balmy rest. Wave not ye cedars, and ye palms be still ; for your Creator sleeps.

ed his care. Then flew to the assembly of the guardians of the earth, who, in subordination to the great Supreme, govern this terrestrial globe, guiding the events of providence. To these was he to express the desire of the blessed spirits, the approaching reconciliation, and the second sabbath.

' O thou who, next to Gabriel presidedst in the great affair of redemption ! guardian spirit of the earth, the mother of the children of immortality, through revolving centuries, art sent to the regions on high, while the ruins of the habitation of the inextinguishable soul are interred under eminences, on which the foot of the passenger never rests. Thou of this once glorious earth the protector, O seraph Eloa ! forgive thy future friend, for making known to mortals, as taught by Sion's muse, thy secret residence, since Eden's creation. If, filled with solitary delight, he is rapt in meditation deep, and the bright round of silent ecstacy : if he has listened to the voice of angels, and his enraptured soul has heard discourses celestial, oh hear ! when bold and sublime, like the youth of heaven, he sings not the mouldering ruins of the world ; but leads man, devoted to death, and rising to immortality, to the assembly of the saints, to the counsel of the guardian angels.

In the silent recess of the unregarded north pole, reign Solitude and eternal Night, whence incessantly flow darkness and clouds, like an overwhelming sea. Thus, at the call of Moses, a black gloom once, O Nile ! concealed thy seven channels, and hid thy everlasting pyramids, the tombs of kings. Never yet has a being whose eye is bounded by the visible horizon, seen these desert tracts, involved in nocturnal stillness, where the human voice was never heard, and where there will be no resurrection ! but dedicated to musings deep, and refined speculations, the seraphim render them glorious, when passing over the mountains sweetly absorbed, in a prophetic calm, they behold the future felicity of mankind. In the centre of these

tracts opens the angelic gate, through which the
guardian spirits descend into their sanctuary.

As in hardy winter, after days dark and gloomy,
the sun rises bright over the snowy mountains,
when clouds and night fly before his all-enlivened
rays, while the icy plains, and hoary frosts, with
brilliant whiteness glitter in his beams : thus Ga-
briel advanced, brightening the dusky eminences
over which he flew. Soon had his foot reached
the sacred gate, which opened spontaneous, sound-
ing like the rustling wings of cherubim, and on
his entrance, closed. The seraph now penetrated
into the depths of the earth, where old ocean slowly
rolls his waves to desart and uninhabited coasts,
while mighty rivers, the sons of ocean, deep re-
sounding, lash the hollow shores. Gabriel still
advancing, his sacred residence soon appeared be-
fore him. The gate, composed of a cloud, gave
way at his approach, and then glowing with celes-
tial brightness, vanished. Darkness rolling under
his rapid feet, fled as he advanced : while far be-
hind, waving flames marked his path. And now
the beauteous seraph entered the angelic assembly.

Where, far from us, the earth turns on its centre,
is a vast concave filled with a pure ether, in the
midst of which is a sun which swims in a luminous
fluid. From this source, life and warmth ascend
into the veins of the earth. The superior orb of
day, jointly with this his never failing assistant,
forms the gay flowery spring ; the fervid summer,
loaded with bending branches, and thee, O Autumn !
rich in golden fruit, and smiling on the mountains
clothed with purple vineyards. But never did this
beneficent star rise or set. Round it in fleecy
clouds distilling dew smiles an eternal morn. He
who fills the heavens and the earth with his pre-
sence, in these clouds makes known his thoughts to

the admiring angels, displaying before them the
wonders of providence. Thus God here reveals
his grace, when after prolific showers, the rainbow
appears in a distant falling cloud, and to thee, O
Earth! declares the divine covenant.

On this sun Gabriel alighted. Around him
assembled the guardians of monarchies, the angels
of war and death, who in the labyrinth of destiny,
convey to the divine hand the directing thread, by
which the Almighty secretly over-rules the actions
of kings, when they, inflated with pride, triumph
in their own strength, and consider their subjects as
made only to administer to their lust and ambition.
There were likewise the guardians of the virtuous,
who conduct the pensive sage, when fond of priva-
cy, he avoids all human schemes of earthly gran-
deur, in silence opening to his mind the books of
endless futurity. These also unseen, add wings to
the inspiring thoughts of the enraptured Christian,
and join their aid when a devout assembly pour
forth their souls in hymns of praise to the great
Redeemer. When the soul of the just departed
Christian, hovering over its late body, sees the
pale and ghastly visage, and all the dismal marks
of the triumph of death over vanquished nature,
then this blessed band, with chearful countenance,
receive him, saying, Beloved soul! the time will
come when we shall gather together all these ruins
of mortality; when the tabernacles of clay, thus
disfigured by the ruthless hand of death, shall, at
the morning of the resurrection, awake from a new
creation. Come then, thou future citizen of hea-
ven, what a delightful prospect lays before thee!
O divine soul! the chief of victors, who has con-
quered death, and triumphed over the grave, waits
to receive thee!

Round the seraph also flocked the souls of those

tender infants who had just entered into life ; but fled weeping with the piteous cries of childhood. Their timid eyes had viewed with astonishment the objects around them, when, not daring to stay on the great theatre, yet unopened to their view, their guardian angels conduct them thence, and animating them with rapturous songs, joined to the harmony of the reviving harp, they in soft and melodious strains tell them, from whence they received their origin ; of the purity of the human soul, when proceeding out of the hands of the All-perfect Spirit ! and with what juvenile lustre the new created suns with their attendant worlds, appeared before the great Creator. The progenitors of the human race, say they, expect you ; a glorious view of him who has crowned you with mercy, awaits you at the eternal throne. Thus do they instruct their worthy disciples in that sublime wisdom, the fleeting shadows of which erring mortals vainly pursue. The souls of the infants now quitting their lucid bowers, joined their faithful guardians, who, encompassing the divine messenger, he made known to the assembled spirits, the orders of the Most High concerning the Messiah. Transported they listened and when he ceased to speak, stood rapt in deep contemplation.

An amiable pair named Benjamin and Jedida, two infant souls in tender friendship joined, at length embracing, thus discoursed, Is it not Jesus, O Jedida ! of whom the seraph spoke ? Ah ! well do I remember, when we were on earth, the ardour with which he folded us in his arms ! How tenderly he pressed us to his throbbing heart ! A tear of benignity and grace fell on his cheek—I kissed it away—I see it still—ever shall I see it. I too remember, answered Jedida, that holding me in his arms, he said to our mothers, who were standing by, resemble these little children, or ye cannot enter into my kingdom. This—this, returned Benjamin, is the Redeemer! the Saviour! our Gracious Friend! the Dispenser of happiness to the human race!

Thus they affectionately conversed, while Gabriel, now bent on a new embassy, ascended. A stream of light rolling down, flowed as he went, with magnificent splendor, from the feet of the immortal. Thus the inhabitants of the moon behold the day of this terraqueous globe illuminate their nights, when dew-dropping clouds descend on the top of their mountains. Gabriel thus ascended into the more exalted atmosphere, amidst the acclamations of rejoicing angels, and of the souls who had left their bodies. Like the arrow flying from the silver bow, and winged for victory, he shot along by the stars and hasted to the sun. Then alighting at Uriel's residence, found on one of the pinnacles of that noble structure, the souls of the fathers, whose fixed looks followed the beams that dispense the new-born day to the land of Canaan. Among these was Adam, the first of men, who appeared with distinguished dignity, standing sublimely pensive. Gabriel and Uriel joined him, and conversing with him on the salvation of man, stood waiting for the sight of the mount of Olives.

THE END OF THE FIRST BOOK.

THE

MESSIAH.

BOOK. II.

THE ARGUMENT.

The souls of the patriarchs see the Messiah awake at break of day ; and the parents of the human race alternately salute him with a hymn. Raphael, John's guardian angel, tells Jesus that this disciple is viewing a demoniac among the sepulchres on the mount of Olives. He goes thither, heals the demoniac, and puts Satan to flight ; who returning to hell gives an account of what he knows of Jesus, and determines his death : but is opposed by Abbadona. Adramelech speaking in support of Satan's determination, all hell approves it ; on which Satan and Adramelech return to the earth, to put their design in execution. Abbadona following them at a distance, sees at the gate of hell, Abdiel, a seraph, once his friend, whom he addresses : but Abdiel taking no notice of him, he proceeds forwards ; bewails the forfeiture of his glory ; despairs of finding grace, and after vainly endeavouring to destroy himself, descends on the earth. Satan and Adramelech also advance to the earth, and alight on the mount of Olives.

THE morn now descending over the woods of waving cedars, Jesus arose. The spirits of the patriarchs saw him with joy from their solar mansion. Among these were the parents of the human race arrayed in heavenly beauty, who thus alternate sang.

Adam began. Fairest of days, said he, of all the stores of time, most sacred ! At thy return, the souls of men, the cherubim and seraphim shall hail thy rising and setting light. Whether descending to the earth, or whether the bright spirits of heaven diffuse thy radiance through the firmament, or thou advancest by the throne of God, thee in festive pomp will we celebrate with hallelujahs jubilant. Thee will we bless with joyful gratulations, O day, in which our ravished eyes first behold the great Messiah arrayed in humility. How beautiful is his form ! how lovely ! how divine !

Eve rejoined, blessed and holy art thou who broughtest him forth—more blessed than Eve, the mother of men. Though innumerable my offspring, I am also the mother of innumerable sinners : but thou, fair daughter of earth ! hast brought forth only one, the great Emanuel, the righteous, the spotless, the divine Messiah ! With wandering eye I view my beloved earth : but thee, O paradise ! I no longer behold : thou wert swept away by the waters of the overwhelming deluge. Thy lofty umbrageous cedars which God himself had planted ; thy tranquil bowers, the mansion of the young virtues, no storm, no thunder, no angel of death has spared. Thou Bethlehem, where Mary brought him forth, where, with maternal ecstasy, she first pressed him to her bosom, be now my Eden. Thou well of David, be the clear spring, where I, just coming from my divine Maker's hand, first saw myself ; and thou homely cottage, where he first wept, be thou to me the bower of primeval innocence. O that I, in Eden, had borne thee ! O that I, just after my fatal transgression, had brought thee forth ! then would I have gone to my Judge, where the earth opened before him, as if to form my grave ; where the rustling of the tree of knowledge produced a dreadful sound ; where his thunders announced the sentence of the curse : where trembling I stood, and fainted with terror. There would I have gone to him. Thee, weeping, would I have embraced, and pressing thee to my fluttering heart, would have cried, forgive me, O my God! and no longer be incensed against me. I have borne the Saviour, the Redeemer, the Prince of Peace.

The first of men then resumed, holy art thou, adorable and eternal, O thou First Cause! thou Prime Source of being, of mercy, of felicity! thou Father of the divine, the holy Jesus, whom thou, all-gracious, hast chosen to redeem mankind, my issue! Their alienation from thee I have ever deplored: Thou, O God! hast beheld my tears— By you, ye seraphim, have they been seen and numbered.—Ye spirits of the dead, the blessed souls of my sleeping descendants, have heard me sigh for the promised happiness of our offspring. But thy divine grace, thy condescending mercy and love to man, changes my paternal concern into rapturous joy.

And now, all gracious Redeemer! Son most dear! returned Eve; while thou bearest our image, the image of mortal man, thee let us implore, to complete the offering made for us. For this thou hast descended from the celestial abodes—for this thou hast veiled thy glories, and art clothed in flesh. O thou Creator and Judge! renew the earth, thine, and our native land, then quick return to heaven; while we, O thou divine, thou spotless Redeemer! hail thy mercy and thy love!

Through the domes of the angelic palace resounded the voice of these fervent souls. The Messiah heard them in his deep recess, as in a sacred solitude, the holy prophet rapt in contemplation, bears, in soft whispers, the voice of the Eternal. Jesus now began to descend from the

top of Olivet. In the midst of the mount, a clus-
ter of palm trees growing on an eminence, reared
their waving heads into the light flimsy clouds of
hovering morning vapours. Under these palms
the Messiah perceived Raphael, John's guardian
angel, absorbed in meditations deep and awful,
while gentle breezes flowing from him, brought
to the Mediator, sounds which none but he could
hear.

With gracious voice, the Messiah spake. Ra-
phael draw near, said he, and invisibly walk by
my side. How hast thou watched the pure soul of
John ? Did his thoughts, O Raphael! resemble
thine ? I watched him, O holy Mediator! an-
swered the seraph, with the utmost care. Holy
dreams hovered round his transported soul. O that
thou hadst seen him, when sleeping, he beheld
thee ! A smile of complacency and love over-
spread his face. Thy seraph also beheld Adam,
when sleeping in the blooming fields of Eden, the
lovely form of Eve just risen into existence, was
presented by his divine Maker to his mind ; but the
pleasure diffused over his countenance, was ex-
ceeded by the pleasing rapture visible in the face
of thy holy disciple. He is now among the gloomy
mansions of death, lamenting over a demoniac,
who, pale as the ghastly corpse, lies stretched in
the dust of the dead. O thou most Gracious !
Wilt thou not see him ? wilt thou not behold the
gentle youth, overcome by sympathising distress,
his heart swelled by the painful feelings of huma-
nity, and his whole frame trembling with horror ?
I myself was so struck at the sight, that the tear
of sorrow quivered in my eye, and I hastily with-
drew.

Raphael ceased. Indignation sparkled in the
eyes of the Mediator, and, raising them up to hea-

ven, he cried, O Father omnipotent . hear me now I call upon thee.   May the enemy of mankind feel the effects of thy justice ; that heaven may rejoice at seeing hell involved in confusion, shame, and terror !

Jesus now drew near to the sepulchres hewn in the cliffs of the rock, where thick and gloomy woods guarded the entrance from the view of the hasty traveller.   Here the morning dawn lowered in chilly coolness, and the sun faintly shot his beams among the tombs.   Samma, thus was the demoniac called, now lay in a swoon by the sepulchre of his youngest and best beloved son, prostrate by the mouldering bones, and the once animated dust that sprung from his own flesh.   Near him stood his other son weeping, with his swelled eyes lift up to heaven.   The fond mother, moved by the entreaties of this wretched parent, had once brought the deceased child they thus lamented, when agitated by the malice of Satan, Samma roved among the dead.   Ah father ! then cried his little Benoni, the darling of his heart, breaking from his mother's hold, while she, filled with terror, hasted after him, —Ah my poor father ! will you not kiss me ? then clinging about his knees, he pressed his hand to his breast.   The father embraced him trembling. The little innocent returned his endearments, and looked up to him with an engaging smile, endeavouring to attract his notice by the little pleasing blandishments of infant fondness.   When the father, suddenly starting, seized the child, and, filled with all the fury of hell, dashed him against the rock : his brains, mixed with blood, discoloured the stone, and with a gentle sigh, his spotless soul left its shattered habitation.   The madness of the wretched parent . then subsided.   He threw himself on the ground ; then rising, snatched up the stiffening corpse, which he folded in his fainting arms : he pressed it to his bosom ; and while the mother rent the air with her shrieks and lamentations, he mourned inconsolable, crying, My son Benoni ! O Benoni, Benoni, my dear son ! while repentant tears gushed from his streaming eyes.

In this state was Samma, who now recovered from his swoon, when Joel, his other son, turning his face, wet with tears, from his father, beheld the Messiah advancing towards the sepulchres, and filled with surprize and joy, cried, O father, here is Jesus, the great prophet, coming towards the tombs ! Satan heard him. and struck with terror, cast a lowring glance through the entrance of the sepulchres. Thus from his dark dwelling, looks the profane atheist, when the loud tempest rides along the flaming clouds, and the tremendous chariots of vengeance awfully roll on high. Satan had hitherto tormented Samma only at a distance, sending forth plagues. from the remotest parts of the dusky tombs ; but now rising and arming himself with the terrors of hell, he launched them at the poor afflicted wretch, who instantly sprung on his feet, but void of strength, he again sunk on the earth. His troubled soul was scarce able to struggle against the assaults of death. But suddenly raised to madness, he was driven by the arch fiend up the rocks. Here, O benevolent Saviour ! Satan would before thy face have dashed him in pieces by casting him down : but thou wast already there. Thy speedy preventing grace supported the helpless, and bore him upon thine immortal wings. The destroyer of mankind, seeing the Saviour approach, trembled with indignation and terror. Jesus now casting down on the demoniac a look of benignity and grace, a divine power issues from his eyes, and Samma, freed from pain, with fear

acknowledges his deliverer : life dawns in that
face, which just before had the awful stamp of
death. With a loud cry, and streaming eyes, he
looks towards heaven. Fain would he speak ; but
only tremulous accents proceed from his faultering
lips : he stretches out his suppliant arms to his
gracious deliverer, and views him enraptured.
Thus the melancholy sage, when bewildered in
thought, shuddering, doubts the eternity of his
future duration ; till a kindred mind, certain of its
immortality, and relying on the promises of the
Almighty, approaches with cheerful looks. The
gloom then disperses, and the illumined soul,
shaking off the painful depression, exults and tri-
umphs, and seems to become a second time im-
mortal.

The Messiah now addressed Satan with a voice
of awful superiority ; Spirit of Destruction, who
art thou, that in my presence hast the presumption
to torture man, the race elected for redemption?
A voice deep roaring answered in wrathful accents,
I am Satan, the sovereign of the world, and reign
supreme over the independent spirits, for whom I
find other employment, than that given to the ce-
lestial songsters. Thy fame, O mortal prophet !
(for Mary could never bring forth an immortal)
has reached the depths of hell ; and I myself, an
honour thou mayest well boast, came to see the
Saviour, whose coming was proclaimed by the
slaves of heaven. But thou becamest a man, an
enthusiastic visionary, like those whom Death, my
son, who is far mightier than thou, has already laid in
the grave. I deemed it beneath me to mind what
those new immortals were doing ; yet not to be
quite inactive, I tormented mankind. This thou
thyself hast seen ; that face has been marked by
the finger of death. I now hasten to hell. My

irresistible foot shall lay waste the earth and the
wide ocean, to open me a commodious passage.
Hell, with joyful acclamations, shall celebrate my
return. If thou darest to oppose me, do it now.
I shall come back with the power of a king, to pro-
tect the world I have conquered. But first die,
thou wretch, added he, impetuously rushing on
Samma.

The Messiah, calm and silent, like the omnipotent
Father, when with a nod he saves or destroys a
world, with a look checked his fury, and rendered
feeble all his boasted power. He fled precipitate,
forgetting in his flight to make the earth and the
ocean feel the force of his irresistible foot. Samma
now descended from the rock, with no less joy than
Nebuchadnezzar flew from the majestic stream of
the Euphrates, when, by the decree of the Almighty,
his reason was restored, and rising erect, he was
able to view the heavens. The terrors of the Lord,
and the roaring waves of the impetuous stream,
no longer passed over him amidst the rolling thun-
der, and the forked lightning, like that seen on
mount Sinai. The prince then went to Babylon's
pensile gardens, not to exalt himself as a God, but
lying prostrate in the dust, with his arms stretched
out towards heaven, he poured forth the warm ef-
fusions of his gratitude to the Eternal. Thus Samma,
hasting to the Messiah, fell at his feet, and cried,
O man of God ! O heavenly prophet ! suffer me
to follow thee ; and let the life thou hast restored
be devoted to thee ! He then rising on his knees,
threw his trembling arms about the Redeemer.
Jesus, casting on him a look of benevolence, mildly
answered, follow me not : but henceforth frequent
the hill of Calvary, where thou shalt see the hope
of Abraham, and of the prophets.

The Messiah had scarcely spoke, when the in-

nocent Joel, with a timid air, addressed himself to
John : Dear Rabbi, said he, lead me to the great
Prophet of God ; for I would speak to him.
The beloved-disciple then taking him by the hand,
presented him to the Saviour, to whom, with inno-
cent simplicity, he thus spake : O great prophet,
why may not my father and I follow thee ? Let
me ask thee too, Why dost thou stay in this dismal
place, where the sight of the bones of the dead chills
my very blood ? Come, O come, thou Man of
God, to our house, to which my father is returning.
My poor mother, I am sure, will be glad to wait
on thee. She will bring thee milk and honey. She
will give thee the best fruit of our trees, she will
cover thee with the wool of the youngest of our
lambs. When summer returns, I will shew thee
those trees in our garden which my father has given
to me, and thou shalt sit under their shade. But
O Benoni ! my dear brother Benoni is dead ! I
must leave him in that tomb. No more, Benoni,
wilt thou go with me to water the flowers : nor
in the cool evening wilt thou fondly wake me !
See there, O divine Prophet ! he lies within that
tomb. Jesus with a tender smile embraced him ;
then wiping away his tears, sent him home, and
turning to John, said, Amiable child ! a mind so
tender and ingenuous have I seldom found in those
of riper years. Thus he spake, and stayed with
John among the sepulchres.

In the mean time, Satan, wrapped in clouds and
vapours, passed through the valley of Jehoshaphat,
and unseen, crossed the Dead Sea. Then reaching
cloud-capped Carmel, he, from thence shot up
into the heavens, where, with look malign, he wan-
dered through the universe, amidst suns and worlds
innumerable ; enraged that, after a long succession
of ages, they still shone with all the beauty and

grandeur :the Thunderer had imparted to them at
their creation.   Then, unwilling that the morning
stars should know him by his gloomy aspect, which
their mingled radiance rendered more conspicuous,
he changed his form, and arrayed himself in ethe-
real light : but soon the effulgent vesture became
insupportable ; when being also disgusted at what
he beheld, which ill suited a mind so foul ; he
hasted back to hell.   Now with rapid descent, he
reached the confines of the mundane system, where
immense spaces opened before him ; and these he
termed the frontiers of more extended realms ;
where he proposed to fix a new empire. Here
as far as the sickening rays of the last stars of the
creation cast a pallid light through the void, he
beheld trasient gleams ; yet saw not hell.   Far
from himself and the blessed spirits, God had in-
closed the abode of terror in perpetual darkness,
For!destruction horrible it was created ; and to
answer the end of punishment, it was dreadfully
pompous, and awfully perfect.   In three nights hell
was formed.   Then God forever turned from it his
face : that face wherewith he smiles with benignity
and grace, on his creatures, transfusing through
their souls the sweetest joy.   Those dismal regions
are guarded by two angels of approved valour.
The almighty himself girded them with arms in-
vincible, that they might there restrain the powers
of darkness, lest Satan, prompted by malice, should
assail the fair creation of God.   To the entrance of
hell, where, with solemn state, the angels sit, de-
scends a lucid path of streaming light, resembling
a river of liquid crystal : that thus remote, they
might not lose the holy joy, and pleasing rapture,
the mingled beauties that the wide creation yield.
    Skirting this luminous way, Satan, involved in a
cloud, reached the gate of hell unseen, and rushing

fiercely through, in haste mounted his burning throne. Among the eyes dimmed by darkness and despair, none saw him but Zophiel, one of the infernal heralds; who, observing a cloud invest the lofty steps, cried to a spirit standing near. Satan, the sovereign of these dark abodes, is at length returned: That cloud of vapours indicates, that he, so long expected by all the gods, is there. While he yet spake, the intervening cloud dispersed, and Satan, with terror and rage on his brow, appeared seated. The servile herald instantly flies to a volcano, which in streams of flaming sulphur used to proclaim Satan's arrival through all the burning land: there mounting on the wings of a tempest, he ascended from the bottom of the mountain up to its summit; where, wrapped in clouds of smoke, is a yawning aperture. There kindling the fiery storm, eruptions terrible proclaim the arch fiend's arrival, while gleaming light illuminating the dark abodes, to the far distant shew hell's monarch, seated high in pageant state. All the inhabitants of the abyss then appear, and their chiefs haste to seat themselves beneath him on the steps of his throne.

Thou muse of Sion, who undismayed, lookest, filled with sacred fervor and solemn awe, down into the abyss of hell, while, when the Most High punishes the sinner, thou readest in the divine countenance, self-approbation and calm tranquillity; O now inspire thy suppliant, and let the mighty voices of the infernals roar in my numbers, as the bellowing storm—as the tempest of God!

First appeared Adramelech, a spirit in guile and malice exceeding Satan, against whom his bosom still boiled with indignant rage, for being the first who attempted the apostacy, which he himself had long before projected. The actions

D

he performed were not to advance Satan's kingdom, but his own. From years immemorial he had been considering how to raise himself to the dominion of hell ; how to engage the prince of the fiery deep in a fresh war against the Eternal : how to cause him to be for ever banished to the infinite space : or, if all failed, how he might subdue him by force of arms. These thoughts had employed his mind ever since the apostate angels, flying before the conquering arm of the Messiah, had been driven down into the tremendous gulph. The superior spirits then assembling, Adramelech appeared ; but instead of martial armour, bore a tablet of polished gold, and slowly advancing, called aloud, Why, O ye kings ! do ye thus ignominiously fly ? Know, ye celestial warriors, ye noble asserters of liberty, that ye shall soon enter new abodes, the mansions of magnificence and immortality. When God had invented thunder, and with it armed the Messiah, who, with a tremendous storm, drove you to this place of woe, I passing by unseen, to the far distant sanctuary of God, entered the awful place, and brought away the golden table of destiny, in which our future fortunes are enrolled. Draw near ye immortals, and read the archives of heaven, Here see the sovereign decree of fate. He then read the following words :

Of the gods over whom Jehovah reigns, one becoming sensible of his divinity, and quitting the heaven of heavens, shall dwell with his divine associates in solitary and gloomy mansions : these will he at first inhabit with pain and reluctance, as he who shall drive them thither inhabited chaos, till, for him, I formed the universe. Such is my will. Dread not, ye celestial spirits, to enter the abodes of terror and dismay. For out of these new worlds shall arise more glorious than those ye have

left.   These Satan shall create : but from me he
shall receive the divine plan.   Thus says Destiny,
the god of gods, I who alone circumscribe all
space, and with my most glorious world encompass
that, with all the orbs and their gods.   Here Adra
melech ceased ; but in vain did the spirits of dark-
ness strive to alleviate their pain by giving credit
to his words.

The Most High, who heard his blasphemies,
said, I am Jehovah, and besides me there is no
other God.   The heavens shall declare my glory,
and the trembling sinner bear witness to my power.
Then proceeded from the mouth of God the mo-
mentous decree.   Deep in the lowest hell rises a
luminous mass, in the midst of the flaming sea,
which runs into the lake of death.   This mass enor-
mous, the circling thunders, in whirling eddies,
tore from its base, when rising high it struck the
proud Adramelech, fraught with lies, and cast
him with his impious tablet into the deadly lake
There seven nights he lay rolling in the abyss.
Long after, he caused himself to be worshipped on
earth as the supreme God, and had a temple erected
to his honour, in which he himself presided, placing
over the high altar the tablet of Destiny, which
none believed.   Thither his partisans resorted, and
like slavish hypocrites, worshipped the visionary
deity, when present, with reverence, and while
absent, with mockery.   From this temple now came
Adramelech, and concealing his secret hatred of
Satan, seated himself on the throne, close by his
side.

Next came Moloch, a warlike spirit.   Lest the
thundering warrior, for so he calls the great Je-
hovah, should descend to seize the plains of hell,
he vainly fortified them with a wall of mountains,
raised with towering battlements.   Oft when the

gloomy dawn rises in sulphurous vapours from the banks of the flaming ocean, the inhabitants of hell see him tottering under the stormy peak of some lofty eminence, while he slowly advances down the declivity of the mountains, when, having cast his load on his new raised mound, which rises towards the high vaulted roof of hell, he stands in the clouds, listening to the echo made by the fall of the ponderous rock, and fancies it to be the noise of the rattling thunder. The souls of the once proud conquerors of the earth then viewing him with astonishment from beneath, he rushes among them from the stupendous heights, while they, winged by fear, fly from the martial fiend. He now went in his sable armour, which resounded as he walked, resembling thunder involved in black clouds. Before him the mountain shook, and behind, the rock trembling, sunk. Thus he advanced to the throne of Satan.

After him appeared Belial, who in mournful silence came from the dreary forests and desert wastes, where the black streams of death, issuing from a source involved in clouds, flow dark and languid to the foot of Satan's throne. Vain, eternally vain, are his endeavours to render the accursed land on its banks, like the bright creation of God. Thou, O Eternal ! laughest at his attempts, when, howling like the tempest, he would imitate the cooling breeze of the zephyrs, and when with impotent arm he attempts to drive the sullen stream before him. At these labours he incessantly toils, while the terrors of God roar in his destructive wings, and desolation, arrayed in deformity, is spread over the trembling abyss. With rage Belial remembers the eternal spring, which like a young seraph, smiles on the ever-blooming flowers of heaven. Fain would he imitate the beauties of

that season in hell's nocturnal vales.   Then frowns
and vents indignant sighs, at seeing the doleful
land lying before him in dreary darkness, for ever
incapable of improvement ; and notwithstanding
all his pains, infinite tracts filled with a dreadful
scene of woe.   Belial, with a brow lowring with
dire dejection, repaired to Satan.   His mind still
boiled with revenge against him who drove him
from the celestial fields, into that land of terror and
desolation, which every succeeding century seemed
to render more intolerable.

Thou Magog, who dwellest in the lake—thou
also amidst thy waters sawest the return of Satan.
Thou camest forth rising in the midst of a roaring
whirlpool, and when thy feet divided the black
stream, the sea, driven before thee, rose like exten-
sive mountains.   Magog cursed the Lord.   The
voice of his wild blasphemies continually flowed
in loud bellowings from his distorted mouth.   Since
his being cast from heaven, he has been ever uttering
execrations against the Eternal ; and filled with
hatred and revenge has been weakly bent on de-
stroying hell, though it should cost him the labour
of millions of ages.   Being now alighted on the
burning land, he spread devastation around, throw-
ing the whole shore with its mountains into the
deep.

Thus did the princes of the infernal regions as-
semble about their king.   Like the islands of the
sea when torn from their foundations, they rushed
on with boisterous uproar and irresistible tumult.
After them crowds of inferior spirits flocked, as the
waves of the ocean roll to the lofty shores.   My-
riads of spirits appeared, who, sentenced to contempt
and endless infamy, chaunted their own exploits to
their harps, which had been cracked by the thunder
of heaven, and sounded the discordant notes of death.

Thus in the midnight hour, the lofty cedars, split
by a tempest, groan, when Boreas in his brazen
chariot sweeps over them, while Lebanon is agitated
and Hermon trembles. Satan sees, and hears them
coming. He starts up in a wild transport, and
casting his eyes over them, beholds the atheists, a
mean grovelling band, among whom was Gog,
their horrid leader, in phrenzy, and in power pre-
eminent. They endeavour to imagine, that what
they saw in heaven was all a dream, the idle pro-
duce of phantastic visions ; and, lost in a labyrinth
of opinion, persuade themselves, that the great
Jehovah, first their Father, and then their Judge,
has no existence. Satan beheld them, with contempt.
For some time he stood lost in thought, then slowly
moved his eyes around, and again sat down. As
menacing storms hover slow and dilatory over
dreary and inhospitable mountains, so Satan sat
frowning and pensive. At length, furious, he opened
his lips, from which a tempest burst forth, and
a thousand claps of impotent thunder issued from
his impious mouth.

Ye formidable bands, if ye are indeed those
who bravely maintained with me bold war in the
plains of heaven, during three dreadful days, hear
with triumph what I shall relate, concerning my
stay on earth. Hear ye also, my friends, the noble
resolution I, your supreme god and king, have ta-
ken to put Jehovah to shame. Sooner shall hell
pass away, sooner shall he annihilate his creation,
and again dwell in solitude, than he shall wrest
from us our dominion over the race of man. Ye
gods, ever unconquered, ever free shall ye remain,
though he should send even hither his Reconciler,
with thousands of his heavenly messengers : nor
shall he rob us of our dominion, though he him-
self should descend to the earth to save mankind.

But against whom do I vent my indignation? Who is this Saviour, this incarnate God who comes clothed in a mortal body? Would the Messiah, who, armed with the thunder of heaven, drove us from the celestial plains, enter the womb of a mortal? or is he, who must soon moulder in the dust, to make war on us, and destroy our empire? Yet there are some here that have timorously fled before him :—who, at his approach, escaped from the emaciated bodies of the mortals they tormented. Ye dastards, tremble before this assembly! hide your faces, and blush in obscurity. Hear it, ye gods! they fled! Why, ye pusillanimous, did ye fly? Why did ye stile this Jesus, who is beneath both you and me, the Son of the eternal God? But that ye may know who he is, hear from me the history of this arrogant impostor. Hear this, ye assembly of gods, with triumph.

From the remotest time, a prophecy has prevailed among the Jews, a nation of all others the most addicted to visions, that a Saviour is to arise, descended from David, one of their kings, who will forever deliver them from their enemies, and raise their monarchy to unparallelled glory. Ye are not ignorant that some of your companions once came with the tidings that they had seen on mount Tabor, a host of rejoicing angels, who, with seeming rapture, and awful reverence, incessantly called on the name of Jesus. That the cedars of the mountain trembled, and the sound of their hymns, uttered in jubilant strains, echoed through the neighbouring rocks, while all Tabor resounded Jesus the Saviour. Then Gabriel, proud and insolent, went in triumph to an Israelitish woman, and giving her the salutation only due to the immortals, in a voice and gesture of reverence, said, From thee shall a king be born, who will protect the portion

of David, and exalt the inheritance of Israel.
His name shall be Jesus. He shall be called the
Son of God, and of his kingdom there shall be no
end. Why, O ye gods of hell! when ye heard of
this, were ye struck with terror? Much more
have I heard, yet continue undismayed. But does
it become us to be apprehensive of danger, because
a mortal Dreamer on our earth assumes the titles of
the Son of God, the Redeemer, and the Saviour?

During this speech, the arch apostate saw arise
the scars made by the Thunderer; but though these
filled him with terror, he strove to rekindle his
boastful rage, and thus continued:

I watched on earth for the extraordinary birth
of this divine infant. He will soon, said I, proceed
from the womb of Mary. Then, swift as the rapid
flash from the lowring clouds, or the thoughts
of the gods, when winged with wrath, will he grow
up towards heaven. In his exaltation, he, with
one foot, covers the sea, and with the other, the
earth. In his dreadful right hand he poises the
sun and moon, and in his left the stars of the morn-
ing. He comes accompanied by Destruction, in
the midst of storms, and rushes irresistibly to vic-
tory. Fly, Satan! ah fly! lest, with his omnipo-
tent thunder he strikes impetuous, and having
hurled thee through a thousand worlds, leaves thee
senseless, and even void of life, in the immense abyss.
Behold, these, ye gods, were my thoughts: but
how far were they from the truth? He came into
the earth a mere human being; a whimpering
child; and, like the other sons of the earth, was no
sooner born, than he mourned his mortality with
infant tears. A choir of heavenly spirits, indeed,
sung at his birth: for sometimes they descend to
take a view of that earth where we rule with ab-
solute sway, and viewing the graves and sepulchres

of the dead, where once was paradise, they, weeping, turn away their eyes; but soon, to assuage their grief, sing hymns of joy, and return to heaven. This was now the case. They hasted back, and left the helpless infant; who then fled from me, while I suffered him to fly; for so cowardly an enemy was beneath my pursuit. Meanwhile my trusty vicegerent, Herod, caused the infants of Bethlehem to be massacred; when the streaming blood; the dying shrieks of the helpless innocents; the agonies of the disconsolate mothers, and the odorous steam of the fresh mangled bodies, mingling with the ascending souls, rendered them a delightful sacrifice. It was I, Herod, who prompted thee to perform this exploit. Let not any inferior spirit claim this honour: an honour which I maintain is due to me alone. Let therefore that vain boaster, who here in hell, would deprive me of this glory, be silent. On the death of Herod, the child was brought back from Egypt. His early years he passed in the lap of his fond mother, and amidst her embraces remained unknown. Afterwards no blaze of Juvenile fire, no impulse of noble valour prompted him to exert his courage. He retired to the lonely deserts, and the dreary wilds. Yet at length he seemed to assume a more distinguished character. One day, when bathing in the river Jordan, on him descended the glory of God on effulgent splendor. This I myself beheld with these immortal eyes. Bright it flowed, as when it issues from the throne of Heaven through long ranks of adoring seraphs. But why it thus descended, whether in honour of the earth-born child, or to observe the watch we kept, is' difficult to tell. However, I instantly heard the rolling thunder bellow from the clouds, mixed with these words; this is my beloved Son, in whom I am well pleased. Thus, to perplex my thoughts, Eloa, or some other

of the heavenly host, uttered these words: **It**
was surely not the voice of God, at least far dif-
ferent did it seem from that, in which he imposed
on us the irksome task of paying homage to his
favorite, the Messiah.   Near Jesus was a fallen
prophet, who, like a savage, roved among the rocks
of the wilderness ; and calling out to this pretended
Saviour, said Behold the Lamb of God, which
taketh away the sins of the world.   Hail thou
who wast before all worlds ! from thee we receive
grace for grace.   God gave the law by Moses ;
but from the anointed of the Lord come grace
and truth.   How lofty ! how prophetic !   Thus
when dreamers praise each other, they wrap them-
selves in a sacred obscurity ; and then we, O ye
immortal gods ! are thought much too mean to be
able to draw aside the fraudful veil.   'Tis true,
the earth-born, of whom the prophet speaks in such
lofty strains, hath already seemed to wake the
dead ; his mighty power, remember it ye princes
of hell, has called to life those, who, fainting under
their pains, have been laid in their tombs—soon
he is to raise the whole human race from sin and
death : from sin, who charms every heart, and reigns
with such despotic sway : from death, the offspring
of the fair flattering charmer, will he also deliver
them : though at my nod he has so often laid in
the dust the whole creation of God.   Ye souls
who, since the formation of the earth I have ga-
thered round me, as numerous as the waves of the
ocean, or as the glittering stars : ye who lament
in eternal night, who, in that night, are tortured
by penal fire ;—in that fire by despair—and in
that despair by me : will then be as free from
death, as the band of the adoring worship-
pers ; while we are to degenerate, and crouching
low, to lie prostrate before him.   Thus what

God's mighty Thunderer was unable to accomplish, this dreamer is to produce. Presumptuous boaster! first free thyself from the lot of humanity, and then awake the dead. Thee will I lay pale and disfigured in the dust. Then will I say to thine eyes, which shall be covered with the veil of eternal night, open and see the dead awake! Then to the ears which hear not, and from which an eternal insensibility shall exclude all sounds, will I say, Hark! the fields, resound with the call, Awake ye dead! And to thy soul that has just taken its flight, and directs its course to hell, doubtless to subdue us, will I call with the voice of a tempest, Make haste, thou who hast conquered death—haste to begin thy triumph! For thee a pompous entry is prepared—the gates of hell open to invite thee in. The deep abyss resounds with shouts of joy—Thee, the gods, and the souls of thy fellow mortals, greet in triumphant songs. Thus in sportive strains he raved: then added, boasting; My great resolutions shall be executed, unless God draws up to heaven the lessening earth, and with it the whole human race.—This Saviour shall die!—he shall die! Thus shall I be both the father and protector of death, and live unconquered through the ages of eternity. —He shall die!—Soon will I, before the face of the Eternal, scatter his mouldering clay in the way to hell!

Thus in a voice hoarse and discordant, spoke the arch-apostate. The great Messiah was still among the lonely sepulchres, when the breath with which the blasphemer ended his impious speech, brought to the holy Jesus a fluttering leaf, on which hung a dying worm. The meek and humble Saviour gave it life; but at the same instant, horrors unutterable entered the bosom of the proud boaster. Behind the step of the high raised throne from which he vented his blasphemies hell sunk, and before it Satan, from the terrors that seized his mind, appeared wrapped in the darkest gloom of night, while all the inhabitants of the dreadful abyss beheld him with motionless amazement.

Below the throne sat Abbadona by himself in deep dejection, ruminating with keenest anguish on the past and the future. Before his face, which was deformed by melancholy, internal anguish, and sad dismay, he beheld tortures accumulated on tortures, extending into eternity. He then looked back to those happy times when he himself was a bright seraph, and the friend of the exalted Abdiel; who on the day of the revolt, bravely vindicated the cause of God, and having zealously contended for the truth before the apostate legions, returned without him to his Creator, invincible and crowned with immortal glory. Abbadona was near escaping with that heroic seraph; but being surrounded with the rapid chariots of Satan, and the bright bands of those who fell from their allegiance, he drew back, and though Abdiel, with looks of menacing love, chid his delay, and strove to hasten his escape from those reprobate bands, inebriated and dazzled with the delusive prospect of his future godhead, he no longer attended to the once powerful eye of his friend, but suffered himself to be carried in triumph to Satan. Now lamenting in pensive silence, he revolves the history of his once spotless innocence, and the fair morning of his days, when he came pure and happy out of the hand of his Creator. At once the Almighty Source of Goodness formed him and Abdiel, when filled with inborn rapture they thus addressed each other: Ah beauteous form, what are we? Where my beloved didst thou first see me? How

long hast thou--how long have I existed ? Come oh
come, my divine friend, embrace me--Admit me into
thy bosom—Let me learn thy thoughts In the
mean time came the glory of God, shining from
afar with ineffable splendor, fraught with bene-
diction.   They looked around and beheld an innu-
merable host of new immortals.   A silver cloud
then gently raised them to the Eternal.   They
saw their Creator . they called him Father, and
enraptured adored him as the source of their
happiness.

Abbadona, tortured by these thoughts, shed a
torrent of tears, and now resolved to oppose the
blasphemous speech of Satan, which had filled
him with horror. He thrice attempted to speak,
but his sighs stopt his utterance. Thus when in
a bloody battle two brothers are mortally wounded
by each others hand, at last each to the other being
mutually known, they are unable to express the
strong sensations of their hearts, and sighs only
proceed from their dying lips. At length Abbadona
thus broke silence :

Though I incur the everlasting displeasure of
this assembly, I will not refrain from speaking.—
Yes Satan, I will boldly speak, and perhaps the
heavy judgments of the Eternal may more lightly
fall on me than on thee. O thou seducer, how I now
hate thee ! This essence, this immortal essence,
which thou hast snatched from its Creator, he will
perpetually require of thee---He will require of
thee the whole assembly of immortal spirits,
by thee involved in ruin. Thou execrable de-
ceiver, with thee I renounce all connection.
I will not participate in thine impotent pro-
ject of putting to death the divine Messiah.
Against whom, O spirit accursed ! dost thou rave ?
It is against him whom thou art forced to confess

is more mighty than thyself! Has not his irresistible thunder sufficiently disfigured thine audacious front? Or cannot the almighty Father defend him against those, by whose delusions man became subject to death? Alas! in that crime I was an accomplice! But mad with rage shall we put to death the great Messiah, and thus perpetually shut against us—us once so many pure and happy spirits, the entrance to future deliverance; or at least prevent some little alleviation of our torment. O Satan! as we all felt increasing pain, when thou gavest the name of thy kingdom to these mansions of night and horrid damnation, so instead of triumph shalt thou return with shame, from thine audacious attempt against God and his Messiah.

Satan heard him with impatient rage, and instantly from the top of his throne, attempted to hurl at his devoted head an enormous rock, but his destructive right hand dropped, shrivelled and void of strength. Then stamping with impotent fury, three times his disappointed malice shook his whole frame, three times he cast a look of malignant fury at Abbadona, while his struggling passions stopped his voice. Abbadona, with an afflicted countenance, still stood before him firm and intrepid.

Now spake Adramelech, the foe of God, of man, and even of Satan. Thou base and abject slave, cried he, I will speak to thee in storms, and will answer thee in a tempest. Darest thou presume to revile the gods? Dare one of the most grovelling spirits of hell to rise up against Satan and me? If thou art tortured, thou slave, it is by thine own thoughts. Fly, thou pusillanimous spirit, from our dominions, the abode of kings—fly into the wide abyss of space, and there importune thy God to erect for thee a kingdom of new tortures, in which thou mayst live for ever. But thou hadst rather perish—perish then, humbly adoring the object of thy terror. Come, Satan, thou who in the midst of heaven knewest thy divine essence, and boldly attempted to dethrone Jehovah—Come, we will soon shew these contemptible spirits the terrors of our arm, by enterprizes that, like a storm, shall at once depress and blind them. Come, ye mazes of impenetrable guile, big with ruin, destruction and death. It is determined that this Saviour shall die: he shall not even save himself. There is no way for his escape; nor shall any guide deliver him from the labyrinth into which he shall enter. But should he even elude our stratagems: shouldst Thou, who dwellest on high, enable him to escape, by enduing him with the sagacity of a god, yet fiery tempests, the agents of our wrath, shall soon take him from our sight—tempests like that with which we formerly attacked the happy Job, the favorite of heaven. Fly—fly from us thou earth, we come against thee armed with all the powers of death and hell. Woe to him who in our world, shall dare to oppose us.

Thus spake Adramelech; and now the whole assembly with unanimous tumult sided with Satan. The stamping of their mighty feet surpassed the noise of falling rocks, and shook the deep profound. Inflated with their future triumphs, the hoarse roar of applauding voices, reached the utmost confines of the dreary regions, all approving the infernal resolution of slaying the blessed Jesus: though an act like this, Time, since he first began his course, had never seen. Its cursed inventors, Satan and Adramelech, with resolutions fell and malignant, descended from their throne; the steps like brazen mountains, resounded under their feet, and the bellowing cry of war and victory accompanied them to the gate of hell.

Abbadona, who alone had remained unmoved, followed at a distance, either still to persuade them from engaging in the dire attempt, or to behold the consequences of the dreadful deed. Now, with steps dilatory and slow he advanced and before he was aware, found himself before the angels who guarded the gate. But how was he confounded, when he saw there the invincible Abdiel! sighing, he held down his head and thought of retiring; then resolved to advance; then trembling and filled with perturbation, determined to fly into the immense abyss of space: but instantly collecting himself he moved towards the seraph. His beating heart spoke the terror of his mind: distressful tears, such as fallen angels weep, fell from his eyes: deep sighs burst from his agonizing breast, and a continual tremor, never felt by mortals, shook his whole frame. Abdiel with an open tranquil eye, stood in fixed attention, gazing up the bright stream of light, and with sweet serenity was viewing the distant worlds, formed by the great Creator, to whom he had ever remained faithful. He saw not Abbadona. As the sun on its natal day poured his resplendent beams on the new-created earth, so shone the bright seraph; but the afflicted Abbadona felt no genial influences from his refulgent rays. Sighing, he cryed to himself in plantive voice, Abdiel, my brother! wilt thou for ever shun me? Wilt thou for ever leave me?—for ever leave me in solitude, far from thee?—Oh grant me thy pity, thou child of light!—Wilt thou not, Abdiel, mourn for me?—Ah, he no longer loves me!—he will for ever cease to love me! Wither, ye ever verdant bowers, under which, in high raised rapture and sweet delight we talked of the tender charms of friendship. Cease to flow, ye celestial streams, where we mingled the sweet em-

brace, and with unpolluted lips sung the praises of
the Eternal—Abdiel, my brother, is for ever dead
to me!   Thou hell, my dark abode, eternal night,
thou mother of torments, join my lamentations, and
when the terrors of God nightly oppress me, may
my sighs and bewailing groans resound in thy
caverns.   Abdiel, my brother, is for ever dead
to me!

Thus unregarded, he, to himself, uttered his
complaints.   He now stood fronting the crystaline
stream of flowing light that leads to the mundane
system.   At first he was afraid of the brightness,
and of the winged lightning, that seemed ad-
vancing towards him.   Immersed in misery, and
confined to solitude, ages had passed since he had
seen the worlds.   Now standing pensive, he cried,
Blessed entrance! oh that I might pass through
thee to those innumerable places, where the Creator
displays his power and grace, and never more tread
the dark kingdom of Damnation!   Ye suns innu–
merable, how much more resplendent was I than
you, ye inanimate children of the Creator, when
first at his almighty voice, your glorious orbs began
to roll!   Now, this gloomy mansion is my place
of residence.   I am an outcast, an object of abhor-
rence to the meanest spirits who maintained their
allegiance to the Omnipotent!   O thou heaven,
seat of purest bliss, the sight of thee fills me·with
remorse!   In thy blissful regions I became a
sinner—there I rose up against the Almighty.
Thou immortal repose, once my sweet associate in
the blessed vale of peace, whither art thou fled?
Alas! thee I have for ever lost, and my Judge
scarce permits me to enjoy, in the midst of my
gloomy horrors, the admiration of his worlds, those
glorious structures that display his omnipotence and
grace   Oh that I might without shuddering, pro–

sume to call him my Creator ! how willingly would
I resign the tender, the endearing name of Father !
how chearfully forego the noble privilege of the
seraphim of being called his children !   O thou,
who art my judge, dare I, abandoned, implore thee
to cast on me one gracious look, while thus involved
in guilt—involved in woe !—Ye dark thoughts,
full of anguish, and thou wild dispair, tyrannic
rage !—for ever rage !—Miserable that I am !
O that I were but blotted from the creation !—
Cursed be the day when the Creator went forth in
his glory, and called me into being—Yes, cursed
be thou, O day ! when the new immortals said, he
is also our brother ; O Eternity ! thou mother of
endless torments ! why didst thou bring it forth ?
And if it must still remain, wherefore is it not dark
and horrid, like the eternal night when the mighty
Thunderer, borne on a tempest, drove us through
the void creation, laden with the anger and curse of
the Omnipotent—But against whom, while doom-
ed to this horrid abyss, darest thou, blasphemer,
complain !—Fall on me ye suns, hide me ye stars,
from the fierce wrath of him, who from the throne of
his eternal justice, both as my enemy and my judge,
fills me with terror and sad dismay. O thou whose
judgements are irrevocable, has eternity no hopes
in store for me ?   O divine Judge, Creator, most
gracious Father !—Alas ! again I offend—I blas-
pheme the Most High—I call him by names not
to be uttered by such an ingrate.—Yet all this he
once was to me—He was once my most gracious
Father—he would have been so still, had I like
Abdiel, my dearest friend, stood firm.—But I, alas !
impious, ungrateful—fled—but whither did I fly ?
Thus he spoke, and looked, dejected into the deep
abyss.   Then lifting up his eyes, glaring with wild
despair, he resumed :

O God, armed with destruction create a fire—a devouring fire that will destroy the spirits which thou, without their consent, hast created immortal. In vain he called, no devouring flame appeared : he then turned and fixing his looks on the worlds, flew up, till spent with fatigue, he alighted on one of the suns, and stopping, suffered his eyes to range over the wide creation, where stars innumerable seemed to press on stars. He perceived a comet in the immensity of space, and approached it from the sun on which he stood. Its sentence was pronounced. Its final period drew nigh, and it was on all sides covered with smoke. Upon it Abbadona threw himself, that he too might perish, but still surviving, he sunk through the inflamed globe, and descended slowly to our earth.

In the mean time Satan and Adramelech approached the earth. They proceeded together, yet alone, each solely taken up with his own infernal thoughts. And now Adramelech descries the earth involved in distant darkness.

There, there it is, cryed he to himself, Yes, there it is. There I, when I have obtained the glory of conquering Satan, shall sole reign as the author of all evil. But why, O earth ! over thee alone ? why not over those stars, whose inhabitants have been already too long happy ? your orbs shall for me perform their courses. Yes, death shall advance from star to star, and in sight of the Eternal, extend his dominion to the utmost confines of the wide creation ! Then shall I not like Satan, successively destroy only single individuals of rational beings, but sweep away entire generations. Before me shall they lie grovelling on the earth, and, writhing themselves with torment, expire. ill I sit on this, on that, or the other star triumphant, and, sole monarch, cast my glad eyes over my infinite domain. Thou, nature whom I shall then have rendered the tomb of thy creatures, shall I delighted behold, while I, laughing, gaze on their corruption, in thy deep and endless grave. Even should the Eternal resolve to form other rational beings of the dust of the tombs, them also will I bring to destruction. Thus shall my never failing skill and intrepidity carry seduction and death from world to world. Then shall I act like myself: and should I be successful in destroying spiritual beings, Satan himself shall perish, and his immortal essence evaporate like smoke. Under him no great and worthy action shall I perform. It is then determined. Spiritual substances shall be reduced to nothing. I will destroy them or perish : for that is better than to live and not to reign. I will summon all my thoughts, to form schemes of destruction. This is the time for performing what has eternally been the subject of my ambition. Now God awakes, and if Satan does not err, has sent a Saviour of mankind, who is to disposses us of a kingdom we have so boldly conquered.—He is not mistaken ; he who is called the Messiah, is the greatest of all the prophets. Yet I shall signalize myself by his overthrow, and all the assembled gods shall esteem me most worthy of the infernal throne. Or, what is still more suitable to my dignity, and more worthy of such an immortal being, I will first destroy Satan : a glorious exploit that will put an end to my servitude !—he shall be subdued, and then shall I reign supreme among the gods.

Thus the proud boastful fiend malignant raved, bewildered by his wishes, in a maze of thought. The Most High, who sees through the darkness of futurity, heard him in silence. Adramelech lost in meditations deep, insensibly wrapped himself in

the gathering clouds : his wringled front glowed
with rage and malice, and fury lowered on his
brow.   At length, at the approach of night, he
again joined Satan, when both descended on the
mount of Olives, they with impatient rage went in
quest of the Messiah, and his faithful followers.
As two murderous chariots armed for slaughter
rush into a valley, against the tranquil general of
an enemy's army, so Adramelech and Satan de-
scended the mountain.

THE END OF THE SECOND BOOK.

THE

MESSIAH.

BOOK. III.

THE ARGUMENT.

The Messiah still continues among the sepulchres. Eloa descends from heaven, and counts his tears. The souls of the patriarchs send the seraph Zemia, from the sun, to observe the words and actions of Jesus, while the darkness of the night prevents their seeing him. The Messiah sleeps for the last time, and while his disciples seek him about the mount of Olives, their guardian angels give Zemia their several characters. Satan appears in a dream to Judas Iscariot in the form of his deceased father. The Messiah awaking comes to his disciples, and mention their approaching flight. Judas, who had concealed himself, over-hears the Messiah, and feels his mind distracted by contending passions.

HAIL earth! my native land, thee I revisit : thou shalt lay me in thy cool bosom among those who sleep in God : thou shalt softly cover these my bones. Yet let me hope first to conclude the sacred song of heavenly love. Then these lips which sung the gracious Friend of man; then these eyes which he has oft filled with tears of joy, shall be closed : then my gentle friends, with frequent gushing grief, shall encircle my grave with ever-verdant laurel, and the spreading palm : there shall I sleep till my new-raised form, awaked from death, rises in heavenly splendor from the silent grave.

And thou harmonious muse of Sion's hill, who
hast carried me to the gloomy regions of hell, and
safe hast brought me back, still trembling: thou,
who in the divine countenance hast seen awful
justice mixed with radiant grace and love, pour on
my enraptured soul celestial light, and teach her
in lofty strains to sing the great Redeemer.

Jesus still remained with John, at the receptacles
of the dead, among the scattered bones of human
bodies, and surrounded by nocturnal darkness.
He sat meditating on himself, the Son of the Eter-
nal Father, sacrificed for man. Before him passed
in horrid form a' numerous train of sins, which
since the creation had received their birth from the
children of Adam ; followed in awful pomp by
those posterity will still produce ; an innumerable
host, flying from the face of God, in the midst-of
whom was Satan their chief and father, driving
sinners from the sacred throne, and gathering them
round' himself. Thus the northern whirlpool, ever
open to destruction, in circling eddies ingulphs the
liquid plain, drawing into its deep abyss unwary
mariners: Jesus beheld the black assembly in
their native forms most hideous, not as when painted
by the passions, they appear to man in the garb
of lavish luxury and proud ambition ; or as when
to the lascivious eye they seem dressed in smiles and
wanton blandishments. The holy Saviour then
looked up to his Father. who, with awful counte-
nance, regarded him ; but though the tremendous
sentence was slowly breaking forth, grace inexpres-
sible beamed from his face. The seraphs say, the
Father then silent dropped the second tear : the
first fell with Adam's curse. While thus each the
other viewed, all nature bowed before them ; full
of awe and expectation, the world stood still, the
stars stopped their courses, and night gazed with

Craig del.

Willis sculp.

Christ & John at the Sepulchres.

Published the 2d June by C Cooke Paternoster Row

all her eyes.   The contemplating cherub in a calm cloud passed by.   The seraph Eloa also riding in celestial vapours came down to the earth, and having counted the tears of love, by the Redeemer shed for man, reascended towards the heavenly plains.   John beheld him rise ; for Jesus had opened his eyes, and enabled him to perceive the seraph.   He saw him, and stood amazed.   Then with ardour embraced the Mediator, and sighing, called him his Saviour and his Lord ; enraptured he thus called him, and filled with joys inexpressible, continued the sweet embrace.

Meanwhile the eleven, who had long been deprived of the sight of Jesus, wandered sorrowful at the foot of the mount of Olives, seeking him amidst the darkness of the night : one alone excepted who no longer paid the same honour, or felt the same tender regard for the Messiah, as the others. Though filled with innocence and unspotted truth, they knew not the purity and sublime nature of their own souls : but they were better known to God.   He had given them minds fit for receiving divine illuminations.   Even he, who proved himself unworthy of the celestial call, might also have received heavenly revelations, had he not afterwards impiously betrayed the blessed Saviour.   For before the souls of the apostles dwelt in tabernacles of clay, golden thrones were prepared for them in heaven, by those of the four and twenty elders. Yet one of these had been covered with clouds, they, however, soon dispersed, and the bright throne again diffused effulgent splendor.   Eloa then came forth, and with a loud voice said, 'This is taken from him, and given to one more worthy.

Their guardian spirits, twelve angels of the earth under the inspection of Gabriel, now ascended to the summit of the mountain, and with tender

complacency, stood unseen, viewing those committed
to their charge, while they, with eyes filled with
anxious tears, carefully sought the divine Media-
tor. Mean while Zemia, an agile spirit, one of
the four who next in authority to Uriel presided
over the globe which enlightens the earth, descended
to them, and thus spoke.

Tell me, ye celestial friends, where is the great
Messiah ? sent by the souls of the fathers, I shall
with awful silence accompany his steps, and with
admiration observe all his words and actions. No
holy expression, no sigh of compassion, will I
suffer to escape unobserved : no look beaming com-
fort, no tear of soft commiseration, shall appear in
his eye, unnoticed. O earth ! too soon dost thou
withdraw from the view of thine ancient inhabitants,
thy fields most lovely, where walks the glorious
Prince of Peace veiled in humanity. Too soon dost
thou fly the day and Uriel's face, while the sun
reluctant lights the other hemisphere. There no
rising hill, no lowly vale, gives delight ; for there
the Saviour is not seen.

Orion, the seraph, Simon's guardian angel, then
replied, Below, among the melancholy sepulchres
hewn deep in the rocks, near the foot of this moun-
tain, stands the great Messiah rapt in meditation.
Zemia beheld him, and remained in silent ecstacy.
He still stood enraptured, while on their swift wings
two fleeting, calm, and silent hours of the night
passed over his head. Then the last balmy sleep
descended on the eye of the Mediator ; for sacred
repose, issuing from the divine sanctuary, was sent
by the almighty Father in a gentle breeze. Jesus
slept. Zemia then turning, entered into the midst
of the spiritual assembly, and in the voice of friend-
ship, thus spake :

Tell me, ye celestial friends, who are those I see

roaming on the monntain dejected and forlorn:
Over their faces hovers sympathising grief, ever
graceful when; as here, there appears a noble mind.
They, perhaps, lament some dear departed friend,
virtuous like themselves. These, O Zemia! Orion
replied, are the holy twelve, whom the Messiah
has chosen for his disciples. Happy are we in
being selected their guardians and friends. Thus
we continually behold their divine Master, and
hear, how he, with sweetest lips of sacred love,
opens to them his heart : how he dispenses his in-
structions : how in sublimest converse he introduces
them to the knowledge of celestial mysteries, or in
parables shews thee, immortal virtue, in all thy
native lustre. Thus impressing his image on their
hearts, he forms them for the glorious employment
of leading man to the high regions of immortality.
Oh how much do we learn from his instructions ;
how vigilant are we rendered by his bright ex-
ample !—and how are ws allured to accompany
him in fervent adoration of the Source of all good,
the supreme Father of angels and of men ! O
Zemia ! wert thou but daily to behold him—wert
thou but witness to his divine friendship, his humi-
lity, his exalted piety, thine heart would overflow
with silent rapture. Delightful is it also to the
immortals to hear his disciples converse of him,
like us, in affectionate effusions of love. Often, O
my friend ! have I said to these my companions,
and I again repeat it, that I have frequently wish-
ed to be of Adam's race, and to live with man in a
state of mortality, if mortality can be without sin.
Perhaps I might then more truly honour the
Messiah ; perhaps I should feel a more ardent af-
fection for my brother, born of the same flesh and
blood. With what rapture might I then deliver
up my life for him who had died for me ? While

stained with my warm innocent blood I would
praise him ; and then my faint sighs, my dying
accents, would sound in the ears of the Most High,
with no less harmony than the lofty strains of Eloa,
when he stands before the throne. Then, Zemia,
thou, or one of these my friends, would, with in-
visible hand, gently close my eyes, and conduct my
departed soul to the Eternal King.

Greatly, O gentle seraph !, replied Zemia, am I
moved by thy words. How hast thou incited me
to join in thy wish to be a brother of man !
Those I there behold are then the holy twelve, the
Messiah's chosen friends. An honour which a se-
raph might well wish to obtain by becoming mor-
tal. I salute you his disciples : ye are worthy of
immortality. You the Redeemer loves as brethren.
Ye shall sit with your Lord on golden thrones to
judge the world. O ye seraphim ! I would hear
the names already recorded in the book of life.
Say first who is he that with quick eye looks around,
and now penetrates the thick grove, perhaps with
impatient eagerness looking for Jesus ? In his
countenance methinks I see the traces of a bold and
determined mind. Tell me the thoughts and emo-
tions of a heart that seems susceptible of the
strongest impressions.

This, replied the seraph Orion, is Simon Peter,
one of the greatest of the disciples. Me has the
Redeemer chosen his guardian angel. Thou, O
Zemia, hast judged aright: he is all that thou
sayest. Shouldst thou see him when full of fervor,
he listens to the voice of his gracious Master ; or
when absent from him, and no longer under his eye ;
or when sleeping, he, in his dreams, beholds his
Saviour : thou, O seraph ! wouldst admire the
sensibility of his heart, and think it still more divine.
Lately Jesus asking his disciples, whom they thought

him, Peter answered, with tears of joy, Thou art
Christ, the son of the living God, But, oh that I
had not heard the Messiah say to Peter, Thou wilt
deny me thrice! how dreadful the prediction! Ah
Simon, my brother! what—oh what were the
thoughts of thine heart? boldly didst thou reply,
I will never deny thee my Redeemer and my Lord.
Yet Jesus again repeated the dreadful words.
Didst thou, Peter, but know how this fills me with
soft compassion, surely thou wouldst, as thou hast
said, rather die than deny thy kind and gracious
Lord. Thou knowest how Jesus loves thee. For
then didst thou observe, that while he thus spake,
he beheld thee with eyes filled with divine sympathy
and grace. Fain, O Peter! would I hope, that
thou wilt not basely deny thy Lord.

The seraph Zemia heard him with deep concern,
and replied, Is it possible that he should be so void
of gratitude and love, as to disown his Saviour,
his faithful, his divine Friend! what honesty and
truth shine in his face! But who is he, on whose
open countenance is painted a glow of virtue and a
detestation of vice, inexorable to the slavish sinner
who knows not God? is he not Peter's friend?
how closely he attends him! with him he con-
verses with all the familiarity of fraternal af-
fection.

Sipha, his guardian angel, answered, right, O
seraph! is thy conjecture. That is Andrew, Peter's
brother. They grew up together from tender in-
fancy, under my care and that of Orion. Often
have I, when his fond mother was affectionately
embracing my infant charge, moulded his heart,
to render it capable of receiving the perfect love
he was afterwards to feel for the Messiah. When
Jesus saw him as he stood by Jordan's silver stream,
he was one of the disciples of John, and still in his

retentive ear resounded the words of that holy,
prophet concerning the mediator, whose coming
was at hand. Jesus, with a look of benignity,
called him. I was present. I beheld a divine
fire pervade his breast; he felt the heavenly·im-
pulse flash upon his soul, and instantly flew to his
saviour.

Now spake Libaniel, Philip's tutelar angel, and
said, He, O Zemia, whom thou seest filled with
social friendship for those two brothers, is Philip.
A smile of benevolence adorns his placid counte-
nance, and the invariable desire of loving as bre-
thren, all whom the Most High created in his own
image, is the ruling passion of his godlike mind.
The great Creator has also tipt his tongue with
mild persuasive eloquence. As at the wakening
morn the dew distils from Hermon, and odours
breathe from the spreading olive, so sweet discourse
proceeds from the lips of Philip.

But who, said Zemia, smiling, is he that with
slow step walks among the cedars? on his face
glows a noble desire of fame. Behold, he appears
like one of those immortal sons of Sion, who con-
secrate their sacred works to posterity, and live in
fame from generation to generation. Their glory
unconfined, becomes boundless and eternal; it
sometimes passes from star to star; and when they,
enraptured, compose hymns to God and his Mes-
siah, we aid the aspiring strains, and sing them in
the heavens.

That, said the seraph Adona, is James the son
of Zebedee. His noble ambition is solely directed
to divine objects: his grand pursuit, to rise to
glory at the great and solemn day, when the Lord
of Life shall awake the dead, and pass sentence on
the sons of man. To his exalted soul, less honour
would be ignominy. On his seeing the Saviour, in

a rapture of joy he ran to meet him.   I saw him
when on Tabor's hallowed mount, Moses and
Elias, sent of God, appeared to the Messiah.   Lo,
bright and glowing clouds encompassed and over-
shadowed them.   Jesus was transfigured : his face
shone more bright than the sun in its meridian
lustre : he was arrayed in silver light.   As in the
holy of holies Aaron the high priest saw the glory
of God, so enraptured by this pomp of celestial
splendor, James admired and contemplated the
glorious appearance. He of the holy twelve, is to be
the first martyr. Thus say the tables of prescience.
He is therefore soon to enter triumphant on the
ample theatre of the eternal state, and to quench
the desires of his longing soul, in the unutterable
delights of never ceasing felicity.

Simon the Canaanite whom thou beholdest sit-
ting, said Megiddon, his tutelar angel, was once a
devout shepherd, whom Jesus called from the field.
His innocent and peaceful life, with his meekness
and simplicity of manners, has gained the heart of
his Lord.   Jesus coming to him on a journey,
he, with hospitable speed, killed a young lamb, and
with assiduous care attended his welcome guest,
transported with the honour of entertaining in his
low cottage the Prophet of God.   Not less grate-
ful was his repast to the Messiah, than that he and
the two angels received from Abraham in the plains
of Mamre.   Come, O Simon !—come, and follow
me, said he, with benignity in his look—follow me,
and leave thy flocks to thy companions.   I am
he, of whom thou, when a youth, heardst the
song of the heavenly host by Bethlehem's limpid
stream.

There is my beloved charge, said Adoram, the
seraph.   Behold James the son of Alpheus.   That
grave and placid countenace is expressive of the

modest virtue which consists not in words, but in
action.   While conscious that he is known to God
though he should be disregarded by man ; forgotten
by posterity, and overlooked by us, his celestial
friends, he would still persevere in his exalted piety
and steady virtue.

Umbriel then stood forth, and stretched out his
hand to Zemia, said, he whom thou seest musing in
the depths of that tall grove, is Thomas, a zealous
disciple.   His mind is continually rapt in medita-
tion, thoughts frequently produce thoughts without
end, and extend before him, like a boundless sea. He
was once almost lost in the dark system of Sadducean
dreams : but was saved by the mighty miracles of
the Messiah.   Then leaving the mazy labyrinths of
entangling error, he came to Jesus.   Yet still, hard
of conviction, he would fill me with solicitude, did I
not know that with his active mind, he has sincerity
of heart, and an ardent love of sacred truth.

Yonder, said the seraph Bildai, is Matthew, who
was educated in the soft luxurious lap of pleasure.
His wealthy parents accustomed him to the sordid
employments of those who, unmindful of their im-
mortal souls, are as insatiably bent on accumulating
shining ore, as if they were to live eternally on this
heavy globe : but on his seeing the blessed Jesus,
the hidden powers of his mind expanded : at a nod
from Christ he followed him, leaving his employ-
ment, which had pressed him down to the earth, to
the groveling souls who have no taste for the more
substantial treasures of heavenly wisdom.   Thus a
brave hero, when called to hazard his life for his
country, breaks from the charms of some fair prin-
cess.   He enters the field.   There the Most High
arrayed in justice, guides the battle, and directs
the hand of death.   The innocents he saves from
the fury of the blood-thirsty enemy, shall with

transports of gratitude proclaim his glory, and if in the midst of slaughter he remembers that he is himself a man, we will chant his name before the Eternal.

Siona, the seraph, then said, that amiable old man with silver locks, is Bartholomew. He is under my care. Observe his devout and engaging countenance. There sacred virtue delights to dwell. By his practice its severities will be rendered more amiable and acceptable to mortals. Thou, O Bartholomew! shalt gather many to Jesus. They shall see thy glorious end, and be struck with thy fortitude, when thou, in the sweat of death, shalt smile on thy murderers, and on thy brethren, with the tranquility of a seraph. Then, ye celestial friends, you will join with me, in wiping the blood from his face, that all may behold his triumph over death, and filled with admiration, turn to the Lord.

That meek and humble disciple, said Elim, is my Lebbeus. Few have such tenderness and sensibility. When I called his immortal spirit from those regions, where souls reside before their union with the body, I found it by a stream which, murmuring like the distant sound of sighs and plaintive moans, creeps along the vale. There, as angels relate, Abbadona lamented, as he returned from Eden, after seeing the mother of mankind, who had lost her spotless innocence. You also well know, that there the seraphs oft bewail the souls intrusted to their care, when after adorning their juvenile years with fair religion, and sanctity of manners, they unhappily blast their blooming virtues, and quitting the nobler pleasures which heaven approves, become infatuated with the false, the shadowy allurements of vice. Alas! how dreadful will be their fate! the angels lament their fall with sighs

F

of pity, and shed such tears, as cannot fall from the
eyes of mortals.   There I found the soul of my dear
Lebbeus, shrouded in tranquil clouds, and listening
with faint perception, to the sound of pensive mur-
murs.   These, where the stronger feelings of the
senses prevail, are disregarded.   Yet when his soul,
clothed with light, entered the body, a slight per-
ception of the melancholy murmurs still remained,
sufficient to impress the mind in its first formation.
Soft in the bosom of a fleecy cloud, I gently con-
veyed the unimbodied spirit to the dwellings of
mortals.   At length his mother brought him forth
in a grove of palms.   I descended invisible from the
top of the rustling branches, and cooled the infant
with refreshing breezes : but even then at the
gloomy sensation that he was born to die, the num-
ber of his tears exceeded that of other mortals.
He passed his youth in tender sorrow, weeping at
the tear shed by a friend, and sympathising in every
woe of his fellow-creatures.   Thus, soft and com-
passionate, has he passed his time with Jesus.
How am I grieved for thee, O Lebbeus ! at the
death of thy Lord, thou, his devout disciple, wilt
sink under the burden of thy grief.   Ah ! support
him, thou gracious Redeemer ! strengthen him in
that hour, thou who pitiest mankind !   Behold
with faultering step he is wandering towards us in
deep affliction.   Here, seraph, of him thou wilt
have a nearer view, and face to face see the softest
and most tender soul.

While Elim was yet speaking, Lebbeus silently
joined them.   Quick the circle of assembled seraphs
widened to admit a mortal.   So the vernal breezes
move before Philomela's plaintive strains.   They
now encompass him, and full of affection, stand as
man with man.   Lebbeus thinking himself alone,
and unobserved, lift up his joined hands, and with

gestures of distress, indulged the transports of his
grief; crying, No where can I find him. Already
one dismal day—already two tedious nights have
fled, and we have not seen him! Ah his cruel
persecutors have at length found and siezed him!
I forsaken, live, though Jesus is dead! Thee have
sinners barbarously slain, and yet I did not see thee
die!—Thine eyes with gentle hand I have not
closed! Say, ye cruel men! where did you mur-
der him? To what dreary desert, to what barren
wild, to what gloomy sepulchre, did ye, inhuman,
drag him, to take away his life? Ah where, my
divine friend, dost thou lie? It is among the dead,
pale and disfigured! The tender grace, the hea-
venly smile of thy compassionate looks, these mur-
derers have stolen!—Thy servants have not seen
thee die! Oh that this heart—this oppressed heart,
might cease to beat!—that my soul, formed for an-
guish, might, like that dusky cloud, fly into the
night of death, that I might there meet my Lord!
Spent with watching, I will lie down and indulge
this heaviness that comes upon me.

Thus lamenting, he sunk into the arms of sleep.
Elim covered him with the slender branches of the
olive; fanned his languid face with his gentle
breath; poured on his head balmy slumbers, and,
while he slept, presented to his mind a dream, in
which he walked conversing with his Lord.

Zemia hung over him full of benevolent sympa-
thy, when a disciple appeared coming from the
gloomy grove before the sepulchres. Tell me, said
he, who is he that ascends the mountain? His
raven locks fall in curls on his ample sloulders, and
a manly beauty appears amidst the austerity of his
countenance; while his head rising supereminent
above those of the other disciples, completes the
dignity of his appearance. But may I, my celestial

friends, presume to say, that if I am not deceived,
I perceive in his countenance, traces of the strongest
agitations of mind, and something that to me ap-
pears mean and sordid. He is, however, a disciple,
and will one day come with Jesus in the clouds of
heaven to judge the world.—But whence, O ye
immortals! is this silence! Will none of you,
my celestial friends, condescend to answer me?
Ah, why do you still continue silent? Have I
formed a mistaken judgment of this disciple, and
does that give you pain? Speak—oh speak—
I own my fault. And thou holy disciple, be not
offended. When thou shalt enjoy the honour of
suffering martyrdom for the truth, and shalt enter
in triumph among the immortals, before these se-
raphs will I atone for my offence, by the most
cordial friendship.

Ah Zemia! must I then answer thee? said
Ithuriel sighing and advancing towards the seraph.
Better would it be for us both, were I to observe,
on this subject, an eternal silence :—Yet I will an-
swer thee. He whom thou seest is Judas Iscariot.
I would not, O seraph, lament over him.—Un-
moved, and without one compassionate tear, would
I behold him. With pious indignation would I
avoid the guilty wretch, had he not been blessed
with a heart formed for every virtue, and passed
his youth unpolluted by crimes—had not the Mes-
siah himself thought him worthy of my care when
his life was pious, holy and irreproachable. But
alas! now he—to add more, would be heaping
sorrow on sorrow! Ah! now I know why, when
in the presence of the Most High, we were dis-
coursing of the souls of the disciples, Eloa the
seraph, on receiving a sign from the Supreme,
descended mournful, and instantly enveloped in
clouds one of the lofty golden seats, set apart for

the twelve disciples, near the Eternal. O that thou, Judas, hadst never been born ! Oh that no seraph had ever mentioned thine immortal soul ! Better —infinitely better would it have been for thee never to have seen the light, than for thee, ungrateful traitor ! to betray thy Lord, and profane the glorious, the sacred office to which thou wert called.

Thus spake the seraph Ithuriel, and with downcast look stood before Zemia, who replied, I shuddering sympathize with thee, and darkness, like that which precedes the dawn, overclouds my eyes. Judas, one of the twelve, and thy charge, O Ithuriel, profane the office of a disciple, and dishonour the gracious Mediator ! this none of the immortals could have believed. Yet, what is his dreadful crime ! What has the abandoned done, before Jesus, and thee, and the celestial spirits : freely tell me though my heart, O Ithuriel ! tremble at the recital.

O seraph ! Ithuriel returned, he hates John, because Christ loves him with greater tenderness than any of his other disciples. And—(fain would he conceal it from himself) he hates the Redeemer ! In an unhappy hour, dishonest avarice took root in his once noble soul : For this is not the vice of youth. Blinded by this base, unsocial passion, he imagines that John will be preferred by the Messiah before the other disciples, and more especially before him, to collect the treasure ; the heavenly treasure, the first fruits of the unbounded wealth of his new kingdom. Thus does he speak ; and this, oft have I heard him murmur with rancorous heart, when in his lonely walks he thought himself unobserved. Once—(long will the horrid image hover in my sight, and fill my heart with silent gloom) Once in the vale Benbinnon, full of inquietude he

gave vent to the agitations of his mind, uttering the
most malignant and impious wishes. Deeply af-
fected, I cast down my eyes, when instantly I beheld
Satan leave him, with an air of bitter mockery and
triumphant smiles ; and then passing by me, gave
me a look of arrogant contempt. At present the
heart of Judas is so torn by the storms of guilty
passions, that I dread lest each black thought, each
fell emotion of his wicked mind, should hurry him
to swift perdition. Oh that thine omnipotent hand,
O God, had held Satan bound in adamantine chains
in the abyss of deepest darkness ! that the immortal
soul thou hast formed for eternal glory, might reco-
ver from her errors, and seize the precious remaining
hours ; that, worthy of her high birth, and the
creative voice by which the Almighty called her to
immortality, and consecrated her to the discipleship,
she, invincible and fearless, might resist the furious
destroyer, with the courage and intrepidity of a se-
raph. But, O thou supreme Wisdom ! thou
Source of Goodness ! be not offended at my
wishes : whatever thou doest, is wisest, most just,
and best.

Dearest seraph, cried Zemia, what says the Me-
diator ?—ah, what does the gracious Mediator say
to his lost disciple ? Can he still see near him the
criminal ? Does he yet love him ? and if he do,
oh ! how does he shew his compassion !

Zemia, constrained by thee, said Ithuriel, I
must reveal all that I would gladly conceal from
myself, from thee, and from the angels. Unworthy
as he is, Jesus still loves him. Full of assiduous
affection, not in words, but by looks of the most
divine benevolence, he lately, when all the disciples
were present, said, Thou art he that will betray me !
But, Zemia, see he approaches, I will retire. I can
no longer bear to look upon the ingrate. Follow

me. Thus saying, Ithuriel hasted away. Zemia
went with him, and Salem, a young seraph who was
John's second guardian, followed them at a dis-
tance ; for God had given to John two tutelar
angels, the chief of whom was Raphael, one of the
most exalted seraphs.

Zemia and Ithuriel now went to Jesus at the se-
pulchres.   There Salem, with radiant countenance,
joined them, and, with a look of cordial affection,
gave them the tender embrace.   A mild joy shone
in Salem's face, and a youthful smile played in his
features.   As the opening gates of a delightful
vernal morn, his mouth poured forth the sweetest
harmony, and from his lips flowed eloquence in soft
mellifluous accents.

Ye seraphs, compose your minds, said he ; there
with Jesus in the tombs, is John, the most amiable
of all the disciples.   Cast your eyes on him, and you
will no longer think of Judas.   Devout as a seraph,
he lives with the Messiah as one of the immortals.
To him the Redeemer opens his heart ; and him
has he chosen his chief confident.   As the friendship
of Gabriel and the exalted Eloa, or as the affection
Abdiel once felt for Abbadona, while living with
him in native innocence, is the friendship that sub-
sists between John and his divine Master.   Of this
he is worthy : for of all the souls of men, the
Creator never formed one more pure and heavenly
than that of John.   I was present when the immor-
tal essence came forth, and beheld a resplendent
rank of young celestial spirits, thus. in flowing
numbers, hail their companion :

We salute thee, holy offspring of the breath
divine !   Beauteous and loving art thou as Salem,
as Raphael heavenly and sublime.   From thee pure
sentiments will flow as dew from the purple clouds
of the morning, and thy humane heart—thy heart,

filled with tender sensations, shall melt, as the eyes of the seraphim, enraptured at the sight of virtue, overflow with sweetest transports. Fair daughter of the breath divine, faithful sister of the soul which once, in its unspotted youth, animated the first of men, we will now conduct thee to the body, thy companion, which smiling nature moulds for thee in proportions just and lovely. It will be beautiful, like the body of the Messiah, which soon the Divine Spirit will form, and which, in manly grace, shall exceed all the sons of Adam. In this thy tender and amiable frame, thy virtues will be proved, till the fair habitation of clay shall be destroyed. It shall then moulder in the dust; but at last thy Salem will seek and awake thee; and if thou hast faithfully performed thy task on earth, will conduct thee, arrayed in celestial beauty, to the embraces of the Messiah, coming in the clouds to judge the world. Thus, enraptured, sang the juvenile spirits of heaven.

Salem ceased. He and the other seraphs, filled with softest affection, remained near John. Thus three brothers encompass a beloved sister, who, in blooming beauty, resembles the fair immortals, while she, with mind untroubled, sleeps on the new blown flowers. Alas! she knows not that her worthy father draws near the end of his virtuous course! With this distressful news her brothers come; but forbear to molest her placid slumbers.

Meanwhile the other disciples, spent with inquietude and fatigue, had fallen asleep: one lay sheltered by the low bending arms of a spreading olive; another in a valley, encompassed by eminences on all sides gently rising; another at the foot of a lofty cedar, which with soft rustling sounds sheds soft repose from its waving top. Some slept in the sepulchres built by the children of the sanguinary city, in honour of the prophets murdered by their fathers : while Judas Iscariot, wearied by the perturbations of his guilty mind, lay near the gentle Lebbeus, his relation and friend.

Satan, who in a secret cave had listened to the characters the angels had given of the disciples, now burst forth, and with fell purpose of dire destruction approached Judas. So in the midnight hour the pestilence silent invades some sleeping city. Death on expanded wings hovers round the walls, breathing poisonous vapours. While the city rests, the sage, still wakeful, sits with his friends, refined in sentiment, under the shade of a leafy bower, regaled with chearful wine. Sober temperance fills the glass, and adds an innocent alacrity to their sublime converse on the charms of friendship, the nature of the soul, and its endless duration. But soon approaches the day of lamentation, Soon death with hollow eyes and countenance terrible, spreads far and wide his baneful influence. Then comes the night of torments and of groans, of heart-rending sighs, and gushing sorrow. Wringing her hands, the tender bride bewails her dearer half, the partner of her soul. Then the distracted mother, whose agonizing heart is deprived of all her little foundlings, curses the day of her birth and theirs. Then even the unfeeling grave-digger stands aghast ; trembling, he joins the crouded dead, and drops into the pit himself had dug.

clouds, and stopping on the tombs, takes a melancholy view of the desert waste, where now solitude

Thus the destroying enemy descended on Judas, and presented to his waking fancy a seducing dream. Quick he enflamed his corrupted heart

which was too much inclined to guilt, with fell
sensations; and thoughts big with rage. So the
red bolt of the heavens, falling on mountains of
sulphur, kindles the ready meterials? then new
subterranean thunders roar, and through the ca-
verns the spreading tempest rolls.   For high mys-
teries, and thoughts apt to inflame the souls of men,
were for his geater condemnation, not unknown to
Satan.   Soon careful solicitude brought back the
seraph Ithuriel to stay by his wretched charge:
but perceiving Satan hovering over him, he trem-
bling stopped; then looking up to the Almighty,
resolved to awake him from his sleep.   Thrice,
with the wings of a storm roaring among the cedars,
he swept over his face: thrice he passed by him
with sounding steps, that made the summit of the
mountain shake.   Yet Judas continued as in the
sleep of death.   To the dreaming disciple Satan,
in the form of his father, appeared with dis-
consolate looks of grief and perturbation ; and
with trembling accents, fraught with guile, thus
spake :

Dost thou here sleep, Judas, careless and at
thine ease? still dost thou continue absent from
Jesus, as if thou knewest not that thou art the
object of his hatred, and that all his other disciples
he prefers to thee? why art thou not continually
near him? why dost thou not attempt to regain
the favour of thy Lord?   Good God! what fault
have I, what crime hast thou committed, that I
should be obliged to leave the region of death to
lament the melancholy fate of thee my son? Dost
thou suppose thou shalt enjoy greater happi-
ness in the new empire Christ is to erect? how
miserably art thou deceived!   Peter and the fa-
vourite sons of Zebedee, will be greater and more
mighty than thee! treasures in a full stream shall

flow to them from the spacious land. All the others too shall receive from the Messiah a much more splendid inheritance than my unhappy son.   Come Judas, I will shew thee his kingdom in all its glory. Rise with me : be not dismayed ; but arm thyself with courage,   Now thou seest before thee that endless chain of mountains, which cast their length-ening shades into that fertile valley.   There gold shall be incessantly dug ; gold, bright and glittering as that of Ophir,; while the valley shall through the prosperous year pour forth a rich exuberance of blessings.   This is the delightful inheritance of the favourite John.   Those hills, covered with vineyards, and those wide-spreading fields, clothed with waving corn, the Messiah has given to Peter. Seest thou all the opulence of that smiling country, where cities rising in lofty splendor, each like Jerusalem, the king's daughter, glitter in the sun, and with their innumerable inhabitants extend along the vale.   Behold how those cities are watered by the limpid streams of a new Jordan, which passes through noble arches in the lofty walls.   Gardens, resembling fertile Eden, wave their blushing fruit, over the golden sands, on its happy shores.   These are the kingdoms of the other disciples.   But now, Judas, my son, observe that far distant mountainous country, wild, stony, and covered with withered shrubs,   How barren, how desolate !   Above it rests night in cold and drisly clouds, and beneath, on the tops of the eminences, a sterile depth of ice and northern snow.   That, O Judas! is thine inheritance.   In those gloomy regions thou, and the birds of night, thy companions, are condemned to wander solitary among the aged oaks.   With what haughty—with what contemptuous airs will the happy disciples look down on thee ! they will pass by without condescending to observe thee !

Ah, Judas, thou weepest with indignation !—but in vain thou weepest !—in vain are all thy tears, while surrounded with despair, thou neglectest to help thyself ! yet listen to me, thy father, and I will disclose to thee my heart. Thou knowest the Messiah delays the promised redemption : the Jews are still in subjection, and he does not appear in haste to erect his new and glorious empire. Thou art also sensible, that the great are most averse to submit to the authority of the Nazarine king, and daily contrive his death. Do thou, therefore, deliver him into the hands of the priests, not to revenge his hatred to thee ; but that he may the sooner overwhelm them with irremediless infamy and confusion, and thus be obliged to found his long expected empire, and to appear before every eye as powerful and as formidable as he really is. By this means thou wilt at once enter into the possession of thine inheritance, and the sooner improve it by labour and industry, by tillage and trade, so as to give it some little resemblance to the more fertile inheritances of thy companions. Meanwhile, of this thou mayst be certain, that the grateful priests will not fail to reward thee for delivering up Jesus. This is the advice of a father ever attentive to thy interest. Fix thine eye upon me, and know me in spite of the paleness of death. Awake. Despise not the admonitions of a parent who is come to revive thy courage ; and let me not return melancholy and dejected to the mansions of the dead.

Satan having thus infected the mind of Iscariot with this deceitful vision, swelled, inflated with pride, like a mountain raised by a volcano, while convulsive earthquakes rock the neighbouring eminences, and sink the surrounding hills. Judas awoke. Furious he started up, crying, Yes, it

was he—it was the voice of my deceased father!
—Thus he spake—thus he looked, when before
me he expired. Ah! it is then but too true that
Jesus hates me! the very dead know that he hates
me! Well, I will haste and put in execution my
father's advice.—But, with what treachery shall
I then act towards the Messiah! May not this
vision be owing to the disgust that rankles in my
heart? or may it not be suggested by Satan?
Hence, ye grovelling, ye timorous surmises! I
already feel that I am enflamed with the disire of
riches—with the impatience of revenge! O my
soul! why art thou so tender, so scrupulous?
visions present themselves before thee—visions en-
join thee revenge.—The command of a vision sanc-
tifies the deed.

Satan heard him thus speak—him who had pre-
viously offended the Almighty, by staining his soul
with base and ignoble passions. He heard him
with pleasure, and glorying in his success, raised
his head still higher, and unseen, looked down on
Judas with triumphant arrogance. Thus on the
top of high Olmypus, a dreadful rock impénds
over the swelling sea, proudly threatening destruc-
tion to the approaching mariners; but soon will
the red lightning, with hedious roar and terrible
confusion, strike it down, and lay it in the lowly
deep. The islands will see its fall and exult in
the avenging thunder.

Satan, now leaving Olivet, with lofty strides stalk-
ed unseen over Jerusalem, and repaired to Caiaphas,
who slept in his still silent palace, by delusive
visions, to infuse into the wicked heart of the ene-
my and high-priest of God, emotions still more
vile. Meanwhile Judas continued on the mount
filled with thoughts malignant as his soul.

The day was rising on the slumbering world

when Jesus awoke, and with him John. Together
they walked up the mount, whence they saw the
disciples still asleep. Jesus then taking the devout
Lebbeus by the hand, said, I, my dear friend, am
here, and still alive. Up sprang the transported
disciple, and embraced him with tears of joy.
Then running to the other disciples, awaked them,
and brought them to their divine Master, when,
affectionately gathering round him, he with a gra-
cious smile thus addressed them.

Come, my pious friends, this day will we re-
joice before we exchange the last embrace. Still
the heavens, from the early clouds, shed the refresh-
ing dews on this favoured land. Behold the
towering cedar planted by my Father's hand, af-
fords her cooling shade; and still I behold man,
formed after the divine image, walking with the
immortals. But this will be no longer seen. Soon
will the darkening sky be wrapped in gloom.
Soon will the earth with dire convulsions tremble.
Soon will man look on me with murderous eye, and
soon will ye all fly from me, your Lord. Weep
not, O Peter ! and thou, my tender, my affectionate
disciple, be not afflicted : for while the bridegroom
is present, no grief is felt by the bride. Comfort
yourselves, ye shall see me again ; Yes, ye shall
see me again at my resurrection—ye shall see
me with all the raptures with which a mother re-
covers her only son.

Thus he spake, but while his face was illumined
with grace and love, his heart was filled with
keenest anguish. He then descended the mount,
accompanied by all his disciples except Judas, who,
standing in the thick shade of tufted trees, had
heard the Saviour's speech, and looking after Jesus
who walked away with quick step, said, He him-
self already knows that a day of darkness hangs

over his head   He is therefore not ignorant of the
manner in which he will treat his persecutors, and
accomplish the great work he has begun.   But
does he know the plot I am meditating against him ?
Does he know that I intend to betray him !—But,
alas ! should I be deceived—should my dream
prove an illusion, and hated as I am, did it come
to encrease my torment ?—Ah cursed be the hour
in which I closed my eyes, and the apparition of my
father appeared to my view ! May shrieks resound
through the mountain !—May dying groans deepen
the horror of the mouldering sepulchres!—Cursed
be the place where I lay !—But why do I thus
rave ? Why give way to such gloomy ideas ?
Why am I thus at variance with myself ?   It
is not my fault if I am deceived.   But dost
thou, hoary, visionary sage, enjoin me to com-
mit a crime, by betraying the Messiah ?—him
whose precepts—whose example I have professed
to follow—him whom I ought to love and reverence ?
May the day—that fatal day, be cursed, when Jesus
chose me—when full of love, and with a look of be-
nevolence, he invited me to follow him ! May it
be covered with clouds and the gloom of night !
May the pestilence walk in darkness, and destructive
diseases slay in the heat of noon ! Let no man
name it ! May it be forgotten of God !—But
whence this agony—this secret horror ? Why, my
bones, do ye tremble ? Why am I so pusillanimous ?
Why do I thus torment myself ?   I will rouze my
courage, and shake off these weak foreboding fears.
My sight did not deceive me, and if it did, can I by
any other means accomplish my desires ? Thus he
raved : meanwhile, since his vision, he had advanced
two dreadful hours nearer to eternity.

THE END OF THE THIRD BOOK.

THE

MESSIAH.

BOOK. IV.

THE ARGUMENT.

Caiaphas assembles the Sanhedrim, relates his dream, and proposes the death of Jesus. Philo, a Pharisee, supposes the dream a fiction, but joins, with great vehemence, in recommending the death of Christ. They are warmly opposed by Gamaliel and Nicodemus. Judas has a private conference with Caiaphas. The Messiah sends Peter and John to prepare the passover. Peter sees Mary the mother of Jesus, Lazarus, Mary his sister, Semida, and Cidli, coming in quest of Jesus. The pious love of Semida and Cidli. Mary proceeds in search of Jesus, who stops at the tomb of Joseph of Arimathea, near Golgatha. He proceeds to Jerusalem, and is met by Judas. Ithuriel, no longer able to continue that traitor's guardian angel, is made Peter's second angel. Jesus institutes the memorial of his death. Judas goes out. Jesus prays with his disciples, and returns to the mount of Olives.

TERRIFIED by a vision, and tortured by anxiety, Caiaphas lay restless on his bed. Sleep fled from his eyes, or if for a few moments they were closed by slumber, he suddenly started, and agitated by his tumultuous thoughts, furiously turned. Thus in a field of slaughter a dying reprobate, hardened in guilt, rolls in agony : The approaching victor, the prancing steed, the harsh din of arms, the shouts of the enemy, the groans of the dying, and all the thundering roar of war,

distract his mind. Covered with ghastly wounds
he lies and seems to sink in wild stupidity among
the dead. Then again reviving, he curses himself,
curses the Most High, and would fain disbelieve
his being. Thus lay Caiaphas, and thus he rose;
ordering the priests and elders of the people to be
suddenly assembled. In the midst of his stately
palace was the hall of the Sanhedrim, built of the
spoils of Lebanon's lofty forest, with all the mag-
nificence that was seen in the works of Solomon.
Thither came the priests and elders. Among the
latter was Joseph of Arimathea, who, super-emi-
nent in wisdom, did honour to the posterity of
Abraham. Serene as the placid moon, riding in
lucid midnight clouds, he repaired to the assembly.
Thither also came Nicodemus, a friend to the
Messiah and to Joseph. Then entered Caiaphas
with proud step, and with a countenance enflamed
by rage, thus spake:

Now ye fathers of Jerusalem, we must take our
final resolution, and with powerful arm destroy our
adversary, lest he destroying us, this be the last time
in which we assemble in this holy Sanhedrim. This
divine priesthood, instituted by the great Jehovah
himself on mount Sinai, and revealed to us by the
greatest of all the prophets—This divine priest-
hood, which continued through all the succeeding
ages, and which neither the towers of Babylon, nor
formidable Rome, seated on her seven hills, could
ever destroy, a wretched visionary, O Israel! is
ready to abolish. To your shame, he has been
suffered to declare with impunity, that he will
destroy the temple of the Lord. Is not all Jerusalem
his? Are not the cities of Judea servilely devoted
to their idolized Prophet? The people grown
blind and superstitious, shun the temple of their
wise forefathers: they flock to remote desarts, to

gaze at his seducing miracles : miracles in which
he is only the agent of Satan.   What can more
effectually blind—what fill with greater amazement
the stupid vulgar, than his raising the dead ?—or
rather awaking the sick from sleep ?   Yet we still
continue in supine indolence, waiting, perhaps, till
his adherents rise in arms, and in some dreadful
tumult, murder us before his face, that he may
shew his power in restoring us to life !   Is it pos-
sible, fathers, that you can thus sit in silent astonish-
ment ? that ye can yet entertain a doubt ?   Yes, ye
incredulous, ye doubt—but doubt now and sleep
forever.   Ye know with what rebellious shouts
Judea has hailed him king.   Never before were
the ways so spread with the branches of the palm.
Never did the air resound with such loud hosannas.
It were indeed to be wished, that instead of those
triumphant acclamations, he had heard the curse
of the Eternal :   that instead of those repeated
hosannas,' his ears had been deafened by the voice
of thunder.   Ye degenerate and unworthy fathers
of the people (pardon these expressions, which pro-
ceed from a mind inflamed with holy indignation)
—not prudence alone, but God himself orders us
to cut him off from the face of the earth.   In
ancient times Jehovah spake to our fathers in
dreams ; and ye yourselves shall judge, whether,
upon this extraordinary occasion, your high priest
has not had a dream from God.

Behold, at midnight when anxious I lay on my
bed, revolving in my mind, what might be the issue
of the late tumults, I dropped asleep.   When lo !
I found myself in the temple, preparing the sacrifice
of atonement.   Already the blood streamed before
me ; already with solemn awe, was I entering the
Holy of Holies, when drawing the vail aside—My
bones still tremble ! still the terrors of God over-

power me !   O ye fathers ! I beheld Aaron in his
sacred vestments, with a menacing brow, advancing
towards me. Holy anger flashed with insupportaole
blaze from his eyes ; the piercing rays which
beamed on me from his breast-plate, shone refulgent,
like Horeb ; the winged cherubs over the ark of
the covenant, fluttered dreadful ; and my ephod,
reduced to ashes, instantly fell to the ground. Fly,
thou disgrace to the priesthood, cryed Aaron in the
voice of terror—fly, miserable that thou art, and no
more presume to degrade thy sacred office, by ap-
pearing here as priest of the Lord. Art thou the high
priest of the great Jehovah ?   (Here he gave me
a furious and vengeful look, like that of a man who
suddenly sees his mortal enemy, whom he is re-
solved to slay)—Art thou the high priest of the
great Jehovah ?   Art thou vested with that sacred
office ?—thou who, criminally supine, canst see
that impious seducer with impunity profane the
holy sanctuary: make a mock of my brother Moses,
of me, and of Abraham, and violate the sabbath of
God ? Go, most miserable ! lest on thy longer
stay, the mercy seat of the Eternal should consume
thee with sacred fire.

At these words I fled. My hair was dishevelled.
Ashes were on my head. Terrified, frantic, and
without my vesture, I ran forth to the people, who
enraged at the sight, attempted my life. Here I
awoke. Three hours full of unutterable anguish
—three hours most horrible, I lay, after this
dreadful vision, as in the agonies of death. Still I
tremble—still my heart beats with terror—still is
my faultering tongue unable distinctly to perform
its office. He must die. From you, fathers,
I expect a speedy determination on the manner of
his death

Here Caiaphas was silent: but after a short

pause, he resumed. Better is it that one should
die, than that all should perish. But in this let
us act with prudent caution. Let it not be at the
feast, lest the infatuated populace should attempt
to save him. Caiaphas ceased.

No sound, nor the least murmur was heard
throughout the full assembly. As if struck dead
by the flash of the heavens, all sat silent and mo-
tionless. Joseph observing the solemn stillness,
resolved to speak in the defence of Jesus, but was
restrained by the fury with which Philo, a dreaded
priest, stepped forth. Too proud to deliver his
sentiments, before affairs were ripe for their being
put in execution, he had never yet publicly men-
tioned Jesus. Great was his character for wisdom,
even with Caiaphas, whom he hated : for he him-
self was a Pharisee. His heavy hollow eyes were
filled with malignant fury, and with rapid and
resentful voice, he thus began:

Caiaphas, in vain dost thou pretend to have re-
ceived a vision from God, as if thou didst not know
that the Eternal never appears to the voluptuous
sensualist, and that no spirits convey revelations to
the hypocritical Sadducees, who disbelieve their
existence. Either thou amusest us by a fiction, or
thou sawest the vision. If the first be the case,
thou here shewest thyself worthy of thy Roman
policy, and thy purchased priesthood : if the latter,
thou, the high priest of God, oughtest to know,
that the Almighty, to punish those who violate
his laws, permits their being deceived by lying
spirits. Thus, that Ahab, the slave of Baal and of
Jezebel, might perish, and the blood of the mur-
dered Naboth no longer cry for vengeance, an
angel of death steps forth from the throne, and
dictates false prophesies to the prophets. When
behold, the rolling chariots bring back the king

mortally wounded. He dies. His blood 'defiles
the field where Naboth was slain. Thy dream
indeed enjoins the punishment of our adversary.
Yet no dream hast thou had, but what has been
furnished by thy fertile invention. Dost thou not
tremble at naming the angel of death? perhaps one
of that order already waits before the eternal throne,
for thy blood, O Caiaphas! destined soon to be
spilt. I plead not for the seditious Jesus, neither do
I hold him innocent. Compared with the Nazarene,
thou art a less offender. Thou art only a dis-
grace to the priesthood of God; but he would
abolish it. This Jesus has been weighed in the
balance in which criminals, however powerful, even
the proud conquerors of nations, are found wanting.
He has been weighed, and is doomed to certain
death. He shall therefore die. With these eyes
I will see him expire: they shall behold his pale
and bloody corse. The earth of the hill on which
he suffers, I will carry into the Holy of Holies: or
at the great altar, lay stones stained with his
smoking blood, as an everlasting memorial. But
how base is thy fear, O Caiaphas! that would
warp us into cowardice, and make us stand in awe
of the giddy rabble. This mean pusillanimity
was never learnt from our forefathers. Let us then
hasten to prevent the thunder—God's avenging
thunder: lest it should not destroy him alone—lest
our eye-balls roll in death, while they behold his
last agonies; and we expire, defiled by being near
him. Did the Tishbite fear the people, when he
slew the priests of the sleeping Baal, whom all
their tempestuous clamour could not awake? His
confidence was in him who made the sacred flame
descend from heaven. But without the assistance
of the descending fire, I will go forth to the people,
and woe to him that shall dare to oppose me, and

once presume to say, that the blood of the dreaming
visionary is not an acceptable oblation to the great
Jehovah !   At a sign from me the multitude shall
join in stoning him.   Before the eyes of all Judea
—before the face of the Romans, shall the rebel
die :   then shall we secure and triumphant sit in
judgment and enter the sanctuary of God rejoicing.

Philo then, with uplifted hands, advanced into
the midst of the assembly, where stopping, he, with
loud voice, made this malignant and profane excla-
mation : Blessed spirit ! wherever thou art, whe-
ther cloathed in heavenly splendor, thou sittest with
Abraham, and assemblest about thee the prophets ;
or whether thou condescendest to visit the congrega-
tions of thy children, and to walk among mortals—
O Spirit of Moses ! to thee I swear, by that eternal
covenant, which thou, by the Divine command,
broughtest from the fiery tempest, that I will take
no rest, till he who hates thee is numbered with
the dead !—till with my hands, full of the Naza-
rene's blood, I come to the high altar, hold it over
my hoary head, and wave it as a thank-offering
before the Lord

Thus he spake, and strove to believe, that the
heart-searching God does not detest such whited
sepulchres.   Yet his conscience called him hypo-
crite.   He felt the just reproach : but full of
inflexible rage, stood with undaunted eye before
the council.

Meanwhile Caiaphas leaned on his golden seat,
trembling with indignation.   His face glowed with
a fury too great for utterance, and he continued
silent, with his eyes fixed on the floor.   When the
Sadducees observing his discomposure, with tumul-
tuous violence rose up against Philo.   So in the
field of hostile slaughter, the foaming steeds of an
iron chariot obtain the reins, when the whizzing

lance, with quivering flight, strikes the rider, who
with his mouth disgorging blood, falls under the
wheels. Then neighing fierce, they threaten with
their flaming eyes : they snuff the wind, and striking
the earth, it trembles under their feet. The en-
raged assembly would have instantly broke up,
had not Gamaliel arisen. Serene wisdom sat on his
venerable countenance, and stretching out his hand,
he, in graceful accents, thus spake :

- O fathers ! if in this tumultuous heat of fiery
rage, calm and sober reason may be suffered to ap-
pear, and you are not enemies to prudence, I entreat
you to hear me. Should the eternal quarrel be
again revived—should the discordant names of
Sadducees and Pharisees produce a perpetual ani-
mosity between you, how will you be able to destroy
the Prophet ? but God has probably sent envy
and variance among you, in order to reserve to his
supreme justice, the office of pronouncing sentence
on the Nazarene. Let us, then, O ye fathers !
leave to the Eternal the vindication of his own
cause. You may be too weak to wield his thunders,
and those mighty arms at which the heavens them-
selves tremble, may sink you in the dust. Be ye si-
lent therefore before the Most High, and, with calm
submission, listen to the approaching Judge. Soon
will he speak, and the earth from the rising to the
setting sun shall astonished hear his voice. If God
speaks to the storm, and says, Do thou tear him in
pieces ! and to the tempest, Do thou scatter his
bones like the dust, and disperse them among the
four winds ! or to the glittering sword, Arm the
avenging hand, and drink the blood of the sinner !
If he says to the abyss, Open, and receive him into
thy bowels, then is he a guilty visionary. But if,
with unexampled power and grace, he continues,
by his heavenly miracles, to diffuse happiness over

the earth : if by his means the blind exulting, lifts up his face to the great luminary of day ; or with enlightened eyes, and overflowing joy, he gazes enraptured on the hand that kindly led him along his darksome way—(Forgive me, if struck by actions great like these, I, in your opinion, speak more highly of him than I ought)—if the deaf ear again hears the benediction of the priest, the song of the bride, and the sacred hallelujah : if by him the dead walk, witness against us, and first lifting their new awakened eyes towards heaven, turn them with pious indignation on us, shew us their tombs, and threaten us with the judgment seat, at which they have already appeared : or if (in which he seems still more divine) he continues to live among us without reproach, and by his astonishing virtue, such godlike miracles are wrought, I conjure you, O ye fathers ! by the living God, I conjure you, to say, whether we ought to condemn him—whether we ought to fight against God. Here Gamaliel ceased, and, with an air of dignity, returned to his seat.

The sun now from his meridian height spread his rays over Jerusalem. At the same time Judas was drawing near, in order to lay his proposal before the Sanhedrim. But first Ithuriel and Satan went thither, and both invisible stood among the priests, where, without being seen, they surveyed the crowded assembly.

Nicodemus sat, and silently surveyed every face. Each member of the court appeared like the self-condemned sinner, when pale and trembling, he hears the thunder roll awful over his head. Even Philo and Caiaphas seemed struck, confounded and disturbed by Gamaliel's words. Nicodemus beholding them with a mixture of contempt and fear, arose, Sweetness and benevolence were visible

in his look, while an air of solemnity and grief
were mixed with that noble dignity that arises from
an approving conscience. His eye, which faithfully
expressed the situation of his mind, mourned and
concealed not its tears. He believed in Christ, and
resolved to acknowledge him before his most inve-
terate enemies. After a moment's pause, lifting up
his hands, he thus spake :

Blessed be thou, O Gamaliel! blessed be the
words of thy lips! the Lord hath appointed thee
his champion, and a two-edged sword hath he put
into thy mouth! thy speech hath divided asunder
our bones, which still shake! still do our feeble
knees fail! darkness still covereth our eyes, and
still God is seen wielding his wrath, to strike
those who oppose his will, into the dust from
whence they sprang! O Gamaliel! may the Most
High, who taught thee this wisdom, who hath en-
dued thee with such magnanimity, be thy protec-
tion! May the Messiah, the sent of God, be thy
Saviour, and the Saviour of thine offspring! But
ye, the persecutors of the great Prophet of God,
I cannot bless—not thee Caiaphas— not thee Philo
—For you I mourn—and if the voice of sorrow
can find an entrance into your hearts—if tears of
compassion, streaming in behalf of innocence, can
move ye—these tears also implore your pity for
spotless virtue! Know, ye fathers, that the sacred
blood being once shed, it will lift up its prevailing
voice like a tempest!—it will call—it will rise to
heaven—to the ear of the Eternal! He will hear
it : he will descend, and give judgment without
mercy to those who have shewn no mercy, by inhu-
manly slaying his holy Prophet. O Judea! Judea!
he will call, where is thy Messiah? if he
be no where to be found, the arm of God, will
throughout all thy land, destroy the men of

blood, who have put to death the Holy One of Israel !

Nicodemus here hung down his head, and weeping, returned to his seat. Still Philo sat with menacing looks, trembling with impotent rage, which his pride struggled in vain to conceal. Disordered by the conflict of contending passions, his eyes became dim, night hovered round him, and darkness hid from his sight the whole assembly. He was ready to sink : no other relief could he obtain, but by his giving fresh motion to his congealed blood, by venting his thoughts. He made the effort. The spirits pent up in his high swoln heart, flushed in his face, and starting up furious, he rushed forward. So when on inaccessible mountains an approaching tempest terrific hangs, one of the black clouds, surcharged with lightning, kindled for destruction, bursts single, and while others strike only the tops of the aspiring cedars, that, armed with a thousand thunders, rolls with repercussive roar through the whole ethereal expanse ; then the mountainous forests blaze, and splendid palaces are reduced to extensive heaps of ruins. As Philo advanced forward, Satan beheld him, and within himself thus said :

Let thy speech be devoted to me : rapid and impetuous let it flow as the floods of hell : terrible as the flaming sea : impassioned as the lofty sounds with which I dispense my orders to the damned : raucorous, and with fury, as the gods of the deep utter their complaints to the immense mountains of the fiery abyss, when the streams of flowing sulphur stop to listen, and glow with a more livid blaze at their execrations. Thus Philo speak, and lead in triumph thy captive hearers. Let thine heart give vent to ideas, such as Adramelech himself would not blush to own. Speak death to the

Nazarene. Thy recompence expect from me. At the sight of his blood thy whole soul shall overflow with such joys as hell affords. And when thou comest to us, I myself will be thy conductor, and introduce thee to those heroic spirits, who delighted in carnage, and in spreading desolation all around. Thus spake Satan, unheard of all but Ithuriel.

Philo, standing with eyes lift up towards heaven, cried, Thou altar of blood, where the lamb of atonement was offered, and ye other sacred altars, once loaded with undefiled sacrifices, which sent up to God a sweet smelling savour ! even thou Holy of Holies ! ye cherubs ! thou mercy seat, where the Eternal once sat, and from the sacred darkness pronounced sentence on the sinner ! thou temple of the Lord, filled with the divine glory ! and thou, O Moriah, where the voice of Jehovah was heard ! when the Nazarene shall lay ye waste, and these sons of Belial, by him protected, shall bring you to destruction, let me—let me be esteemed guiltless of your ruin. When our children with anxious looks, and trembling knees, wringing their hands, seek the God of their fathers, and do not find him—when they seek in vain the Lord, because the Nazarene has erected his throne, where Jehovah himself resided above the cherubim ! let it be known, that of this I am innocent. If idolaters bring polluted incense to the sacred place, where hung the veil, where once the high-priest alone went with humble reverence to the mercy seat ! may my afflicted eyes never behold the impious deed ! may God rather close them in death, than permit them to see this abomination of desolation, fall on his people ! All in my power will I do to avert the impending evil. And, hear me, O God of Israel ! If ever from thy lofty throne thou heardest the petition of a mortal, prostrate in the dust, of this lowly earth—

if at the command of Moses the earth swallowed
up Corah, Dathan, and Abiram—if at Elijah's
prayer, the fire descended on the messengers sent
by the king, and consumed them from the top of
Carmel—hear me, O God of Israel ! while I curse
them who revile thee and defend the foe of thy pro-
phet Moses.   May thy end O Nicodemus be like
the end of the Impostor, and thy grave like the
grave of the sower of sediton !—May it be among
the graves of the murderers, who were stoned at a
distance from the temple and the altar.   When
thou diest, may thy heart be hardened !—may it be
obdurate and inflexible ! may not God suffer thee
to weep, lest weeping thou shouldest turn to him !
for thou has wept for the impious, and thy servile
eye, in opposition to the Eternal, has shed profane
tears.   Thou too, O Gamaliel ! hast espoused the
cause of the seducer.   May a horrid gloom—may
black darkness cover thine eyes, then mayest thou
wait in vain for relief from the Nazarene, and pine
away with fruitless grief ! may deafness close thine
ear, and horror thy life : then lie till the Nazarene
awake thee—till thou rot.   And if thou hast declared
to the stupid herd who, like thyself, idolize this
pretended Saviour, that he will raise thee up, may
that many headed beast trample on thy grave,
and mock both thee and thy Prophet.   When thy
soul, divested of its covering of flesh, stands trem-
bling before the judgement seat to bear her sentence,
then, O God ! stretch out thy dreaded arm, and
strike the appalled sinner—strike also Nicodemus,
and fulfil on both the curse I, for thine honour pro-
nounce.   But reserve thy fiercest anger, before
which the mountains tremble, and all hell is dismayed,
for a still more guilty sinner—Wrap thyself in ten
thousand thunders, then go forth and strike the
Nazarene.   I have been young, and now am old,

yet have I continually worshipped and adored thee
after the manner of our fathers ; permit, not then,
O God, my dying eyes to behold the Nazarene
triumphant.   Should he conquer, thine eternal
covenant, thine holiness, thine oath, and the blessing
thou gavest to Abraham and to his prosterity, are
all vain—are all annulled.   Then will I, before all
Judea, renounce thy laws and ordinances—then
will I live without thee—without thee will I lay
my drooping head in the silent grave.   If thine
arm doth not cut off the Impostor, never didst
thou appear to Moses !   The burning bush at the
foot of mount Horeb was all an illusion !   Thou
didst not in tremendous state descend on the top of
Sinai, nor did the trumpet sound, or the thunder
roar, or the mountain shake !   Then both we and
our forefathers from time immemorial, have, of all
the nations upon earth, been the most worthy of
pity !   For no law came down from heaven, and
thou art not the God of Israel.

Here Philo, with wrathful countenance, returned
to his place. Nicodemus stood with down-cast eyes,
like one who patient under oppression experiences
in his own breast all that dignity and elevation
of sentiment, which arises from conscious virtue
and purity of heart.   Gravity sat in his face, and
in his soul was heaven.   The godlike man was
filled with awful thoughts, and revolved in his mind
the solemn night when he discoursed with the
Messiah on mysteries sublime.   While the Saviour
spake, enraptured, he beheld his heavenly smile,
his look of grace, the more than human lustre of his
eyes : he saw the display of paradisaical innocence,
the lofty, the resplendent trace of the Son of God.
This now filled him with silent ecstacy ; he was too
highly blessed to be afraid of man.   Elevated by
a flaming ardor, an heavenly awe to himself he

seemed as if standing in the presence of God, before
the assembled race of man, at the general Judgment.
On him were fixed the looks of the whole assembly.
His eye was serene, filled with the irresistible fire
of awful virtue ; his air commanding attention, and
he thus began.

Happy am I, who with these eyes have seen the
Messiah ! Happy am I, in having beheld the Hope
of Israel ! the deliverer, whom Abraham, while
solitary walking in the grove of Mamre, oft longed
to see ! whom David would, with joyful transport,
by his prayers, have brought down from the arms
of the Father ! whom the prophets with holy tears
longed to behold ! but whom God gave to us the
unworthy ! Thou, the First-born of the Father,
full of grace and truth, didst divide the heavens, and
come down to bless thy people. Yet these term
thee a visionary and a sinner. O thou guiltless :—
thou most innocent !—who are they that thus de-
fame thee ? When didst thou invent lying visions ?
When was thy soul polluted by sin ? did the divine
Jesus stand before the assembled Israelites, when
thou, O Philo ! wast present ? didst thou not then
hear him cry aloud, Who among you is able to con-
vict me of sin ? Where, Philo, was then this furi-
ous wrath—those lips, slanderous and profane ?
why didst thou and thy surrounding companions
stand speechless ? why at first did an universal
silence reign, and every ear remain fixed in expec-
tation ? There were seen faces full of rapturous
joy, while others were filled with anxious fear,
dreading lest some should step forth and witness
against him. How aweful was this silence !—this
suspence ! but when among the innumerable mul-
titude none stepped forth—when none could find
cause of accusation against the great Prophet of
God, suddenly the voices of the applauding people

on all sides ascended to the skies, while with the
loud acclaim Moriah shook, and the woody sum-
mit of Olivet trembled ! Then, flocked to him
the once blind and dumb, and with an effusion of
joy, returned him their most grateful thanks. Then
the numberless crowds, he had before miraculously
fed in the deserts hasted to bless this Friend of man.
Then was heard among the people the loud voice of
the youth whom at the gate of Nain, he had restored
to life. Oh more than man ! cried he, thou Son
of the living God ; the hand which I stretch out
to thee was once stiff ! These eyes that weep—
that weep at seeing thee, O thou divine were
closed ! This soul which exulting, is filled with
fervent love, had quitted its fleshly abode ! They
were carrying me to the tombs of the dead !—But
thou to these stiffened limbs—to these closed eyes,
didst life and animating heat impart ! Again I saw
the earth and sky, and by me stood my trembling
mother !—Thou calledst back the departed soul !—
They carried me not to my tomb !—Thou art more
than man ! thou art not a sinner ! Save me, thou
Son of the Eternal God ! thou the promised seed !
the joy of thy mother ! the joy of the earth, by thee
redeemed.

Thus he spake, while Philo, with downcast eyes,
sat poring on the ground. Then, after a moment's
pause, he resumed, Why, O Philo ! didst thou
silent stand before all Judea ?—Yet why need I
here relate these events !—Ye already know them.
Hadst thou, Philo, eyes to see—hadst thou ears to
hear—wert not thine understanding wrapt in dark-
ness, and thine heart plunged in the gall of bitter-
ness, long wouldest thou have known him to have
been the Son of the Eternal Father ! or wert thou
too stupid for this, thou shouldest have stood in
awe of God, and have reverently waited in the dust,

till the Judge of the whole earth had justified him from heaven, or sent destruction on his head.

O Religion thou offspring of God ! thou sacred friend of man ! fair daughter of truth ! sublimest teacher of celestial virtue ! best blessing sent from heaven ! immortal like thy divine parent ! lovely as the angels of God ! and sweet as the eternal life ! Thou art the creatress of elevated sentiments ; the mother of pure devotion ; or, as a seraph has named thee, thou art Excellence inexpressible, when thy lucent beams descend into the noble soul ! But in the minds of the proud hypocrite, and of the wicked bigot, how art thou transformed ! thou art then the daughter of the first incendiary ! a priestess that delights in blood ! No longer bearest thou thy native lovely form ; fair as light, most meek and humble ! thou then art black as everlasting night, and smeared by the blood slain by thy murderous hand ! Thou art an hideous fiend that hoverest over altars smoking with human victims ! Thou, presumptuous, stealest the thunder reserved by the Sovereign Judge for his own use ! Thy foot stands on hell ! thy head, menacing, towers to heaven !—Thou teachest the wicked to murder thy best friend. But—O Religion !—Religion !—dost thou breathe murder ? dost thou delight in slaughter ? dost thou animate the breast of the assassin ?—No. Some spirit of hell assumes thy name !—some spirit of darkness wears thy garb, to fulfil the counsels of the damned—O Religion, ever fair and lovely !—O Religion, most injured ! actions like these are far from thee, thou offspring of the God of grace and mercy ! thou fountain of peace and salvation ! thou sweetest charm of life ! —of death !—of heaven !————

My soul is enflamed with pious ardor, yet while

rapt in contemplation of this amazing subject, I am
filled with pity for you. An abhorrence, mixed with
compassion seizes my soul, while I reflect on your
insensibility to every humane, every generous senti-
ment : that you have rendered yourselves unable to
distinguish between religion, and the thirst of
blood : that your dark minds can scarce discern the
bright beams that irradiate the fair form of amiable
innocence ! But little doth innocence regard her
not being seen by you, while she is seen by the pure
Source of all Good, and by the enraptured spirits
of heaven ! Innocence will not fear, though con-
demned by the abject sinner, while seraphs stand
and admire, and the Eternal, seated on his lofty
throne, smiles benignant. Oh when the sons of
earth rise and witness against her, how little, how
contemptible do they appear ! But what ap-
pearance will they make, when standing before the
whole assembly of the awakened dead ?—when all
the host of heaven shall witness against them !—
when the loud voice of a cherub shall call the saints
they have persecuted !—when the Lord himself
shall speak, and lead them triumphant into glory !
How will they then, seized with horror, call to
the hills to hide them ! to the mountains to fall
upon their heads ! to the sea to overwhelm them
with its waves ! and to desolation to reduce them to
nothing ! that they may be hid from those they
have unjustly condemned, and not meet the eye of
the dreadful righteous ! that they may be hid
from the tremendous wrath of the mighty Judge,
who will espouse the cause of the innocent !
Strengthen me, ye lofty ideas of the solemn, the
universal judgment ! May ye be to me as the
mount of God, to which I may fly, when—O my
dying Lord ! thy last look strikes through my soul !
—Too plainly do I already feel the strong emotions

that will then swell my heart. When I think of
thy approaching death, a two-edged sword seems
to glitter over my head.—In vain, ye lofty ideas of
the coming judgment, do ye elevate my soul—a full
heart, swelled with grief like mine, attends not the
awful trump. Shalt thou die ?—thou divine—
thou who, when young, I have carried in these
arms, and clasped to my heart, with silent joyful
admiration ? Men, distinguished by their wisdom
and learning, with amazement gathered round thee
and improved by thy discourse ! Even legions of
celestial spirits issued from the everlasting gates,
and descended to hear the words of thy mouth :
then, enraptured, returned, singing thy praise.
Behold thou commandest the tempest, and the
tempest rejoices to obey. The storm is hushed.
Thou risest and walkest on the sea : thou treadest
on the fluid waters.—The heavens see thee walking
on the liquid deep !—Shalt thou die ?—Yes, if
such be the sacred decree of the Eternal, thou shalt
die—If the Most High has resolved not to interpose,
but to suffer these most impious to dip their guilty
hands in thy sacred blood—thou shalt die ! but I
will weep over thy grave. I will go to the holy
brook of Bethlehem, where Mary bore thee.—
There will I bewail thy death !—there will I die !
—I will lament over thee, thou best of all the hu-
man race ! thou Son of God ! thou Angel of the
Covenant ! thou Prince of Peace ! May my tomb
be near to that of the righteous Jesus—near the
bones that rest in peace and safety, to awake to
life eternal !—Yet why do I delay to leave this
assembly ! Guiltless and undefiled I leave it—
God has heard me—me who am pure from shedding
innocent blood : now thou Judge of the earth, call
me to thyself ! for I have no part in the council
of sinners.

Having thus spoke, he for a few moments stood silent, and then with a countenance of angelic serenity, cried, Philo, thou cursest me, but thee I bless. This I have learned from my Lord and Saviour, whom thou wouldst slay—For thou wouldst slay gentle mercy and forgiving grace. Listen, oh listen to my advice, and know him. When thou standest on the brink of death—When the innocent blood thou hast spilt terrifies thee and overflows thy soul like a deluge—when thy revengeful voice echoes back, and pierces thine ear like a tempest—when thou shalt hear, amidst the darkening gloom of encreasing horrors, the Judge of the earth, preceded by the trumpet's terrific sound : the stroke of the glittering sword whetted for destruction : the fiery arrows drunk with the blood of the cruel : then will thoughts far different from those that now employ thy mind, rush on thy soul. Thou wilt then in the bitterest agonies, and with the most doleful cries, bowing and writhing thy limbs, supplicate and implore his mercy ; and then—then in that awful and tremendous moment of expiring nature, may God hear thy supplications, pity thy tears and thy groans, and regard thee with compassion.

He then passed through the crowd, accompanied by Joseph. The seraph Ithuriel, seeing the devout Nicodemus leave the assembly, rose with extended wings, and enraptured hovered in the air. His eyes beamed with resplendent joy, and a heavenly smile adorned his face. So one of the celestial host, filled with divine love, and ecstatic rapture, stands on one of the blooming hills that encompass the eternal throne, while Eloa, in the divine presence, joining his melodious lyre, sings the rewards of virtue, and the ecstacies of friends meeting in the blissful regions : Meanwhile the listening angel is, lost in admiration : the speaking strings, in sounds mellifluous, swell with higher, and still higher strains, while each thought rises on thought, till he spreads his golden wings, and rising, flutters enraptured, dissolved in joys unutterable. Thus hovered Ithuriel, while to himself he said, O human race ! with what blessings shall ye be crowned, if after the great Redeemer's death, ye rise to such sublime perfection, and each Christian resembles this righteous man ! Regardless of Satan he suffered him to hear his words. The arch-apostate perceived his ecstacy, and felt with pain the triumph of the towering seraph, who ascended towards heaven. Nicodemus, addressing himself to Joseph, as they left the assembly, cried, My dear friend, thou seemest covered with shame ! This pierced the soul of Joseph ; who already secretly lamented his timid silence : trembled, and unable to speak, he left Nicodemus, and filled with inward anguish, lift up his humbled eyes with grief towards heaven.

When Nicodemus retired, the whole assembly were struck with profound consternation ; for he had transfixed their souls, and filled them with the deepest wounds. They then strove to benumb the internal sense of pain ; but on the great, the decisive day of judgment, these wounds shall open and bleed afresh ; eternally bleed ; for no longer shall they be able to stiffle the secret monitor within.

All were now silent ; and the council was suddenly risen, when Judas—the detestable Judas, entered. Wondering, they saw him pass through the crowded hall, and, with a composed air, approach the high-priest, who, with wicked joy, inclined his head to hear him, and then admitted him to a private audience. This being ended, Caiaphas returned to the council, and said, Some

there are in Israel who do not bow to the idol.
This man is one of his disciples, and yet he has
the courage to adhere to the ordinances of our fa-
thers. He deserves a reward. Judas took the
silver, and, transported at the honour done him
by the pontiff, walked with an arrogant air of dig-
nity out of the council. The reward indeed appear-
ed to him too small ; but he flattered himself with
the hope that it would be greatly enlarged, when,
by his zeal and activity, he should carry his
treachery into successful execution. Philo, how-
ever, with a look of hatred, had viewed the disciple
pass along ; for he was secretly vexed, that one
of the lowest of the people should have a share in
that honour which he had proposed to arrogate
entirely to himself. Yet on his return, the dis-
sembling hypocrite gave him a smile of approbation,
and continued looking at Judas till he had left the
assembly. Thus the first of murderers, with a
look of mockery and triumph, follows with his eye
the ambitious conqueror rushing into the battle.
It is he that inspires him with habitual cruelty,
and bids the idle dream of everlasting fame flutter
at his heart, and sparkle in his eye, while the ver-
dant laurel seems to sprout around his brow. The
din and tumult of the armed field sounds delightful
in his ear, and without emotion he hears the groans
of the dying. He has forgotten that both he and
they are Christans. He has forgotten that the
thunder of the last judgment, shall awake both him
and them ! So Judas, accompanied by the eyes and
wishes of the Pharisees, absorbed in golden dreams,
went in quest of Jesus.

Forth from the banks of the brook of Cedron
came the adorable Messiah, walking through the
grove of palms that shades the valley. There be-
holding the city, and his assembled enemies, he

cried, No more, O Jerusalem ! will I lament thy
children.   See here are the sepulchres of the saints
whom thou hast slain ! yet many of thy sons will
one day be mine, and join with you, my disciples,
in bearing witness of me !   I will now accomplish
my almighty Father's will.   Go Peter, and thou
John, my faithful, my beloved disciples, to the city,
where you will see within the walls a man bearing
a pitcher of water.   With affectionate amazement
will he cast his eyes on you.   Follow his steps, and
where he enters, ask the good man of the house,
saying, ' Where is the guest-chamber, that the
Master may eat with his disciples ?   He will cour-
teously conduct you to a large upper room : and
there make ready.

The two disciples found every thing as Jesus had
said.   While the lamb was preparing, Peter,
who eagerly expected his Lord, ascended to the
flat roof of the house, to see if he could perceive
him coming.   But while his eye was wandering in
search of his Lord, he beheld Mary, the mother
of Jesus, accompanied by a few friends.   She ap-
peared fatigued and in pain ; for several days had
she sought her son, and passed each tedious night
in tears.   Yet serene she walked, though uncon-
scious of the dignity she derived from her native
purity and unsullied virtue.   She had an humble
heart, which pride had never entered, and a noble
soul worthy of the first daughter of Eve, if Eve
had never sinned.   Thus she advanced amidst her
friends.   Close by her side was Lazarus, from
his short death awaked, filled with heavenly sen-
sations, and secure of immortal life.   His downcast
eye appeared filled with mysterious thoughts, blend-
ded with dignity inexpressible by mortal speech,
and only felt by the happy dying Christian, who
smiles at the hour of death.   He was then rapt in

meditation, on the separation of his soul, and
its return to the body, when at the Messiah's call
he arose from the dust. He was followed by his
sister Mary, who devoutly listened to Christ, had
been melted by his discourse, when chusing the
better part, she sat weeping at his feet. Paleness
and languor now overspread her countenance. In
her eyes stood the quivering tear, which she strove
to restrain. Nathaniel, whom Jesus had pronounced
to be without guile, had gained her heart, and
both he and her heavenly brother, who had been
restored to life, divided the tender virgins thoughts.
Unmoved she felt the approach of death: yet
already sympathized in the grief that would be felt
by Nathaniel, and her half immortal brother. Near
her walked the modest Cidli, the daughter of Jairus.
Scarce had twelve guiltless years passed over her
head, when in the chearful gaiety of blooming life,
she lay down in a peaceful field, and died in the
presence of her mother. Then came the gracious
Messiah, and calling her back to life restored her
to her afflicted, now transported parent. In heaven-
ly sanctity, she bore the traces of her resurrection,
and already appeared half divine: but she was still
a stranger to the glory that was to crown her future
life, and had not yet obtained the full blown beauty
of ripened age: yet was her pious soul impressed
with a noble love. Such was the Shulamite, the
fairest of the daughters of Israel, when awaked by
her mother under the apple-tree, she followed her
guiding steps into the myrtle grove, under the
refreshing coolness of the inviting shades, where
in clouds of spicy fragrance, the heavenly loves
hovered invisible: inspired by them, she there
first inhaled sublime sensations, and trembling wish-
ed to find the youth who, created for her, was
inflamed with the same sacred emotions. Thus

on the arm of the devout
arus. She was accompanied
by Semida, whom the Saviour had raised from the
dead by the walls of Nain. He was in the bloom
of life; his hair hung in curls on his shoulders,
and he appeared as beautiful as David, when sitting
by Bethlehem's limpid stream, he was ravished at
hearing the Almighty's voice. But the smile of
David sat not on the face of Semida.

Now Mary, the mother of Jesus, lifting up her
eyes, discovered Peter. Speedily she hasted to-
wards him hoping to find her son. Peter and John
had descended into the hall, and went to meet her.
They beheld her and stood amazed, so strongly was
the elevation of her mind expressed in her face,
with such dignity was her form invested by him,
who before his being man, was Creator, and such
again will he appear, when at his call the dust of
the dead shall form new and immortal bodies, and
again clothe the souls they before invested. Her
attendants, two of the most amiable daughters of
Judea, and who most deserved her affection, walked
on each side with sweet and humble modesty. As
above all the mountains of Judea, Tabor, the
resplendent witness of the bright transfiguration
rises supereminent, so amidst these holy women
Mary rose graceful. When among these favoured
disciples she saw not Jesus, she stood oppressed
with grief: but at length recovering her speech,
she turned to John, and smiling, while the big tear,
with trembling lustre, glittered in her eye, thus
addressed him :

He whom I have often borne in my arms—he
who oft with looks of filial love has lain nearest my
heart—I tremble at calling my son: for too exalted
is he for a mortal mother—too great is his power—
too great his miracles for one born and beloved of

me!—Where, O dearest John! ah! where is the
Son of the Eternal? Long have I, with solicitous
inquietude every where sought him—sought to
prevent his coming to Jerusalem, the profane, the
murderous city that seeks his life. They would
put him to death, whom mine arms have borne;
whom my breast has nourished; whom my tearful
eyes have viewed with maternal tenderness.

The pious John with gentle voice replied: By
the command of the Lord, we here prepare the
feast of the passover. Soon will he return from
Bethany. O Mary! wait his coming, and then
reveal all that thine heart, with such maternal
fondness, longs to express; and its great emotions
so worthy of the holy Prophet.

All were now silent. The sister of Lazarus,
who had oft enraptured, listened to Jesus, gently
leaned on her beloved Cidli, and to Cidli, Semida
drew near, with downcast looks. She, no stranger
to the pain that long had swelled the heart of
Semida, looked aside at him; in his melancholy
eyes she read the sensations of his soul, and behold-
ing the dignity with which suffering virtue adorns
the countenance, her heart melted, and she indulged
these tender thoughts.

Generous youth! for me he passes his life in
grief, his days in sorrow! Oh that I were worthy
of thee, and that thy Cidli deserved thy pure and
heavenly love! Long have I wished to be thine, to
learn from thee, why virtue is so lovely and so
blessed. Thee I love as in ancient times, the
daughters of Jerusalem loved! I love thee as a
young lamb, that at thy nod delights to play before
thee; as the lily of the valley is brought forth
and nourished by the early day, so in thy pure em-
brace would I be formed for thy eternal love! Ah
my mother, why hast thou renewed to me the

severe command of heaven ?—but I am silent—I
obey the wisdom of an affectionate parent, and the
voice of God speaking in her ! to him am I de-
voted ! I am raised from the dead ! too little do I
belong to the earth to be given to a mortal ! cease
then, thou amiable youth, thine affectionate, thy
tender sighs ! Oh that I might again delighted
behold that face dressed in chearful smiles, and
wet with no tears but those of joy ! pleased may I
again behold thee, as when a youth, thou smilest
at seeing me escape from my mother's fondling arms
to run to thine.

Affected by these tender sentiments, her tears
forced their way, which Semida perceived, though
Cidli abashed, covered her face with her veil. He
then softly stole dejected from the company, and
when alone, looked on the ground, in plaintive ac-
cents, cried :

Why does she weep ? No longer could I be-
hold her tears. Ye precious drops, which silent
stand trembling on her glittering eye, were but one
of you shed for me, that one would be to me rest
and consolation ! I still incessantly grieve—grieve
for her ! My mind so full of soft solicitude is
filled with thoughts of her ! O thou immortal
part of me ! thou soul that inhabits this tabernacle
of clay !—or thou reason, inform me of my fate,
and disperse the clouds that hang over me. Tired
am I of weeping—tired am I of being thus over-
clouded with perpetual gloom. Why, when I see
her, who, perhaps, is no longer mortal—why, when
she is absent, is she still the subject of my thoughts ?
Why does my full heart then feel sensations before
unknown ? How tender are my ideas, all center-
ing in love ! Why flows from Cidli's lips such
soft, such silver sounds ? Why does her speaking
eye, from which her soul looks out, fill my throb-

bing heart with such strong, such dear emotions ?
each pure as innocent, and noble as the actions
of the wise. Why does grief with sable wing,
hover over my head, when I·imagine she loves me
not ?—Torturing thought be gone ! Ah, then
am I hastning to the grave, to which I was once so
near !—Often do I then attempt, with powerful
arms, to combat my sorrow. My soul assembles
every sentiment that can evince its high birth and
native dignity : I endeavour to inspire it with
firmness, by the idea of its immortality : but,
alas ! it is all in vain, I still weep. Why am I
obliged to feel this everlasting flame ? Oh, why
does my heart become so miserable, by aspiring
to an union with an heart so pure ? Why do I still
incessantly repeat her name ? But can I ever
cease to remember her ?—Ah what voice divine is
this, that in sacred whispers, and in harmonious
strains, which none but tender souls can hear, tells
me that my love shall be eternal ? I will then ever
love thee !—be thou silent or reserved, thou shalt
ever be the object of my love ! Ah, Cidli, could I
with humble awe, presume to think that thou wert
formed for me, how tranquil would be my heart !
Thy love, O Cidli ! would fill my soul with joy !
Oh, that I might be allowed to indulge the pleasing
thought, that thou, heavenly fair, wilt be for ever
mine !—mine through the endless duration of eter-
nity ! My love of thee has taught me to know
the exalted charms of virtue, once to me invisible !
My heart with glad solicitude obeys her precepts.
Thy voice, O duty ! I hear from afar—thy secret
whispers silent lead me : their divine sound, has
struck mine ear, and not in vain ! With child-like
innocence, my obedient heart fulfils thine easy
injunctions ; nor shall the possession of her who is
dearer to me than the whole creation, be polluted

by guilt. What a gift, O Cidli! wouldst thou
be to me! how would I thank the giver, and
borne on thy purity, as on wings, approach nearer
to the supremely Amiable, who has formed thee
thus lovely!—who has rendered my heart so ten-
der and thine so divine! As at thy birth, thy
mother dissolved in transport, gazed on thee; and
as she hung over thy dying face, when thou ex-
piredst in her embrace, deaf to the sound of the ap-
proaching foot, and to the soothing voice of the
helpers in Juda: so has my soul been agitated by
the sensations, the transports, raised by each mo-

hang over thee, view thy purity, the sublimity of
thine ideas, the dignity of thy conceptions, till I

from heaven into the heart of man! But when
invaded by other thoughts, and lying in silent
nocturnal gloom, my soul becomes dissolved in
tender sorrow; I then appear abandoned by all,
and confined to a painful solitude! thou art no
longer with me, and the whole creation is to me
a spacious void! Oh for the sake of that virtue
and love, and inward beauty, which raise thy spot-
less soul above the dust of the earth; or by what
is still more precious and exalted—by thy awaking
from death, and by thine immortality, when clothed
in light, thou shalt dwell among the blest inhabi-
tants of heaven, and by the crowns, the rewards of
virtue, I conjure thee, my dear Cidli, tell me if
thine heart feels the same sensations for me; if it
knows the love I feel?

Oh the elevated, the sweet, the rapturous idea!
she has been raised from the dead!—I too have
been awaked from death—perhaps to die no more!
and ooth to a higher life—Vanish, ye deceitful

dreams ; ye rash desires.—How may I be involved
in your dangerous seductions ! to what an excess
may I be carried by my love for Cidli !—Yet can
I with too much ardour love her—her with whom
in that exalted life, I more desire to live, than here
in the dust below ! With her, whether on high,
or upon earth, I long to join in love to the Eternal !
and in pouring out our souls in grateful affection
to our Lord and our Redeemer !—But is he not
now in danger of being put to death ?—No, I can-
not believe that he can die who has raised me from
the dead ?—How often has he already eluded the
persecutor's rage !—but when dangers threaten
his sacred life, ought I to indulge these thoughts
of love ?—O pardon me, thou divine Jesus ! let
all my private griefs be lost in my concern for
thee ! and thou, my soul, fix thine whole attention
on the designs of these most hardened—most un-
grateful men, against thy Lord, thy Saviour.
Semida now leaving Jerusalem, hasted to the silent,
the lonely rock, in which had been lately hewn his
sepulchre.

Meanwhile the mother of Jesus, with anxious
look, addressed herself to John. He does not
come, I will go, said she, and meet him—I will
go and meet my son, the Messiah.—I will find him,
if his cruel enemies have not dipped their hands in
his blood, and numbered him among the holy
prophets who sleep in death ! if he yet lives—if I
be worthy to behold the lovely form, the attractive
graces of my prophetic son, and his countenance
beaming love divine, will once more condescend to
smile on his enraptured mother, I will lose my an-
guish at his feet, where he graciously suffered Mary
Magdalene, who is not his mother, to weep. With
awful reverence will I also prostrate myself before
him—I will grasp his knees—I too will wet his

feet with my tears! Then looking up to his face benign, I'll say, By that ecstatic; that transporting rapture that was diffused through my whole soul, when the immortals struck my ears with heavenly harmony, and in divine hymns sung thy nativity! If ever I was dear to thee—if thou still rememberest the filial affection with which thou returnedst thy mother's joy, when, after solicitous search, I found thee in sacred dignity among the priests, who, by thy words were filled with mute amazement: Then, O my Son! I flew to thee with open arms.—I pressed thee to my heart, and lifting up my eyes, adored the great Jehovah! Oh, by that ecstatic joy, the foretaste of eternal felicity; by thy humanity and gentle condescension to all, have compassion on me, disappoint the designs of thine enemies, and do not die. Thus she spake, and then hasted to meet her Son, with the rapidity with which an ardent and devout ejaculation ascends to him by whom it is inspired.

The great Messiah beheld his mother advancing towards him, not with the eye of sense, but with that intuitive perception by which he penetrates the thoughts of the enraptured seraph. Ah! I will, after my resurrection, said he, have pity on thee, with a pity beyond that of a mother to her only son! and then turned aside.

Now advanced the grey evening. Silence reigned all around, and he slowly walked to the hill of Golgotha, near which was a solitary sepulchre hewn in the rock, wherein no mouldering corse had yet returned to its original dust. This had been formed by the devout Joseph of Arimathea, that on the last day, when death shall end his reign, he might there rise from the earth. He knew not for whom he had ordered it to be hewn: or that there was to be laid the body of the great

Messiah ! Jesus stood by the sepulchre, and casting up to the hill of Golgotha, a look of sacred grief, thus gave utterance to his divine thoughts.

Now declines the day. Now comes the prayerful night resting on Gethsemane. Soon will the day again enlighten that hill, and the dawning morn arise on Golgotha. Then thou, who containest the bones of the meanest sinners, shalt become an altar, on which the willing victim shall be slain ! soon will it bleed ! Welcome death for the human race ! Then will my gracious Father look down on me from his exalted throne, where I once sat in his embrace ! Me will the angels of God behold, and those for whom I die ! Welcome death for the heirs of eternal life !— There, in the bosom of the Father, have I sat, the Creator of man, and the Friend of the created ! I am now, O man, become thy Brother ! and though once arrayed in celestial splendor, yet wounded will I die, bleeding on thy hill, O Golgotha !—Then—(Here he turned, and looked into the sepulchre)—then will this body pass two nights and one day within the silent mansion of that cool tomb, in a softer sleep than that of Adam, when the great mystery of death was first unfolded, and he, one melancholy evening, heard the decree, Thou must lie down and die. Many centuries has he slept, and over him has the feet of his descendants walked, while he hears not the sound. They too are dead, and on their bones the feet of their offspring have, careless, trod ! But amidst the joys of a blissful eternity, can any felicity be compared to mine ? the righteous shall all transported awake—in peace, in rejoicing and triumph awake ! When my body has slept in this narrow mansion, and I have raised to endless life the bones of the dead, then every care, every doubt will cease—every tear be for ever wiped away! Death will be the introduction to triumphant joy and sweet sensations. Nor the grim tyrant, nor the threatening tomb, shall appear on the new earth. This reflection benumbs all human sensation. The blessed in lucid white shall walk serene. Many shall bear wounds like those of the Son of Man—resplendent wounds! They shall hymn the Victor, and call him by the tender names of son and brother. What earthly mortal, what inhabitant of heaven can count their number? Old things shall then be done away, and behold all things shall become new. But first Golgotha must see me die, and that sepulchre inclose this mortal frame.

The Messiah then quickened his pace. Judas, lurking in the dim twilight, found him near the wall of Jerusalem, and silent mingled among the saints, forming on his deceitful countenance the look of innocence, while his heart felt the sting of guilt. Ithuriel, who had gone before him, had heard from the top of an olive the approaching step of the Messiah, and descending as Jesus passed by, walked with him invisible, and in accents soft as the last thoughts of the dying Christian, thus spake :

Thou, O Saviour! knowest that thou art betrayed by Judas—by him who has been instructed by thine example—by him who has seen thy miracles—by him to whom thy lips have unfolded the mysteries of eternal life, and whom thou hast condescended to call thy disciple. Still the harmonious voice of the sublime Eloa fills my ear : still are open his lips, calling me to haste down to earth, to be the tutelar spirit of Judas! but, ah, I leave the sinner! no longer can I be his guardian! against him shall I witness on the great day of retribution!—against him shall I speak with the voice of thunder. Between the resplendent seats of those that are worthy to sit with thee, judging the world, will I come forth, clothed in darkness, and extending my hand towards the cloud that will envelop thy throne, will I say, O thou whose blood trickled down from the cross! O thou who hast bled and died by the hands of those thou lovedst! Judas Iscariot has drank iniquity, and against this dreadful day has steeped his soul in blackest guilt. He has called down destruction on his head, and deserved the fate of the reprobate. Let him be driven from the presence of the Lord. His guilt be upon himself: I am innocent of the blood of the sinner:

Here the immortal paused, but looking at the Mediator, and reading in his eye, that he might farther disclose his concern, he thus continued:

Alas! what different thoughts did I once entertain of the disciple of the gracious Friend of Man. Thou, Judas, said I, shalt, by thy glorious wounds, bear witness of thy Lord, and when thou diest a martyr for the truth, thou shalt hear the sublime songs we shall sing before the Victors. Oh, didst thou but thus die, thy soul would be arrayed in light, and thy friend would then, rejoicing, conduct thee in triumph to the Messiah, the first of Conquerors. Among the golden seats, placed for the twelve elected by the Messiah, I should have pointed out that raised for thee. At the sight of the radiant seat, and of him who sits on the throne, thy soul would overflow with transport! I should have stiled thee my friend, my brother! with softest voice I should have called thee my fellow seraph! Then would my Judas explain to me the mysteries of Christianity:

his sensations when the Spirit which inspired the
holy prophets, descended upon him from heaven—
when thou 'O Judas ! receivedst the fortitude to
despise death—when taught by the Holy Spirit,
thy heart prayed in words unutterable, and tasted
of the innocence of Paradise.—But these thoughts
are fled. As the smiling spring drops her flowers,
as the bloom of life fades, ere it is ripened by
time, so all is passed away. Forsaken am I by
the disciple ! Lately was I the guardian angel of
a saint : but now solitary I walk among the
angels, who look upon me with silent sympathy.
Speak the word, O divine Messiah ! shall I return
to the celestial regions ? or am I worthy to be-
hold thy death ?

Jesus, with a composed look, answered the
seraph, Simon Peter will also be tempted by the
malicious destroyer, I therefore appoint thee his
angel. Two have been given to John ; Peter must
have the same number. He shall hereafter bear
the celestial hymns, sung by those who shall join
the triumphant host above, and in his death will
he resemble me.

On hearing this the seraph with fervid joy,
flew to embrace Orion, his fellow guardian.
Jesus now hasted to celebrate the last convivial
feast with his disciples, and passing by the splendid
palaces of luxurious sinners, entered the more
peaceful dwelling of an obscure upright man. The
disciples silently reclined around the table on
which was placed the lamb of the covenant. Next
to the Messiah was John, on whose face sat an
affectionate smile. With sweet serenity Jesus then
looked round on his disciples : his eye dispensed
peace, soft repose, and a pleasing melancholy,
full of deep contemplation and calm heart-felt
felicity. So Joseph appeared among his brethren,

after feeling the first raptures, when his tears, his speaking tears ceased to flow ; when he no longer hung on his brother Benjamin, and he knew that his aged father was still alive.

Jesus now, with a mournful look, cried, Greatly have I desired to eat this repast with you, my disciples, before I suffer—soon will be accomplished the predictions of those who spake of me. Ye know the prophet that was worthy to see the divine appearance, who heard the voice of the seraphs over a throne in the temple, while the heavens resounded with their festal hallelujahs, and their crying to each other, Holy, holy, holy, is the Lord of Hosts ! the whole earth is full of his glory ! then the posts of the doors moved at the voice of him that cried : the temple was filled with smoke : the sanctuary with clouds of votive incense. Then was I present with my Father ; with him was I in the temple : for before Abraham was, I am—before this sacred land with the mountain of God arose from the waters—before the world itself was formed, I was.—But these thoughts, in all their amplitude, ye cannot yet comprehend. This divine prophet, who saw the glory of the Most High, at length cried, Lo, I behold in futurity, a branch springing out of the stem of Jesse, that shall grow up before the Lord as a tender plant, and as a root out of a dry ground. His form is changed—his beauty withered. Every solace of life is fled, and all the smiles of the blooming year. He is despised and rejected of men : a man of sorrows, and acquainted with grief. Men are silent at the affliction of his soul. They turn away their faces from him. Yet hath he borne our griefs, and carried our sorrows. For our transgressions he is wounded, and with his stripes are we healed. Like the wandering

sheep have we gone astray: we have turned every
one to our own way: the Lord hath therefore
laid on him the iniquity of us all. . Oppressed
and afflicted, he opens not his mouth : meek, like
the lamb, is he led to the slaughter, and as a
sheep before her shearers, is dumb.   From prison
and from judgment is he taken, and who shall
declare the generation of the redeemed, who are
numerous as the host of heaven. He hath given
his life an offering for sin, he shall therefore see
his seed, a race of new immortals, who having
died to sin, have awaked to righteousness, and
with him shall enjoy eternal life.

Thus spake the Redeemer, and then continued
long silent, with his eyes lift up to heaven.   At
length he resumed.   This, O my disciples ! is the
last time in which I shall keep this feast with you.
For never more shall I taste the fruit of the cheer-
ful vine, till I drink it new in my Father's king-
dom.   In the realms of joy are many mansions
—these I go to prepare for you.   There I shall
see you again, and with the assembled fathers,
commence new festivals, spiritual repasts, of per-
petual duration.

Jesus ceased, and still all were silent.   Thus
silent were the holy people on mount Moriah,
when Solomon, the wisest of the sons of Abraham,
at the prayer of consecration, laid his crown at the
foot of the altar, before the Eternal.   Then was
the temple filled with a cloud.   The priests, be-
holding the glory of the Lord, were unable to
continue their sacrifices, and the jubilant hallelujahs
ceased.   Not a word was then heard, till one of
the supplicants, transported with sacred awe, lift
up his face to the cloud, and with tremulous voice,
and arms stretched forth towards heaven, cried,
Holy, holy, holy !   Thus silent were the dis-

ciples, till Lebbeus, turning to Judas, with soft
voice, said :

Alas ! 'tis now too certian, that whatever the
other disciples may say or think of his frequent
discourses on death, that the Son of Man is about
to die. Come death, relief from misery, the re-
pose of the weary traveller, take pity on me!
for when Jesus, my Lord, is led to death like a
lamb to the slaughter, thou wilt be my sole con-
solation !—His sighs now stopped his voice. The
Messiah observed him and Judas, and giving
him a look of mingled benevolence and grief, said
to his disciples, How shall I tell you, my friends,
that one of you will betray me !

Seized with sudden grief and astonishment, all
cried, Lord is it I ? The Messiah answered, It
is one of you who now keep the paschal feast with
me. Here his countenance assumed the severity
of the judge, and he added, The Son of Man
goeth, as the prophets have written of him ;
but woe to him by whom he is betrayed : good
were it for that man that he had never been born.
Judas then, with a low voice, repeating, Is it I?
Jesus whispering, answered, Thou knowest that it
is thyself.

Now thoughts of grace and eternal salvation
again brighten the Mediator's countenance. He
rises to institute the sacred Eucharist, uttering the
solemn words which so many boldly profane, by
absurd superstition, by ignorance, and by more
hateful vice. But in vain do they wear the fair
garb of Christianity, or the well painted mask ;
for while, with polluted hearts, they chant the
praises of the spotless Redeemer, they call down
on themselves the sentence of eternal death. He
who godlike lived, and filled with benevolence,
died on the cross, is not the Saviour of the cruel,

the impious, the lewd, the dissolute : while steeped in impenitence, and wallowing in vice, meek-eyed mercy, ever gracious, ever pure, stretches not out her hand to them.   All now received from him the bread, the emblem of his broken body, and the sacred cup, typical of his streaming blood —with humility and awful silence they received them from his hand.   When John, seized with a sudden transport, sunk down at his feet, kissed them, and wetted them with his tears.

Jesus then looking up towards heaven, with a gracious smile, cried, O Father ! permit him to see my glory.   John then arising beheld at the end of the chamber a bright assembly of angels, who knew that he saw them.   Rapt in an ecstatic transport, he beheld the sublime Gabriel, with motionless astonishment : enraptured he saw the brightness of the celestial Raphael, and him he honoured : with delight unutterable, he also perceived Salem in an human form, who, with a smile of friendship, opened his arms, and him he loved.   Now, turning his ravished eyes, he discovered in the Messiah's placid countenance, traces of his celestial glory, and sunk speechless on his bosom.   Gabriel then rose on his extended wings, and transported with love, said to Jesus, O thou great Messiah, embrace me, as thou embracest thy disciple !   To him the Messiah answered, Thou, O Gabriel ! shall attend on me, when I sit on my throne, and shall be seated with Eloa, in the presence of the Most High.   Gabriel bowed adoring.

At last came Judas, and with the familiarity and dissembled love of John, threw himself at the feet of Jesus.   Judas arise, said the Messiah, and gave him the cup, the memorial of his death. Judas received it unmoved.   Then the Saviour, viewing him, was troubled in spirit, and, with a loud voice, cried, I know those whom I have chosen : yet one of you will betray me. This I now tell you, that ye may believe when it is accomplished, and that ye may know the rewards prepared for him that continues faithful unto the end. He that receiveth my word shall be saved. Whosoever receiveth you, receiveth me ; and whosoever receiveth me, receiveth him that sent me. But the traitor will not obtain the crown of life. I repeat it again, one of you will betray the Son of Man !

Sorrow was again spread over each countenance. Peter then made a sign to John, who still lay reclined on the breast of the Redeemer, and, whispering, asked, Who is it ? He it is, said the Saviour with low voice, to whom I, with tender affection, and brotherly love, give this sop. He then gave it to Judas. John trembled ; but his humanity kept him silent.

Judas now abruptly left the room. Night was come, and he was surrounded with all its terrors. Widely he cast his eyes into the dark obscure, and thus spake to himself : He then certainly knows it ! Now will the smooth, the fawning John, reveal it to them all—All will know what the heart of Jesus has intrusted to him—They will all know what I have done—Be it so—These new kings must fly before they have obtained their kingdoms. John may perhaps soon learn to lay aside his insidious smiles, and Peter, when in bonds, will be less bold !—With what imperious accents did Jesus speak ! With what a stern air, and commanding voice did he cry, Judas arise ! How different the language he uses to his favorite John !—Kings indeed are not to be commanded ! I will however see them again, before they obtain their kingdoms—in bonds will I see them!—but theird friend will die!—Is it possible? who will believe that he can die, who has raised others from the dead?—He die!—What wilt thou relent? O my suffering heart! banish all humanity!—If he die he must surely be a visionary, and not the sent of God—Our priests are men of wisdom—they are the ministers of Jehovah, the King of kings—yet they always hated him!—They respect, and would maintain the laws of Moses—They have engaged me in their interest: but they will not go so far as to put him to death—I would only see him in bonds, and then hear him. Perhaps he will for a moment forget the exalted merit of his favorite disciples, and, condescend to look upon the slighted Judas!—but I must hasten—the lords of Jerusalem expect me.

He then proceeded to the high priest's palace. The assembly of the disciples was now holy, and unpolluted by guilt. Thus when the Christian youth returned from the interment of Ananias and Sapphira, with fairer beauty shone the congregation in the eye of the Lord; for their sacred unanimity was disturbed by no selfish, no sordid disposition. In the meanwhile Jesus, with divine majesty and composure, thus addressed his disciples.

Now is the Son of Man glorified: now is the infinite, the boundless mercy of the Most High glorified in him. Though at present his splendor is veiled by the body of flesh, soon shall even this human frame be invested with celestial beauty. —But your grief interrupts my speech.—Why, my children, do you weep?—'tis true I shall soon leave you: ye shall seek me, but shall not find me: for ye know not whither I go; and whither I go ye cannot come—But cease your tears. Ye shall see me again. My dear children, I give

you a new commandment—a commandment more
noble, more exalted than all the traditional ob-
servances of the scribes and elders; Love each
other as I have loved you : for by your tender,
your mutual, your disinterested affection, shall all
men know that ye are my disciples.

Simon Peter then arose, and said, Whither,
Lord, dost thou go ? Whither I go, said the
Redeemer, thou canst not follow me ; but thou
shalt at length follow my steps, and walk in the
path I tread. Why, O my Lord, said Peter,
with an eager and amiable warmth ; why cannot
I follow thee now ? To preserve thy life will
I lay down my own ! Thou, Simon, lay down
thy life ! returned Jesus ; alas ! how little dost
thou know thyself ! I repeat it again, that ere
the early cock proclaims the opening dawn, thou
wilt deny me thrice !

The Redeemer then asking if they were all
present, the disciples, oppressed with melancholy
answered, We are here. Christ then returned,
The voice of one I no longer distinguish. To
this Lebbeus replied, trembling, Judas Iscariot
is wanting. Jesus was standing ; but he now
kneeled, and the apostles placed themselves on
their knees around him. The blessed Saviour
then lifting up his eyes, prayed with a loud voice :
O Father ! the hour is come, glorify thine only
begotten Son, that thy Son may also glorify thee.
To his power hast thou committed all mortals,
that he may at length raise them from the dead,
and bestow on them everlasting felicity. This,
O my God ! is eternal life, to know thee, and
Christ whom thou hast sent, as the Prince of
Peace, and the King of Glory. Already, O
Father ! do I behold in spirit the accomplishment
of the important work. Thee have I glorified

here on earth, and the work thou gavest me to do,
I have finished. Now crowns and regal honours
await me at thy 'right hand! give me the glory I
enjoyed with thee, ere I, by thy power, created
the earth and its inhabitants. Thy tremendous—
thy gracious name have I declared to those thou
gavest me out of this guilty world: thine they
were: thou gavest them me; and to the wisdom
which I taught them, they have faithfully ad-
hered. Now do they know that what thou teachest
me, I have taught to them. This knowledge they
with duty and with reverence have received;
deep in their hearts have they lodged the divine
truth, that thou hast sent me. For them, O Fa-
ther! do I pray—for them I now pray, and not
for the world. All who are mine are thine;
those that are thine are mine, and the subject of
my joy and my glory. Now do I quit this earthly
globe, to return to thy celestial throne—to thee,
O Father! but they remain on earth the scorn of
sinners, and exposed to misery! Keep then, O
holy Father! those whom thou hast given me,
that they, as brethren, may live in amity, and like
us unite in the great work of love and grace
divine. While clothed in this terrestrial frame,
I have taken care of them, and watched over
their immortal souls. Here they are, O my Father,
none have I lost, but the son of perdition! he
ungrateful, has deserted me, and is become a wit-
ness to the truth of the prophets. Now come I
to thee. Thus I speak while I am still with them,
that they may think on my glory and rejoice in
my joy. The words of thy love have they heard,
and sinners have hated them, as they hated me.
Yet I pray not that thou wouldst take them
from the earth: but only that thou wouldst
shield them from their persecutors;—from the

spirits of destruction; for they like me walk in innocence. Sanctify them, O God! through thy truth: thy word is truth. As thou hast sent me, I send them: for them I lay down my life, that they may be pure and holy, and ready to suffer for the cause of truth and virtue. Yet, O my Father! I pray not for my disciples alone; but for those they shall convert—for those my children, who will one day, like the dew of the morning, be born to me through thy word. May they all be one, as thou, Father, art in me, and I in thee, so may they be one in us: that the world may believe that thou hast sent me. The glory I receive from thee I give to them, that they may be one, even as we are one, and all fulfil thy gracious intentions, that the sinners of the earth, filled with admiration, may perceive that I was sent from heaven. Love them, O my God! whom thou hast given me, as the first fruits of thy Son's love to man; may these be where I am, and behold that glory, which thou, gracious Father, gavest me, before the heavens were stretched around this earthly ball. The world knew thee not; but I have known thee. To these my friends, have I disclosed the important purposes for which I was sent, and will farther disclose them, that thy love to me may penetrate their hearts, and their immortal souls be filled with love to thee, and their Redeemer.

Now Jesus arose, and went forth with his disciples. At length, drawing near to the brook of Cedron, and hearing the nightly breeze play in the branches of some olives that stood on an eminence, he said to Gabriel, in the depth of the garden, on the sloping side of the mountain, is a solitary spot, shaded by a grove of palms, there assembled the angels. Thus the Saviour spake, and was now drawing near to the accomplishment of such exalted deeds, as since the creation of the earth and the heavens, or since the birth of the angels, had never been known; such as were never seen in the boundless theatre of infinite space. But no outward acclamations, no vain testimonies of applause, the pleasing and fit attendants on the exploits of vulgar heroes, surrounded the great Messiah, while he went forth to conquer sin and death.

THE END OF THE FOURTH BOOK.

THE

M E S S I A H.

BOOK. V.

THE ARGUMENT.

God descends towards the earth, and is met by the wise
men of the east, newly released from their bodies, one of
whom addresses the Most High. He is seen by the first
inhabitant of a guiltless world, who relates to his happy
offspring, what he has heard of the fall of man, and the
coming of the Messiah. God rests on Taber. Jesus
prays, when Adramelech coming to insult him, is by a
look put to flight. The Messiah comes to his disciples,
whom he finds asleep. He then returns to pray. Abba-
dona comes, and after mistaking John for the Messiah,
finds him, and gives vent to his thoughts. The Messiah
again returns to his sleeping disciples, and a third time
prostrates himself in prayer, when God sends Eloa to
comfort him by singing a triumphant song on his future
glory. All the angels, except Eloa and Gabriel, withdraw,
and God himself returns to his celestial throne.

ARRAYED in awful dignity, Jehovah sat on
his exalted throne, and near him was Eloa,
who, with humble reverence, and low prostration,
said, May I presume, O Eternal! to ask, Why
sits terror on thy brow? Why does anger flash
from thine eyes? What means this thunder which
rolls tremendous? Thou lookest on the stars,
and they hide their heads. Silent are the cherubim
and seraphim—Of all the numberless myriads of
angelic spirits, none do I hear chanting grateful
praise, none in lofty strains hymning the great

Messiah : but all, with reverential awe, veil their faces with their wings. Wilt thou, O God ! arise, and destroy the kingdom of Satan ? . Wilt thou, O Most Righteous ! go forth to chastise the blasphemer ! and to reduce to nothing the deep abyss of hell his dominion ? Shall the name of him whom thou hast created no longer remain in the book of the living ? Then shall I see him lying prostrate, O thou adorable Source of Justice !— lying prostrate before thee, vanquished by thine anger, while the howling of his despair shall pervade the regions of eternal night, and . reach even the gates of heaven. Then shall the stars in their courses proclaim, There lies the arch apostate, reduced to destruction. If this be thy will, O thou Sovereign Judge ! arm me with thy power, and permit me to march out against the blasphemer. Let me be encompassed with impenetrable gloom ; give me a thousand thunders, and clothe me in thy divine strength, that before thy face, I may crush at the very gate of death, the menacing chief of thine accursed foes. O Jehovah, how dreadful art thou in judgment ! long had I existed when the earth was formed ; for my days are not the days of a mortal, who shoots up, spreads his leaves and florishes, then withers, sinks and dies : yet never have I seen thee thus arrayed in terror ! O thou Omnipotent ! forgive my having taken upon me to speak to thee. I am but a vapour. Be not offended against me, O my Maker ! view me not with that piercing look which thou now castest on the earth, lest thy finite seraph die, and no longer be remembered in the sanctuary of his God.

The Messiah, said the Eternal, has placed himself between me and the human race. I descend to Judge him. He is on the earth wehre he expects my decree. Come, follow me, arrayed in all thy celestial beauty. He, guiltless, suffers for sinners: he, ever merciful, will bleed for his very murderers; and even lay down his life, not for his friends: but for his cruel, his merciless enemies.

Thus spake the Almighty, and arose from his eternal throne. Loud thunder now resounded through the high arch of heaven. The holy mountains shook: the clouds of sacred darkness which encompassed the sanctuary, three times flew back, and at the fourth, the lofty seat of judgment was seen to tremble. The Most High proceeded through the solar way that leads down to earth. At the end of the bright path illumined by suns, he was met by a seraph, who was conducting six righteous souls, who had lately left their bodies: they were arrayed in glory, and their new ethereal forms shone with resplendent beams. These were six wise men of the happy east, who, guided by a swift moving star, first brought their gifts, and paid their adorations to Jesus—to Jesus, the heavenly babe, encompassed by ministering angels.

Hadad, for so the first was called, left his beloved consort, the fairest of the daughters of Bethurim. At his decease she burst into no lamentations. This in a sacred hour of love she had vowed to Hadad: certain of his and her immortality, she suppressed her tears—she forgot to weep: Yet their mutual love exceeded that of mortals.

Selima, during a life of piety, and fervent devotion, had borne his misfortunes with resignation. He died, and entered on everlasting happiness.

Zimri taught the people: but they treated him with contempt, and persisted in their vices. Yet when dying, he prevailed on one of them to lead a divine life, and then expired.

K

Mirja brought up five sons, whom, by his, example, and instructions, he inspired with the love of virtue. They enjoyed her pure, her intellectual treasures : this was their riches : they neither had, nor needed other wealth : but looking forward to a more blissful state, they, with resignation, beheld their pious father die.

Beled's eyes smiling in death, were closed by his once mortal enemy, who wept over him. Beled had revenged himself by his magnanimity ; for he had generously given him half his kingdom. On which the hatred of enmity gave way to the soft sensations of friendship. He who had endeavoured to dethrone Beled, now became charmed with his virtues, and lived like him.

Sunith used to sing in Parphar's grove to the youth of Bethlehem, and with him were his three holy daughters. Thee have the cedars—thee, has Jedidoth's flowing stream bewailed to its lonely banks ! Ah thee, have thy veiled daughters, O Sunith ! lamented to their harps, with virgin tears.

The piercing eye of these spirits penetrated the wide expanse, and they saw a distant approaching glance of the divine glory. Their senses now refined and fitted for everlasting joys, became more strong, more exquisite. The glory of the Lord passed over them, and the seraph, with humble adoration, cried aloud, Behold the great Jehovah !—

Selima now filled with rapture, essayed to speak, when his new voice, flowing in soft melody and silver sounds, filled him with pleasing surprise. O thou whom I behold, said he ; by what name, thou Source of being, of light and joy !—by what worthy name shall I, transported, call thee ?—thee whom my eyes now first behold !

God ! Jehovah ! Father ! Or wouldst thou rather be named the Inexpressible ? Or the Father of thy holy Son Jesus, who, at Bethlehem, assumed the human form : whom we, with troops of rejoicing angels saw ? Hail eternal Father of the everlasting Son ! to thee be raised incessant hallelujahs ! In thee exults the immortal soul, born of thine inspiring breath, and the heiress of eternal life. Thou most blessed ! most incomprehensible ! among men have I heard thee named love ; yet how dreadful, how terrible dost thou now appear ! Oh comest thou forth to slay thine enemies ? Shall the abode of sinners be utterly destroyed ? Wilt thou exterminate those that yet disown thy Son ? No, thou art merciful and gracious ! Thou wilt not be rigorous in judgment ! For them—even for them, the unthankful and the evil, hast thou sent the great Messiah ! Hail thou eternal Father of the everlasting Son ! Then Selima, with the other souls, worshipped in humble prostration.

At the other end of the luminous path, Eloa, with agile motion, leapt into his resplendent chariot, in which he had carried Elijah up to heaven, when, O Dothan on thy cloud-enveloped mountains, he was seen by Elisha. Eloa stood erect. He rushed forward like an impetuous storm: Then resounded the golden axis. Then backward flew his hair and vesture, like shining clouds. With firm foot the immortal stood immoveable. In his right hand he carried on high a storm ; at each elevated thought thunders burst from the tempest. Thus he followed the mighty Jehovah through luminous paths enlightened by suns. The Almighty now passed through the vast assemblage of stars, called the milky way: named among the immortals the resting place of the Omnipotent:

for when the first celestial sabbath saw the world
completed, there the Eternal stopped ¡ to view
his works.

The Almighty now approached a star, the
dwelling of rational beings, men formed like us,
but free from vice, and exempt from death.
Their first progenitor stood among his guiltless
offspring in all the bloom, in all the vigour of
manly youth, though a long series of ages had
passed over his head. His eyes, which time had
not dimmed, beheld with pleasure his happy
descendants ; nor were they incapable of shedding
the pleasing tear of joy. His quick ear was
not closed to the voice of the Most High ; to the
instructions of the seraph ; nor to the language
of his numerous offspring, from whom he with
pleasure heard the endearing appellation of father.
At his right side stood the mother of men, her
children, beautiful as when the Creator first led
her, immortal fair ! to the embraces of her spouse ;
even age had added to her charms, and she now
appeared more lovely than her blooming daughters.
At his left hand was his first-born, his worthy son,
the image of his father, arrayed in heavenly inno-
cence. Around them stood their descendants of
different generations ; and scattered about them,
on the smiling turf, reclined their youngest off-
spring, whose waving locks falling in curls, were
crowned with flowers, beautiful as those that, on
this earth, once enamelled the plains of paradise.
With pleasure they gazed on their primeval
parents, while their young hearts panted to imitate
their virtues. The fathers and mothers had brought
the lovely infants born the preceding year, to re-
ceive the first dear embrace, and pious benedic-
tion of their original ancestors. When the
happy father of this blessed race of immortal

beings, lifting up his eyes towards heaven, to invoke the divine benediction, beheld the face of God. The smile of benignity and paternal love now gave place to a look of solemn and reverential awe, mingled with gratitude; then bowing in humble worship, he cried:

Behold and adore, O my children, the great Eternal! from whom both you and I received our life. 'Tis he who has clothed those vales with beauteous flowers: those blooming groves with fragrant blossoms and blushing fruit, together hanging on each bending bough; and has crowned the summit of these mountains with golden clouds; yet neither to the flowery vale, the blooming grove, or to the aspiring mountain, has he given immortal souls. These were his gifts to you my children! Neither to hill, nor grove, nor vale, has he given your lovely features, nor the human form, so convenient, so august: nor the face significant, expressive of the soul's deepest thoughts: no look of rapturous joy sublime, with grateful eye raised up to heaven: no voice to transmit the great sensations of the glowing heart to fellow minds; or to join the lofty strains of the adoring angels! To me he appeared in the waving groves of Paradise, then a small but delightful garden, though it has now spread over this spacious country. There, with benignant grace, he first appeared to me, when from earth he had formed me man, and blessing me, led your mother to my embraces. Speak, ye cedars, rustling speak—speak, for under your branches I saw him walk! Stay, thou rapid stream—stay, for there I saw him pass thy waves! Whisper, ye gentle gales, as when with smiling grace he descended from these towering hills! Stand still before him, O earth, and suspend thy course, as once thou

stoodst still, when he passed over thee ; when
round his face sublime the moving heavens flowed !
when his right hand poised the glowing suns, and
in his left he held the revolving planets !   . , .

May I presume, O Eternal ! again enraptured
to look on thee ?   O Father ! disperse the tre-
mendous gloom with which thou art encompassed.
Remove from thine eyes that awful displeasure,
which sure none but an immortal can behold and,
live !   By whom, O my God ! art thou offended ?
—can it be by those thou lovest ?—Perhaps 'tis
by a guilty people who fell and ventured (a
thought I can scarce conceive !) to provoke the
All-gracious, the Omnipotent.—

Hear me, O my children, and attend to my
words.—Long have I been silent, lest I should
give inquietude to your tender, your happy minds,
and melancholy should disturb your sacred rest.
Far from us, on one of the worlds enlightened by
another sun, are men whose form resembles ours ;
but having forfeited their native innocence, are
no longer immortal.   You justly wonder, and well
you may, that he who was created for an eternal
duration, and was one of the most admirable of the
works of the great Omnipotent, should basely forfeit
his immortality.   But it is not the everlasting spirit
—the never dying soul that is become mortal : it is
the body which returns to the earth, of which it
was made.   This they call dying.   The immortal
soul having lost its beauty, its innocence, is con-
ducted to the righteous judgment seat of God,
there to receive a sentence according to the works
done in the body.—Ye awful, ye dreadful thoughts
fly far from me ! I stand aghast at the dread
idea ! On that tremendous tribunal, God alone, the
Creator and Judge, can think.   With what over-
whelming terror does the mere idea of death fill

an immortal ! It is preceded by something dreadful, which those unhappy creatures call pain. The dying can scarce with trembling tongue utter a mournful farewel !—With difficulty he respires ! —A cold sweat rises on his altered face !—Faint and slow beats his heart !—His eye-strings break ! —His eyes become fixed, and no longer see !— From them the face of the earth and heavens are vanished ! they are lost in the abyss of night !— He no longer hears the voice of man, nor the tender sighs of love and friendship !—He himself cannot speak ! His heart ceases to beat ! he dies ! The form once the most lovely becomes loathsome ! —It is buried in the earth, and concealed from human sight ! Thus the daughter expires in the arms of her fond mother, who wishes to accompany her in death. The father presses to his heart his only son, who expires in blooming youth. Fathers, mothers, the comforters and supports of their unhappy children, die in the midst of the cries of their desolate family. The beloved spouse perishes in the embraces of her husband, Love, that celestial sensation, is the sole image that has remained on that earth of its primitive felicity; but it is only a faint image of it, that never exists but in the hearts of the few virtuous. Alas ! it renders even them happy but for a moment !—A moment—and they die—God shews them no pity : he relents not at the parting sigh of the pious spouse, at the fervor of her supplications, and her earnest entreaties for one hour more : nor at the despair of the trembling youth embracing her in speechless sorrow : nor at the afflicted virtue, to which love and its tender sensibilities, sometimes raise the mortal pair.

Here he ceased, interrupted by the lamentations of his affrighted children. The fathers pressed

their sons, and the mothers their terrified daughters
to their trembling breasts. The boys grasped the
knees of the stooping fathers, and kissed from the
parent's eye the manly tear. Hand in hand sat
brothers and sisters with their timorous looks fixed
on each other! and on the bosoms of the beloved
fair sunk, trembling, the immortal youths; who
felt life beat with a higher pulse, while reclined
on the breast of the celestial maids. But now the
father of that spotless race, recalling his fortitude,
thus resumed, while his fair consort fondly leaned
on his shoulder.

Oh may it not be these whom God in his wrath,
is now visiting: Alas! they have, perhaps, too
much offended their gracious Creator; and having
filled up the measure of their iniquities, he is
going to exterminate them. Ah! ye kindred race,
originally designed like us, for immortality, had
you but known our affectionate love;—had you
but foreseen our sorrow for you; never, surely,
would you, by your crimes have drawn down the
vengeance of your and our Almighty Friend!
O kindred race! should the earth be your grave,
and God at once destroy all its rational inhabitants,
we will pity those whom God has slain—but we
shall despise ye too—our pity will be mingled
with contempt.—How could ye, ungrateful, offend
such unbounded goodness?—Yet to this race, O
Almighty Father! thou hast sent thy beloved
Son, the glorious Messiah! All the seraphs, in
their visits to us, with the applauding angels,
have proclaimed that he shall be their Redeemer
—that one day he shall raise the dead to life, and
that we ourselves shall see them. Behold, the
Most High turns his face from us, and now descends
to the earth. How wonderful, O God, art thou
in thy judgments! How inscrutable are the wise

perfect, ever unchangeable ! Let

thy blessings be poured on these mine offspring !
With faces veiled the cherubim and seraphim
worship before thine exalted throne ! Thee im-
mortal men adore from this sacred earth !—thee
mortal men, whom thou slayest, adore in the dust !
Thus he uttered the effusions of his soul, while
his fixed eyes followed the divine effulgence.

The Almighty now drew near to the earth.
From a towering assemblage of clouds, Eloa saw
the great Messiah, and there, wrapt in obscurity,
in gentle accents thus spake. O thou gracious
Redeemer ! how greatly is thy labouring mind
distressed, while thus imploring and procuring
mercy for sinful man ! What finite intellect can

depths of sovereign wisdom, and of grace divine ?
—But let me be silent, and, rapt in wonder,
adore ! Thus spake Eloa, and then, stretching
out his arms towards the earth, in silence poured
forth his benedictions.

God now descended on mount Tabor, and,
shrouded in a solemn midnight cloud, viewed
this whole terraqueous globe, with idolatrous
altars and sinners covered. Over its extensive
plains was spread the empire of death, witnessing
against man. He saw all the sins, from the
creation to the final day of retribution—the sins
of the idolators ; those of Jehovah's servants ;
and the sins of christians, still more horrid, rise
in the clouds before the sovereign Judge : before
him they arose in hideous forms, unshrouded
from night. They arose from the abyss in which
they were buried by the guilty heart, that, un-
grateful, rebelled against the all-gracious Creator.

The hideous host was led by the crimes of those capacious souls, who beheld thee, O sacred virtue! in all thy celestial beauty, yet obeyed not thy pleasing dictates; but self-convicted with black impiety, and redoubled guilt, opposed the generous feelings of humanity and heavenly grace, struggling in their breasts, and witnessing between themselves and God. In gigantic forms they appeared before him who directs the thunder, and guides the forked lightning; for inexorable conscience, with irresistible voice, summoned them to approach. An universal accusation now ascended to heaven. On the fluttering wings of the wind were borne the soft sighs of suffering virtue. Loud as the roar of waves rushing impetuous, resounded the groans and lamentations of the dying from the bloody field of slaughter, witnessing against the ambitious potentates of the earth; and the voice of thunder was given to the blood of the martyrs, crying, O thou who in thine awful hand holdest the balance of judgment, behold the innocent blood that has been shed—shed for thy sake, O thou most holy, just, and true! The Almighty then revolving in his infinite mind, the virtues of the various orders of intelligent beings who had continued faithful, and weighed the actions of the wicked. His anger was kindled. The earth then shook to its centre; but he supported it with his hand lest it should be scattered through the immensity of space. Then turning towards Eloa, the seraph at once knew the intimations of the divine countenance, and ascended into the air As from the ark of the covenant rose the luminous cloud, the guide of the people of Israel when led by Moses, they from desert to desert moved their tents; thus silent on a midnight cloud stood the seraph, with his eyes fixed on the

mount of Olives. Him the blessed Saviour then
beheld, and instantly hasted to Gethsemane, to pour
out his soul in fervent prayer for man. Filled
with inward distress he went, followed by three
of his disciples. These he at length left behind,
and withdrew alone to a silent solitary spot,
where, unobserved by man, he might give vent
to the great, the painful sensations that swelled his
heart.

Thou hast led me, O harmonious muse of Sion!
to the sanctuary; but the Holy of Holies I have
not seen. Oh had I the soft melodious voice with
which the exalted seraph sings: did the terrific
trump, which shook the solid base of Sion's mount,
resound from my lips: did thunders speak from my
right hand the thoughts which the celestial harps
cannot resound; Yet, O adorable Messiah! should
I fail in singing thy passion, the mighty con-
flicts of thy great, thy generous, thy tender
soul!

Thou, O Moses, once boldly prayed to see the
great Jehovah face to face; but wast concealed in
the sheltering rock while the glory of God
passed by; yet from afar beheld the resplendent
beauty of the Eternal; I am more frail than thee;
yet may the Spirit of Truth overshadow me with
his downy wings, and help my feeble sight, that
I may see the blessed Jesus struggling in the agonies
of his dreadful passion!

Prostrate in the dust of the earth, which trem-
bled with silent terror, lay the gracious Messiah,
with his guiltless eyes and hands lift up towards
Tabor. Seen by no mortal eye, his looks were
fixed on his Father's face: distressful thoughts,
filled with horror, pressed in swift succession on
his soul, and his whole frame shook with un-
utterable agony. His terrors still increased:

the anguish of his heavenly mind became more intense ; and instead of sweat, the starting blood trickled from the face of the adorable, the gracious sufferer. Then raising his head from the ground, his streaming tears, mixed with the purple drops, while lifting up his hands and eyes, he thus addressed the Sovereign Judge :

O my Father ! when this world was formed, soon died the first men—soon was each hour marked with dying sinners ! Already have ages past blasted by thy curse. Now is arrived the awful time, when by my death I shall purchase immortality for man. When the earth was scarcely formed, ere the mouldering corse returned to dust, I chose this hour of suffering, and ardent cried, Lo, I come to do thy will, O my God ! Now— now is arrived the awful time ! Hail ye who sleep in God, ye shall awake !—I who formed the earth was born to die !—to die on its surface !— to die that man might live ! But how heavily the lot of mortality hangs upon me ! O thou who holdest the sword of justice ! let the hours of anguish pass with rapid flight ! To thee, O Father ! every thing is possible—let therefore this bitter cup pass from me !—Yet not my will ; but thine be done. My uplifted eyes watch at midnight, and can no longer weep : my trembling arms are stretched towards thee for help : but alas ! I do not find it—Faint with weeping, I sink to the ground—To my grave !—But I resign myself to thy will—thy will, O Father ! be done.

Having thus spoke, he lay prostrate on his face in solemn silence, then raising himself up on his trembling arms, looked forward into the gloom. Here passed before him terrifying images of eternal death. He beheld reprobate souls curse the day of their creation. He heard the dismal howls of the deep abyss · the winged voice of anguish, like falling cataracts, bellowing loud. Then the voices of mankind sunk in one boundless sigh· of deep-rooted despair. Jesus sypathized in their distress, and, filled with unutterable compassion, felt their misery.

. Adramelech from a barren rock had long viewed the Messiah; but now descending, in order to come to· him, he, with triumph and exultation saw before him a snicide reeking in his own blood: the accents ·of whose· despair, and the bitter sighs of returning humanity and remorse, echoed through all the neighbouring hills. At this spectacle the apostate spirit increasing in insolence, resolved to mock the great Messiah. With disdainful pride in his haughty eye, and lost in an, ocean of impious thoughts he stood, resolving to give to his infernal ideas a voice like that of the black bursting cloud: but Jesus turning, and casting· on him that majestic look of awful dignity with· which he will judge the world, the rancorous spirit felt the powerful glance, and trembling sunk abased. Bewildered amidst a whirl of impetuous crowding thoughts, he stood without thought. All around him was a void: no longer did he see the heavens and the earth; no longer the Messiah: himself alone he beheld. At length with difficulty collecting his weakened strength, he fled.

The Mediator now leaving the gloomy solitude, walked towards his disciples, that after such suffering, such lonely anguish, he might enjoy the human solace of seeing the face of man. Silent·he drew near, and found them asleep.

· The surrounding heavens now rejoiced, and solemnized the second sabbath since·the creation; one still more sacred than the first. At length, the final, the decisive day of judgment being passed, the third will arise with unutterable glory, and extend thoughout eternity. At its celebration the Messiah himself will preside. All knew that the great high-priest was accomplishing the redemption: for thus God had said :

When the thunders shall roll from pole to pole, and the harmony of the spheres be changed to the ocean's roar: when ranks of wandering stars shall tremble through the vast extent of the heavens: when upon you come the terrors of the Lord, and from your heads suddenly fall your golden crowns ; then has the Messiah begun his severest sufferings.

' Now sang the heavenly host, Past is the first hour of the exalted sufferings of the great Messiah, the Redeemer of man ! Past is the hour which to the good brings eternal rest. ' '

Meanwhile the Messiah stood looking on his disciples, whom he saw fast in the arms of sleep. He considered with complacency the serious air spread over the face of the exalted James. Thus graveland serene sleeps the happy Christian before his death. On the affectionate John reclined Peter ; but he was not like John, filled with smiling tranquillity. Over the beloved disciple, Salem, one of his guardian angels, still hovered. Jesus now said, Simon Peter thou sleepest ! what, couldst thou not watch with me one hour ? Ah soon will quiet slumbers cease to close those weeping eyes ! Watch and pray lest the tempter surprise thee. Thou, indeed art willing ; but thine heavenly spirit is pressed down by thine earthly frame. Jesus then returned, and again fell on his face and prayed.

On the other side of the mountain Abbadona, veiled in a thick cloud, advanced, saying to himself ; Ah ! where shall I at length find the gracious

Saviour, the Redeemer ; Alas ! I am unworthy to
see this best of men.   Yet Satan has seen him !——
O thou divine Prophet ! where—oh where shall
I seek thee !—where shall I find thee !' Through
every desert have I roved.   Every river have I
traced from its source.   In the solitude of every
sequestered grove, my trembling feet have wan-
dered.   To the cedar have I said, Oh tell me—in
rs tell me, dost thou conceal him ?'
mountains I cried, Bow down your
solitary tops' at my tears, that I may see the divine
Jesus, who, perhaps, sleeps on your summits ! I'
am unworthy to see thy face—ah unworthy am I;
O Jesus ! to behold thy benignent' smiles !   Thou'
only art the Saviour of men !—Me thou wilt
not save !—Thou hearest not the plaintive voice
of an immortal !—Alas ! thou art only the Saviour
of men.

He then saw before him the sleeping disciples.
Near him lay John, smiling in his placid slumbers.
He saw him, and struck with fear, trembling, drew
back.   Long he paused : but at length cried, If
thou art he whom I seek—If thou art the divine
man who came to redeem mankind from sin and
misery, with tears—with incessant tears—with
everlasting sighs will I hail thee, thou amiable
Redeemer ! thy countenance has the lineaments of
celestial purity, and the traces of a tender and
generous soul.   Yes, thou art he !—Thee have I
sought—sweet tranquillity, the rich reward of
virtue, hovers round thee !   But I tremble at
seeing thy soft repose.   Turn—oh turn thy face
from me ; or I must look aside, and weep.

While Abbadona thus spake, Peter awaking,
called out, Ah John ! I have seen the Master in
a dream, who looked at me with mingled dis-
pleasure and compassion.

This the fallen seraph heard, and stood amazed. Now favoured by the silence of the night, he distinguished a mournful voice. Inclining his attentive ear to the place whence it came, he more distinctly heard the soft and doleful accents. He was moved, and stood some time irresolute.

Shall I proceed, said he, and view the man who there in sounds of anguish and distress, struggles with death, and the thoughts of judgment? Shall I see the blood of the murdered, who, perhaps quietly returning home, through the shades of night, quickened his steps, to embrace his affectionate wife, and to caress with parental pleasure his lisping children, hanging about the neck of their mother, when some lurking foe, some barbarian in the dark, bent on murder, gave him a mortal wound! Perhaps his life was crowned with virtue, and his deportment adorned by wisdom! Ah shall I see him! Shall I see his dying pangs!—his florid cheeks change to deadly paleness! Shall I hear his last groans—his expiring sigh! Ah blood murtherously shed! terrific blood of innocence—thou bearest witness against me at that inexorable judgment-seat where the soft voice of mercy is not heard! Unhappy that I am! I was concerned in seducing the human race—in rendering them subject to death!—The blood—the innocent blood here shed; and that which through successive ages will flow, is spilt by me. Ah! I hear its frightful voice, rising against me to heaven, and demanding vengeance—vengeance everlasting on my guilty head! Why did I come to the earth, which on all sides offers to my view the scattered bones of the children of Adam? In vain do I endeavour to turn from them my affrighted eyes. My conscience, fatal attendant! leads me, in spite of myself, to the gloomy tombs, where are laid so many victims which I have contributed to murder! Thou dreadful calm which reignest in the habitations of the dead freezest my heart with fear and horror! Yet he whom I have irritated, comes in silence—Thunders and clouds go before him! The word of his mouth is death! is judgment without mercy!

A prey to these dreadful ideas, he advanced with slow and dilatory step towards the mournful voice. Now he beheld the gracious Saviour who, with his face to the earth, still lay in humble prostration. Seized with fear Abbadona stepped back, and was silently moving round him, when Gabriel advanced from the thick concealing shade. Abbadona saw him, and trembling, retired. The inhabitant of heaven now drew near, and bowing his ear over the Saviour, with-held in his wondering eye the starting tear. Absorbed in thought he stood, listening with reverential awe to the Messiah, with an ear which, at the distance of a thousand times a thousand miles, hears the songs of the enraptured spirits that surround the throne. He now distinguished the soft thrilling sound of the slow flowing blood of the trembling Mediator, as it ran from vein to vein. Much louder did he hear in his divine heart the inexpressible, the heavy sighs which swelling with mercy, and with love to man, were more delightful to the Father's ear, than the song of all the heavenly host. The seraph thus discovered the Saviour's passion, and folding his hands, with his eyes lift up to heaven, rose into the clouds.

Abbadona now seeing Gabriel, and a multitude of the heavenly host, with their eyes beaming compassion, in expressive silence, looking down on the Messiah, remained aghast, and trembling, cast on him a look of mingled fear and surprise,

L

The Saviour now from the ensanguined dust slowly
raised his face, at which redoubled terror encom-
passed the fallen seraph : yet he again recovered :
again gave vent to the new ideas which filled his
mind.   Sometimes he suppressed his timorous
thoughts, and sometimes disturbed the silence of the
night by his sighs and lamentations.

O thou whom I here see struggling with death !
cried he ; by what name shall I call thee ?   Art
thou formed of the dust ? a son of earth, a sinner
ripe for judgment, shudders at the last day, and at
the opening tomb.—Yes, thou art—but a divine
lustre adorns thy human form ! Thine eye, from
which shines innocence, and truth, and love to
God and man, bespeaks thee superior to the grave
and to corruption !   Thy face is not that of a
sinner !—not thus looks the wretch rejected of the
Most High ! Surely thou art more than man !
Methinks I here perceive a mystery deeper than
my thoughts can fathom ! A bright labyrinth
all divine !—Ah ! I still discover more !—But,
who is he ?—O fallen spirit ! turn—turn thine
eyes away from him.—A sudden thought has
darted into my astonished mind—A great, a dread-
ful idea ! Alas ! an awful resemblance do I per-
ceive—Fly, fly, ye dread surmises !—Stream not
around me, ye terrors of eternal death—Ah ! I
perceive a concealed resemblance of the great
Messiah, who descending in his flaming chariot,
rushed upon us, armed with ten thousand thunders,
and hurling destruction, drove us before him,
vanquished and dismayed.   Then immortality
became a curse ; life eternal, death.   Alas ! we
had before fled from innocence—from every celes-
tial joy, the lot of the righteous !—Jehovah him-
self had ceased to be our father !   Once, while
hurled headlong through the deep abyss, I turned

my face, and saw him behind me—saw the dreadful Son of God !—lightning flashed from his eyes ! —high he stood—his chariot then the sable seat of judgment—under him was darkness and death— Him had the Father clothed with omnipotence !— him, the radiant image of his mercy, had he armed with destruction ! At his thunders, and the force of his avenging arm, nature shuddered, and all the depths of creation trembled ! No more did I see him—My eye was lost in the palpable gloom ! Thus confounded, I was carried away through storms and thunder—through the howlings of affrighted nature, despairing, though immortal ! —I see him still !—still I see him !—his face had something that resembled that of this man here bowed in the dust—this more than man !

Here he paused, and continued for some time as if lost in thought ; then in a low voice cried, Ah ! is he—is he the Son of the Eternal ?—the Messiah ?—the dreadful Victor ?—but he suffers ! —he is struggling with death !—boundless is the anguish that shakes his divine soul !—he laments in the dust !—his swelling veins, pressed by the anguish of his benevolent mind, bedew his face with blood—To me no misery is sure unknown, yet I know not how to name his anguish. Remote in distant gloom I see new thoughts big with wonders approach, in mazy labyrinths involved. The Son of the great Jehovah, the brightness of his Father's glory descends from heaven ; assumes the human form ; preaches repentance ; suffers for man, and, to give life and immortality to his mortal brethren, dies !—With what awful reverence the angels approach ! Even nature seems to observe a reverential silence, as if her Creator was present. Oh, if thou art the dread Messiah, the only begotten of the Father, I ought to fly, lost

seeing me trembling at thy feet, thy wrath be
kindled, and thou instantly sit in judgment
against me!—But thou lookest not on me!—Yet
to thee my thoughts are not unknown.—May I
venture to indulge the ideas which now first
begin to arise in my mind?—Of men art thou
the Saviour! and not of the more exalted angels!
O gracious Messiah! hadst thou condescended to
become a seraph; hadst thou deigned to enligten
us by thine instructions; hadst thou for us lain
extended in the celestial plains, as here on earth, and
with supplicating heart, and hands and eyes lift up to
the throne of the Majesty on High, how would
I then, O thou divine!—how would I then have
embraced thee! With what joyful transports
should I have hailed my Saviour and my Lord!
What rapturous hosannas should I sing! With
what ecstacy should I join the harmony of the
harp to my exulting strains!—Ye children of
Adam, the favorites of the Most High, may the
curse of everlasting fire fall on the heads of those,
who ungratefully spurn at his offered grace, and
on each heart insensible to the boundless love of
your Redeemer! Ye tribes of the redeemed, that
shall hereafter resort to him, should you profane
the sacred blood which drops from that face, may
this blood rise up against you, and ye be esteemed
his cruel murderers!—To you I call, ye apostates
from grace—to you who, after having tasted of
the heavenly gift, shall draw back to perdition!
—when the dreadful gulph of eternity shall first
lie before you, and ye are filled with the tremendous
thought, that you, like us are cast out from God,
the first and the best of beings!—then will I,
looking through gloomy tracts of misery and night,
on the new distresses of your immortal souls, cry,
Hail torment everlasting! Hail misery without

end ! This ye have chosen for a shadow ! for this ye have resigned everlasting felicity ! let this be your portion, and your reward ! Then will I tear myself from the iron arms of hell, and ascending to the throne of the exalted Saviour, with a voice that shall pervade both heaven and earth, will I cry, Oh ! why dost thou, Most Gracious redeem only the repentant sinners of the human race, and not the angels ! 'Tis true, hell hates thee—but I, forsaken—I who feel more noble sentiments, do not hate thee.—Too long alas ! too long have I, weary of my existence, and of a dreadful immortality, poured forth lamentations, and tears of blood ! Abbadona having thus given a loose to his disturbed thoughts, hastily ascended into the air and disappeared.

The Messiah now, a second time, arose from the dust, again to behold the face of man ; and again the heavenly host rejoiced and sang, Past is the second hour of the exalted sufferings of the great Messiah the Redeemer of Man ! Past is the hour which to the good brings eternal rest !

But soon the blessed Saviour left his slumbering disciples, and went a third time to prostrate himself before the Sovereign Judge. Around him the sable curtain of night was spread, over the heavens, and he was encompassed by the deepest gloom. Thus the last night before the day of awful retribution, will he clothed in the blackest veil of darkness, hastily bringing on the coming morn. The loud thunder, and the sounding trump will then soon be heard : soon the joining bones and the buzzing field, teeming with resurrection. Then from his exalted throne, the same Jesus shall call the world to judgment.

The Father, now looking down from Tabor,

saw the agonies of the Messiah. Below, at
the foot of the mountain, stood Eloa, silent;
his head was enveloped in clouds, and his
pensive looks were directed to the earth. The
Most High now called Eloa, who instantly arose
in silence through the gloom and stood before
him. Then to Eloa, the Eternal said, Thou hast
seen the sufferings of the Messiah; go sing to
him a triumphant song, of the saints, that from
his sufferings and death shall be sanctified, and
raised to immortal life; and of the glory with
which he shall be crowned when he shall reign
at my right hand.

Trembling, with lowest reverence, the seraph
answered. But when face to face I behold the
great Messiah, disfigured by his bloody sweat:
when I see the benignant smile that adorned
his countenance, lost in the melancholy traces
of his inward anguish; and in his pleasing
features distorted by grief, can but obscurely
discern his greatness, shall I not be struck
speechless? Will not the strong emotions I
shall then feel, prevent the harmony of my ce-
lestial song? Shall I not be encompassed by
all the Saviour's terrors?

With mild grace, God replied, Who raised
thy flaming courage high above the heavens?
From whom hadst thou thy triumphant song,
when my thunders, cast from the hand of the
Messiah, pursued the chief of the rebel host,
and thou thyself rode on the wings of the
tempest? Who strengthened thine heart and
enabled thee to see the death of the first man,
and, in him the death of all the children of Adam?
Haste, I myself will lead thee, and shouldst
thou, at the near view of his sufferings, trem-
ble, he will teach thee to mingle with thy

tremulous accents, the pleasing sounds of triumph.

Thus spake the Almighty. The seraph went forth, Jordan roared and thunder issued from Tabor. Slowly he descended from the mount of Olives, when dreadful gusts of midnight winds wafted to him the suppliant sounds uttered by the great Messiah, and a silent tremor seized the astonished seraph. But when advancing nearer he observed his distressful countenance that shewed his bitter anguish, he stood deprived of all his native beauty and heavenly splendor; and seeming no longer an high immortal seraph, he resembled an inhabitant of the earth. Now the Saviour cast on him a look of dignity, mingled with a gracious smile, and with the glance, the seraph's immortal beauty and celestial radiance returned, when rising in a cloud, skirted with gold, he thus triumphant sung:

Thou, Son of the Most High, what grateful rapture does a look from thee inspire! I am found worthy to contemplate thine awful, thy divine sensations, and from afar to view the mystery of thine agonies, and thy love to man. Ye devout, ye sacred emotions, continue to transport me beyond the limits of my finite ideas; bear me from this gloom to the divine glory. Hail almighty Father, and thou Son divine!—Thus shall the blessed children of the resurrection feel sensations new and sublime. As from deep amazement the Mediator has awakened me, so, ye offspring of Adam, shall he awaken you! This joyful tremor, this rapturous exultation ye also shall feel, when ye, transported, rise to eternal life! Then thou, O holy Saviour of men, who here liest prostrate in the dust, shall sit on thy resplendent throne, and summon the inhabitants to come to judgment! With what effusions of joy will thy faithful servants behold thee on thy judgment seat! With eyes sparkling with rapture, they will view the radiant marks of thy wounds, the memorials of thy love imprinted by thy dying on the cross. Thee, O Jesus! shall they celebrate with ceaseless hallelujahs. They shall transported feel that they are immortal, and shall triumph in the glorious thought, that because thou livest, they shall live also, they shall for ever possess thy love, and for ever share thy glory!

Thus sang Eloa, while the divine Redeemer blessed the adoring seraph, with a look of grace and benignity: then bowed towards heaven in tearful silence. Thus the expiring lamb, without blemish, and without spot, wept, while he lay bleeding on the sacred altar. The angels, who with downcast look had viewed the Redeemer, unable longer to bear the sight of his anguish, withdrew. Gabriel kept his station, but veiled his face. Eloa also remained ; but wrapt his head in a midnight cloud.

The earth stood still. Thrice it shook, as if preparing for its dissolution, and thrice it was restrained by the Great Jehovah. The Saviour now rising from the ground, the host of heaven again sang in jubilant strains, Past is the third hour of his exalted sufferings : past is the hour which to the repentant sinner brings everlasting rest. Thus sang the heavenly host, while God ascended to his eternal throne.

THE END OF THE FIFTH BOOK.

THE

MESSIAH.

BOOK. VI.

THE ARGUMENT.

The Messiah is seized and bound. The assembled priests
are filled with consternation at being informed that the
guard were struck dead. Their fears are removed by
the arrival of a second and a third messenger. Jesus
being taken before Annas, Philo goes thither, and brings
him to Caiaphas. John expresses the agitations of his
mind. Portia, Pilate's wife, comes to see Jesus. The
speeches of Philo and Caiaphas, with the evidence
given by the suborned witnesses. Jesus, on declaring
that he is the Son of God, is condemned. Eloa and
Gabriel discourse on his sufferings. Portia deeply af-
fected withdraws, and prays to the chief of the gods.
Peter, in deep distress, tells John, that he has denied his
Master, then leaves him, and deplores his guilt.

AS' the dying Christian, when approaching
death shakes each relaxing nerve, prizes
the solemn moments more than he esteemed whole
days before; for then his Almighty Father claims
his last obedience, the last struggles of his virtue,
which flowing from a heart now freed from gro-
velling passions, rises towards the Source of Per-
fection; the soul then plumes her wings, and soars
on high, numbering the sacred minutes by fervent
prayer; while the all-seeing God looks down
propitious, and angels prepare the immortal crown:
so the hours of the great, the mystic sabbath be-

came more solemn, as the gracious, the divine
Redeemer hasted to bleed and die. Eloa, rapt
in the contemplation of the great Messiah's distress
and the importance of this sacred time; soon unveiled
his face to Gabriel, and thus addressed his celestial
friend :

Didst thou see his sufferings ?—Didst thou be-
hold the anguish of his great and benevolent mind ?
My admiration and surprise, no words in our celes-
tial language can express !—Alas ! what has he
still to suffer !—On every moment seems to hang
an eternity !

Thousands of years, answered Gabriel, have
elapsed since first I strove to learn the future won-
ders of his love—to obtain some knowledge, though
obscure, of the Messiah's promised grace to man
Yet how have I erred ! Oh let us admire in si-
lence ! We are encompassed by a holy labyrinth
of wonders. We see nothing around us but tombs,
and from them shall proceed angels of light. Happy
mortals, sweet be your slumbers ! Then Jesus—
But ah behold ! Who is he that advances with
wild gesture encompassed with lights ? Who are
those wretches who seem sent from the abyss of
hell ?—But he who equally created the grains of
sand, and the flaming suns—who equally reign
over the worm and the seraph, knows their inmost
thoughts, and is fully acquainted with all their
vile designs ! What do I see ? Judas at their
head ! he is their conductor ! the traitor will not
thus elated walk when the last trump shall call
forth the dust from those hills which cover them
from the Judge !

While he thus spake, the multitude lift up
their torches, and sought through the mazy groves
The great Emanuel perceived them, and sent
against them a black cloud which hung over them

spreading terror all around. Damp horror seised their minds : but the perfidious Judas defying the powerful admonition, and arming himself against the voice of conscience, softly cried, Where is he? His favorites say they saw him on mount. Tabor, arrayed in celestial splendor ; but they shall soon see him in bonds ; and all their schemes of grandeur shall vanish—But O my coward heart thou tremblest ! Can the coolness and gloom of night shake the courage of a man ? Finish thy work, and dare to pursue the road to wealth and happiness. Thus he spake to himself, and hasted forward.

The Saviour seeing them approach, said to himself, Far, very far are the eternal mansions from this abode of sinners. The humble path I now tread leads to the grave, yet will I walk in it. But it will shine refulgent, when the dead shall arise and the general judgment remove the veil.

Judas Iscariot led the band. The priests had commanded that he should take armed men and seek for Jesus among the sepulchres. These were ordered to bind him, and to bring him before the council. Judas knew the place of solemn prayer, the solitary recess where, during the silence of the night, Jesus used to pour out his soul to the Most High, in fervent supplications for man. The ungrateful traitor had said to the band, Whomsoever I kiss, is he : take him, and lead him away. But still the night had mercy on that perfidious disciple, and delayed his giving the insidious kiss. Yet soon the band with impotent fury advanced to the sleeping disciples ; when the Redeemer, moving towards them with awful dignity, said, Whom seek ye ? With rage and tumult, waving their flaming lights, they cried, Jesus the Nazarene. Now were come the other disciples ; and now the angels who had

retired, again came, and fixed their eyes on the
Messiah, who, with that divine composure, with
which he had commanded the agitated waves to
be still, answered, I am he. Struck by his voice,
they all fell speechless at his feet, and with them
Judas. Thus lie in the martial field the dead.
Thus stretched among the slain lies the furious
warrior, when the sedate chief, from the quiet
centre of the battle, sends around him destruction.
But at length they awoke from their trance, and
the traitor also arose from the earth. Over him
hovered the angel of death, and he seemed on the
point of being called to judgment; but concealin
the horrors of his mind, and the rancour of his
heart, with an affected air of serene friendship,
he went up to the holy Jesus, and crying, Hail
Master! saluted him. Now had he filled up the
measure of his guilt, and by the basest and mos
impious action, had, like an infernal spirit, opened
a way to the deep abyss of terror and dismay
Yet the meek, the humble, the divine Jesus, fille
with compassion, looked up to the traitor with a
eye of pity, saying, Ah Judas! betrayest thou tb
Son of Man with a kiss? Ah unhappy Judas
wherefore art thou come? Then gently resigne
himself up to the multitude.

Peter no sooner beheld this, than his passion
being enflamed, he, with eager impatience, brok
through the disciples; drew his sword, and rush
ing with an intrepid countenance, on the multitude
struck at the servant of the high priest, and cut o
his ear. But the gracious Friend of mankind
smiling benignant, instantly healed the wound, an
then looking on Peter, checked his ardour, saying
O my disciple! put up thy sword, and be a
peace. Knowest thou not, that were I to pra
for help to my Father, he would send me fro

heaven legions of mighty angels ? but how then
would the Scripture be fulfilled ? Then turning
to the multitude, who rudely bound him, he cried,
Are ye come out as against a thief with swords
and staves to seize me ; as against a vile malefactor,
who had escaped from the hands of justice ?
Were not I daily with you teaching in the temple ?
To you have I taught the way of life : you have I
instructed to shun the path of death and of destruc-
tion : Ye then laid not your hands upon me.
But this is your hour for accomplishing this work
of darkness.   Here he ceased, and now was come to
the brook of Cedron.

In the mean time the council of the priests and
elders had assembled in the stately palace of
Caiaphas and there remained agitated on the waves
of fluctuating hope and fear.   Their inquietude
and anxious murmurs did not escape the greedy
ears of the alarmed populace, who, filled with
curiosity, crowded the marble stair-case that led
to the council chamber, and filled with astonish-
ment, trembling blessed the Holy Prophet, or
stamping vented their maledictions.   The priests
now growing impatient, said to each other, None
of our messengers are returned.   What can detain
them ?   What means this delay ?   He who has
betrayed his master, has, perhaps, also betrayed us.
Or, the Nazarene, according to his frequent prac-
tice, has, by some illusion, escaped.

Thus were they discoursing, when one of their
messengers hastily entered the hall, with his hair
erect, and a cold sweat covered his pallid coun-
tenance, which was distorted by fear and terror.
For some time he stood speechless, while all be-
held him with looks of astonishment ; but at length
recovering, he cried in a trembling voice, Ye
priests and rabbies, we went according to your

orders, and at last found Jesus of Nazareth beyond
the brook, not far from the sepulchres.   The
sepulchres filled with horror did not affright us;
but the sky was hung with blacker clouds than
ever the eyes of man beheld!   Yet the band
marched forward, while I stood at a distance.
Soon I saw the prophet.   Then was I seized—I
know not how it was ;—but then was I seized with
a shivering, that shook my whole frame !—Yet
though they stood so near, they did not know
him ; but rushed on those that were about him.
He then cried with a firm voice, Whom do ye
seek?   Our men, still undaunted, called out
Jesus the Nazarene.   Then—methinks I hear him
still !—All my joints tremble !—He answered, as
with the voice of death, I am he !   No sooner
had he spoke the words, than they all fell on their
faces !—They now lie dead, and I only have escaped
to bring the dreadful news.

The priests at hearing these words, changed
colour, and remained as motionless as the rocks.
Philo, the hardened Philo, was alone able to speak,
and his rage overcoming his fear, he cried with a
furious voice, Thou, wretch, art either one of his
disciples, or art affrighted by the phantoms of the
night.   The open sepulchres made thee giddy,
and filled thee with the thoughts of death.
Fancy represented to thee the dead.   The men
we sent live ; they would not fall down at his
words.

While he yet spake, another messenger entered,
and cried, Ye priests and fathers, much have we
suffered. Before him have we sunk to the earth : for
his look was dreadful, and death was in the
words of his mouth.   But yet we have taken
and bound him.   He himself held out his hands,
and suffered us to bind them.   We took him,

trembling, lest we should again hear the powerful,
the fatal words. But now he comes along, with
silent patience, and has already entered the walls
of Jerusalem.

Scarce had he finished, when a third messenger
entered, whose looks of joy shewed that he brought
welcome tidings to the enemies of heavenly grace
and spotless virtue. Bowing he spoke, and, in
glad accents, cried, Blessed be you, ye priests of
the living God, and ye venerable fathers ! may all
who rise against you, and all the enemies of the
Lord, be destroyed, like this Galilean ! We are
bringing him bound with bonds, which neither
his words nor smiling countenance will be able to
unloose. All his followers have left him, and
he is now near the palace. May God give you his
blood !

He had no sooner concluded, than Satan entered
the assembly, and with him an infernal joy that
fascinated the priests, causing to hover before their
eyes the appearance of the streaming blood of the
Victim, and the paleness of his approaching death ;
while their ears were struck with the voice of his
torments. They then imagined his lips closed in
everlasting silence, while over his bones passed the
feet of the saints. Long did they remain under
this delirium : but Jesus not appearing, their fears
and rage at length returned. They then sent other
messengers and with them went Philo.

The guard had stopped by the way, and taken
Jesus to Annas, one of the chief priests ; for, while
the heavy vapours of the night were falling, the
hoary priest had left his bed to see the man who,
he imagined, had spread confusion through Judea.
John followed at a distance. Genial sleep had
now fled from his eyes, and melancholy sat on his
faded cheek. At length, recollecting that this

priest was void of that rancour which corroded the
heart of Caiaphas, he suppressed his timorous
dejection, and entering the hall, saw his beloved
Lord standing as a criminal before Annas, who
thus spake:

Thou art to be tried by Caiaphas. If thou art
innocent, as the great works thou hast done have
spread abroad thy fame, not only the nations of the
earth, but the God of Abraham, and his children,
will protect thee! Say then, what hast thou
taught? Who were thy disciples? Didst thou
teach the laws of Moses?—Didst thou—did thy
disciples observe them?

Annas now paused; he wondered at the prophet-
like mien with which Jesus stood before him! and
admired his composed dignity, undebased by pride.
The great Emanuel condescended thus to answer:
Freely I taught in the synagogues and in the tem-
ple; whither the Jews always resort. Why then
askest thou me? ask them who heard me.

While he thus spake, Philo rushed in. The
assembly was instantly in a tumult. Then an officer
who had the soul of a slave, committed against the
gracious Saviour, an action of such mean inhuma-
nity, that it was thought worthy of being foretold
by the prophets. Philo, with imperious voice,
now cried, Away with this seditious fellow,
that he may receive sentence of death; on
which the guard of the blessed Redeemer again
seized him, and, unresisted, took him thence.

John no sooner saw the Messiah in Philo's power,
than his face became overspread with a mortal
paleness; his eyes were dimmed; he trembled, and
grief took possession of his heart. At last, with
unsteady step, leaving the palace, he beheld, at a
distance, the moving torches. I will follow—No—
I dare not now follow thee, cried he; yet I entreat

thee, O thou best of men, that if God has decreed
that they shall be suffered to put thee to death, I
who have loved thee, and still love thee, with
an affection that exceeds that of a brother, may be
permitted to die with thee! that I may not see
thee struggle in the agonies of death, nor hear
the last—last blessing that proceed from thy fal-
tering lips!—Is there no deliverer?—no deliverer
upon earth?—none in heaven? Do ye too sleep,
ye angels, who sang, when his exulting mother
brought him forth? Alas! when your hosannas
resounded in her ears, little did she think of his
terrible death!—There is no other deliverer, but
thee alone, O God! the deliverer of the living
and the dead! O thou omnipotent Father of man-
kind, have mercy on me, and let him not die!—
Let not him die, who is the most holy of all the
children of Adam!—O thou Source of Mercy!
give these murderers—these cruel murderers, a
heart! fill their souls with the gentle feelings of
humanity!—Ah! I no longer see him! the moving
lights disappear!—Now,—now—they sentence him
to die!—May their cruel souls melt, O Jesus, at
beholding thy suffering virtue!—But who is this
roving in the dark? Is it not Peter? He has,
perhaps, heard our dear Master condemned to
suffer death.—How hastily he walks!—Now he
stands still—I no longer hear his footsteps.—How
solitary is this place!—How silent this dreadful
night!—Ah! this silence is fled.—What tumul-
tuous noise is that?—Perhaps they are hastily,
under the cover of the night, dragging him to
death, lest the compassion of the people should
deliver him—lest the melting stones, or their weep-
ing swords should see his death; and that the an-
gels alone may behold his blood!—Ah! have
pity!—have pity on him—Have pity on me! and,

O thou Father of Mercies, who hast compassion
on all thy works, let him not die !

Thus, in broken sentences, intermixed with
sighs, he, weeping, gave vent to his thoughts,
while he slowly moved to the high priest's pa-
lace,. and there continued standing without in the
dark.

Philo, the furious leader of the brutal troop
that guarded Jesus, hasted before them to the
council, where they perceived by his triumphant
look, his lofty deportment, and flaming eyes, that
he who had healed the sick, and raised the dead,
was safe in custody, and near the palace. Before
they had time to applaud Philo's active zeal, the
Messiah was brought in ; and seeing him entering,
they trembled with mingled rage and joy. With
a serene countenance he ascended the steps, and
stood before the judgment seat. All dignity, even
the dignity of a mortal prophet, had he now laid
aside, and appeared as tranquil as if only viewing
the fall of some murmuring stream ; or, as if his
mind, after being long elevated with the sublimity
of divine converse, was now relaxed, while he
indulged a short interval of pleasing and familiar
contemplations. He retained only some traces of
his heaven-born excellence ; but these were such
as no angel could assume, and none but those celes-
tial spirits fully discover. Philo and Caiaphas,
filled with rancour, had their eyes rivetted to the
floor. The seat of judgment gave the latter the
privilege of speaking first, and the former,
from pride, envy, and jealousy, was ready to
assume the same privilege : yet both continued
silent.

On the side of the palace, where a few lonely
lamps presented a dim light, was a circular staircase
that led to a gallery in the judgment hall, where

leaning on a marble balustrade, Portia, the wife
of Pilate, stood among other women, in the bloom
of beauty. Her person alone was young, for her
mind was adorned with the wisdom of riper age.
In her the fair blossoms blowed, and produced
fruit, as in the mother of the Gracchi, to enrich
the degenerate Romans. Prompted by the desire
of seeing the great Prophet, Portia had hasted
thither, with a few attendants; for the ostentation
of grandeur, and every idea of superiority, she had
laid aside. Eternal providence had directed her
steps; and while the rancorous hatred of the
priests filled her gentle mind with all the vehe-
mence of indignation; she, with admiration and
earnest solicitude, saw him who had raised the
dead stand with calm composure, before his
persecutors. With different passions was he
viewed by Philo, and thus spake the hypocrite :
Bring him nearer, and bind him faster. But
before we begin his trial, let us lift up holy hands
to God, and praise him, for having, at length
pronounced his sentence, and his no longer proving
us, by keeping silence. Here he lift up his hands,
and added; O Jehovah ! hear the prayer of thy
people. Thus may all perish who rise up against
thee; may their name, and the place of their
abode be forgotten ! May they never be remem-
bered, except where the bones of the dead lie
scattered, and where the hills have drunk the
blood of those that rebel against thee ! Yes, we
will praise thee ! we will praise thee ! we will
encompass thine altars, rejoicing, and Israel shall
be a song of triumph: The sinner shall bleed;
for hitherto Judah hath shut his eyes, and yet did
see : hath stopped his ears, and yet did hear : but
at length the wild illusion is vanished; and we
behold him bound who pretended to have been

before Abraham. 'Often, indeed, have the peop
with manly resolution, plucked off the gallir
shackles of error, and taken up stones to slay tl
blasphemer! Yet again they suffered themselv
to be deceived.—But, O thou Impostor! this d₁
is the period of their blindness, and of thy deceii
Though the people here present are but few
number, yet among these, many will, at our ca
witness against thee. The high priest will summ₁
them forth. Meanwhile I charge thee, and c₁
all Judea to witness the truth of the accusation-
I charge thee with blasphemy and sedition. Th₁
who hast cried in a manger, hast made thyself
God: hast pretended to forgive sins, and to rai
the dead: but thy mother and thy kindred sh₁
soon see thee expire. Then awake thyself! Th₁
shalt not enjoy such soft slumbers as those th₁
hast raised. Thou shalt lie down with the slai
whom God has rejected. There sleep—there f₁
the iron sleep of death, where the revolving s
and the wandering moon shall drink up corrup
fumes, till death is satiated, and Golgotha beco
white with human bones. Thus—thus mayest th
lie, and if there be a greater, a more horrid cur
streaming with seven-fold imprecations, whi₁
midnight hears, and the howling graves join in
tering, may it alight.—Here the bloated lips
the blasphemer were instantly stiffened, and l₁
distorted visage overspread with the paleness
death. In the moment when he began to denoun
his dreadful curses, his conscience, in vain, sm
him, for having no fear of the Almighty; ₁
now an angel of death, invisible to all besid
with a look of terror, stood before him, and th
addressed the hardened sinner.

The curses that proceed from thy mouth,
thou most execrable hypocrite! shall fall on th

self. The dark, the bloody hour of thy dissolution approaches with rapid wing. Soon will it come, O thou most flagitious hypocrite ! Soon wilt thou suffer a death as dreadful as ever mortal died, without the least mercy, the least token of relenting favour from thy Creator and thy Judge. When midnight surrounds thee, when death walks in the blackest gloom, when the king of terrors has struck the important blow, and thy struggling spirit, filled with horror, takes its flight ; then, in the valley of Benhinnon, shalt thou see my face.

Thus spake the angel of death, in whose lowring front were gathered clouds of wrath. From his lofty glaring eye flashed revenge. He stood like a towering rock, and on his shoulders fell his hair, black as the shades of night. Yet did not the destroyer smite him : but he encompassed him with his terrors, and made the accents of death roar around him. Philo, as much as mortal can, experienced the horrors of the damned ; horrors rushing upon his soul · with instantaneous and overwhelming rapidity. He was struck with sad dismay : his strength failed him : he was visibly seized with an universal trembling. Still the terrors of God ran through the very marrow in his bones : but as a worm, crushed by the foot of the passenger, curls writhing upwards its convulsed frame, and rears aloft its head : thus, with distorted efforts, he at length, after a long pause, struggling strove to proceed ; but only added, What I, overpowered by the offender's guilt, cover with silence, the issue will unfold. Thou high priest make haste to try him. He ceased, stiffened by fear, and unable farther to vent his rage.

A profound silence now reigned throughout the assembly. Portia had examined Jesus, and was struck at the noble serenity of his countenance

during the impious, the inhuman speech of his
inveterate foe; her eye beamed with pity, her
heart beat with redoubled strength, and sublime
ideas filled her mind.   Her eager looks now ranged
over the whole assembly, to see if she could find
no generous and noble soul, who, like her, admired
the Prophet. But she sought in vain, goodness
of heart was not to be found among a people ripe
for destruction, who were soon to see in flaming
ruins their boasted temple, where Jehovah now no
longer dwelt. One, however, she observed warming
himself at a fire in the outer room with the crowd,
who, with fierce looks' seemed to reproach him;
when turning pale, he with confusion looked wildly
round, and then fixed his eyes on Jesus. Ah!
said she to herself, that is surely the Prophet's
friend, he wishes his deliverance : he, perhaps,
seeks to deliver him, and fain would he teach the
rude populace to walk in the fair path marked
out by this wise man ; like him to live a life of
sobriety and the purest virtue ; like him to be the
tender friend of the human race, and, without
ostentation, to delight in doing good. But they,
void of understanding, threaten to drag him also
before the priests and elders. This strikes him
with terror : he trembles, and wanting the firm-
ness of this good Prophet, shrinks at the menace
of death.   Perhaps the afflicted mother of the
much injured Jesus, suffused in tears, besought
him to go and save from death the dearest, the
best of Sons. Oh with what pain, with what
agony of grief would his amiable, his blessed
mother have been filled, had she been here, and
heard the rancorous speech of that odious Pharisee!
—But why—oh why do I feel this deep concern
for this unknown mother ?—Why is my heart
filled with these strange emotions for a man whose

person I never before have seen, though often have
I heard of his virtues ? Do I wish to have brought
forth one who has so noble a mind, and to have
given him as a blessing to the world?—O thou
mother !—thou happy mother ! pride thyself in
him, and may thy life flow serene !—May thine eye
not see him expire ! Yet his death will afford an
instructive lesson to the world.

Now the high priest, rising from his seat, cried,
Though all Judea feels the burthen which the
man before us has laid on every shoulder, and the
whole world too well knows that he has impious-
ly rebelled against the Great Jehovah, who has
displayed his terrors on mount Moriah ! that he
has rebelled against the priests of the Most High
God ; and against the great Cæsar : though not
Caiaphas alone, but all Judea, demand that sen-
tence should be passed against him, and that death
should strike the blow, yet will we examine wit-
nesses, and hear his defence. 'Tis true, Israel is
not now assembled, and most of the witnesses are
involved in the shades of night—O ye devout
people who now sleep, soon will ye awake to
purer festivals than those in which the traitor
joined ;—for among the few who are here, wit-
nesses will not be wanting. Let him who works
righteousness and loves his country, stand forth,
and declare the truth.

Thus spake Caiaphas. Then came forth wit-
nesses false and corrupt. They had received the
hire of iniquity, and Philo, with most industrious
care had busily employed himself in filling their
narrow grovelling minds with calumny and the
basest malice. One with an inflamed look, leering
on the Messiah, cried :

How he profaned the temple we all know : but
in no instance did he violate that sacred place

with greater impiety, than when he drove away
those worthy persons, the dealers in offerings. We
were assembled to pray, when coming with fury
he turned the sellers of the beasts for the sacrifices,
out of the holy portico. What veneration can he
have for the Eternal, who was guilty of such vio-
lence in his temple, as to drive away the offerings
by which God is honoured?

After him appeared another, who with equal
folly and malice misrepresented the divine zeal of
the blessed Jesus: falsely adding, that he would have
taken possession of the temple; and from thence
have fallen on Jurusalem; but that his followers,
who, with repeated shouts, had in the wilderness
hailed him king, here proved false, and obliged
him to fly.

Then arose a Levite, who, with a contemptuous
air, cried, Has he not blasphemed the Most High
by his enormous pride, in pretending that he had
the power to forgive sins? On the holy Sabbath
he connived at his disciples, when they, regardless
of the sacred day, plucked ears of standing corn!
On the holy Sabbath too he restored the withered
hand! and yet this profane offender, who thus breaks
the commandments which the Most High deliver-
ed to Moses on mount Sinai, pretends to forgive
sins.

Now spake the fourth. With contemptuous smile
he arose, and in the voice of ridicule, said; I too
must give witness: but what need is there, O
fathers, of witness against one who, giddy with his
vain enterprizes, builds on the most romantic
dreams? He has said, and people no wiser than
himself stared and wondered.—He has said, I say,
that he would destroy the temple, and within three
days a new one should arise from the dust, built
by himself. This before me, he presumed to utter.

A man whose hair was whitened by time, then disgraced his hoary locks by his puerile sentiments. This sinner, said he, keeps company with publicans. I myself was one of that number, and maintain, that from them he was learnt to despise Moses, and to heal diseases on the Sabbath.

Thus they witnessed, while looks of expectation were darted on all sides on Jesus, each impatient to hear his defence. So around the dying christian, whose mind is filled with rapturous hopes and dawning joys, stands a crowd of base mockers whispering, The animating dream of immortal life will, like himself, soon disappear. Yet still he enjoys the reviving prospect of endless bliss ; prays for himself and for them, and smiles at the grave. Thus the expecting crowd gazed on Jesus. But silent was the Prince of Peace. On which Caiaphas, prompted by impetuous rage, cried :

Thou sinner, hearest thou in silence what these witness against thee ? But the Messiah still continued to hold his peace ; on which the haughty pontiff, still more exasperated, raising his voice, cried, Speak : I conjure thee by the living God, to answer, whether thou be Christ, the only begotten Son of the Father ? Jesus replied, Thou hast said it. Caiaphas now stood up : his eyes flaming destruction. Satan joined in the same look, while Abaddon, the angel of death, who attended Philo, thus indulged his rapid thoughts :

Were he to esteem these murderers worthy of an answer, it would be that of mercy. But the anger of the Most High is kindled, and the wicked and impenitent will be reserved for judgment. The last day will at length arrive. Thou great and terrible day of the Lord, wilt arise in all thy dreadful lustre ; then will I salute thee, thou day of retribution, as the fairest of all the sons of

Eternity; for then the balance of justice shall be
held forth, and every man be judged according to
his works. I will hail thee, O festive day !, when
the righteous shall triumph, and with palms in their
hands shall encompass the now persecuted and
insulted Messiah; while these earth-born rebels
against the Eternal will be involved in woe, and
cast from the presence of Lord, and the glory of
his power. I will therefore veil myself, and be
silent: but my silence is the forerunner of death
and vengeance.

In an instant these thoughts passed through the
angels mind. He then fixed his eyes on Caiaphas,
who had condemned the Messiah before be spake.
Meanwhile the Saviour lift up his eyes to heaven,
and then fixing them on the high-priest's face, cried,
I say unto thee, hereafter ye shall see the Son of
Man sitting on the right hand of power, and coming
in the clouds of heaven.

Thus shall Jesus open the last day, when he
shall come in tremendous glory, descending amidst
the songs of angels, and their sounding harps.
Here the Saviour opened a sudden view of futurity;
and with no less rapidity, from the amazed eye,
closed the tremendous scene.

Caiaphas, now impelled by a torrent of rage,
observed no measures, but stepping forth impetu-
ous, with death lowring on his brow, rent his gar-
ment, and rolling his fiery eyes, called out to the
mute assembly, Speak, ye have heard his blas-
phemies! What need have we of farther wit-
nesses? You have heard what he says. Speak;
What think ye? Then all cried out, Let him
die! Let him die!—Yes, let him die! rejoined
Philo, swelling with rage ; I must give vent to the
fulness of my heart: Let him die the accursed
death of the cross ! a sharp and lingering death.

Let his mouldering bones receive no sepulture ! Let his corpse putrify in the parching sun ! and on the day when God shall call forth the dead, may he continue deaf, and not hear the divine voice. Here lie ceased, and the multitude in wild confusion, rushed on the holy Jesus.———

O sacred muse of Sion's hill ! lend me the veil with which thou coverest thy face; when singing thy orisons before the Eternal : that I like the blessed spirits on high, with humble reverence, may cover mine eyes, adoring. Gabriel and Eloa now standing apart and unseen, thus discoursed :

"O Eloa, how deep are the mysteries of the Most High ! How inscrutable are his ways ! Nothing have I seen that equals the deep humiliation of the Son—of him who shone with such resplendent glory !—of him who on high subdued the rebel host !—of him before whom the bodies of the dead, shaken by his creative voice, shall, at his call, awake, and the earth suffer, as in the throws of child-birth, when he, attended by the loud resounding trump, the angels of death, and the falling stars, shall come to judgment.

Behold, cried Eloa, at the formation of this terrestrial globe, he spake, and the light diffused abroad its enlivening rays. A storm, replete with animating life, rushed before him ; and a thousand times a thousand living beings assembled on his right hand. At his command the sun, glowing with invigorating and reviving light, turned on its center. Then arose the harmony of the spheres ! then he created the visible heavens !

Behold, at his command, replied Gabriel, eternal night fled and skulked at a distance from the wide creation ! Eloa, thou wast by when he stood over the dark abyss : when at his call appeared an

enormous mass inert and deformed: it spread
before him like broken suns, or the ruins of an
hundred worlds. He bid it glow, and then through
the regions of death arose the blue sulphureous
blaze! Then was torture known; then did the
yells of anguish reverberate through the deep pro-
found

Thus discoursed these great celestial spirits.
Meanwhile Portia, unable longer to bear the in-
sults offered to the divine Jesus, went up to the
top of the palace: where, having for some time
silently indulged her tears, she lift up her watry
eyes, and her fair hands towards the lowering sky,
and thus gave vent to the painful sensations of her
troubled mind: O thou first of beings, who
createdst the world from chaos, and gavest to man
a heart formed to feel the mild sensations of
humanity! whatever be thy name, God! Jupiter!
or Jehovah! the God of Romulus, or of Abraham!
—O thou Father and Judge of all, may I presume
to pour out my lamentations before thee! What
offence has this peaceable, this righteous man com-
mitted, that he should be inhumanly put to death?
Dost thou, with delight look down from high
Olympus on suffering virtue? To man indeed
it affords an awful admiration, a wonder mixed
with terror: but canst thou who hast formed
the stars, be filled with wonder? No—in thee
amazement has no place! More sublime are the
sensations of the God of gods! Surely thy divine
eyes cannot, without pity, behold the guiltless
suffer? nor wilt thou fail to reward him, who,
thus calmly resigned, offers up himself a sacrifice
to virtue, and to thee! as for me, compassion
flows down my cheeks. But thou, where there is
no trembling tear, canst discern the hidden an-
guish of suffering virtue. O thou Father of gods

and men, reward, and behold, if possible, this righteous man with admiration !

As she now stooped over the balustrade that encompassed the flat roof of the palace, she heard below mournful accents, that seemed to proceed from a person in despair. These sounds of grief were uttered by Peter. John, who had continued standing at the door, hearing Peter's groans, and the plaintive broken accents that burst from him, with tender pity cried, Ah! Peter, is he yet living? Thou weepest !—thou art silent !—John ! returned Peter, leave me—leave me to die alone ! —I cannot survive my guilt !· Our gracious Master is lost ! But more lost am I !—O Judas ! Judas ! thou execrable disciple, hast betrayed him !—I too have been false ; before all who have asked me, I, miserable that I am, have denied him ! Fly from me, John, and leave me to die in silence. Do thou—do thou also die—Jesus is sentenced to suffer death ; and I like a base, a pusillanimous wretch, have publicly before sinners, denied him !

Thus Peter, in the agony of his grief, confessed his guilt to John, who, struck with surprise and concern, continued silent. The repentant disciple then hasted from him, and stood in the dark, by the dew besprinkled corner stone of that spacious building, against which faintly leaning, he sunk down, and declining upon it his drooping head, long wept in silence. But at last in broken sentences, thus expressed the emotions of his agitated mind. O death ! let thy hideous form now for ever cease to affright me !—Turn, O Jesus ! turn away that tender, that killing look !—Ah ! I, ungrateful ! have committed the foulest, the blackest deed ! I, like a base coward, have denied thee, my friend ! my gracious Master !—thee whom I loved—thee who lovedst me with an affection superior to that of the kindest friend !— thee whose godlike virtues, whose benevolence, whose piety, more than thy miracles, render thee all divine ! O my grovelling timorous soul, what hast thou done ?—in the great day of retribution, my dear Lord will disown me !—disown me before his faithful disciples, and all the holy angels !— This—this I deserve. Yet, O Jesus, whom I still love ! compassionate my anguish, and let me not hear the dreadful words, Depart from me, I know thee not !—O horrid—horrid thought ! Alas ! alas ! what have I done ? The more I think of my crime, the deeper I feel its envenomed sting ! Thus with conscious shame, and deep remorse, shall I languish out my wretched life, and lingering die !

Here he ceased, and silent indulged his tears. Near him stood Orion, his guardian angel, who with soft pity, and seraphic joy, observed his penitential sorrow. Peter now falling on his bended knees, cast up his tearful eyes towards heaven, and, in a low voice cried, Thou awful Judge supreme, the Father of men and angels, and of my Lord, thy blessed Son ! Oh pity—pity my distress ! Thou knowest the anguish of this contrite heart ! I have denied—basely denied Jesus, my Lord ! my gracious Master ! and my Friend ! Yet extend thy mercy to me, ungrateful ! Forgive, forgive this soul, so dastardly, and so vile. He will die ! Unworthy am I to die with my dear Lord—But before he bows his head to the grave—before he gives his last blessing to his faithful disciples, may I once more see him cast a gracious look on me and may his dying eyes cheer me with forgiveness ! To thee, O Jesus ! would I then sue for pardon, and not for a blessing. I would entreat thee to let me hear from thy lips that thou forgivest me: for my guilt will not permit me to say, My Lord, hast thou but one blessing, and that confined to these thy righteous, thy faithful disciples!—Then if by my tears, my humble sorrow, my deep contrition, I prevail on thee to let me hear that I have obtained forgiveness, I will go, and before the whole world acknowledge thee as my Lord—While it is thy will, O my adorable Creator, that I should live among men, it shall be my sweetest employment to seek out the good, the pious, the pure of heart, to whom, with incessant grief and tears, will I say, Yes, I knew Jesus, the most holy, the dearest, the best of men, the Son of the Most High God! Yet was I unworthy to know him!— I was one of his chosen disciples!—He loved us all —he loved me—yet I, unworthy, did not return his love! for in the hour of his distress, my courage failed, and I no longer loved the most holy of men, the best, the most divine! His kind, his generous heart overflowed with benevolence; he lived for others, and not to himself. He fed the poor: he healed the sick: he raised the dead to life. Hence he was hated!—hence he was murdered by wretches dead to humanity! I will teach you the words of wisdom that fell from his gracious lips. But first, arise, ye men, and come away, let us go to his grave, and weep!—Ah! his grave! how dreadful the thought!—O Jesus! thou divine Jesus! Where wilt thou rest in peace?—Where will the rage of the cruel leave thee a grave?

Thus with deep anguish, and humble fervor, Peter deplored his ingratitude to him, whom the sinners of the earth, in their words acknowledge, and in their actions deny: but he wept, and obtained the martyr's crown.

THE END OF THE SIXTH BOOK.

THE

MESSIAH.

BOOK. VII

THE ARGUMENT.

Eloa welcomes the returning morn with an hymn. The
Messiah is led to Pilate, and accused by Caiaphas and
Philo. The dreadful despair and death of Judas. Mary
comes, sees her divine Son standing before the Roman
governor, and filled with grief, applies to Portia, who
comforts her, and tells her dream. The Messiah is
sent to Herod, who expecting to see him work a miracle
is disappointed : when Caiaphas observing his dissatis-
faction, accuses Jesus, who, after being treated with deri-
sion, is sent back to Pilate. That governor endeavours
to save him ; put is prevailed on to release Barabbas,
and condemn Jesus. He is scourged, arrayed in a pur-
ple robe, and crowned with thorns, and in this condition
Pilate shews him to the people to excite their compassion,
but finding all in vain, he delivers him to the priests,
who cause him to be led to crucifixion.

ELOA now stood amidst the purple blushes of
the opening morn, encompassed by the
guardians of the earth, and in slow and solemn
strains joined his lyre to his melodious voice.

To thee, eternity, is born this awful day—this
day of blood ! It hastes to appear. It rises in the
heavens replete with mercy, and with grace divine.
Hail, all gracious Father ! who gavest thy Son to
die for man ! and from blackest guilt bringest
forth smiling peace and immortality. Hail, Saviour

meek and holy! This awful day shall shew thy
love to man, while all the wondering host above,
enraptured shall admire thy condescension, and
extol thy divine philanthropy and grace. Ye
cherubim and seraphim tune your golden harps,
and chant his praise, who now will bleed and die,
that man may live. Thou now shalt bruise the
serpent's head, and break the sting of death. From
the earth shall angels rise; and quitting their
mortal clay, appear in radiant forms; while
eternal rest shall close the train of thine exalted
triumphs.

Hail blessed day, replete with mercy, and with
grace divine! Behold the sun now begins to
smile with more refulgent lustre on this earthly
globe...See how his slanting rays dart along the
nether sky! Hail day of sacred rest, 'and solemn
joy in heaven, in which the seraphs lay their crowns
before the eternal throne adoring. Let all the
wide creation join to praise the suffering Jesus,
and suns and worlds innumerable admire and cele-
brate his mercy, and his love divine.

Thus sang Eloa, while his sacred hymn resounded
through the heavens. Now had the high-priest
assembled his creatures in the inner hall, where
sitting in council, they conspired against the holy
Jesus. There in deep consultation, they debated on
the methods by which they might bring over Pilate
to join their bloody purpose; on the measures to
be taken with the multitude; and on the manner
in which the Saviour should die. But the proud
Philo despising them too much to attend to their
advice, abruptly left the assembly, and sought the
Messiah, whom he found sitting with the guard
at the declining fire. Before him, with menacing
port, and quick step, he walked to and fro: till, at
length, he fixed his threatening eye, gleaming with

revengeful fury on Jesus.　He then stood still :
but amidst all the ebullitions of rage he foresaw,
with fluttering anxiety, a train of difficulties that
opposed his design : these he provided against,
by placing before his mind every expedient which
eloquence, the authority of the priests, or any
external object might afford : leaving nothing to
chance.　At length, recollecting that Jesus might
be rescued by the furious populace, his heart began
to fail ; but checking his fears, and summoning all
his courage, he resolved to put him to death, or
to perish in the attempt.　Then considering that
the time for executing his fell purpose was now
arrived, his heart again fluttered ; but he soon
suppressed the tumult within, and now full of his
resolutions, the slight airy web prepared by vain
precautions, he returned to the council ; where he
instantly cried, with a loud voice, Still, fathers do
you delay !　Does not the dawn already appear ?
—Shall he yet live till the evening ?

Rouzed at Philo's words, the council suddenly
broke up ; and the guard rudely laying their hands
on the blessed Jesus, they with a formidable body
of the priests, scribes, and elders, led him to Pilate.
Cold was the breath of the morning ; and the
glimmering light of the rising day now unveiled to
Jesus the temple, which was only for a few hours
to prefigure a nobler sacrifice, than was ever
offered on its smoking altars.　From that struc-
ture he turned his eyes to heaven.　He was hurried
along, and early as it was, was soon attended by a
numerous multitude : for report had not concealed
the transactions of the night.　Messengers were
dispatched to inform Pilate of their coming, and
they had scarcely arrived, when that governor, to
his great surprise, beheld all the tribe of Judah
appear before him, only to bring a dubious charge

against a single man.   Having pressed up the
ample stair-case, which led to the judgment hall,
they stopped in an open gallery before it, called
Gabbatha, where Pilate had caused his seat to be
placed : for the approaching festival did not per-
mit their entering the court of justice.   There, in
superb state, sat Pilate on the seat of judgment,
who immediately cried, Of what do the elders
of Israel accuse the prisoner ? and—How ! added
he, interrupting himself, do I see Caiaphas himself
here ?   This he spake aloud, with his eyes fixed
more on Jesus than on the assembly.   The high-
priest then advancing nearer, said : We flatter
ourselves, that Pilate hath such an opinion of the
fathers of Israel as to be persuaded that they
would not have brought this man before him, were
he not a criminal.   Yes, Pilate, he is a criminal,
and his crime greater than has ever been committed
since Israel has enjoyed the happiness of being
under thy government.   With such indignation
has his guilt filled the fathers of Judea, that they
are unable to represent before thee, in a clear light,
the impious opposition this Jesus has made against
the laws of our prophet, and the holy temple !
or how the sorcerer, by his fascinating speeches,
and a thousand pretended miracles, has seduced
the people !   Long, very long, O Pilate ! has he
deserved death.——

Here Pilate interrupting him, cried, Then take
him, and judge him according to your law.   Why,
O Roman ! resumed the high priest, dost thou
mock us ?   Thou canst not but know, that it is
not lawful for us to put any man to death.   Here
he paused, vexed that Pilate should oblige them
to recollect their lost freedom : but soon continued,
Thou knowest what submission, what unreserved
obedience and unshaken fidelity we have shewn to

Tiberius, our Sovereign, and the father of his country. This Jesus whom thou seest before thee, has assembled the people in the wilderness of Judea, where, by his factious speeches, he hath incited them to shake off their subjection to Cæsar, and to make him king. He pretended to be the person foretold by the prophets as the deliverer of Judah. He searched into their inmost thoughts, learnt their sentiments, sympathized in their concerns, and when they were hungry in the desert, supplied them with food. How greatly he has by these means attached them to himself, appears from the manner in which he made his public entry into Jerusalem—But I shall not attempt to describe the odious pomp and rejoicings of that profane day. Thou thyself must have observed them, and have heard the rude acclamations, the hosannas, the frantic exultations of the maddening populace, which doubtless shook even this solid edifice.

At this Pilate only smiled: on which Philo, repressing the heat of his malice, and all the fury of ungoverned rage, calmly began, Could I, O thou wise Roman, imagine, that thou wouldst suffer thyself to be so deceived by a specious shew of humility, as to believe the proud traitor incapable of forming ambitious schemes of rebellion, I should continue silent. But thou knowest mankind.— This Jesus, however contemptible he may seem, while bound and a prisoner, made a very different appearance in the deserts of Galilee. I beg, O Pilate, thy patient hearing, while I lay before thee a slight sketch of his projects. First, by the arts already mentioned by the high-priest, he practised on the infatuated multitude. He then proceeded to try how far he could govern them. But how did the trial answer his presumptuous attempt?

Confident discourses, eloquence sublime, now indeed lying dormant, and fictitious miracles, gave him success. His projects ripening apace, he moved the multitude to make him king. They flocked about him, and the air resounded with their applause. This he perceived, and the more to inflame their zeal, withdrew from their sight. This succeeded. They went in quest of him, and the rolling stream was swelled by the accession of new currents. At length finding their strength equal to the end proposed, he no longer avoided them; but entered Jerusalem in triumph. Yet, however great was the attachment of the multitude to him, it went not so far as to induce them to compel the fathers of Jerusalem to go out and meet their king. And be assured, O Pilate! that had they dared to make the attempt, there is not a hoary head among all those thou seest before thee, nor any of us who serve at the altar, who would not with joy have bled in the cause of God, and of Cæsar.

The divine Messiah, without shewing the least emotion, remained plunged in profound meditations. He thought on the sufferings that were to purchase the redemption of man. The most cruel death summoned him to the altar, while those who raged around him were only the sacrificers, and these he scarce observed. Thus the commander, chosen to revenge the injuries done to his country, flies to the bloody battle, without regarding the dust that rises under his feet. Pilate, though a Roman, was filled with amazement at the silence of the Mediator. Thou hearest, said he, the heavy charge that is brought against thee, and yet art silent—Perhaps thou art unwilling to defend thyself before this tumultuous assembly. Follow me. Jesus then followed the Roman governor into the judgment hall.

Now inquietude and uncertainty seized on the priests, who trembled and turned pale.

Judas a more abandoned sinner than they, who with guilt of deeper dye, had ungratefully betrayed his divine friend, seeing the approach of that death, to which he found the impatient priests were resolved to lead him, suddenly started up, and hastily rushed out of the assembly, then pressing through the waving multitude, flew to the temple, where Caiaphas, dreading an insurrection, had posted a number of priests. This the traitor knew, and now had entered the sacred structure, where reigned an awful silence. At the sight of the veil, hanging before the Holy of Holies, he hastily turned aside ; he was seized with a sudden tremor ; paleness sat on his cheek, guilt and horror on his brow. Then going with frantic gesture up to the priests, he cried aloud, Take back your silver. I have sinned in betraying the blood of the innocent, which, wretch that I am, now falls on my head ! He then throws the money at their feet, and rolling his eyes, in wild despair, rushes out of the temple, and out of Jerusalem, flying from the sight of man. He stops, and looks around. He runs. Again he stands still. Again he flies. Then hastily casts his eyes about to see whether he be observed by mortal eye. At length no human being appears in sight, and the noise of the city dies on his ear.

Judas then clenching his hands, and stamping, cried, Oh how my guilt stares me in the face, and tears this obdurate, this black, this cruel heart ! I cannot—I must not bear it ! This nameless agony will not—no, it will not, after death, be more dreadful ! O horror most horrible ! O rage —rage, too long am I in thy power ! When these eyes are closed—these ears are deaf—I shall

not see him stretched on the cross !—I shall not
see his trickling blood ! nor hear his faultering
voice !—But he who spoke on Horeb said, Thou
shalt do no murder !—He did—But I have no
God !—Thou despair shalt be my God ! Thou
commandest me to die !—I will obey—I will die !
—Ah ! why do I tremble ? why feel this inward
conflict ? Why, O my soul ! dost thou shudder
at the dreadful deed ? Nature rises against it !
It starts back from destruction ! Wouldst thou live
—live branded as the most treacherous—most
ungrateful—most accursed !—Have I not betrayed
—nay, murdered the holy Jesus—once my friend ?
for this the grave opens wide its gaping jaws—and
hell !—Oh horror—horror inexpressible !—Sure
hell cannot be worse !—I'll know the worst. Die
wretch die !—kill also the soul, which would
carry its wretchedness beyond the grave.—Thought,
thou art my torment—my curse !—I would kill
thought ! Thou thinking principle, so wretched,
and that yet shudders at this dread deed of black
despair, to thee I wish destruction ! Thus, with
wandering look he spake, and then with fury cursed,
and raged against the Eternal.

Ithuriel, and Obaddon, the angel of death, had
followed his steps. They saw him stop under a
spreading tree, and perceived on his countenance
the hideous traces of despair, when Ithuriel, with
precipitate voice, said to Obaddon, Behold he is
going to die by his own hand ! I who have been
his angel, was willing once more to see him ; but I
abandon him to thee, and to the dread effects of
his rash despair. Yes, I was once his guardian,
but thou angel of death seize thy victim, I veil
myself, and fly from this scene of horror and turn
away my eyes. Then Obaddon, rising to the
summit of an adjacent hill, stretched towards

heaven his right hand, in which be held a flaming sword, and uttered the solemn words pronounced by the angels of death, when man filling up the measure of his guilt, impiously deserts the post allotted him by the great Creator, and flying in the face of sovereign mercy, which ever smiles on true repentance, murders himself.

O death, I conjure thee, by the awful name of the great Omnipotent, to make this man thy prey! His blood be upon himself. Behold thou, to thee, extinguishest the sun. Life and death lie before thee: but thou, wretched mortal, shortenest the time appointed thee by sovereign wisdom, and chusest death. Withdraw thy light, O sun! and on him come the agonies of expiring nature! O grave, open wide thy tremendous jaws! and seize him, O corruption! His blood be upon himself.

Judas heard the voice of the immortal. Thus, at midnight, the wandering traveller, in a lonely forest, listens to the distant storm which howls in the mountains, and tears up the cloud-topped cedars on their lofty summits. Filled with all the frenzy of despair, he answered, Too well I know that voice: It is the dying voice of Jesus! thou demandest my blood!—Thou shalt be satisfied. Thus crying, with look wild and furious, he leapt from the crag of a shelving rock, and was suspended in the air. Obaddon himself was astonished, and started back. The amazed struggling soul, ere the breaking of his convulsed heart, thrice shook his whole frame; and at the fourth, the stretching cord, by which he hung, broke: he fell on the craggy rock, and death drove his frantic spirit from its earthly mansion. It arose upwards. Volatile spirits followed from the squalid corpse, and, swifter than thought, gathered round it, and became an aerial body, that with clearer eyes, the soul might behold the dreadful abyss, and, with finer and more terrifying ear, distinguish the thunders of the awful Judge rolling on high : but it was a body odious to the sight, weak, and only sensible of pain. Soon had the soul recovered from this stupor of death. It began to think, and said, Am I again sensible ?—What am I now ?—How light I raise myself on high in the air ! Are these bones ?—No, they are not—but yet I have a body !—How mysterious !—Who am I ?—Dreadful are my perceptions ! I feel myself miserable !—Am I Judas, who died by his own hands ?—Where am I ?—Who is he on the hill —that bright figure, who casts a dreadful look towards me ?—Oh that mine eyes had remained closed in darkness !—but they see more clearly ; —more clearly still ! ah, how dreadfully clear ' —Let me be gone !—O horror ! horror ! it is the Judge of the earth !—I cannot escape !— and that is my frightful corpse ! O that I could enter it again !

Now the guilty spirit, amazed and confounded, sunk to the ground. Arise, called Obaddon from the hill, sink not down to the earth. I am not the Judge of the world ; but Obaddon, the angel of death, one of his messengers. Hear thy sentence. This is the first, and worse is that which will follow.

To death everlasting art thou adjudged ! Thou hast betrayed thy Lord, the gracious Messiah ! Thou hast rebelled against the omnipotent Jehovah ! and hast murdered thyself ! Therefore he who holds the scales in his right hand, and in his left death, hath said, The terrors that shall gather round the head of the traitor are beyond measure ; beyond the reach of numbers. First shew him the bleeding Redeemer fixed on the cross. Then at a distance let him see the bright mansions of everlasting felicity, and then convey him to the gloomy regions of eternal night!

Thus the angel announced the sentence. On which the trembling ghost, now rendered by its terrors still blacker and more horrible, followed Obaddon at a distance.

In the mean time Jesus was in the judgment hall with Pilate, who said, Art thou the king of the Jews? -The Saviour, looking on the Roman with a placid gravity, answered, If my kingdom were of this world, then would my servants fight: but my kingdom is not on earth. How then, returned Pilate, canst thou be a king? I am, said Jesus. I came down to earth, and was born to lead mankind to the truth. They that are of the truth listen to my voice.

Here Pilate changed the discourse, and with the air of a politician, willing to elude the decision of an affair which he thinks beneath his farther enquiry, said with a smile, What is truth? Then returned with Jesus to the multitude, and addressing himself to the priests, said, I cannot find that he is guilty of any crime; much less that he is worthy of death. It does not appear to me, that he has really engaged in any seditious practices: but as ye have mentioned Galilee as the principal scene of his rebellion, I will send him to Herod, who is now in Jerusalem, and let him, if he pleases, punish him. The affair seems to relate to something in your law, of which Herod is a better judge than I.

After a sleepless night, the mother of the most amiable of the sons of men, came to Jerusalem with the first appearance of the dawn, and hasted to the temple in search of her divine Son; but not finding him, stood depressed with anxiety and grief, till a hoarse murmur from the governor's palace reached her ears. She then moved towards the sound without any idea of the cause from which it arose, and mingled with the crowds which from every part of Jeruselem were flocking to the judgment-seat. Melancholy, but entirely at ease with respect to the cause of the tumult, she drew near to the solemn place, when she observed Lebbeus, who, no sooner met her eye, than he hastily withdrew. Ah, cried she to herself, he shuns me! Why does he turn aside! This thought drew the sword which the divine providence had ordained, should pierce through her soul. Mary then entering the place called Gabbatha, and raising her head, saw Jesus. Her angel, on beholding the paleness of death overspread her face, and the tender anguish that appeared in her eyes, turned aside. Yet she, though her sight grew dim, and her ears seemed stunned, went forward, and trembling, proceeded towards the judgment-seat, where she at once saw her son, his powerful accusers, with the Roman governor sitting in judgment, and heard the voices of the multitude clamourously demanding his death. What could she do? To whose mercy could she have recourse? She looked around and saw no pity. She raised her eyes to heaven, but from thence received no relief. In this extremity her bleeding heart in silent fervor, thus offered up its petitions to him who perfectly knows every idea of the human mind.

O thou who causedst the miraculous birth of this my dear Son to be made known to me by an angel, before I had, by thy power, conceived: who in Bethlehem's vale gave him to me, that I might rejoice with a mother's joy, in concert with those with whom never mother rejoiced: with a joy which the angelic hosts themselves in their hymns at his birth, did not fully express : oh let me not see the wicked prevail against him ! Thou who graciously lent an ear to the supplications of the mother of Samuel, when at thine altar, she mingled her petitions with her tears, hear my sighs, and pity the distress of my soul. O God most merciful ! consider the anguish of my heart. Thou gavest me the tenderness of a mother ; thou gavest me the best of sons—Of all human beings the best. O thou who createdst the heavens, and hast directed the sons and daughters of affliction to fly to thee for relief, if my petition be agreeable to thy divine will, suffer not these cruel men to put to death my Son, the holy Jesus.

Here her distress grew too great to permit her even to give vent to her thoughts. Meanwhile the stream of the impetuous multitude drove her aside out of his view With much difficulty she now made way through the crowd : she stood still : then pressed forward, seeking for his disciples ; but not finding them, she veiled herself, and freely indulged her tears. At length, lifting up her eyes, she saw herself close by the other side of the Roman palace : then sighing, she said to herself, Perhaps some humane, some tender mind may dwell in this riotous house ; perhaps a mother, who is not above sympathizing in a mother's grief. Oh that this were but the case !—Many mothers report of thee O Portia ! that thou hast a benevolent heart.—O ye angels, who at the manger sang the nativity of my Son ! may she pity my distress !

Mary instantly ascended the marble steps, took off her veil, and entered the empty, silent rooms. Soon she saw a graceful Roman lady, issue forth from a distant chamber, on the side next the hall of judgment, who, beholding Mary, stood surprised, while her limbs appeared to tremble under her loose robe. The mother of Jesus, though her countenance was clouded by grief, in all her gestures shewed a dignity that was admired even by the angels: for true dignity is best understood by the celestial spirits; and now, with a graceful humility, she approached the fair Roman, who instantly cried, Say—oh say, who art thou? for never have I beheld such noble sorrow.

Mary now interrupting her, said, If thou feelest in thine heart the compassion that sits on thy countenance, lead me—oh lead me to the amiable, the humane Portia. The lovely Roman matron, now still more amazed, answered with softest voice, I am Portia. Thou Portia! returned Mary, filled with an agreeable surprise. On seeing thee a secret wish arose in my mind, that Portia was such as thou appearest. And art thou indeed that Roman lady?—But thou canst know little of the grief felt by a mother belonging to a people whom thou hatest, yet the women of Israel extol thy gentleness and humanity. I am the mother of him whom Pilate is now judging, whom cruel men have unjustly accused, though he has committed no offence; for he is holy, and his life irreproachable.

Portia stood viewing her with rapturous admiration; while her mind rising above the dejections of compassion, she at first seemed lost in amazement. At length she cried, And is he thy Son, and thou the most blessed of women? Art thou the mother of the divine Jesus? Art thou Mary? Then turning from her, she, with audible voice, thus lift up her thoughts, and her eyes to heaven.

O ye Gods! she is his mother! upon you, ye nobler, ye better Gods I call, who have been revealed to me in a dream—a dream filled with

important realities. O thou Supreme! Jupiter is
not thy name, nor Apollo; but whatever thou
art called, thou hast sent to me the mother of the
greatest, the wisest, the best of men! if indeed
he be a man: sent her a supplicant to me!—oh let
her not offer her supplications to me! but rather
let her lead me to her exalted Son, that he may
deliver me from darkness and doubt! that by
casting upon me a distant look, he may unfold the
knowledge of the Most High God, and the won-
derous mysteries I long to know.

Portia again turned herself towards Mary, who,
with an affectionate look, met the Roman matron's
eye, and then cried: How art thou moved!—Doth
Portia pity me?—Oh then am I happy—then am
I indeed a most happy mother! No mother ever
loved a son with a love like mine. But, O fair
Roman! let me conjure thee by thy heart so full
of compassion, not to implore thy Gods. It is thou
thyself must help my Son; they have no power to
help him: nor canst thou, if the Most High has
decreed that he shall die. Yet if Pilate keeps his
hands unstained with the blood of the innocent,
with more confidence will he appear before the
judgment-seat of God.

Portia earnestly fixing her eyes on Mary, thus,
with gentle voice, replied: Oh I scarcely know
what I say, or what emotions swell my heart! but,
let this be thy consolation; I will strive to help
thee—thee whom my soul loveth. Know too, O
Mary! that I do not, as thou supposest, call on
those Gods. A holy dream, from which I am but
just risen, has taught me better Gods, and to them
have I prayed. A celestial, a terrible dream, the
like of which hath never before been presented to
my imagination—I would have helped thee, Mary,
even though I had not the happiness of seeing thee:

for the vision that appeared before me, had already, with a powerful voice, spoke in thy behalf : but the end of it was dreadful and mysterious. At my awaking, strong were the impressions it had made upon my mind, and I was hasting to see the mighty prisoner, when behold, the Gods sent me his mother !

Here she beckoned to a female slave, who stood at a respectful distance in the passage ; for on leaving her apartment, she had given orders that a slave should be sent to attend her. She was now come, and Portia, addressing herself to her, said, Go to Pilate, and let him know from me, that he who is now before him is a divine person, that therefore I entreat him not to condemn the righteous. For this morning it was the will of the Gods, that a vision in his behalf should trouble me while I slept. Then turning to Mary, she added, Cease now, thou tender mother, to dwell on thy sorrows. I will lead thee into my garden : we will walk among the flowers opening to the morning sun : where we shall be free from this alarming noise, and there I will relate to thee my instructive dream.

Portia was now silent, and Mary, unable to express her gratitude and joy, made no reply. They walked down into the garden, while the noble pagan was rapt in amazement, and in reflections which had never before employed the faculties of her mind. Her angel had infused the dream, and from the strong and warm sensations with which she was affected, now awaked new thoughts, that the greatest certainty and force, he might touch the finest strings of her heart : but at length, rousing herself from these contemplations, she thus addressed herself to Mary.

Socrates,—thou indeed knowest him not ; but

MESSIAH

Port– Socrates indeed thou knowest him not

Published by I British Museum 1808

my mind exults at his very name ; for the noblest
life that ever man lived, he crowned with a dignity
in death, that did honour to such a life. That
eminent sage, has always been the object of my
highest admiration. Him I saw in a dream : for
he gave me to know his immortal name. I, Socrates,
said he, whom thou admirest, am come to thee
from, the regions beyond the grave. Cease to
place thine admiration on me. The Deity is not
what we thought him. I in the shades of rigid
wisdom, and thou at the altars, have gone astray.
To reveal to thee the wonders of the Most High
would exceed my commission. I only lead thee
to the first step of the outer court of the temple.
Perhaps, in these wonderful days, in which the
greatest and most important event is seen on earth,
a better a more exalted spirit may come, and lead
thee farther in the way of truth and holiness. But
thus much I may declare to thee, and this know-
ledge thou hast procured by thy singular goodness.
Socrates no longer suffers from the cruelty of the
wicked. There is no Elysium, no infernal judges,
no Tartarus. These are only weak and chimerical
fictions, the offspring of ignorance and error.
Another Judge judges beyond the grave, whose
wisdom comprehends all knowledge, whose justice
is impartial, whose power is boundless, and whose
goodness is infinite. Other suns shine than the
fabulous luminaries of Elysium, and the felicity
of the blest is pure, ineffable, eternal. But all
actions are numbered, weighed, and measured,
how then must the highest apparent virtues sink
in real value ! how is the boasted worth of the
hypocrite scattered like dust before the whirlwind !
The sincere are rewarded : their involuntary errors
receive forgiveness. Thus I, on account of the
sincerity of my heart, have obtained grace, and

me happy. On earth I loved virtue.; here I drink full draughts from its pure celestial spring. O Portia! Portia! how different is the state on the other side the tomb, from that we have imagined. Your formidable Rome, is no more than a large assemblage of busy ants, and one sympathizing virtuous tear is of more value than a world. Oh deserve to shed such tears! The celestial spirits are now solemnizing a mystery which has not been. unfolded to me, and which I, rapt in wonder and. surprise, can only admire at an awful distance. The greatest of mankind, if I may presume to call him a man, suffers more than the sufferings of a mortal, and paying the lowest obedience to the, Most High God, perfects all virtue. He suffers for the human race. Behold, thine eyes have seen him. Pilate now sits in judgment on thy Redeemer: but should his blood be shed, louder will it cry, than any innocent blood ever spilt.

Here the venerable phantom paused, and then crying, Observe! instantly vanished. I looked around me, and, behold, a black cloud soon covered, all the azure sky with darkness, and descending, hovered over the graves, which trembling, opened. Over one of them the cloud separated, forming a lucid chasm, through which ascended a man stained with blood, followed by the eyes of multitudes dispersed on the graves, who looked upwards with, stretched out arms, as if longing to follow him, till he ascended above the clouds, which soon dispersed. After this I looked, and behold many bled and died for him who had ascended on high. The earth drank their blood, and trembled. I saw the sufferers die; nobly did they suffer, and better were they than the men among whom we live. Now arose a tempest; dreadful it marched along, spreading a thick gloom over all nature. Terrified

I awoke.—Here she abruptly paused. Thus the
mind, trembling, starts back from a train of thoughts,
on finding that the last verges too near on the awful
depths of providence.

Mary, now filled with new sensations, lift up
her eyes to heaven; and then casting an affectionate
look on the fair virtuous Roman, thus answered,
What shall I say to thee, O Portia? I do not
comprehend all the sublime truths contained in
thine amazing vision. . But how much do I honour
thee, O thou favoured of heaven! Spirits of an
higher order will come, and lead thee into the
sanctuary of God.   Silent as I am, when with
pleasure and admiration I listen to thy discourse,
permit me now to say, that he who created the
revolving heavens, with as much ease as these
blooming flowers, is the true and only God.   It is
he who has given to the human race a life of labour,
of fleeting joys and transient sorrows, that we may
not forget the value of our immortal souls, nor
cease to remember that immortality dwells beyond
the grave.   He is called Jehovah, the Creator, the
blessed and only Potentate, the King of kings, and
the Lord of lords.   He was the God of Adam, the
first of men; the God of Abraham our father.
The worship we pay him, whatever the proud may
say, the pious among us acknowledge to be involved
in obscurity.   Yet it was prescribed by the Eternal
himself, who can and will remove the veil.   He is
now removing it.   Jesus, the great prophet, the
worker of mighty miracles, the messenger of the
Most High God, whom with inexpressible joy,
reverence and astonishment, I call my Son, came
to remove the veil.   That I was to bear him, that
his name was to be Jesus, that he is to redeem
mankind, were revealed to me by an immortal being,
one of those spirits whom we call angels; but

though they are, like us, created, the deities of the Greeks and formidable Romans, did they really exist, would be but as mere mortals, compared with these exalted beings. When I brought forth the wonderful child, though mean was the place, an host of these bright immortals celebrated his nativity, with hymns of joy and triumph.

: Portia now overcome by her amazement, lift up her joined hands and her eyes towards heaven, and sinking down on her knees, prayed. She strove to pronounce the word Jehovah : but feeling a secret awe, which would not suffer her yet to presume to mention the tremendous name, she arose, and giving Mary a look of sympathetic sorrow, cried, He shall not die. .

Ah he will !—he will ! returned Mary. Long has this thought clouded my life with grief and melancholy. For he himself, O Portia ! has said it. He is resolved, to lay down his precious life : this appears to me, and his pious disciples, most mysterious.—Ah now my wounded heart bleeds afresh ! Thy divine vision begins to open to my mind.—May God—the God of Abraham bless thee !—but oh turn from me thy weeping eyes ! —In vain do thy tears, O Portia, speak comfort to my soul !—He is determined to die !— to die !

Here her voice failed her. Long they stood without being able to lift up their eyes to each other, weeping in silence. At length, as the dying saint casts a look at her friend, the amiable, the disconsolate mother, lift up her head, and cast her swimming eyes on Portia, who, with answering look of tender sympathy, took her by the hand, and said, O, thou best of mothers ! thou most honourable among women.! I will go with thee—I will mourn with thee at the sepulchre of the dead !

. While they thus interchanged cordial discourse,
the high priest, attended by the multitude, hurried
the great Messiah to Herod, whose stately palace
already rang with the cry, that Pilate was sending
thither Jesus of Galilee, who had performed such
mighty miracles. That prince hastily assembled
his courtiers; and being seated, thus addressed
them: This day will instruct us in the truth, or
free us from error. You have all heard what fame
has published of Jesus of Nazareth, of his healing
the sick with a word, and, with a word, raising the
dead! Yet he could not save himself from bonds,
and is at last in our hands! What an unexpected
event!—Here he ceased, dissembling the satisfac-
tion that lurked in his proud obdurate heart. The
greatest of all the prophets, said he to himself, is
going to appear before me as a vile criminal, and
I shall see him tremble at my feet. I shall be his
judge. I will order him to perform a miracle.
should he comply, I shall have the pleasure of
seeing it, and the honour of its being done at my
command; and should he not, yet still will plead
before me this celebrated prophet, before whom
Israel has strewed palms, and sung hosannas.

Herod's indulgence of these vain contemplations
was interrupted by the priests, who, with loud
and hasty steps, entered the hall. The benevolent
Jesus was still at a distance among the multitude,
who pressed around him, endeavouring to see him:
some stormed, others raged. Some uttering curses,
reproached him, and others wept. The great
Messiah walked amidst the tumult with silent
resignation, filled with ideas too sublime for the
narrow powers of a mere human mind to conceive.
He looked forward, to the state of his pious fol-
lowers after his decease, when the Comforter should
pour raptures into their transported souls, and

enlightening their understandings, lead them into
all truth. Many of these, his faithful friends,
were among the multitude, pressing towards him,
to obtain his last blessing, while the crowding
populace drove them back. . Often did they renew
their efforts ; ..but they renewed them in 'vain.
Amidst these were the disciples ; Peter, with
heavy heart and languid eye, that in silent language
spake his grief. John, and Lebbeus, were also
there 'with Nathanael, and many of the seventy
followers of the Lord. Among the crowd were also
several of the female friends of Christ ; Mary Mag-
dalen, with Mary, the mother of the sons of Zebe-
dee ; but not the sister of Lazarus': she lay at the
point of death. The first of these fair disciples was
unable to repress the ardour of her soul ; for
seeing by her one whose eyes the divine Jesus had
opened, filled with devout fervour she cried aloud,
Oh, if thou still rememberest the hour when he
gave thee to behold the glorious light of the sun,
and all the blaze of day, help me—oh help me !—
convey me through this maddening crowd, that my
eyes may once more see my Lord—that I may once
more receive his last blessing !—Oh they will kill
him !—they, cruel men, will murder my Lord !
but in vain were her entreaties, in vain did the
grateful man endeavour to assist her. Mean while
Peter, dispirited by the anguish of his mind, at
length desisted from all attempts to advance nearer
to his gracious Master : but John, ascending an
eminence, obtained a distant sight of the blessed
Saviour ; and then lifting up his eyes to heaven,
gave vent to his full heart in silent prayer. Mean-
while Lebbeus, addressing himself to the other
Mary, who, overpowered with grief, covered her
face, said, O thou mother of the sons of Zebedee !
happy parent ! look up to heaven, look up with

comfort! How great is her grief who bore the
spotless, the righteous, the divine Jesus! Where-
ever I turn my eyes, methinks she appears before
me! I feel, I feel her sorrows! I sympathize in
the tender, the painful emotions of her melting
soul—of her bursting heart! Pity, Oh pity me,
ye angels of death! shorten her sorrows; and that
she may not see her holy Son expire, oh remove her
to the world of peace and joy!

At length the future Judge of the World entered
Herod's palace, and was led before that prince;
who, on his seeing him, was struck with amaze-
ment: amidst all the swellings of pride, he was
astonished at beholding such dignity, such sedate
composure. For some time he sat viewing him with
a penetrating look till his pride suppressing his
amazement, he thus spake:

Thou prophet, the fame of thy miracles has
spread over the whole country, and has reached
even my ears. Yet the voice of fame, seldom re-
presenting things as they really are, generally says
too much or too little. Shew me then what I
am to think of the miracles she, perhaps, has too
sparingly attributed to thee. Not that I doubt of
thy having performed them: I would only see them
performed that I too may admire them. For as
thou wert before Abraham, so thou art greater
than Moses, and all the succeeding prophets.
Thou oughtest then, to exalt thyself above them
by thy superior miracles. That thou mayst not
hesitate in thy choice, I have selected some, all of
a sublime nature, and worthy of thee. Yonder
rises Moriah; above which thou seest the roof
of the temple, and its lofty glittering pinnacles;
Do thou say, Bow ye pinnacles, and do homage to
the Prophet. Within the temple lie the remains
of David, how would that holy king rejoice at the

sight of Jerusalem ! ,with what amazement should
we be filled at seeing him ! Call, therefore, O
prophet ! to the bones of the king, that he may
fly from the dark and lonely tomb, and appear
alive among us. But thou art silent. If neither
of these please thee, speak to the waters of Jordan,
saying, arise, O Jordan ! turn thy limpid stream,
and flow round Jerusalem ; defend her splendid
towers, and then roll back thy waters to Genazareth.
Or command Sion to rise nearer to heaven, or to
place its lofty summit on the top of Olivet, that the
people may, with amazement, behold its far pro-
jecting shade. Thus spake Herod, without knowing
to whom he directed his discourse. He knew not
that both the aspiring mountain, and the proud
tyrant of conquered nations, when compared with
the humble, the divine Jesus, were no more than
elevated dust.

Herod now once more exclaimed, What art thou
still silent ? the Messiah then beheld him with a
look of awful dignity : which he mistaking for con-
tempt, arose full of wrath. When Caiaphas ob-
serving his passion, seized the favourable moment,
and leering on the Messiah, with malignant sneer,
thus spake :

Thou thyself, great Herod, seest what kind of
man this prophet is. Behold when thou demandest
a miracle he is silent ! Can he perform miracles ?
The vulgar imagine that he can, and we have
some weak men among the elders, who are of the
same opinion. Can he who, though often admo-
nished, has had the insolence to oppose the covenant,
and the law of Moses, be sent of God, and endued
by the great Jehovah with the power of working
miracles ? But his profanation of the covenant
delivered on Sinai, when involved in smoak, amidst
the terrors of God, the summoning tempest, and

the sound of the trumpet, Caiaphas might avenge.
But, Herod, it belongs to thee to punish a rebel
who has pretended to be a king, and gathering all
Judea around him, has made his triumphant entry
into Jerusalem. The people strewed his path
with the branches of the palm : they spread their
apparel on the ground, crying, Hosanna to the son
of David, Hosanna to the king of Israel, Hosanna to
him who comes in the name of the Lord ; strew
palms ; pour forth your hosannas ; let hosannas
resound through the highest heavens. Sion echoed
back these seditious acclamations, and the portico
on Moria reverberated the sound. I, therefore,
conjure thee by the ashes of the holy David ; and
by the sacred remains of thy father Herod the Great,
to punish these impious profanations.

Philo now smiled on Caiaphas, though he
was the object of his hatred ; while Herod,
with bitter mockery, ordered a' white robe to be
put upon Jesus, like those worn by the Romans
when candidates for an office. Pilate, added
he, has judged rightly, and knowing his high
merit, will inaugurate him as king, by adding to
his hosannas and his palms, the purple and the
crown.

Herod spoke and withdrew. The guards of
the prince then put a white garment on the holy
Jesus, and having insulted him by their cruel
mockery, he was sent back to Pilate. The mul-
titude being now greatly-increased, by the vast
resort of people who came to celebrate the feast of
the passover, Jesus was accompanied by an innu-
merable crowd, and every part of the city was
thronged by a wild concourse. This Philo un-
daunted sees, just as a pilot, on observing the
approaching waves, rejoices in his skill, and in
the buoyancy of the supporting flood. Though

he knows that the people are still divided, and that
many thousands are warmly attached to Jesus,
he remains uumoved. He assembles about him
the Pharisees, hastily gives the word, and they as
readily disperse themselves among the, yielding
crowd. Thus from the cup of a mortal foe poison
flows, and every drop is death. The Pharisees
haste to inflame the multitude, and the many-
tongued orators emulate his rancour, his eloquence,
and specious blandishments ; each according to
his different disposition venting exclamations, re-
proaches or curses. Thus from different mouths
resounded,

Think ye, that he has performed miracles ?
Herod has asked for a miracle ; but he asked in
vain. Ye saw how mute he stood.—Accursed be
he who vilifies our father Abraham. Accursed be
he whose whole life has been a profanation of the
law !—Behold his accusers are the priests of the
Most High God !—Has Jehovah sent to us one
whom he abandons ? He has abandoned him—ye
see bim in bonds.—The heathens in his trial are
too mild, too merciful.—Men and brethren, ye are
the holy people ! for you shines the temple ! for
you the altars blaze ! for you the flame of the
offerings on the high altar rises up to heaven ! To
you the dust of the prophets, to you the holy ashes
of Abraham, call for revenge ! Come then and
revenge the greatest of our fathers. By such
acclamations, the Pharisese drew thousands to their
side. Few stood neuter and suspended in doubt :
Yet still, some continued virtuous and faithful :
These were thinly scattered amidst the multitude.
Thus when a wild hurricane has laid waste the
forests that cover the extended summits of the
mountains, still stand a few solitary cedars that have
resisted its fury.

In the mean while Pilate, in order to save Jesus, had caused a prisoner, who, before his being apprehended, had been the terror of the country, to be privately brought into the judgment-hall, and the priests and people were no sooner returned than he was exposed to their view on an eminence, in the open gallery called Gabbatha, His glaring eyes rolled: he bit his lips, and held his panting breath. Rage, not remorse, bowed his bushy head; and shaking his naked nervous arm, he rattled his chains. On the right hand of this fell murderer, Pilate placed the divine Redeemer. The assassin viewed him clothed in a white robe, when the idea that Jesus, or himself was to be immediately led to death, struck him like a fiery dart, and with anxious solicitude agitated his big swelling heart.

Now Pilate, pointing to the benevolent Jesus, said, Ye brought this man to me, for seducing the people from their allegiance to Cæsar. I have heard him, but do not find that he is guilty of the charge; neither does Herod. I cannot therefore consent to his death. But as on your festival, I am to deliver to you a prisoner, I will order him to be scourged, and then release him. Here he paused, but observing, that with dissatisfied looks they continued silent, he resumed. But ye hear not reason—Tell me, which shall I deliver to you, this Barabbas, a robber and a murderer, or Jesus, whom ye call the king of the Jews?

In the mean time Portia's messenger came to him, and said, The man whom thou judgest is a divine person: Portia therefore entreats thee not to condemn the righteous; for this morning it was the will of the Gods, that, on his behalf, she should suffer many things in a dream. Philo was now alarmed, especially when his emissaries coming in,

let him know, that many of the people declared for
Jesus.   Suddenly were heard from afar the melan-
choly cries of those who had been deaf, lame, blind,
and even dead, calling Jesus the holy, the benevo-
lent, the divine friend of mankind ; but the raging
murmurs of the nearer crowd, stifled the sound of
their exclamations and complaints ; as the cries of
an helpless child, in the midst of a forest, are
drowned by the bellowing storm : or as the wise
instructions of the sage, are lost before the repeti-
tion of the sounding exploits of the great.   Philo
was sensible of the danger of having his malevolent
views rendered abortive. He knew Pilate's design
in placing the murderer with the prophet, in the
view of the people : but relying on his popu-
larity, he, with an indignant air, left the Ro-
man, proud of the chains, which, by his oratory,
he could throw on the minds of the people, and
stepped forth, while Pilate, with mingled contempt
and anger, observed him from the seat of judg-
ment.

  Philo made a sign to the people, and they were
silent before him : he then with ardent look said :
With but few words, ye men of Israel, can I this
day address you. Ye know me. I hate the despiser
of Moses.   I curse him, who, whatever his soothing
lips may pretend, curses Moses by his life.   From
this disposition, from my zeal for our great pro-
phet, I now come to lay before you felicity and
destruction.   Chuse, ye Israelites, chuse whether
Barabbas shall be saved, or Jesus. Barabbas,
we all know, is a murderer.   Pilate also knows it,
and did he not aim at inspiring you with a misplaced
compassion, he would not raise up him as a com-
petitor for your favour with this Jesus, who would
fascinate our minds with the specious semblance of
innocence.   But I shall not presume to penetrate

into Pilate's designs. "We are a conquered people,
and it becomes us to be silent ; but Philo cannot
conceal from you, ye Israelites, that ye stand on
the brink of ruin, and, with grief, with anguish
of heart I speak it, ye are perhaps inclined to chuse
destruction. Yet the descendants of such great,
such holy ancestors, shall not thus sink into per-
dition. This Jesus—this man of cruelty knows,
that, when he had filled up the measure of his
seditions, the Romans would come and extirpate
us. Thousands stood around him when he talked
of the siege of this city, the sinking state, of the
temple of God being levelled with the dust. So
blinded were, ye, that ye were filled with admira-
tion. But he had no mercy on you. He foresees
the miseries of Jerusalem : he knows that he, and
he alone is the cause of her approaching anguish,
yet persists in his rebellious practices. He sees
the smoak of the burning temple, which sinks on
Moria, never more to rise. He sees the altar for
burnt offerings thrown down. He beholds the
stately Jerusalem weeping ! she who sat as a queen
among the cities, covered with ashes—bereaved of
her children—alas ! they lie unburied ! they lie
exposed, in the eye of day, turning to putrifaction !
while the young, whom torturing anguish and
devouring grief have spared, are seized by the
furious warrior, and their tender bones dashed
against the ruins of this their native city !—Alas ! no
father sees them !—their fathers died in the field
of battle !—no mother weeps over them ! the
mothers had long been consumed by emaciating
grief ! All this he sees—he sees void of pity,
insensible to mercy !

He had no sooner ended, than the other priests
shouted their assent, as a signal to the people.
But little want was there of such dreadful, such

malignant representations, to raise a tumult in their hearts, which their own vices had already implanted there.

Pilate, who had sat lost in thought, now again cried; Which of these two shall I deliver up to you? Imediately Barabbas! was resounded from every side, with such fury, that the angels who encompassed Jesus, trembling, turned aside their faces; and Barabbas! Barabbas! was still the cry. At length Pilate's amazement being suppressed by his indignation, he cried, What then shall I do with Jesus, your king. At this, stamping with fury, they bellowed out, Crucify him! crucify him! The Roman once more endeavouring to calm their rage, added, But what is his crime! He has done nothing worthy of death. At this their fury burst out with a more violent flame, which being still blowed up by the voices of the enraged priests, the people, stammering, pale, and grinding their teeth, cried, with vengeful looks, Crucify him! crucify him! crucify him! Sion, and the forsaken temple on Moriah resounded with the noise, whilst their feet filled the air with a cloud of dust.

Pilate, seeing that all his endeavours to save Jesus were in vain, with a weakness unworthy of a Roman, passed sentence upon him whom he had declared innocent. Struck with fear, he had before left the judgment seat, but now ascending it again, a slave, by his command, brought him water in a vessel of Corinthian brass, when making a sign to the people, they, with a mixture of perplexity and wonder, stood looking at him in silence. The slave pouring the water on his hands, he solemnly washed them before the multitude. At this instant the angel which in ancient times passed over the dwellings in the land of Goshen, sparing those that were sprinkled with the blood of the lamb, armed with the terrors of God, hovered over Judea, to devote the people to utter destruction, and fixing his eyes on the countenance of the divine Messiah, there perceived their rejection, accompanied with a tear. Then that angel of death began those words of the curse, which proclaim through heaven the sentence of the Sovereign Judge, when nations are ripe for destruction. His voice seemed like the sound of earthquakes, the remote harbingers of death. Then he engraved the sentence on an iron tablet, and placed it near the Judge's throne.

Pilate, making a sign to the slave to retire, again addressed himself to the multitude, crying, Ye furious and inexorable men, I am innocent of the blood of this just person. See ye to it. On which, pronouncing sentence on themselves, they cried, His blood be upon us and our children. Pale horror, sepulchral silence, and a cold shivering, followed the words : but not remorse.

Now Pilate having ordered the crowd to make way, they opened to form a passage, and Jesus was taken into the judgment hall to be scourged, while Barabbas, being set at liberty, joined the multitude. The savage murderer, on finding that he was free from his chains, shook himself, and leaping, shouted forth his obstreporous joy. He stood still : he was silent : he ran : he again stopped : the people trembled, and wherever he came, drove back. Yet Philo gazed upon him with pleasure. He too would have gladly accompanied the Redeemer : but it not being lawful for him at that time to enter the judgment hall, he walked before the door, and often stopped to listen. With joy would he have seen his sufferings : with joy and triumph would he have heard the voice of his pain.

But, O thou muse of Sion ! who, filled with

grief turnedst away thy face from the divine, the
suffering Redeemer, sing in mournful strains,
the scourge, the reed, the purple mantle, and the
crown !

The guard, a brutal band, assembling round him,
rudely strip off his garment. Thus in the parched de-
sart, where no refreshing stream gladdens the plain,
and dispenses fertility, the furious winds strip off
the leaves from a solitary tree, that had offorded
shelter to the faint and weary traveller. They
then drag the Lord of Life, and bind him to a
pillar. The blood follows every stroke. The
precious blood of the holy, the benevolent Jesus,
in crimson streams falls from his back. Then Eloa,
at the dreadful sight, sinks down, and, with the
humiliation of a mortal, lies prostrate in the dust.
At length, laying aside the blushing scourge, and
loosing him from his pillar, over his shoulders
they throw a purple robe ; in his hand they put
a reed, and press upon his drooping head an en-
circling crown of thorns, from which the drops
of blood fall trickling round. Then bowing with
insulting mockery—But the trembling harp drops
from my feeble hand, and my faultering voice in
vain attempts to sing all the sufferings of the eter-
nal Son.

Pilate, seeing the calmness with which the divine,
the humble Jesus bore pain and insult, once more
endeavoured to fill the people with the commisera-
tion he himself felt, and, giving a sign to the
Redeemer, went out of the judgment hall, followed
by the patient all-gracious Sufferer. The multitude
seeing them coming, again pressed forward, till
Pilate, having commanded silence, cried aloud, Ye
men of Israel, I bring him out once more, to inform
you, that he has done nothing worthy of death.
Then Jesus advancing nearer, they had a full view

of him in his purple robe and bloody crown.
Pilate now stretching out his hand, and looking
first on Jesus, and then on them, in a compassionate
accent cried, Behold the Man! At this instant
the great Redeemer gave orders to the angels,
which trembling, hovered round him: for his
divine looks needed not words to express their
meaning: they instantly read this gracious com-
mand, Give to my disciples, and all my faithful
followers, internal and celestial consolations; when
I on the uplifted cross shall bleed and die, and lie
among those that sleep in death!

Pilate had hoped to impress the minds of the Jews
with sentiments of compassion: but they still
shewed their insensibility to all the tender feelings
of humanity: for the clamours of the cruel priests
were a constant prelude to the loud cry of, Crucify
him! crucify him! At length being filled with
indignation, Pilate hastily answered, Take him
away then, and crucify him: for I find no fault
in him, and then angrily turning from them, retired.

Caiaphas, now hasting after the Roman, said, O
Pilate! we have a law, and by that law he ought
to die, because he has made himself the Son of God.
At hearing the words, the Son of God, Pilate
trembled, and taking Jesus back to the judgment
hall, with anxious solicitude, cried, Tell me whence
art thou? Jesus made no answer, at which the
governor being offended, said, Speakest thou not
to me? Knowest thou not that I have power to
crucify, and power to release thee? Then the
Messiah calmly answered, No power couldst thou
have against me, were it not given thee from above,
therefore they that delivered me to thee have the
greater sin.

Pilate then went back to the assembled people,
when reading, in his resentful gestures, the motives

P

to his return, they cried aloud, If thou, O Pilate! releasest this man, thou art not Cæsar's friend— Whosoever maketh himself a king, rebels against Cæsar. The governor, provoked, and struck with double fear, wanted the resolution to support his dignity; and only answered with mockery and a contemptuous sneer, What, shall I crucify your king? On which the chief priests hastily replied We have no king but Cæsar.

Now the multitude surrounded the divine Jesus, and in savage triumph led him to death, while the pusillanimous Roman withdrew into his palace.

THE END OF THE SEVENTH BOOK.

THE

MESSIAH.

BOOK. VIII.

THE ARGUMENT.

Eloa descends from the throne of God, and proclaims that now the Redeemer is led to death, on which the angels of the earth form a circle round mount Calvary, also named Golgotha. Then having consecrated that hill, he worships the Messiah. Gabriel conducts the souls of the fathers from the sun to the mount of Olives, and Adam addresses the earth. Satan and Adramelech, hovering in triumph, are put to flight by Eloa. Jesus is nailed to the cross. The thoughts of Adam. The convertion of one of the malefactors. Uriel places a planet before the sun, and then conducts to the earth the souls of all the future generations of mankind. Eve, seeing them coming, addresses them. Eloa ascends to heaven. Eve is affected at seeing Mary. Two angels of death fly round the cross. Eve addresses the Saviour, and the souls of the children yet unborn.

COME thou who, on Sion's sacred mount, hast oft beheld the most holy of the high celestial choir : thou who from him hast learned what the eternal Spirit taught, now sing the dying Saviour, the greatest of the dead. Come, O muse of Sion ! divine instructress ! come—trembling thyself, lead thy trembling votary—lead me to the awful crucifixion. Filled with holy terror, I would see the expiring Redeemer; behold his fixed eyes, his pallid cheek, his open wounds, his precious blood !—Ah! he faints, he bleeds, he reclines his drooping head ! he bleeds, he faints, his eyes are closed in darkness ! speechless is he who formed the tongue, and dead is the Lord of Life !

From the presence of the Almighty Father, Eloa darted down with flight more swift than rays of light, beaming from the bright orb of day : even the immortals could scarce discern his rapid course. In his left hand he held a celestial crown, and in his right, a golden trumpet, from which he breathed heavenly notes, while all the spheres joined their harmony. Then the exalted seraph sang in strains mellifluous and sublime.

Rejoice, ye sons of heaven, rejoice! and all ye celestial spirits, whether seated on the flaming suns, or encompassing the throne of the great Omnipotent, join with soft commiseration and exalted joy, to celebrate the great Sabbath of redeeming love. Join all ye spirits in wonder and in praise. Rejoice, the hour is come—the awful hour, in which the Lord of Life will die for man. The gracious victim is already on his way. Join all ye heavenly hosts, in rapturous strains, to celebrate his love to man.

His voice spread through the heavens. The blessed spirits had already anticipated the awful, the joyful sound. Eloa instantly hovered over mount Calvary, while the angels of the earth hastened round him. He called, and about him they formed a radiant circle, close arranged, extending far and wide. Then, leaving the centre of this resplendent ring, he descended on the top of the mount. Thrice, with humble reverence, he bowed his face to the dust, then standing erect, lift up his hands, and cast his eyes down on the

Messiah, who, amidst insulting crowds, was slowly moving towards Calvary, groaning under the weight of the ponderous cross. Then Eloa stretching out his arms over the mount, cried, Hear, ye heavens, and rejoice! Thou hell give ear and tremble! In the name of the all-gracious Father, whose sovereign goodness laid the plan of mercy; in that of the great, the suffering Redeemer, who, full of benignity and soft compassion, is coming here to bleed and die, and in that of the Holy Spirit, the Sanctifier, the Comforter of repentant sinners, by whom they shall be led into all truth, thee, O mount, I consecrate for the death of the Son. Holy, holy, holy is he who was, and is, and is to come!

Thus did Eloa consecrate the mount, while overpowering amazement dimmed the effulgence of the great immortal, who now seeing the Son of Man near the mount, bending with tottering step, under the galling cross; a heavy burden for shoulders torn by cruel stripes! he prostrated himself on the parched grass, and with folded hands, thus poured out his soul.

O thou who drawest near to thy altar, to die the most ignominious, and therefore the most astonishing, the most glorious of all deaths! Thou Friend of man, Creator, yet Child of Bethlehem, born of a race doomed to the grave!—Thou weepest, while to thee we sing triumphant hymns. Thou humblest thyself so low as to suffer on Golgotha. The heavenly host are lost in wonder, while rapt in the contemplation of thy love to man. O thou Son of God! the incarnate Messiah, once immortal! the Accomplisher of all that is amazing, highest, best!—of all that is most glorious, most admirable, most divine! the Restorer of innocence! the Lamb of God, which taketh away the sins of

the world! the Reviver of the dead! the De-
stroyer of death everlasting! the Judge of the
earth! Hear my lowly supplications, attend to
the voice that addresses thee from the dust on
which thou art to bleed. O thou Saviour of man,
when thine eyes fail, when the paleness of death
everspreads thy face, when the heavens shall
trembling pass away, and the sun withdraw his
light, then from the overshadowing night, in which
thy life departs, strengthen me, O thou great Ac-
complisher of the redemption of man!—strengthen
me, that I, helpless, trembling, and forlorn, may not
sink among the sepulchres of the earth—and when
in the hovering twilight, the convulsed creation
shall appear to swim before my disordered sight,
may I see thee expire! O death of the Son, how
near dost thou approach! From the first who be-
came mortal, till the last of the race of Adam,
the happy influences of thy death, O thou Messiah!
shall extend, and all arise at the sound of the last
trump. Hail, ye redeemed, who shall come re-
joicing, having washed your robes, and made them
white in the blood of the Lamb!

Eloa now arose, and around Calvary marshalled
the angels of the earth in wide extended circles.
They assembled on low and floating clouds, that
covered the broad summit of the mountain, or
hovered in deep contemplation above the cedars,
moving with their waving tops. He himself stood
on a pinnacle of the temple. A mighty host
encompassed the mount; these were the dispensers
of the providence of the Omnipotent. Here were
the angels of death and of judgment, the guardians
of mankind, and of the future Christians, who,
being the protectors of the martyrs, have the chief
place at his throne, for whom the palm-bearing
martyrs die.

Meanwhile Gabriel, whom the divine Sufferer had sent to the sun, alighted at Uriel's residence, and standing before the souls of the parents of mankind, thus addressed them :

! Draw near ye parents of the human race, and behold your Saviour. Here, with his trembling right hand he directed their sight, and then added : The Redeemer is dragging his cross ; near the foot of the hill of death ! On its summit, ye shall behold him bleeding on that torturing cross for you, and for your children !—O ye redeemed ! he goes—he hastens to prepare eternal life for generations yet unborn !

Thus spake the seraph, and then flew towards the earth. Silent, with mingled grief and joy, the human spirits follow : they haste ; their celerity can only be surpassed by the ideas of the devout soul ranging with holy rapture from star to star. Gabriel leads the radiant band, and now they reach the mount of Olives, on which Adam alighting first, sinks down, and kisses the earth.

O earth ! maternal land ! said he, do I again behold thee ! How many ages are passed away, since at my death, or rather my revival to a nobler, a better life, thou receivedst my frail cumbrous body into thy peaceful bosom ! Never since that awful—happy moment, have I trod on thy surface. Thy bosom is now filled with the remains of my offspring. I salute thee, O earth ! I salute you, ye remains of the dead, my children. Ye shall awake ! Yes, my dear children, ye shall awake ! The hours approach that shall deliver the earth from the curse brought upon it by my sin, and at length your dust, my children, rising, shall bless the gracious Saviour, who now dies for you and me. Behold the incarnate Messiah, the earth-born

Creator comes !—Behold, he comes to die—to die
for you !

Thus spake the first of men ; then silently look-
ing towards Calvary, a heavenly melancholy, a
sacred awe, thrilled through his whole ethereal
frame.

On the temple stood Eloa, whence he descried
the crowd of happy human souls that descended
with Gabriel. Then turning his face, he perceived
on high over the cross, Satan and Adramelech
wheeling about with looks of wild exultation :
Satan transported with the work he should soon
accomplish, and both pleased with the thoughts of
future deeds, productive of misery. He sees them
above the clouds of the moving earth, with im-
mense circuits, measuring the vast empyreal vault.
Eloa, now vested in his full glory, instantly arose
from the temple towards the immortal offenders, ar-
rayed in all the lustre of this most solemn day,
and surrounded by the terrors of the Most High.
Before him light breezes became bellowing storms,
and his progress was as the march of an army,
under whose feet the rocks tremble. The mighty
sound, and no less awful effulgence of the celestial
spirit, proclaimed his approach. The apostates
saw and heard him coming ; they strove in vain
to conceal their confusion : they stopped and be-
came still of more sable hue. So in the abyss of
the lowest hell stand two rocks, covered with the
darkest nocturnal gloom. With one stroke of his
extended wings, the seraph then reached the spirits
accursed, and thus, with commanding voice, spake :
Ye whose names are mentioned in the abyss, be
gone. Ye see the luminous circle of the pure,
the exalted immortals ; fly, and free the sacred
place from your profane presence. The extent

of the most distant radiance of the blessed shall
indicate your limits ; within the compass of their
beams, presume not either to soar above the clouds
or to creep along the dust of the earth.

Thus the seraph delivered his commands. As
when two storms descend in black clouds on two
of the mountains of the Alps, the rapid thunder
bursts in their bosoms, and rolls through the wind-
ing valleys ; so the proud infernal spirits prepare
to answer Eloa. All the terrors of rage, all the
rancour of revenge, gather in the wrinkles of their
brows, and flash from their flaming eyes : but
Eloa beholding them with majestic look, and
stedfast gaze, checked the thunder ere it burst,
crying, with a commanding voice, Be ye silent—
fly—Did I come with that triumphant strength,
with which I am endued by the Omnipotent, my
thunder, hurled from this uplifted arm, should
drive ye beyond the bounds of the wide creation.
But I come in the name of the Son of Adam, who
there bears his cross ! and in the name of that
Conqueror of hell and death, command you to fly.
They fled : but first changed blacker than the
gloom of midnight, and were pursued by terrors
which drove them aside among the ruins of Go-
morrah in the Dead sea. With joy the angels and
the souls of the blessed saw their disgraceful flight,
while Eloa, arrayed in all his glory, returned to a
pinnacle of the temple.

The holy Jesus was come to the hill of death,
when, faint with suffering and fatigue, he sunk
under the burthen of the cumberous cross. The
blood-thirsty multitude then forced a fearful tra-
veller, who had just descended the declivity, to
bear the cross. Among those who followed, some
soft and gentle minds, free from rage, beheld him
with compassion, and lamented his fate ; yet their

hearts being attached to vanity, scarcely did they know whom they pitied. This sorrow, fleeting and transitory as a morning dream, arose from no devout sensation of soul, Jesus heard their lamentations, and turning towards them, said, Why do ye weep, O ye daughters of Jerusalem! Weep not for me : but weep for yourselves and for your children : for the day of distress and anguish approaches ; the dreadful day, when they shall say, Blessed are the barren ! the womb that never bare, and the breast that never gave suck ! Then will they say to the mountains, fall on us, and to the hills, cover us. For if this be done to me, what shall be done to the sinner?

Having at length reached the summit of the hill, Jesus lifts up his eyes to the Sovereign Judge. Meanwhile the executioners take the cross, and set it up among the bones of the dead. Now the solemn day shines with fainter light ; yet still the smallest of the animal creation sport in the extended fields of vital air. Soon the earth gently trembles through its depths profound ; whirling storms sweep along its surface, and howl through its hollow caverns : the cross shakes, and near it stands the Prince of Peace.

Adam, on perceiving him, could no longer contain his transports : with glowing cheek, and hair flying back, he rapidly advanced to the slope of the mountain : then sunk to the earth, while the celestial radiance, which beamed from his immortal eyes, was dimmed. He lay dissolved in tears of joy, and love, and gratitude, which were mingled, with a flood of sorrow and amazement. While all these passions, in pleasing confusion, rushed upon his soul, his thoughts burst into speech, and the angelic circle heard his suppliant voice, when lifting up his eyes, he thus spake :

O thou Son! thou Saviour! thou the great Messiah, and my Lord! the immortals weep, when absorbed in thy love, they, with silent admiration, mention thy thousand thousand glories, thus eclipsed—thus brightened by thy sufferings! Ah I call thee Son; then struck with wonder, pause and weep with them! Jesus my Son!—rapture is in the thought! Whither—Oh whither shall I retire to bear the pleasing, joyful grief of this inexpressible salvation? O ye angels who were before me, yet not before him, look down—with wonder and amazement look down on Jesus my Son!. Thee, O earth, I bless, and thee, O dust, from which I was formed!—O joy!—thou plenitude of joys eternal, that fill all the desires of the immortals!. Oh the great, the profound, the heavenly plan! It was thine, O Jehovah'! thine was the glorious, the gracious plan of redemption! thy loving-kindness and compassion exceed the ideas of the rapt seraph! —and thou, O Jesus! didst leave the splendor that surrounds thy throne, and all the pure, the refined, the ineffable delights of heaven to descend to earth—to become my Son—to redeem my offspring from the power of sin—to perfect redemption for man, by obtaining a glorious victory over temptations, sufferings, and death! Thus dost thou bruise the serpent's head. Rejoice, O my immortal soul! in the wonders of his love—eternal praises are due to. him, who by his sufferings and death for us procures eternal felicity! Stand still, ye immortal souls, and wondering,. behold this abyss —this wide abyss of joy! What, ye heavens, are the moments of a mortal life to the joys of immortality? Yet each of these is divine—each moment when well employed, bears on its rapid wings eternal repose! This shall I—this shall you, my children, enjoy! Lend me your voice, ye celestial spirits, that through the whole creation I may aloud proclaim, that the great Redeemer is now entering the shadow of death. Arise mankind from the squalid earth—arise, lift up your heads; come and wash your souls in tears of pity, love, and joy! The Messiah your Creator! Brother! Friend! is on the verge of the opening grave. Ye, my children, are his beloved; for you he dies! Come, all ye my children, to your dying Redeemer —ye who dwell in palaces roofed with gold, lay down your crowns and come—Ye cottagers, leave your lowly hurdled huts and come. Alas! they hear not my voice—they hear not the voice of love—O thou who offerest thyself a willing sacrifice! let me with overflowing gratitude, for ever admire thy condescending love. Complete—oh complete, thou gracious Sufferer, the mighty work. And now—But ah! what inexpressible melancholy rushes upon my heart!—What sympathetic sorrow penetrates the deep recesses of my soul! Now, O Jesus! thou enterest the dismal path of death! Strengthen, O Eternal Father! me; the first of sinners, who have already seen corruption, that with melting soul, I may behold my Son, my Lord, die—die for repenting sinners!

Adam was silent. In the mean time the mighty, the humble Sufferer approached nearer to the cross, and lifting up his hand, held it before his face, then bowing low, said what no angel heard, nor no creature understood: but Jehovah from his lofty throne, now environed with sable clouds, answered. The words of the Most High reached the distant limits of the wide expanse of heaven, and the throne of judgment trembled. The executioners came up to the Redeemer: then all the worlds, with wide extended roar, stopped at the points of their orbits, whence they were to proclaim the redemption.

They stood still: the thunder of the poles died away, and sunk into silence: silent was the whole motionless creation, shewing to all under heaven the hour of sacrifice. Thou also, O world of sinners and of graves, stood still! Now the angels, arrayed in all their unfading glories, looked down. Jehovah himself looked down, and supported the sinking earth: he looked down on Jesus, whom, with barbarous hands, they nailed to the cross.

As when almighty death has overspread the creation, and a world sleeps in silent corruption, no living being standing on the dust of the dead; so, in solemn silence, the angels, and thine Omnipotent Father, O crucified Jesus! looked on thee: But when thy blood first started forth from thy hands and feet, then the amazement of the seraphim grew too strong for silence, they burst into mingled sounds of exultation and mourning. Now were the heavens filled with new adorations. Once more, and again once more, Eloa cast his wondering eyes on the bleeding Jesus: and then with a dignity with which he had never appeared to any of the immortals, in an extacy of admiration, he flew into the heaven of heavens, and with a voice that resembled the sound made by the stars in their circular courses, cried, The blood of the Saviour flows! Then flying into the immense abyss, he repeated, The blood of the Saviour flows! He next, with more calm astonishment, bends his course to the earth. As he returned through the region of creation, he saw the archangels on the suns: worshipping they stood, while from their golden altars a flame arose, like the crimson blush of the morning, and ascended to the Judge's throne. Beneath, through the wide creation, sacrifices blazed, as types of the bleeding sacrifice on the cross. Thus the seventy elders of God's chosen people saw on Sinai the appearance of the glory of the Most High : or thus arose the sacred cloud, and pillar of fire from the tabernacle, to guide the people on their way.

Still the god-like Saviour bleeds ; and looking down with divine benignity and grace on the people of Judea, who were crowded together in one great throng from Jerusalem to the cross, he meekly cried, Father, forgive them ; for they know not what they do.

Silent amazement accompanied the voice of love through a part of the crowded multitude, who lift up their faces to the bleeding Redeemer, and beheld him overspread with a deadly paleness. This was all that mortal eyes could see. The souls of the pious dead saw diviner, more mysterious things. They observed his struggling life, which death could not destroy, had not he borne- a commission from the Supreme Sovereign of all. They perceived what convulsive terrors shook his mortal frame, while forsaken by his Almighty Father, he hung on the lofty cross ! How great the salvation procured by those purple streams ! What love and compassion were shewn by his bearing his cruel wounds ! Behold, he lift up his eyes to heaven, seeking ease from pain ! but no ease he found, every moment repeated the most dreadful death. With him, as a farther debasement, were crucified two malefactors, one on his right hand, the other on his left. Of these, one, an obdurate sinner, grown grey in guilt, turning his sullen distorted face to the Mediator, cried, if thou be Christ, save thyself and us, and come down from the accursed tree.

The other criminal was in all the vigour of blooming youth : he was not abandoned, though he had been seduced by sin ; and now rising superior to his tortures, he boldly reproved his fellow sufferer, crying, Ah, dost thou not fear God, when death—when condemnation are so near? What we suffer, alas! we suffer justly for our crimes; but this man, added he, looking on Jesus, has committed no crime. Then writhing his body towards the Redeemer, he strove to show his veneration, by lowly bowing his head. The effort tore his lengthening wounds, and the blood gushed forth in larger streams; but disregarding the pain, and the streaming blood, bending still lower, he cried, Lord remember me, when thou enterest into thy kingdom.

The Mediator, with a divine smile, beaming benignity and grace, looked on the agonizing sinner, and, with a gentle voice, replied, This day shalt thou be with me in Paradise. With devout trembling the malefactor heard the reviving words, which thrilled through his soul. With blissful ecstacy his eyes, which swam in tears of joy, remained fixed on the divine Sufferer, the Friend of man, and till his faultering speech began to fail, he attempted, in broken sentences, to express his new and exalted sensations, the delightful foretaste of eternal felicity. What was I? Oh what am I now? cried he, with a look of transport, that banished from his face the traces of pain. Such misery before, and now such joy! Oh this extatic tremor!—these sweet—these rapturous sensations! What dawning felicity breaks in upon my soul! Who is he that hangs next me on the cross? Is he a pious, a just, a holy prophet?—He is much more—ah, much more—surely he is the Son of God, the Messiah, sent from heaven! His kingdom then is far—far exalted above the earth! O ye men and angels, this is the promised Messiah! yet how deeply does he humble himself! He stoops to

suffer this painful death! he stoops still lower—
he stoops to save me! How incomprehensible!
Oh be thou ever beloved by me, while, lost in won-
der, I cannot comprehend this grace! Greater art
thou than the highest angel; for, surely an angel
could not thus have transformed my soul—could
not, with such sublime rapture, have raised it to
God! Yes, thou art the divine Messiah, and
thine—thine I shall be for ever!

Thus he spake, and then hung absorbed in silent
rapturous astonishment. Whenever he cast up his
eyes towards heaven, or on the extended earth, all
seemed to smile. The peace of God had rested
upon him. At a glance from the Redeemer one of
the seraphim now hastily lett the circle, which en-
compassed Calvary, and stood under the cross.
The import of the divine look was, Thou seraph
bring the redeemed to me, after his death. He in-
stantly returned to the angelic circle. This was
the invincible Abdiel, who by the appointment of
the Most High was now an angel of death, and
kept the gate of hell. Instantly troops of other
angels surrounded him, and asked his commission.
Abdiel with transport answered, I received orders
ofter the death of that criminal, to conduct him to
the Messiah, who hath given him salvation. The
delightful task fills me with sweetest joy. A sin-
ner is delivered, and delivered in the hour when the
gracious Saviour is bleeding—is dying for man!
To conduct this purified soul, thus prepared for
heaven to its Redeemer is a delightful task!
Congratulate me, O ye angels! on the blissful
office.

In the mean while Uriel, the angel of the sun,
had long stood on a mount of that shining globe,
ready for his progressive flight; and now the time
was come for executing the commands he had re-

ceived. Radiant he arose, and proceeded through the heavens with steady wing, to a remote planet, which the Omnipotent had ordered him to place before the sun, that the life of the divine Redeemer might expire under a more awful covert than that of the night. Already the seraph stood over the pole of the star—of that star where dwell the souls who, before their birth, are removed into this momentary mortal life of probation. There Uriel looked down on the souls of future generations, and calling the star by its immortal name, thus spake :

Adamida, he who has assigned thee thy station, commands thee to leave thine orbit, and to place thyself opposite to that sun, to prevent any of its rays reaching the earth.

The heavenly orbs heard the commanding voice reverberate from the mountains of Adamida. The star tremulous turned its thundering poles, and the whole creation resounded ; when with terrific haste, Adamida, in obedience to the divine command, flew amidst overwhelming storms, rushing clouds, falling mountains, and swelling seas. Uriel stood on the pole of the star, but so lost in deep contemplation on Golgotha, that he heard not the wild tumultuous roar. Now, O sun ! it had reached thy region. At the sight of the new solar orb, the tender human souls were filled with astonishment, and raised themselves above the planet's ascending clouds. Adamida then slackened her course, and advanced before the sun, covered its face, and intercepted all its rays.

The earth was silent at the descending twilight, and as the gloom increased, deeper was the silence. Terrifying shades and palpable darkness came on. The birds ceased their notes, and sought the thickest groves : the very insects hurried to their retreats,

and the wild beasts of the deserts fled to their
lonely dens.   A death-like stillness reigned through
the air.   The human race, standing aghast, looked
up to heaven. The darkness became still more
dark.   What a night in the midst of day !   The
intercepting planet had, to all human eyes, extin-
guished the sun ! How terrifying the awful night
which was thus involved in sable clouds the ex-
tended fields, and was rendered doubly terrible by
this solemn silence !

But Jesus, amidst the terrifying gloom, hung
unterrified on the lofty cross, while the blood and
sweat of death trickled from his dying members.
At the sight, silent nature was struck with conster-
nation, like that felt by a virtuous friend on his
hearing that he whom he loved is snatched away
by a premature death.   Or as the generous citizen
remains immoveable, and contemplates with eyes
that shed no tears, the melancholy and venerable
remains of the brave patriot who has died for his
country : but soon awakened by grief, his emotions
shake his whole frame, and raise a tempest in his
sympathizing soul. - In such dismay the earth then
lay, and thus shook.   The foundations of Gol-
gotha quaked : the darkened cross trembled, and
widened the wounds of the divine Sufferer, while
his life issued forth in larger streams.   Now stood
the multitude fixed by deep rooted horror, wildly
gazing towards the cross.   Dreadfully flowed the
sacred blood, by them unjustly shed.   On them
it came, and on their children.   Fain would they
have turned aside their faces ; but irresistibly impel-
led by terror, their eyes were continually directed
towards the bloody cross

Uriel, having still another command to execute,
descended from the pole of fixed Adamida, to the
unborn souls on its surface.   They saw the celes-

tial intelligence approach; already they were in bodies of the human form, though of an etherial texture, tinged with the gay splendor of a ruddy evening cloud. Follow me, said Ithuriel : I come from the great Eternal, to take you to yonder earth, overshadowed by the world on which you live. Ye shall see the Saviour of man—your Saviour : but yet ye know him not. A remote beam of immortal felicity will dart upon you. Follow me, ye blessed, who when born, will become candidates for immortal life, and all the joys of heaven. —Come and behold the awful scene. To him who now dies on the cross, every knee shall at length bow, and every tongue confess that he is Lord and Redeemer.

The conducting spirit extended his wings, and flew encompassed by the souls. Thus the pious sage, fond of meditation, and high celestial converse, hastes by moon-light into a lonely forest, there in devout raptures to contemplate on thee, O thou Infinite and Supreme ! so amidst the souls, the transported seraph, rapt in thought, speeds his way, and draws near to the earth.

The progenitors of mankind saw the numberless band coming in the dusky clouds : myriads of myriads of immortals ; a majestic train of thinking beings, that have existed ever since the creation ! Now the mother of men, astonished, turned from the cross her attentive eye. The children come—they come ! all the unborn—the Christians come ! Thus spake the general mother to the father of men. But soon she again fixed her eyes on the bloody cross, adding, These are my immortals ! But ah, by what name do they call thee, O thou who bleedest, who diest for them ! With what hosannas shall they hymn thee, thus disfigured with wounds ? Oh that you, ye children of salva-

tion !—ye Christians ! were now born ; that thou-
sands and thousands of weeping mothers led you
to the cross ! Oh that you already knew the most
holy of those born of women : him who,' when he
first entered this mortal state, wept at Bethlehem !
But O Adam ! they will know him, they will know
the dear Saviour, the Son of the Eternal ! But as
the flower whose stalk is broken by the boisterous
wind, hangs its still beauteous head and dies, so
some of you, my beloved children, will fall by the
murderous sword of persecution ; and hanging
your heads, will smile in death. You, happy mar-
tyrs, your mother congratulates. Ye are the chosen,
the exalted witnesses of the greatest and most im-
portant of all deaths. O ye glorious sufferers
for the cause of truth, of virtue, of your Redeemer !
Your pale and hollow cheeks will assume the
soft blush of celestial beauty : Your wounds will
shine with refulgent splendour : your dying groans
be changed to sweetest strains of heavenly harmony,
and rapturous songs of joy and triumph.

The great Emanuel now lifting up his eyes, filled
with celestial love, beheld the unborn souls : his
look drew forth a sacred tear on every cheek, and
each soul trembling with holy awe, felt new sen-
sations.

Now the colour of life instantaneously flushed
on the face of the dying Jesus ; but as instantane-
ously vanished, never to return : his faded cheeks
became sunk, and his head hung on his breast :
with difficulty he raised it up towards heaven ;
but unable to sustain its weight, soon it dropped.
The pendant sky formed an arch round Golgotha,
more silent and dreadful than the sepulchral vault,
and sable clouds of wide extent hung over the
cross. In an instant the silence ceased, and a noise
ushered in by no murmuring sound, suddenly

burst from the earth, with a roar so tremendous,
that the sepulchres of the dead, and the pinnacles
of the temple shook. This was the forerunner
of a tempest, which, rushing on the lofty cedars,
tore them up by the roots, and made the towers of
Jerusalem quake. Then loud thunder rolled
through the sky, and the deafening clap bursting
over the Dead sea, its affrighted waters foamed,
and the heavens and the earth trembled.

Silence, with steady foot, again stood on the
earth, again the gloom began to disperse, and the
unborn, the human race, and the dead, speechless
gazed on the Redeemer. Meanwhile our general
mother, with soothing melancholy, now her sweet
companion, viewed the divine Saviour, under his
lingering death. On beholding him, her eyes were
dimmed by obscuring affliction, and soft sympathetic sorrow. The Messiah now downward bent
his looks on a fair mortal, whom with fixed regard
he viewed, while she with drooping head, and a
countenance pale and mournful, trembling, stood
at the foot of the cross, involved in silent sorrow :
her eyes fixed by grief on the ground, shed no
tears ; for the kind relief of those heart-easing drops
was with-held. This, said the first of women, is
surely the Saviour's mother—Thy grief, O my
daughter, tells me that thou art she who bore thy
Lord and mine.—Thou art Mary. What thou
now feelest, I felt for my dear murdered Abel,
when he lay breathless, with his own blood distained—How I pity thee—thy grief equals what I
then felt, O thou tender mother of my dear dying
Jesus ! Thus to herself she spake, while with an
affectionate look, her eyes hung on Mary : nor yet
had they left her beloved daughter, had not two angels of death, with awful, solemn flight, approached from the east. Silent and slow they came.

Destrction sat on their faces, and their vesture was
the gloom of night. Sent by the Supreme Lord,
they approached the cross, and so tremendous was
their appearance, that the souls of the progenitors
of the human race sunk nearer to the earth, and
images of death, with the terrors of sepulchral
corruption, hovered around the immortals.

The angels of death standing on the hill, face to
face, viewed the dying Saviour, then one rising to
the right, and the other to the left, with sounding
pinions, seven times flew round the cross. Two
wings covered their feet, two trembling wings their
faces, and with two they flow. These, when ex-
panded, sent forth groans and sighs, and sounds of
death. Dreadful the angels hovered. The ter-
rors of God sat on their expanded wings, and seven
times they flew around. The dying Jesus, raising
his languid head, looked at the angels of death,
then cast up his eyes to heaven, and cried, with a
voice which none but his almighty Father heard,
Ah cease to encrease the torture of these wounds!
O my God forbear! Instantly the two angels bent
their airy flight towards heaven; but first cast a
dreadful look on Jerusalem, and on her inhabitants
who stood around. On their ascent they left the
etherial spectators under deeper dejection, and pen-
siveness more profound. With disordered counte-
nances they stand looking on the graves, then at
each other, and then towards heaven: but soon
they again turn their faces to him who bleeds
on the cross. Innumerable they stand, and though
every eye speaks grief or consternation, no immor-
tal eyes express such tenderness as those of the mo-
ther of men. She bows her head towards the
earth, the grave of her descendants, and spreads
her raised arms to heaven. Now she lays her
mournful brow in the dust: now folds her hands.

She rises, and earnestly looks around.   At length,
with faultering voice, she gives utterance to her
thoughts, and from her lips, immortal harmony
flows forth in sighs.

May I, O thou divine, Messiah! presume to call
thee Son ?—It was my crime that brought thee
down from heaven, and nailed thee to the cross.
Had it not been for me, who have exposed my off-
spring to sin and death, thou wouldst not have been
my Son,—thou wouldst not now hang bleeding on
thy gaping wounds: nor ever, ever die !   What
an exchange has my guilt brought on thee, O thou
most loving and beloved ! thou hast exchanged
bliss for misery ! life and ineffable joy, for torment
unutterable, and all the agonies of expiring nature !
I—alas ! I was the cause ! yet turn—turn not
away from me thy dying eyes.   Thine all-gracious
Father, the prime sou
has condescended to forgive me—Thou too hast
pitied—hast forgiven me, O my Redeemer, and
the Redeemer of my offspring ! the high arch of
heaven resounded, and the throne of the Eternal
echoed back thy praise, when thou, the beloved of
thy Father, offeredst to give thy life for repentant
sinners, that we might enjoy life everlasting.—
And now thou diest—I stand abs lved by boundless
grace—But thou diest !—This overwhelms my
soul—It throws back immortality into the grave !
O thou divine Saviour, allow me to weep for thee,
and forgive—forgive the soothing tears of an
immortal ! Yes, O thou dear Redeemer ! thou
hast forgiven me.—Forgive me, also, O my pious
offspring ! for when me, your last groans, when me,
your dying sighs curse, as your murderer ; then
let your hearts bless me ; for I am also the mother
of the Saviour, of the Prince of Grace, of the Au-
thor and the Finisher of your faith, who dies that

you may live ! Curse me not then, O my children !
for I, when mortal, often shed the kindly tear for
you, and when my struggling heart failed, for you
I dying wept, and poured forth tears for those
who, after me, were to sink into corruption. When
ye now, O my pious, my virtuous children, expire,
ye shall sleep in Jesus, and be conveyed to the
realms of ineffable delight !—conveyed to him,
whom ye now see bleeding on the cross ! Then
curse not your mother, O my children ! for though
I rendered you mortal, Jesus Christ is also my Son,
and he will clothe you with immortality ! But,
O my dear Lord ! my Redeemer ! my best be-
loved ! whose kindness and grace no words can
express, thou diest ! Oh that this sorrowful hour
were passed, and that thou hadst escaped from pain,
to the felicity that awaits thee at the right hand
of the Majesty on high.—Now my dear Jesus bends
his looks on me ! O ye seraphim rejoice, he turns
his face to me ! Let the gates of heaven echo back
the sound, that the great, the divine Redeemer once
more turns his face to the mother of mortals ! The
joys of eternity already shine around me ! I lift up
my eyes to the Most High, the Omnipotent God,
whom the heaven of heavens cannot contain ! I
stretch forth my hands to his beloved Son ! the
Brightness of his Father's glory, the Restorer of
innocence ! the Reviver of the dead ! the Judge
of the earth ! the Redeemer of man ! and with
amazement attempt to express my gratitude : but
words cannot describe what I feel : my soul swells
with rapture. I am lost in transport, in extasy,
in joy unutterable ! Bless the Lord, O my chil-
dren ! bless the great Omnipotent, the original
source of joy, of love, of happiness ! Oh pour out
your souls in grateful praise to the Lord your Re-
deemer, and everlasting Friend. By his bloody

sweat in Gethsemane ; by those wounds, and that pure blood now shed for you ; by his drooping head, his dim and languid eyes, his countenance disfigured by pain and approaching death, I conjure you to love and imitate your Lord, your Friend, your Saviour. In his name I bless you, O mine offspring ! and may the blessing of the Lord always rest upon you !

THE END OF THE EIGHTH BOOK.

BOOK. IX.

THE ARGUMENT.

Eloa returns from the throne of God, and relates what he has seen. The behaviour of Peter, who joins Samma and a stranger, and afterwards successively meets Lebbeus, his brother Andrew, Joseph, and Nicodemus, and then returns to Golgotha, where he sees John, and the female friends of Jesus. A conversation between Abraham and Moses. They are joined by Isaac. Abraham and Isaac address the Messiah. A cherub conducts the souls of some pious heathens to the cross. Christ speaks to John and Mary. Abaddona, assuming the appearance of an angel of light, comes to the cross ; but being known by Abdiel, flies. Obaddon conducts the soul of Judas to the cross, then gives him a distant view of heaven, and at length conveys him to hell.

ELOA now filled with deep contemplation, slowly hovered over the pinnacles of the temple, and then came to the assembly of the progenitors of the human race : whom he thus addressed :

Before I communicate my thoughts, oh join in prayer with me. Ere I speak, I will offer my adorations. All then, with humble prostration, in silence adored the Infinite and Eternal, and silent rose. Eloa still continued rapt in thought ; but at last said :

To the First of beings, to him whom no name can express, no thought conceive, I have just soar-

ed, desiring to see him face to face, in all his t
mendous glory. I reached the suns that gild t
radient path to heaven, and they were dimmed.
then ascended to the celestial throne, where dar
ness progressive deepened beyond darkness ; but
words can express the deepness of the sable clo
in which the Eternal was involved, nor the aw
terrors with which he was environed. I sto
amidst the profound silence of the fair creatio
I sunk prostrate, adoring the great Omnipotent
silence. Thus Eloa spake, and veiling his fa
withdrew.

The head of the divine Jesus now hanging up
his breast, he seemed to slumber. The storm
the blasphemous multitude was laid, and all w
calm as the ocean reclining on the peaceful shor
Those who revered the Saviour walked about t
skirts of Golgotha, where with weeping eyes, th
might obtain a distant view of the Redeemer.
each avoided the others ; their afflicted bea
allowing them no tongue for converse, hitt
converse adding pain to their distress. On
the beloved disciple, and the tender mother
Jesus, continued with each other at the foot
the cross.

The disciple who had sworn that he knew not
divine Master, was now walking solitarily abo
the mountain. Thus by the winding shore wa
ders a son, within sight of a rock on which b
father was wrecked ; speechless he walks, with l
eyes fixed on the spot where his tender pare
perished, and lifting them up to heaven, burs
into bitter lamentations : Peter now faint wi
weeping, stood on an eminence near mount Ca
vary, too weak to express his grief, too weak
lift up his supplicating hands to heaven. Itburie
his guardian angel, with pity beheld his grief, a

infused into his heart some drops of consolation.
This, though an immortal, was all he could give.
The afflicted disciple felt the lenient balm thrill
through his soul, and now looking up, with long-
ing eyes, sought his friends, desiring to receive
from them reproof and comfort. He stood with
his eyes directed t wards Jerusalem; for up the
hill of death he did not dare to look. At length,
his eyes were drawn aside by a distant murmuring
sound, which arose from the strangers, who, being
come to the festival, were hastening to obtain a
sight of the crucified Prophet. To them Peter
went, and among the more silent groups of people,
sought his fellow disciples, but none he found.
At length the conversation of two men suspended
his search; one of a swarthy complexion, richly
dressed in a foreign robe, asked a man of an open
countenance, who held by the hand his little son;
for what crime the malefactor, on the middle and
more lofty cross, was put to death? His crime!
said the other, with an air of surprize; he is put
to death because he hath given health to the sick,
feet to the lame, ears to the deaf, eyes to the
blind! because he relieved the possessed, of which
number I was one, and freed us from our torments!
because he even raised the dead! because by his
powerful preaching he opened to our enraptured
souls the gates of eternal bliss! because his life
was holy, blameless, divine!

Here seeing Peter, he stretched out his hand
towards him, and said, This is one of the chosen
friends of the great prophet, who daily saw and
heard from him the words of truth. Do thou in-
form us, added he, turning to Peter—inform this
stranger and me, why they put this divine person to
death. Comply, O thou man of God! with my
request, and turn not away thine eyes from me.

Thou knowest him. Thee he loved! for thou wast one of his chosen disciples. Brothers have less love for each other, than thou and John have for him.

Peter still turned from them, not because he was known; for now he was prepared to die; but his being Joined with the faithful John, pierced his very soul. My friends, said he at last, with faultering voice, There dies the holy!—Then bursting into tears, he hid himself among the crowd.

Thus he left Samma and Joel, with the favourite of queen Candace; the eunuch, afterwards baptized by Philip. These, filled with admiration, now moved slowly towards Golgotha. Meanwhile, Peter discovered at a distance Lebbeus, who stood, leaning with a dejected look, against a withered tree, and going towards him, with a faint trembling voice, said, Ah Lebbeus! hast thou too seen him on the cross? Thou, in thy grief, canst dare to lift up thine eyes to him; but I—oh pity—pity my misery!—Here, here it bleeds! added he, laying his hand on his breast: Here my swelling, tortured heart bleeds! Will not my dear friend speak to me? Will he not afford me one word of consolation?—Thou art silent—still art thou silent. In vain Lebbeus strove to give utterance to the strong emotions of his mind. Yet the agitations that appeared in his countenance, and his falling tears were not speechless. But no comfort could Peter's soul receive from them. With heavy heart he left that affectionate disciple, and depressed with a new load of woe, again hid himself in the crowd. At length, having once more escaped from the multitude, he suddenly saw before him his brother Andrew. Him he would have shunned; but receiving a sign to retire farther from the people, Peter followed him, and, on joining him, cried, My bro-.

ther ;—my dear brother !—Then embraced him : not indeed with his usual fervour, for with feeble grasp he held him, and hung on his neck weeping. O my dear Peter, returned Andrew, with more composed affliction ; fain would I, but I cannot suppress my grief ! My heart bleeds as well as thine ! I mourn for thee—the best of Men ! the most faithful, the most loving Friend ! the Son of God !—thou—alas !—before his enemies —hast denied !

Meek-hearted grief, sacred to him whom he had denied, and effusions of cordial thanks for his brother's fidelity, appeared in Peter's eyes : but speechless were his lips. They then walked hand in hand, with their eyes still suffused in tears, which scarce allowed them the power of sight, till, at length, overcome by the langour of grief, their hands sunk, and losing their hold they parted. Peter, still disconsolate, and still earnestly breathing after consolation, walked alone ! but not far : soon he cast his eyes on two persons whom he esteemed, yet strove to avoid ; but was too near. Does the dear disciple of the divine Teacher not know us ? said Joseph of Arimathea. We also, O Simon ! are his disciples, We were so in secret, but now we are ready to acknowledge him before all the people. Nicodemus, my worthy friend, who cannot be unknown to thee, has boldly declared for Christ before the sanhedrim : with unshaken courage he, before them all, spake in his defence : but I alas ! too late acknowledge him. I was intimidated—coward as I was, I did not dare to express my thoughts before that impious assembly ! Forbear, dear Joseph, said Nicodemus, to afflict thy tender mind. Thou camest away with me, and hast already owned the divine Jesus.

to heaven, cried, Hear, O hear, Thou God, and
Father of the holy Jesus ! the voice of my sup-
plications. Him whom I so faintly owned while he
lived, may I, before all the world, undauntedly
acknowledge when dead.

Here Joseph was silent. His petition arose to
the eternal throne, and with the grant descended
divine grace. Nicodemus now addressing himself
to Peter, said, O Simon ! thy heart seems steeped
in bitterness, and thou turnest thy face from us.
We share thy grief, we feel like thee, the death
that is now seizing the holiest, the best of men !
Perhaps he is now expiring ! But, O thou, his dear
disciple ! let thy gracious words pour into our
souls an healing balm ; and let not thy melancholy
eye upbraid us with having so long, only in private,
acknowledged the divine Jesus—thy Lord and ours.
As a tree seized by the blustering winds, quivering
bends its lofty top, so Peter, hanging down his
head, stood trembling. Overpowered by remorse,
he hid his face in his garment. Then fled, seeking
rest in greater pain. He hasted back to Golgotha,
and with labouring steps, ascended the hill. He
now more freely breathes, He ventures to raise
his eyes to the lofty cross ; but not to the awful
face of his dying Lord. Under it he beheld, near
each other, John and the mother of the sacred vic-
tim, motionless, silent, and with eyes which, through
excess of grief, shed no tears. At a small distance
stood many of the faithful, who had followed the
Saviour out of Galilee. Though low their birth,
though obscure their rank, though mean their
appearance, sacred history has transmitted the
names of some of that virtuous band to posterity:
Mary Magdalene, Mary the mother of James and
Joses, Mary the mother of the sons of Zebedee,
and thou, O Mary, who now didst behold, extended

on the cross, thy divine Son, the best and most amiable of the race of men. These, with many others, from the warmth of their affection, ventured to stand near their dying Lord.

Mary Magdalene had sunk on the ground; longing for death.—Carried away by the torrent of her sorrow, she abandoned every hope ; every idea of the Saviour's miracles, and lay impassioned on the hill, filling the air with her complaints. The mother of Joses, though herself inconsolable, prompted hy the tenderness of her soul, attempted to give her the comfort she herself could not feel ; and, with the soft voice of pity, strove to alleviate her distress : but soon the agony of her own grief rendered her silent. Meanwhile the mother of the two sons of Zebedee, pale and faded with grief, stood weeping in the dreary gloom, with uplifted eyes, and wringing her hands, seemed to say, How long will the divine vengeance be delayed ? Soon will it fall on this cruel people !

But none with more fervour of soul ; none with more cordial compassion, viewed the dying Jesus, than the converted criminal. This escaped not the notice of the immortals, more especially of those who were once of the human race ; while the chief object of their exalted sensations was the grace of the Redeemer. Abraham, enraptured with the thought of his salvation, observed him with warm affection ; till at length the affecting sympathy with which the already happy convert beheld the Holy Sufferer, struck the patriarch with such mingled pity and joy, that, breaking forth from his mute astonishment, he turned to Moses, who stood by his side ; and the exalted father of the twelve-tribed Hebrews, thus spake to the inspired legislator, the builder of the tabernacle :

R

What we, O son ! behold—what these few hours
display, will furnish us with discourse through the
endless ages of eternity. Thou sawest the glory
of God on Horeb ; I in Mamre's sacred grove :
mild was then its appearance : then the divine lips
sounded melodious grace. Thus sweet, thus ravish-
ingly soft was the voice of the Saviour, when he
spake pardon to the criminal. O thou pure, thou
spotless Jesus, thou suffering Messiah, how great
is my joy at the redemption thou procurest for
sinners, my children ! my jubilant songs shall join
those of the heavenly host ! See how this new dis-
ciple smiles, at his approaching death ! How the
mercies of the Most High---how the divine bene-
volence of the great Redeemer swell his struggling
heart ! How the transports of eternal life beam
around him ! Yet, though the repose of a better
life is so near, with what soft compassion does he
look on the sufferings of his gracious Saviour !—
That my abandoned children should thus ungrate-
fully, with cruel hands, slay the Lord of Life,
would, was I mortal, fill me with such grief as to
bow me down to the grave ! What Gabriel in vain
strove to conceal from me, let me communicate to
thee ; and then may the dread idea be for ever
banished from my mind. The gracious Redeemer,
who, with the marks of these wounds, shall come
to judge the world, has already foretold the fate
of these abandoned sinners : nay, they have impre-
cated the divine vengeance on themselves. The
heathen governor sought to save him, and, with
reluctance, passed sentence ; while they cried out,
His blood be upon us and our children. Oh that
no angel of death had engraved the dreadful words
on an eternal rock, and placed it by the throne of
the Most High. I see—I see nations coming from

the ends of the earth to pay homage to the divine
Jesus ; to listen to his precepts, and to bow before
him, their Lord and Saviour. But among these I
see not my children.

Moses answered, Thou father of Isaac, of Jacob,
and of the faithful who adhered to the worship of
Jehovah, when the multitude flocked to graven
images : thou Father of her who bore the Re-
deemer, and of him who accomplishes the great
work of redemption ! O Abraham ! lift up thine
eyes and behold. What I shall say, is to thee al-
ready known : but 'tis good frequently to gaze
on the fair face of truth. There are a people of
judgment and of grace. The Unsearchable, who
points with his right hand to mercy, and with his
left to judgment, hath placed the Jews on a rock,
that all generations of men, all the sons of the dust,
may clearly see that they have the power of chus-
ing life and death ; whosoever, therefore, on ob-
serving the monitory rock, will not look up to it
to see and learn, is his own destroyer : he condemns
himself.

Abraham listened with grateful smile to his
words, and replied, Perhaps when they have long
served as a proof to the nations, they will forsake
the ways of sin, and then the son will no longer
hear the iniquities of the father. Then, O Moses,
then perhaps they will return—Sweetest transports
flow in upon me, and peace from God smiles all
around ! Oh then will they return to the great
Redeemer ! the Saviour of all mankind !—to him
who by day in a cloud, and in the night by a pil-
lar of fire, led their forefathers to the land of
Canaan, and on the cross now bleeds for them.
Return, return, O my children !—return to him
who is ready to save !—to him—to him—whom

ye are now putting to death !—to the Lamb that
will soon be slain !—to eternal life !

Here with supplicating look, he raised his eyes
to heaven. Isaac, his beloved son, once the com-
fort of his declining age, seeing him, came in his
juvenile form, with a smile of joy, mingled with
concern, and instantly cried, Ah father, in thy
countenance I see the warm emotions of thy mind !
But alas ! our children cruelly slay him, who
sanctified himself for them ! Yet, O Jehovah !
thou wilt at length have mercy on them ! thou wilt
bear them on eagles' wings to their Saviour ! At
this delightful thought felicity comes hovering
round me, and extatic bliss rushes upon my exult-
ing soul ! Yet one idea fills me with sacred awe.
—Well dost thou remember, when on yonder sa-
cred mount—(for ever sacred let it be to me !)
—thou ledst me to the altar. Thy son more cheer-
ful than thyself, went by thy side, rejoicing that
he was going with thee to sacrifice to the Eternal :
but when I lay bound on the wood, and the light-
ed brand flamed by my side ; when I lifted up my
eyes swimming in tears to heaven ; when you gave
me the parting kiss ; then turning from me drew
the glittering blade, and held destruction over thy
son—But I pass over that trying hour, since crown-
ed with ages of purest joy—Then thine Isaac
was surely chosen to prefigure the Son of the
Most High—the sacrifice that now bleeds on
Golgotha. This fills me with a sweet and rap-
turous melancholy that overpowers my immortal
soul.

Thus Isaac spake, and Abraham in soft accents
replied, Let us bow before the Redeemer. In-
stantly they kneeled : one of Abraham's arms en-
closed that of his son, and their folded hands were

raised to Golgotha.   The father then cried, O thou
sacred source of joy to believers ! thou Son of the
Supreme Father ! what have I felt since a mortal
mother bore thee at Bethlehem ?   The angels,
lost in astonishment, comprehend not the wonders
of thy grace and love.   Thou the inspiring theme
of their jubilant songs, condescendest to shroud
thyself in a mean and humble life.   Scarce could
the spirits on high know thee under the lowly dis-
guise.   O thou in whom the brightness of thy Fa-
ther's glory shone ! thou hast walked the steep,
the solitary way of mortality ; and now art thou
come to its solemn, its momentous period—to thy
last, thy most painful sufferings, which, long before
I was born on this earth, thou, O my Saviour, and
the Saviour of all that come to thee, didst chuse !
—didst chuse for man !—and now thou bleedest—
thou diest !—Oh ! thou art far superior to our
compassion ! Yet we feel the great, the dreadful
stroke, with which death strikes thee, and at which
the immense creation trembles.   Have mercy on us,
O God Most High ! thou spring of never failing
mercy and of grace ! that we may not too deeply
feel the sufferings of thy Son.   Have mercy—have
mercy on all who, rapt in admiration, surround
the Saviour—on all, like us, allied to the dust.

Here Abraham ceased, and both were silent,
till Isaac asked, Who are the souls that cherub
is leading to the cross ?   The radiant band ap-
proached from the distant sky, beautiful as the
rising morn.   They had quitted their tabernacles
of flesh, and came from all the nations of the earth,
extending from pole to pole, where their bodies
had been consumed by the quick devouring flames
of the funeral pile, or committed to the silent grave.
Their hearts were sincere and pure, if the purity of
mortals deserves the name.   Animated by the love

of virtue, fairest ornament of the human mind, and ever lovely in the eyes of the Universal Parent, they passed through this inferior life ; but had not been illumined by the light of an external revelation. Thousands of these happy souls were led by the meditative cherub, while seized with their first astonishment at the glories of their new state of existence, they with silent rapture adored the Sovereign Lord of all, who is no respecter of persons, and whose tender mercies are over all his works. To them the cherub turned his face, when Abraham and the other patriarchs heard him thus address the souls, while they approached the gloom surrounded cross.

What ye, blessed spirits, see, consider with all the powers your new and rapturous sensations will allow. Here is fresh subject for your love, your gratitude, your devout astonishment. None born of woman can without the Mediator, who there bleeds for you, see the Eternal. Ye happy souls, to you I now reveal the great mystery of eternity. The divine victim expiring before you is Jesus. He offered himself a sacrifice for sinners condemned to die. Though the Son of the Most High, he was born on earth, horn of a mortal mother, who there stands at the foot of the cross. Fastings, prayers, adorations, instructions, miraculous acts of beneficence, sufferings on sufferings, filled up the life of the gracious Saviour : and now—(the joys of eternity hang upon the great event)—now he dies—he dies for all the sons of earth—he dies for you !—Had he not from the beginning been chosen the Redeemer, all would have died ; but through his obedience all shall be made alive. God is pleased with your sincere endeavours to know and obey him, and, happy souls, for his sake your sincerity is accepted : He whom ye strove to know,

has seen your tears ; has heard your petitions to be
freed from sin, which ye felt, which ye conquered,
though ye knew not all its evils. Hence your
prayers have ascended to the highest heavens and
were acceptable to him who searcheth the hearts of
the sons of men. Prostrate yourselves to the
bleeding Jesus your Friend, your Redeemer, your
Intercessor ! Oh give thanks to the great Media-
tor ! to the Dispenser of eternal life ! to the suf-
fering Jesus, the Son of the Most High God !

    These souls, filled with inexpressible blissful
sensations, mingled with gentle dejection and as-
tonishment, sunk in rapturous adoration of the
gracious Saviour, who had loved them before the
foundation of the world, and was now dying to per-
fect the redemption of the human race.

    Salim and Selith, the guardian angels of John
and Mary, observing the grateful prostration of
these enraptured souls, Salim cried, How sensible
of their felicity, O Selith, are these new immor-
tals ! How the joys of heaven already flow in upon
them ! O my friend ! What a spectacle worthy of
angels ! They are for ever delivered from the trou-
bles of mortal life ; from the afflictions which fall
so thick and heavy on the inhabitants of the earth !
Alas ! the dear persons under our care are far from
enjoying their repose ! They were lately so filled
with sublime sensations, as scarce to feel the heavy
clog of mortality ; but now, those pale cheeks, those
agonizing looks, those bleeding wounds, have chilled
the extasies of the mother and the friend ! I, O
Selith, also feel them !—I feel the cruel nails that
pierce their souls ! I, replied Selith, have seen many
of the afflicted : but no distress like theirs ! Yet is
my compassion mixed with wonder. Is it not
strange, that they who are beloved by the Eternal,
should thus deeply suffer ? yet with pleasure I

reflect, that God frequently imparts consolation to his suffering servants, when every ray of hope seems vanished. And, O Salim! if my ardent desire of seeing them again favoured by divine consolation, does not deceive me, I now see emanations of comfort beaming from the benevolent eyes of the Messiah.

Thus spake Selith. He erred not; for the Redeemer would no longer withhold his pity from John and the afflicted Mary; but cast down on them a look whence reviving effusions streamed into their fainting souls. Then inclining his divine face towards them, Mary, with trembling expectation, listened, while, to her ear the voice of her gracious Saviour, thus descended; Mother, behold thy Son. Then to the disciple he said, Behold thy mother! John and Mary transported, looked at each other filled with surprize, and shedding tears of gratitude.

The dying Jesus still continued suspended in keenest torture. An horrid silence encompassed the hill of death, and the earth incessantly trembled through its secret caverns. Yet in the neighbourhood of Jerusalem, its latent trepidations were not felt. Once did the concussion reach the rebellious city: but it only raised an obscure sensation: something of a distant terror of impending vengeance, for the blood that was then flowing, seized the hearts of the multitude.

The secret convulsions of Nature reached a rocky mountain far from Olivet, where into a gloomy cave, Abbadona had retired to mourn in the depths of the earth. He was sitting on the declivity of a subterranean rock, viewing with fixed attention a torrent which fell at his feet. His listening ear was following the roar of the foaming stream, which flowing from the summit of the lofty mountain, was dashed from cliff to cliff, when suddenly he felt under him a progressive trembling, and the rocks fell from their aspiring heights. Abbadona, terrified at the convulsive pangs of nature, cried, Does the earth lament that she has brought forth children ? and is she tired of bearing her mouldering issue in her bosom, which is now become a perpetual grave to them ? Thus thronged with human bodies, she is within dreadful, while without she is clothed with a verdant robe, and adorned with blooming flowers. Or, alas ! does she lament the great, the divine person, whom I, in midnight darkness, saw in humble prostration, suffering !—Ah, what is his fate ! Why do I delay

justice nearer me, when exposed on the open earth, than when here ? No where can I escape from justice ! should I fly from the creation, still would she follow me ? I will then seek him, I will see the issue of his dreadful sufferings, and penetrate into the mystery of this great event—But if he is always encompassed by this heavenly host, how shall I approach him ? How sustain their looks ? Dare I to imitate their splendor ? Dare I to transform myself into an angel of light ? Alas ! the God of truth would, with his pointed lightning, strip off the disguise, and the angels see me in my hideous form. But Satan has been permitted to appear like an angel of light ! he who has provoked the Most High by greater crimes—by incessant acts of deepest guilt ! Ah this disguise is not to conceal any base design, harboured in my tortured heart ! But shall Abbadona use disguise ?—Retire, retire, O wretch, rejected and forlorn !—retire, and in secret contemplate thy misery !—Am I excluded then from going ? and must I not know the end of his wondrous sufferings ?—But, how should I be able to behold the looks of the angels and not fly?

Thus fluctuating, and still dubious he arose from the cavern: but scarce had he alighted on the surface of the earth, when with astonishment he drew back: for then seeing her involved in the dreadful gloom of night, he cried, with a tremulous voice, At mid-day, overspread with such thick darkness! Is the earth ripe for judgment? Is she now to be destroyed? Doth the Omnipotent hold her in the hollow of his hand?—But wherefore? Does the wonderful Sufferer lie buried in her bosom? and does God require him of her sons?—But can the Messiah die?—Wherever I turn, perplexity dwells, on each new idea. Much better is it for me to haste and seek him—to see, and by that means, to learn than to sit alone, lost in fruitless conjectures.

Thus resolved, he stood on the tree-crowned summit of a lofty mountain, and amidst the shrouding darkness, long with quick eye, sought the holy city. At length he perceived it, when through hovering clouds, it seemed like a heap of ruins. Now, trembling, he tries to assume a bright etherial form and all the juvenile beauty with which he shone in the blissful vale of peace: but awkward is the imitation. Radient tresses indeed flow beneath his shoulders, which are adorned with golden wings; within his eyes he retains his tears, and the lustre of the dawning day overspreads his lucid countenance. Thus arrayed in beauty he, with trembling flight, chuses his way through the thickest gloom. In traversing the coast of the Dead Sea, he hears an unusual noise in the agitated waters: with the roar of the waves are intermingled the groans of anguish, and the howls of despair. So, when guilty cities are swallowed up

by an earthquake, there resounds from the open-
ing abyss, the cries of the dying, mixed with the
fall of polluted temples and marble palaces; at
which the pale traveller, filled with terror, flies.
Thus the affrighted Abbadona hears the roaring of
the Dead Sea, mingled with the groans and bel-
lowing of Satan and Adramelech.   He knows
them, and with fluttering wing, leaves the doleful
shore.

He now draws near to the angelic circle.   At the
august appearance he is suddenly overpowered by
an insurmountable terror, and his mimic lustre
fades.   The angel solely immersed in the contem-
plation of the holy the dying Messiah, observed
not his approach : but he escaped not Eloa's
piercing eye.   He instantly knew him, and thus
said to himself, The forsaken of God, this fearful
soul-tormented seraph, would then behold the cru-
cified Jesus !   Already has he seen his passion in
the garden.   He seeks him again !—How restless
—how miserable is his state !—A prey to inces-
sant remorse !   Long, very long has he been dis-
solved in these bitter tears of anguish !—O God,
thou Sovereign Judge, all thy purposes on Abba-
dona thou wilt accomplish ! thy ways are ever just
and righteous.   Then in humble prostration, he
prayed in silence.   On his rising, he made a sign
to an angel, who instantly stood before him. Haste,
blessed spirit, said Eloa, haste to the angels, and
to the progenitors of the human race, and thus ad-
dress them.   Abbadona, trembling and anxious, is
drawing towards us.   Should he venture to mingle
with you, oh forbid him not ; for in extreme dis-
tress he comes, to obtain an awful view of the Re-
deemer.   Let none order him to fly.   Let none
discountenance a mind so humbled.   Indulge him

in this afflictive alleviation of his anguish. About the cross are greater sinners than Abbadona.

The fallen seraph hovered, trembling, about the angelic assembly. He hesitated ; fluttered forward ; stopt ; alighted on the ground. He was suddenly desirous of returning back. He then animated himself with the thought, that none but the Messiah could be encompassed by so spacious, so pompous a circle of angels. He now flew amidst them.' The angels turned and saw him ; they saw the faint disguise. Abbadona wore a ghasty smile ; a lustre that irradiates none of the blessed, mingled with fixed horror and predominant grief, which he strove in vain to conceal. With silent commiseration they suffered him to pass, and he approached the cloud topped hill ! but seeing those on each cross, he swiftly turned aside. No, I will not see them, said he ; I will not see the faces of the dying ! Their sufferings pierce me too deep, and present to my thoughts images of horror ! too loudly do they accuse me to the Sovereign Judge ! Unhappy creatures ! my companions in guilt and misery, who have rendered yourselves so guilty that your own brethren have made you such terrible examples !—But I will not enquire whether the justice or cruelty of those like yourselves have inflicted on you this dreadful death—Let me fly— let me escape from this distressful sight. But where shall I find him whom I seek ? This assembly of the heavenly host has not descended to the earth in vain : they doubtless incircle him. He is then in this sacred place : but where ? When I saw him in the garden it was covered with an horrible darkness—that on this hill, strewed with bones, is still more horrible. But can he not be seen ?—O that some angel would point him out !

—Dare I, unhappy, ask an angel to shew me him ?
Did they know me by this tremor, by this melan-
choly confusion, they would order me to retire.—
But rapt in divine contemplations on this holy per-
son, they observe not me—Ah, wretch ! how de-
based art thou ! thou darest not lift up thy bash-
ful eye to the faithful ministers of God ; and yet
on this hill of sculls presumest to appear before
them, while adorned with all their radiant splen-
dor !   Perhaps here, where dying malefactors
afford the most manifest proof of the fall of man,
Jesus concludes his earthly sufferings.   Perhaps,
prostrate among human bones, he is here offering
up his supplications to the Sovereign Judge.   Ah,
must I again turn my face towards this mount of
death !

He then turned, hovering slow and timid around
the hill, till descending, he sought with quick and
piercing eye under the crosses.   There he found
John, and careful watched his looks.—Meanwhile
the gracious Saviour still hung on the darkened
cross, and every feature of his agonizing counte-
nance seemed to wish for the repose of the grave.

Abbadona at length recovering from his first
emotions,—softly cried, It is impossible—it is im-
possible—It cannot be—He die !—It is impossible !
But why do I delay to obtain conviction ? Then
lifting up his eyes, he suddenly added, I see him
—I am not deceived—It is he !—Yes, it is he !—
he whom I saw on the mount of Olives, prostrate,
weeping, and pouring out his soul in prayer for
man !

He now sunk upon the hill, and resumed, Here
will I in the dust wait the issue of this solemn
tremendous scene, and if I may be permitted, will
see the divine Sufferer die !—Ah what is this that
arises in my mind like the opening dawn of rest ?

Is it the stupefaction of anguish, or a ray of re-
viving hope ?—of the best hope I dare entertain—
the hope of annihilation ? Oh deceive me not, thou
mere ideal hope—Thou dost not—Thou art more
than imaginary. Methinks I now dare fly to the
Sovereign Judge, and humbly implore him to grant
me annihilation ! Ah then I shall be no more !—
No more shall feel the burning torment ! Then
at once will my existence cease ! I shall be blotted
from the race of immortal beings ! be forgotten by
the angels, by the whole creation, by God himself !
Behold, I bow my head, O Jehovah ! to thine om-
nipotence ; and do thou, my Sovereign Judge con-
descend to exterminate me from thy creation by an
invisible touch of thine almighty hand, or by a sub-
til blaze darted from thy refulgent splendor.

Such were the supplications of Abbadona, which
he presumed to hope would be accomplished.
Filled with mingled joy and terror, he glided along
the earth, and looked up to the bloody cross, to the
dying Redeemer, visible in obscurity, striving to
retain his borrowed splendor. But while he thus
strove, and his fears and terrors still returned, he
perceived hovering on the right side of the more
lofty cross, his beloved, now his dreadful Abdiel,
once his friend, his brother ; for with him was he
created. Surrounding gloom instantly veiled from
his sight the radiant circle of angels, and to him
the whole creation appeared too narrow. Every
appertinence of an happy immortal, all the graces,
all the powers of a fair etherial spirit, he suddenly
strove to assume, to prevent his being known by
Abdiel ; and hasting as if dispatched on some high
behests, from remote worlds to others more remote,
he had stopped, but dared not stay ; he thus, with
quick speech, addressed himself to Abdiel.

Tell me, dear seraph, (for thou, perhaps, mayest

know) when will the Saviour expire? I am ordered·
to be expeditious ; yet, wherever I am, I could·
wish, with the lowliest adorations, to solemnize
that important·moment.

Abdiel, at hearing his voice, turned towards the·
unhappy, and, with a gravity softened by compas-
sion, answered Abbadona!—As the face of a bloom-
ing youth blasted by a sulphureous flash darted·
from the clouds, is suddenly overspread by the livid·
paleness of death, so gloom issuing from the abyss,
instantly covered 'the face of Abbadona. All the
heavenly host beheld his transformation. When,
struck with·fear and shame, he suddenly flew, with·
rapidity, from the bright circle of the celestial·
spirits, unable to bear their looks or their splen-
dour.

The fallen seraph ascended far into the sky, and
then sunk down on·a mountain, from whence at the
same time arose on the ·opposite side a spirit, far
more black·and miserable than he who had fled.
One of the bright inhabitants of heaven seeing him,
said to his companion, Who is that wretch accursed
advancing towards us, from yonder hill ? How ·has
the hand of justice branded his wrinkled front !
How is he deformed by odious guilt ! Yet he ·pre-
sumes to fly towards this· bright assembly !—But·
see, the mighty Obaddon is driving forward the
wretched spirit. Ah ! it·is the ghost of the trai-
tor !

Now·the angel of death brought the trembling
caitif near to the cross ; and all the celestials saw
him·so black,·that he seemed a spot in the darkness
which encompassed·the globe. He appeared as
distressed with agonizing terror, as if, wherever
he flew,·over him enkindling lightnings blazed,
and under him the earth opened, while that darted
at ·his head avenging fires·; and this, with equal

fury prepared to swallow him. Thus, with wild
anguish, the soul of Judas approached the cross,
with his eyes fixed on Obaddon! who, waving in
his right hand his flaming sword, drove him, re-
luctant; till, alighting on a sable cloud, he, with
imperious voice, thus spake :

Behold! there lies Bethany—here the palace of
Caiaphas—here below, the house where thou, un-
grateful, didst partake of the memorials of the
Saviour's death—There is Gethsemane—that is thy
carcase—dost thou tremble?—tremble still—but
open not thy mouth in curses. Here, stretching
out the flaming sword towards the middle cross,
which rose pre-eminent, he added, That is Jesus
Christ, once thy Lord!—He dies!—he dies for
men! to sweeten their life, their death! to deliver
them from torment like thine, and to exalt them to
the regions of eternal bliss! Those wounds, whence
flow his redeeming blood, shall shine, with en-
rapturing lustre, when he comes to judge the
world! Now turn, thou wretched spirit, and fol-
low me. Overwhelmed with despair, Judas turned
aside, and Obaddon quick relieved the angelic
circle from a sight so hateful. They now wing
their way among the stars. The traitor is terrified
at the immense extent of the silent creation. The
dread idea of the omnipresent God rushes upon his
mind with all its terrors ; and long he trembles
before he dares to utter this request :

O thou most dreadful of the angels! let me
entreat—let me implore thee not to carry me to the
throne of the Eternal Judge—but, with that dread
flaming sword, to put an end to my wretched being.

Obey, and be silent, said Obaddon, driving him
forward, till at length, at his command, he stood
on one of the suns, and near him that angel of death.
There he shewed the traitor the heaven of heavens,

where the Most High visibly displays his glory, and the blessed enraptured spirits enjoy the beatific vision. Though the throne of God was now encompassed with sacred darkness, and instead of eternal hallelujahs, and the triumphant joy of the saints, reigned stillest silence : yet heaven was still worthy of being the residence of Him who is the Author of all beauty; the Source of all perfection, and to the most exalted of the blessed, was still the region of boundless joy, of ineffable felicity. This said Obaddon to the wretched spirit, is the heaven of the Most High God, the theatre on which he displays the most blissful manifestations of his exuberant glory, which he graciously imparts to those who make him the object of their grateful love. At present the Eternal hides his face from all finite beings, and sits shrouded on his throne in sacred obscurity : but still mine eyes perceive the divine glory. That celestial, that blooming mountain is called Sion ; upon its top he who now dies, for man will often shew himself resplendent in grace, to those who on earth, were his pious followers. Those twelve golden thrones thou seest on Sion, shining like the sun in its splendour, were, by the august Rewarder of virtue appointed for the twelve faithful disciples of the divine Jesus : and, seated on these, they shall one day judge the earth. Thou wast one of his disciples. That throne was thine. But thou hast forfeited the seat of bliss ; and it will be given to another more worthy. Sue not for destruction. Fruitless are all thy lamentations. Behold, so many of the celestial glories as thine eyes are able to discover, so many torments has God measured out to thee. In vain, feeble wretch, theu strivest to forbear looking up to heaven. Learn to know the omnipotence of the Supreme Judge. Like a rock in the sea, which no storm can

move, shalt thou here stand and contemplate, that
Jesus Christ dies on the cross to raise those who
love him to this heaven : to this state of unutterable
glory.

At these words Obaddon left him, and flew up
towards heaven, till arriving at one of the celestial
suns he prayed. At length rising from his orisons,
and returning to the traitor, who stood wildly
gazing and filled with unutterable misery, he cried,
Away, thou wicked spectre, I now lead thee to hell,
thine everlasting dwelling. Thus, with the hoarse
voice of terror sounding like redoubled claps of
thunder, spake the angel of death, and then precipi-
tated his flight down towards hell. From afar they
heard the noise of the infernal deep, which roaring
struck the confines of the creation and undulated
to the nearest stars. In that space where God has
set bounds to infinitude, hell rolls her torrents of
liquid fire. There no order submissive reigns
above or below ; no law of motion swift or slow.
Sometimes with unusual rapidity they move, such
is the command of the Sovereign Judge, to punish
the fresh crimes of her inhabitants with flames
more vehement, and sharper darts of ever-dying
death. Now with rageful impatience, and hideous
sound, mingled with groans, and yells, and shrieks,
they fly up into the wide expanse. Meanwhile the
traitor and his potent guide quit the confines of
the fair creation, and all the worlds innumerable,
and, with extended wings, sink down to the gates of
hell. The angel of death stationed there knows
Obaddon, sees the criminal writhing and struggling
to escape, while the dread of the flaming sword
forces his reluctant submission. He unfolds the
wide adamantine gates, which harsh grating with
jarring sound impetuous turn their broad hinges,
and at once discover the deep the dread abyss tre-,

mendous and most horrible. Not mountains heaped
on mountains would fill up the enormous entrance :
these would only render the passage more rugged.
No path leads down to hell's hideous deeps. Close
by the gate rocks cleft with gusts of liquid fire,
fall down in ruins wild, while dismay pale and
giddy at what is seen and heard, looks speechless
down with eyes wide staring and face aghast, into
the flaming gulph. The executioner of the divine
vengeance, with the infernal Judas, stood at this
gaping grave : the grave where Death never dies
—never sleeps. The seraph then turning aside,
pointed his flaming sword down into the deep abyss,
and cried, This is the abode of the damned, and
this, O wretch ! is thine abode ! Jesus Christ, once
thy gracious Lord, descended from heaven, lived
a life of sorrow, breathing benevolence and love
to man, and is now dying on the cross, to save man-
kind from this place of everlasting woe !

　Thus he spake, and hurled the struggling spec-
tre into the abyss. Then with rapidity soared from
the precincts of the fiery deep, to the fair creation.
Now he comes to the altar on which the divine vic-
tim was offered, and stands waiting farther orders
from the Omnipotent.

THE END OF THE NINTH BOOK.

THE

MESSIAH.

BOOK X.

THE ARGUMENT.

God looks down from his throne, while the Messiah casts his eyes on the sepulchre, and prays; then with a look fills Satan and Adramelech with terror. Many elevated souls are now given to the earth, one of whom delivers his thoughts of the dying Redeemer. A character of these souls. A conversation between Simeon and John the Baptist. Miriam and Deborah lament the dying Saviour in a hymn. Lazarus comforts Lebbeus. Uriel gives notice that the first of the angels of death is descending to the earth. The impression this makes on Enoch, Abel, Seth, David, Job, and more particularly on our first parents, who descend to the sepulchre of Jesus, and pray. The angel of death descends, addresses the Messiah, and makes known the divine command. The Messiah dies.

STILL farther do I travel in my tremendous path, still nearer draw to the Saviour's death —to his death who breathed nought but love divine, and whose love supports my fainting powers. O let me not, presumptuous, too boldly sing the great Redeemer! nor without solemn dignity attune my song! Look down propitious, on me, who am but dust, O thou, by whose omnipotence I am environed! Thou seest all the conceptions of my mind, ere into thought they rise, nor is there a word that trembles on my tongue to thee unknown. O

my Redeemer! enlighten me, and when I stumble
forgive! A ray of thy light, a drop of thy grace
is to the famished soul fulness, and to its thirst, the
refreshing stream.

The throne, which was wont to shine serene in
visible beauty, now stood involved in the thickest
gloom of night : solitary it stood, around it no im-
mortal adored, save an angel of death, who pros-
trate beneath the lowest step, with raised hands and
suppliant eyes, looked up with fixed attention.
Meanwhile Jehovah through the bright dust of
scattered suns, and worlds obscure, through silent
nature looked, with awful'view, understood or · felt
by none but him on whom the eternal eye was fixed.
Death, now so near, the Saviour's whole frame
pervades. The worlds tremble through all their
secret powers. Troubled, enraptured, silent, stand
all the immortals, contemplating the Son of God,
on whose divine face a more deadly paleness sits.
His weary languid eyes are faintly cast on his near
sepulchre, hewn out of a lonely rock among trees
of antient growth, and with a mind still filled with
benignity and soft compassion, which no pain could
expel, he thus pours forth in secret sighs the yet
warm thoughts of his expiring soul. There in the
sleep of death soon wilt thou, my body, lie. For
this I assumed thee. Yet though thou shalt lie
down in death, thou shalt not see corruption. O
my gracious Father! "wipe every tear from every
eye" that shall then weep for me!—Have pity on
them, when thou shalt bring them to their latest
hour!—Have pity on all who believe in thy be-
loved Son, who now dies for the sins of the world!
O Father! have compassion on all who, in their
struggles with death, shall fly to thee for grace and
consolation. Have compassion on those, who shall
be brought by many tribulations to the grave : who

in poverty shall live, and yet shall not deny thee : who while they keep a conscience void of offence both towards thee and towards man, shall become the scorn and mockery of sinners : who, true to their friends, bless even their enemies : who, by their actions, shew their love to their brethren, their love to mankind !   Have compassion on those, who undazzled by the honours, the wealth, the dignities of life, shall use them for the good of others ; themselves regardless of the glittering toys, and all the distinctions of vanity.   Oh be merciful to those who, loaded by thy gifts, shall constantly employ them in thy service, and to thy glory : in their last hour shew them the light of thy countenance : when their eyes sink in death, and their aspiring souls are ready to take their flight to their great Creator, then visit them with thy consolations, and receive them to the world of eternal peace and joy.   O holy Father ! God of love ! by the blood which flows from these wounds, on which my body is suspended ; by the ensanguined crown of thorns that encircles my head, and by all my agonies and sufferings, I conjure thee, in the name of that love that has induced me to suffer the ignominy and death of the cross, to accomplish the salvation of mankind, to hear me, and grant that they whom I love may remain faithful to the end—may die in comfort, and, rising to eternal life, receive the bright crown of unfading and immortal glory.

Thus silent prayed the great, the dying Messiah. Then turning his benevolent eyes from the sepulchre, he looked with stern brow on the Dead Sea, where lay Satan and Adramelech.   His eyes now darted convulsive terrors and deep dismay into the depths of that tempestuous lake, and both the apostate spirits sunk in the lowest misery.   Then was fulfilled the sentence of the Eternal, that the

Seed of the woman should bruise the serpent's head.
Satan in the midst of his anguish stamped into atoms
one of. the subterranean rocks, and intermingling
his faultering accents with languid howlings, thus
began :

' Feelest thou, like me, the inflamed, unquench-
able tortures, which death, eternal death, pours
into the deepest recesses of this immortal substance ?
In vain would I give thee an idea of what I suffer :
but hell affords not images so frightful, so terrible,
as to enable me to describe what I suffer. Judge
my anguish, that will allow me to be sensible of no
other joy than that of seeing thee suffer ! Judge
my humiliation, and the excess of my despair, when,
in spite of myself, I am forced to acknowledge that
he is omnipotent !—Yes, he is omnipotent, and I
the blackest monster of the abyss ! The lowest—
the lowest I lie, and all hell is upon me ! With all
its torments am I oppressed ! to all the terrors
of the fiery gulph, my boasted empire, am I aban-
doned !—But did he, by his thunders precipitate
us into this gulph ? No, an angel bid us fly—our
boasted courage sunk, and we like cowards fled !—
But in whose name did his messenger utter that
command ?—Oh ! what new vengeance threatens
my rebellious head !—The great name I dare not
utter ! He in whose name we fled—he whom we
persecuted, now perhaps dies ! A new, a more
fiery dart of destruction flies with this thought
through all my immortal powers. Darkness on
darkness surrounds me. The obscure mystery
affords not the least glimmering ray—Ah ! this is
misery—all, all around me is misery ! Even the
hope, the wretched, the agonizing hope of anni-
hilation vanishes. Ye worlds, and thou heaven,
turn ye to chaos—be confounded with hell ! and
hide me from the wrath of the Omnipotent.

The proud Adramelech, could scare with sobbing anguish and despairing look, reply, Help me—thou accursed, help me. I suffer the pangs of ever-dying death. Once I could hate thee with furious hatred, but now I can no more !—I sink under the excess of my misery !—I would curse thee, but cannot ; I would curse myself for imploring help of thee ! O monster !—O Satan ! help me, I conjure thee help me !—This he uttered bellowing loud, and laying his iron hands on Satan, continued, It would be a satisfaction to me to detest, and to curse thee—I will—I will. Here fainting with the effort, he sunk and fell.

Thus both experienced the vengeance sent forth from the mighty Victor ; and so far Terror stretched her crushing arm, that the lowest hell resounded with the howlings of despair.

O muse of Sion ! no farther unveil the dreary abodes of pain and horror. Another and a nobler scene opens before thee, a scene of sacred melancholy, of holy adoration, and of grace divine.

Jesus now turning his eyes from the Dead sea, viewed the celestial bands that dissolved in pious grief, and rapt in sacred wonder, surrounded the cross. The soft sensations of eternal love appeared in the looks of the divine Saviour ! and long did they dwell on those souls who had never entered a mortal frame, or sanctified the dust. Now approached one of those happy periods in which the earth was blessed with many noble minds, that spread their influence through future ages. 'Tis true, the fame of virtuous deeds doth not always float along the stream of time ; yet the great effects of fair examples are seen conquering disgust and error ; and, with a progress secret but sure, flowing into the deeds of posterity. Thus, though the stone thrown into water sinks, on the surface wider

and still wider circles, quivering spread around,
Now one of the most exalted of those unembodied
spirits, perceiving a glimpse of the light, which,
during her stay on earth, was to beam pure
sanctification and radiant truth, thus indulged her
thoughts.

Still more and more do I feel, that he is the great
Messiah. Innumerable and powerful as the suns
that gild the starry fields of light whence we came,
but with influence much more benign, are the
thoughts I read in his countenance.—But how
different is his appearance from that of our friends
the angels !—Ah he resembles the men by whom
he is surrounded ! but in his form alone he resem-
bles them. In their faces is something gloomy,
and averse to their Creator. Ah ! what is man ?
We must also be of their number ; like them we
must be clothed in mortal bodies ; like them
must live awhile and then return to the Eternal.
O thou Father of angels and of men, be thy decrees
accomplished ! Thy divine will be done ! and
thine, O thou Messiah ! Of all that is difficult
to conceive, this is most inconceivable, that thou,
once arrayed in thy Father's glory, sufferest—There
thou, raised above the hill, art suspended ; there
thy passing life seems to flow away : and ye angels
who once resolved my questions, are now silent.
Yet within myself I feel that this departing life,
to which, O thou divine ! hast condescended to
submit, is of importance to me—to me, perhaps
of more importance, than to the flaming seraph—
I love the suffering Messiah more than I can tell.
O my God, accomplish what thou hast begun,
complete my inflamed, my continual, my devout
breathings after felicity ! Thou alone, O thou
Infinite Source of perfection, art my felicity ! In
thy presence is eternal joy.

Thus meditated the transported spirit, and not fruitless were its meditations. God, who oft in distant periods prepares what he is determined to accomplish, thus forms the soul for a life of probation, and for the succeeding joys of eternal, ineffable felicity.

Let time now fly with joyful wings, Around the cross stood waiting with devout fervor, the future guardians of the souls who drew near to a mortal life.

Trembling with solicitous joy, the attendant angels stood while from the Redeemer's eye issued the great command, Go and live; believe and come. Their angels then smiling, received their charge and led them forth.

Relate, O Sion's muse! their life: relate their gifts and graces, while, dwelling in tabernacles of clay, they passed their mortal pilgrimage, in sacred love and pious ardour; imitating the bright example of their Saviour. The effects of the new sensations they had experienced on beholding Jesus on the cross, took root in all, and at length unfolding with their increasing perceptions, became mingled with the resplendent grace that flows from above.

One of the fairest of these souls was that of Timothy. He was yet in the bloom of youth, when he began, with humble and ardent zeal to watch over the church committed to his care, and, undaunted, ventured to preach a dying, a risen Jesus. He was instructed by Paul, who brought to him the knowledge of the Lord, out of that awful, that dazzling light which beamed conviction. The pure soul of Timothy learnt, with tremulous joy, the way to eternal felicity, and taught it to thousands. Thousands too were converted by his death; when having nobly finished his course, he fell by the executioner's sword. Like Paul and Cephas, he shone in the church as a bright resplendent luminary

Thou, Antipas, didst early receive the glorious rewards prepared for the faithful. Then the Judge of the earth, in his sentence on the church of Patmos, mentioned thine immortal name. With inflexible fidelity, with pure, with warm affection thou lovedst thy crucified Lord, lovedst him till death.

· Hermas, with tears of joy, sang the Mediater.—Sang him who died, who rose again, who ascended on high, and led captivity captive.—Sang the Son of God, the Saviour of frail and mortal man—The Son of God, who shall raise the dead, and judge the world. His hymns were sung by Christians retired to solitary caves, when Hermas receiving an intimation of the will of the Most High, left the choir of his rejoicing brethren, joyfully suffered death, and went to join the more exalted choir above.

Phebe, desirous of doing good, and winning souls, left the narrow limits that confine her sex, and generously devoted herself to the service of the church. She kindly strove to remove the distresses of the indigent; to help the sick; to comfort the dying. Heaven-born Charity, her dear companion, was always with her; but she fled from applause, and was known only to the pious, and to the angels.

From every fluctuating doubt of false wisdom, Herodian was at length freed, and convinced that he who was not more exalted by his miracles than by the sublime truths he punished, had made known the Eternal Father's will; dispersed the shades of death, and marked the path that leads to heaven. Through what intricate mazes of thorny speculation did he wander, before he reached the light which God, at length, poured around him! In what painful, what fruitless researches did he engage, before he found the lightness of the scale of human knowledge, and the preponderating weight of that of heavenly wisdom!

Epaphras was powerful in prayer. Like Paul, he was esteemed worthy to suffer for the sake of the crucified Jesus. He was thrown into the prison of a tyrant. The prisoner heard his prayers for the churches, and the blessings derived from his supplications chiefly streamed down oo his beloved Colossians. With them he watched and strove with unwearied diligence. His zeal and fervor were blessed with success. They flourished and spread their branches, they blossomed and brought forth the fruits of sanctification, righteousness, and peace. 'Laodicea too, partook of the benefits of his instructions, and by his exhortations and prayers many souls were inflamed with love to the crucified Saviour. But at last Laodicea sunk into a cool indifference. The beloved disciple of Jesus then sent from Patmos the sentence of the Judge, which was mingled with mercy and with grace. On her repentance he promised that she should still be clothed in white garments, and still receive the victoy's crown.

Persis was one of those favourites of heaven whom God, through tribulation, leads to eternal rest. Resigned amidst her sufferings, she mingled her tears of affliction with those of gratitude and joy, when in silent prayer she poured out her soul to her Maker and Friend.

Not from a love of fame, the partial, the lukewarm rewarder of Virtue, often her cruel persecutor, and malevolent slanderer, was Apelles actuated; nor from a fondness for the esteem of the wise, who

however sagacious, know not the secret springs
action ; for the act alone is visible to the bodi
eye, the intention only to the mind of the age
His love of the Omniscient, whose piercing vie
penetrates the secret purposes of the soul, with tl
exalted rewards promised to the pure in heart, we
the animating motives that excited him to practi
the most exalted virtues.

The merit of Flavius Ciemens arose not fro
his divesting himself of the lustre derived from b
affinity to Cæsar. It was easy to despise the tyran
but the courtiers accused him of being immerse
in indolence unbecoming a Roman ; of being de
to business, honour, and his country. His nob
soul, though not insensible to the sting of the
reproaches, still persevered in his adherence to tl
duties of christianity, duties which be esteemed tl
most exalted and sublime. Thus he became wo
thy of the martyr's crown. Fain would he hav
performed nearer the throne those actions whic
instructed and animated the saints ; but knowin
that his generous labours for the good of mankin
would there be lost on servile flatterers, and the
luxurious lord, he confined himself within
more contracted sphere, and enjoyed the oppo
tunity of doing good, and improving his immort
soul.

Lucius, though wrapped in the entangling n
of business, with a mind free and undisturbe
discharged his duty with unwearied zeal ; neithe
proud of his merit, nor discouraged when th
seed he sowed seemed not to shoot. Sedulous in re
deeming time, he knew how to banish the world ; t
spare some sacred hours for prayer and meditation
some happy hours for the gentle offices of meek
eyed mercy and of smiling charity ; and throug
this pleasing course entered into life eternal.

Ye females emulate the virtues of Tryphena. Ye also live among unbelievers. Her tender heart felt the purest, the noblest, the most virtuous passion. The youth was beautiful, and adorned with every amiable quality; but he sacrificed to idols, and was inflexibly attached to their worship. Tryphena apprehended danger from his easy-flowing eloquence, and still more from the soft passion that swelled her heart: she therefore struggled and triumphed over it. Serenity and joy were the rewards of her pious resolution, not to hazard a soul destined for immortality.

Linus, who before his martyrdom, bravely disdained to accept of proffered life, purchased by apostacy, was superior to the frivolous enjoyments which too often ensnare even the good. When alone, he employed himself in searching his own heart; and when in company with his friends, who had pure and noble sentiments, he loved to compare their actions with the examples and precepts of the words of God, the original source of sublime thoughts and heavenly sentiments. He loved to disperse the gloom that hovers over the grave, and to lose himself in the bright ecstatic prospect of a resurrection to eternal glory.

Ignatius loaded with chains and condemned to suffer death, by the order of Trajan, who on this occasion forgot his natural humanity, triumphed in bearing ignominy for his beloved Lord. No meaner reproach could be brought against this great, this exalted saint, than his too earnestly striving for the honours that encircle the martyr's brow. The eagerness of the sons of vice and folly in pursuit of pleasure, could only exceed the ardour with which he longed to obtain the radiant crown; if there can be excess in aspiring after such a prize. His setting glories shone with the same

mild influence, as that with which they rose. I
valuable is the conclusion of the life of
Christian ! How beautiful to his companion
the victory, appears the sweat of the conque
when he has obtained his prize, and the g
reward is ready ! He strengthened, he anim.
with the prospect of eternal felicity, the bretl
who flocked once more to see him, and to rec
his last blessing. Those whom his eyes, swimm:
in the kindly drops of joy, could not behold, by
letters he exhorted, comforted, and inflamed v
love to the divine Redeemer, till being cru
dragged to the amphitheatre, he was there,
wild beasts, torn in pieces.

The parents of the young and amiable Clau
were heathens ; heathens were her brothers
sisters. Her father was a man of probity ; a
tionate was her mother ; her brothers and sis
were worthy of esteem. Claudia loved them,
shared their love. Yet she alone became
Christian. She then. lamented their error,
boldly persevering, in spite of opposition, die
the faith of her Lord.

Far from the busy world lived Amplias, w
to a deep knowledge of human frailty, united
ardent and steady desire to fulfil the great,
astonishing command, Be ye perfect, even as y
heavenly Father is perfect. From the radi
seat of heaven streamed this injunction, like
divine light on the inhabitants of the dust.
looked, he never turned from the narrow g
through which it beamed ; but with vigor
perseverance, falling and rising, climbed the rugt
steep.

Phlegon had travelled over the bright cir
of Grecian literature, and great were his cart
possessions ; yet that did not inflate him w

vanity, nor these sink him into voluptuousness.
Wherever he directed his steps, silent flowed
the balm of humanity. He clothed the naked ;
he gave health to the sick : he lavished blessings
still more precious, these were salutary counsels
to the diseases of the mind, diseases worse than
those of the body. He dispensed healing comfort
to the soul entangled in the web of doubts, and
many wavering Christians, who were ready to
forsake the bleeding Friend of the human race,
he brought back into the path to heaven. From
real humility, he seemed a stranger to worldly
wisdom, and to know nothing but Jesus—Jesus
the Redeemer from sin, the surest support in life

doubts and scruples, his profound knowledge flowed
like an inexhaustible spring, and the thirsty travel-
ler was refreshed with copious draughts.

Tryphosa, kind by nature, and still more kind
from duty, was the best of mothers. She carefully
instructed her offspring in the knowledge of Christ.
Indefatigable in the resources of prudence and
virtue she finished the work she was appointed to
perform ; and was an ornament to the church :
yet her many good actions were concealed. But
scarce had she brought forth her last son, when
she expired weeping. She bewailed him, and
died. Then the blessing of the Eternal descended
on her family. Her elder sons educated the infant ;
who, at length, died a martyr. The seraphs re-
ceived the happy spirit from the arms of death :

she welcomed her son on his arrival at the regions
of unutterable felicity.

To forbear revenge, when revenge is justice, is
great : to love the offender, is noble : to alleviate
his distresses by private offices of kindness, is divine.

·Thus didst thou—with reverence write thy name—
·thus didst thou, E$_{ras_{tus}}$! When thine exalted
soul entered the celestial abodes, angels, rising from
·their golden seats congratulated thee and hailed
thine arrival with songs of triumph.

These were the souls which their guardian an-
gels led from the cross of the dying Jesus, into a
life of probation. With expanded wings they
descended from mount Olivet, and came to Geth-
semane. At the garden where the Son of the Eter-
nal suffered his agony, they were seized with awe.
Those who stood under the palms saluted them
with cordial love: These were Simeon, and the
great prophet, who had the honour to baptize the
divine Jesus, and to see the Holy Spirit hovering
over him like a dove, while the voice of the Most
High, descending from heaven, pronounced, This
is my beloved Son in whom I am well pleased.
Here were also Esaiah, the great prophet of the
crucified Jesus, and Ezekiel, who beheld a type of
the resurrection; when crying, Hear, ye dry bones;
the bones shook, and the dead awoke. Here too
were Noah, who found grace in the eyes of the
Lord ; righteous Lot ; Melchisedek, a prophet,
priest, and king ; Joseph and Benjamin his brother ;
David and Jonathan; fair Miriam, the sister of Mo-
ses, and Deborah, who sang the mercies of God, her
saviour, and the saviour of the host of Israel.

Simeon now cried, Blessed souls ! go and enter
your frail habitations of clay. May ye bring ma-
ny to salvation ! May ye diffuse benevolence and
love through all the descendants of Adam : benevo-
lence purer and more sublime than the philosophers
ever taught. Ah John, how happy is their fate !
How exalted will be their reward ! Does not this
sight brighten the gloomy ideas that stream from the
hill of Golgotha ?

The harbinger of the Lord returned, Had I words to express my thoughts, could floods of mournful or joyous tears reveal what I feel, then, O Simeon, would I tell what I have felt, since the gracious Messiah has been dying on the cross. But silence best becomes me.

Thy words, returned Simeon, pierce through my soul. I was exulting in the end of his sufferings, and the glories that await him on the right hand of the Majesty on High. But how hast thou brought me back! Ah! he whom, weeping, I embraced—he whom, speechless, I held in my arms, till God restoring my voice, I burst into prayers and thanksgivings—he—he bleeds—he bleeds on the cross!—with malefactors bleeds!—While his heart still glows with love to man—with love to his murderers—he bleeds—he dies! But I will hold my peace till all be accomplished.

Then Deborah and Miriam, after a long and mournfull silence, burst into plaintive songs, flowing with melting softness. For the voices of the immortals rise in spontaneous harmony to express such sensations as those of Deborah and Miriam. Hence she who, on Ephraim's mount, gave her name to the spreading palm, and Amram's daughter, thus in alternate verses sang.

O thou, once the most lovely of human beings! thou who wast the fairest of the sons of men! how are thy features changed by the livid traces of death!

, My heart is plunged in softest sorrow, and clouds of grief surround me ; yet still to me he appears the most beautiful of men : of all the creation the most lovely : fairer than the sons of light, when glowing with fervor, they adore the Eternal.

Mourn ye Cedars of Lebanon, which to the

T 2

weary afford a refreshing shade : the sighing
cedar is cut down : of the cedar is formed his
cross.

Mourn ye flowers of the vale, which grow on
the banks of the silver stream ; ye must not encircle
the Saviour's head : it is already crowned with
piercing thorns.

Unwearied he lift up his hands to his Father
in behalf of sinners. His feet, unwearied, vi-
sited the dwellings of affliction. Now are they
pierced. His hands and feet are pierced with
cruel wounds.

His divine brow, he on that mount, bows to the
dust : from it runs mingled blood and sweat. Alas !
how is it now wounded by cruel thorns !—by his
bloody crown !

The soul of his mother is wounded as with
a sword. Ah thou Son most gracious and
divine ! have compassion on thy mother, and
comfort her, lest at the foot of thy cross, she
die !

Ah, were I his mother, and already in the life
of bliss, a sword would still pierce through my
soul.

O Miriam ! his compassion-beaming eyes are
almost extinguished, and hard he draws his breath,
which still breathes nought but love. Soon,
ah soon will his last looks be directed towards the
heavens.

O Deborah ! a mortal paleness sits on his
faded cheeks, wet with the trickling drops of
love. Soon will his divine head sink, to rise no
more.

Thou, who shinest above, O celestial Jerusalem !
burst into tears of joy. Soon will the hour of
affliction be past.

Thou, who sinnest below, O terrestrial Jerusalem !

burst into tears of grief; for soon, at thy barbarous hands, will the Sovereign Judge require his blood.

The stars in their courses stand still, and the Creation is struck dumb at the sufferings of her Creator!—At the sufferings of Jesus! the everlasting High Priest! the Redeemer! the Prince of Peace!

The earth also stands still, and from you who dwell on its surface, the sun has withdrawn his light. For this is Jesus! the everlasting High Priest! the Redeemer! the Prince of Peace! Hallelujah.

Thus responsive sang Deborah and Miriam. The blessed Saviour now visibly approaching the moment of death, most of the faithful withdrew, unable to bear the awful sight. With fixed eye and unsteady step, Lebbeus retired, followed at a distance by Lazarus, who was involved in more composed distress. Lebbeus entering a ruinous sepulchre near the foot of the mount of Olives, and leaning on a piece of the fallen rock, sunk down upon his knees, and rested his head on the craggy stone. When Lazarus stopping at the entrance, with gentle voice, that would attract the ear of languishing sorrow, and make her stoop to listen, thus spake:

Sink not, my friend, beneath thy grief. Lift up thy face from the damp, the silent tomb, and let me see thee look at me. Ah dost thou no longer know the voice of him whom thou hast always loved?—of him who has returned thy love?—I am Lazarus, whose death cost thee so many tears, whom Jesus restored to life. Oh with what transports of joy, that seemed too big for utterance, didst thou then, with faultering voice, thank our divine Master! Before we returned him our, grateful thanks, this body lay in the grave, and corruption began to seize upon it. How often have we discoursed on that event!—Thou like the other disciples, thoughtest that his kingdom was to be on earth, ere it began in heaven; yet never couldst thou solve the doubts that kept me from seeking some earthly meaning in the sublime discourses of our Lord. But shake off, O my friend! this depressing grief. Open to me thine afflicted heart. Thou shalt lament him—thou shalt lament the divine Saviour, who lingering in acutest pain, has during successive hours been dying on the cross. Yet sink not under thy grief. He can, if he pleases, descend from the fatal tree. But though he die, he will never see corruption. Can he who was before Abraham, who descended from heaven to raise mankind to the mansions of bliss— can he be subject to corruption?

Lebbeus still leaned on the rock, yet turning his face towards Lazarus, with fixed eyes looked up to his friend, who running to him, embraced him; brought him out of that sepulchre, and seizing his hand, cried, Raise thine eyes, O Lebbeus, and behold. I perceive the presence of God in this scene of gloomy horror. With what solemnity it is distinguished by the Almighty! How has he clothed the heavens and earth with his terrors! May not God, by the death of the Holy One of Israel, be accomplishing those things we did not understand? Since the divine Saviour has been bleeding, I have felt—(how shall I express my thoughts in just and worthy terms)—I have felt sensations soothing and peaceful, that have softened my affliction. Every thing round me appears sacred. Wherever I turn, I find the traces of the Eternal, the marks of his omnipresence. This sacred tranquillity is filled with divine sensations. Since the gracious Sufferer has been bleeding on the cross, I have heard a soft breezy fluttering, as if bands of the immortals were hovering near me. The same I heard when my soul had quitted its frail habitation. Celestial beings also frequently glance before my eyes with rapid flight. This, my dear friend, diffuses through my soul a divine calm, the peace of God, and dawning felicity.

Here Lazarus paused, when Lebbeus, fixing his looks upon him, suddenly called out, Thou art struck with amazement !—Ah, who is it ? On whom dost thou gaze with such joyful transport ?

Lazarus, on recovering his speech, answered, Just now a celestial spirit shot over me.—Never before have I had such a view of the glory of an immortal !—of the bliss of the other world ! He has perhaps brought from heaven some divine message : for his flight was swift as the quickest thought. Having thus with faultering rapture spoke, he embraced Lebbeus, and then added, He will not—No, he at whose birth the host of heaven rejoiced will not see corruption !

It was Uriel whose lustre had struck the eyes of Lazarus. The immortal had left the sun, to fly to the progenitors of the human race. I must inform you, said he, with his face glowing with the rapidity of his flight, that the chief angel of death descends from heaven, with course direct towards the earth. The flames of the Lord blaze before him ; the flutter of his wings has the sound of the roaring storm, and etherial silence flies at his approach. Was his flaming sword to touch a world, the enkindled dust would instantly be dispersed through the immensity of space. Dreadful is his look— more dreadful than when on the guilty earth he poured the overwhelming deluge, and as the minister of the general destruction, emptied the oceans, of the celestial waters. Soon will ye see him, and at the sight terror shall come upon you, as it did upon me. Deep inexpressible sorrow is impressed on his awful countenance. Ah he is sent to bring death to the Mediator ! and to denounce the judgments of the Almighty on you guilty city ! Uriel then trembling, turned aside, and mingled with the angels.

Amazement, mute and motionless, seized the souls of the patriarchs, followed by a dejection too deep for words to express. Struck with the thought that Christ, the Son of God, was in a few moments to expire, the souls for whom he was dying, though redeemed from sin, seemed to sink back into their former earthly life, and to feel sensations of guil t, which remembrance clothed in all its dread array.

Enoch leaned with his left hand on a tomb, and raised his right towards heaven. Though he had walked with God ; though he had not fallen by the hand of Death, or had ever mouldered in the grave, yet in the eye of infinite Wisdom, and spotless Purity, he was not free from sin ; but by his faith and repentance he pleased God, and was translated. Had the earth been dissolved, and the great lamp of heaven extinguished, he would have remained undismayed : but at the near approach of the Saviour's death, grief streamed through his inmost powers ; and the angels, the patriarchs, the unborn souls, and every mortal vanished from his sight. Scarce could his eye discern him who shed his blood.

Near him Abel lay on a rock in silent prostration. This son of Adam was adorned with the sweetest innocence that mortal knows, with fervent piety, and gentle love, yet died by a murderous brother's haud. His eyes were now alternately lift up to

heaven, and cast on the cross, while he lamented
that the Saviour of the world, the Son of righ-
teousness should suffer a more cruel death than
he.

Seth, the worthy brother of the first dead, and
an early preacher of righteousness, had often,
through the many centuries of his long life, medita-
ted on the promised Seed, who should bruise the
serpent's head ; but had been able to form no
idea of the dreadful sufferings of the mighty Victor.
Now, with trembling heart and flammering tongue,
he cried, O thou Judge of all !—thou Judge of
whatever was, and is, and is to come !—Then
pausing, cast his looks to· heaven, to· the cross,
to the redeemed, and to the sepulchres of the
dead.

Long had darkness covered the eyes of David :
Long had he trembled ; yet, since the coming of
Uriel, he stood looking up to him, who drew near
to the grave. At length, recovering his speech,
these broken sentences flowed from his lips : O
God ! my Saviour's God ! Why hast thou forsa-
ken him ? He pours forth his sighs before thee :
but thou delayest to help him. The basest of sin-
ners have laughed him to scorn—have derided his
confidence in thee. He is poured out like water :
his heart is melted within him : his tongue cleaveth
to the roof of his mouth, and soon wilt thou, O
Death, lay him in the dust. Wild beasts, and not
men, encompass him. They stand and look upon
him whom they have pierced—Ah, how they have
pierced his hands and his feet ! They have stretch-
ed him on the cross, and all his bones may be num-
bered ! O God most merciful and gracious, how
unsearchable are all thy ways ! Soon will he leave
his mortal frame—soon will be ascend on high,
triumph over the grave, and lead Captivity captive.

Then will his death be declared to the ends. of the earth, that all the generations of men may bow before him !

Job, made perfect by sufferings, the trials of his faith and virtue, had been encompassed by the terrors of the Omnipotent : but, unable longer to think of the crucified Saviour's death, he soared from the depths of affliction, crying, He will live ! —he will live ! He will rise the conqueror of death and hell ! Then shall my eyes see thee !— They shall see thee, my Lord ! my Redeemer : my Saviour ! in all thy glory !

Thus were the faithful affected by the expectation of the angel of death. But none felt the near approach of the Mediator's death with such lively grief as the first parents of the human race : who, when Uriel descended, were standing close to each other, with their eyes fastened on the Saviour, feeling through all their vital powers, some resemblance of the terror inspired by the angel who drove them out of Paradise. Thus, at the last day, the blessed, struck by the trumpets powerful clangor, the trembling earth teeming with resurrection, and their own sensations of returning life, will be lost in wonder and astonishment : but at length, friends enraptured will know their friends, and brothers their brothers, whom, while absorbed in amazement, they had not seen. So Eve, at length, took by the hand the father of men, and, with words scarce rising to sound, cried, Say, O Adam, shall we seek some deep, some humble abyss : and there prostrate ourselves, imploring the Almighty to alleviate the pains of his death ?

Adam, with a look of love, replied, O mother of the human race ! much too mean are we to intercede for him with his Almighty Father. Were Job, Noah, Daniel, and even Eloa, the most

exalted of the celestial spirits, with ardent fervor
to join with us, vain would be our supplications.
The dispensations of God are all conducted by
unerring wisdom—by infinite goodness. He does
not see fit to interpose, and therefore no comfort—
no consolation will the Saviour receive amidst his
anguish. Such are the decrees of the Almigh-
ty, whose ways are inscrutable. Ah ! I am fil-
led with a new idea, which perhaps flows from
God, follow me, and do what thou seest me per-
form.

Now with mournful flight they descended from
the mount of Olives to the hill of death, and stop-
ped at the sepulchre, where the gracious Saviour,
like his brethren of the dust, was to sleep. Before
the entrance of that house of death was rolled a
large and ponderous block of stone, on one side of
which stood the father, and on the other the mo-
ther of the human race. The idea of the near se-
pulchre of the crucified Jesus, pierced her soul,
like an arrow from the quiver of the Almighty, and
she sunk on the stone. Adam, raising his hands,
thrice uttered, in silence, the name of the redeemer;
while with an attentive look of mingled love and
grief, he viewed his face, now more pale than that
of death. Soon overcome with the sight, he sunk
in the dust, and placing his sorrowful brow on his
folded bands, fixed his eyes on the ground, from
which God had formed his mortal frame, and in
loud prayer raised his suppliant voice, while the
angels, and the exalted souls of his happy de-
scendants heard his impassioned orisons.

Lord God, merciful gracious ! and thou the vic-
tim of the sins of man ! our High priest, Prophet
and King ! hear from thy bloody altar the fervent
prayer we offer up to thee from thy gloomy sepul-
chre ! God has pardoned our crime, and has per-

mitted us for many ages, to behold thy divine fac
with rapturous joy! Our sin was pardoned c
account of that death thou art now suffering
Permit, O source of mercy! that on this solen
day, in which thou restorest to the vision of t
Father, all who resist not thy gracious purpose
on this day in which thou reconcilest all; blotte
out the sins of all; and savest man from etern
death: Permit, O divine Mediator! that on th
day when thou also offerest thyself.for me, I m
recollect my sin, with humble and bitter grief.
is not that I fear to be cited a second time befo
thy dread tribunal, I have seen the face of Go
and thou art now entered into the Holy of holie
However permit me thou Judge of the earth, wl
hast humbled thyself even to this death of the cros
once more to confess what I was, and to presume
recollect my forgiven crimes.

Here sacred melancholy and devout transpo
suppressed his utterance. Eve silent, with expre
sive countenance, had accompanied his prayer, ai
now added with audible voice: O thou who a
devoted to death! on this day of blood—on th
day, when, O my beloved Redeemer! thy mort
frame is to lie down in the grave, let Eve, the fir
of women, also mention her crime, with such gra
forgiven, and acknowledge it with tears of humili
and grateful love! Here Adam resumed, Y
'twas we began the fatal trespass; we proceede
we completed the dire offence. O deed of horro
slight was the prohibition—how easy to perform
We received it from God, the first, the best
beings! our Creator! who formed us of the dus
and gave us souls to know, and tongues to prai
his goodness: who, while we were blessed wi
innocence, filled our minds with inborn joy, a
sweet sensations: who rewarded our ardent praye

with pleasing rapture; every new resolution not
to. taste of the fair forbidden fruit, every act of
obedience before our wretched fall, with sublimest
delight: who continually reminded us of his pre-
sence and sovereign wisdom, by ten thousand living
creatures, whose admirable texture incessantly re-
warded speculation with new discoveries, and in-
creasing wonder; who gave to me, the mother of
mankind, and me to her: whose apparent glory
bestowed on us, raised us nearer to him, than all
the surrounding creation.—Yet presumptuous and
ungrateful we vainly strove, O thou Source of
Being! to seize thy power, thy glory, and to
become like thee divine.—But, gracious Father,
thou hast forgiven us. Thee let us for ever adore
with warmest gratitude and awful love. And O
thou divine Saviour of men, the Effluence of thy
Father's splendor! may these sufferings be re-
paid with glory, and honour, and affectionate
obedience! May all the wide creation hail
thy goodness, and all mankind proclaim thy grace!

Thus Adam gave vent to the strong sensations
of his mind, and with him our general mother:
he with loud voice, and she in silent thought.
Then the countenance of the divine Redeemer
beamed on them divine mercy, heavenly tranquillity,
and that peace of God which passeth knowledge.
Enraptured, they felt these effusions of the Media-
tor's love, and the first of men filled with ecstatic
ardor, stretching his arms towards the cross, thus
cried:

O my Saviour, and the Saviour of mankind, my
children! thy love exceeds all thought: nor can
words express my thanks; for " eternity itself is
too short to utter all thy praise." Here will I
stay till thou bowest thy head in death. But
amidst the pain thou sufferest for sinners hear my

supplications for my offspring—for all who shal
hereafter dwell on earth. In the imperfect dawn o
infant thought may they feel thy love and lisp th
praise! O guide their blooming years; cheris
the tender plants that they may early bring fortl
fruit! Irradiate those with transcendent virtue
and truth divine, who, in riper age, are to enlighte
the earth, and teach the ways of God to man
May the traveller never slumber in the coolin
shade, or on the brink of the refreshing stream
while he loses sight of the radiant crown whic
God holds out from afar; and captivated by gro
velling present joy, forgets the glorious future re
compence! And may all who cease to attend t
the soft voice of love and grace, be called by afflic
tion from the error of their ways. O my children
my children! how inexpressible is the condescen
sion and grace of him who dies on the cross for you
May your stony hearts be touched by his all co
quering love! With contrite souls may ye hea
the voice of the blood which now flows fron
Calvary in streams of mercy and of grace!—

But what bliss pours in upon me! what jo
pervades my inmost powers! while I contemplat
the glories that await the righteous dead! Fro
them the beatific vision is before death concealed
They soon enjoy it all— are ravished with ineffab
delight, and with triumphant joy behold the
Lord—their Saviour! Oh when thou after tl
final judgment, shalt free the earth from the cur
brought upon it by my sin, and shalt create
anew blooming like Eden, then, innumerable as tl
sands of the sea, as the drops of the morning de
glittering in the fields, and as the stars that shir
in the firmament, by the multitude of those who er
ter into thy glory!

Eloa now called with a voice that shook the s

lid base of Moria, and made the courts of the temple tremble, crying, He comes. He comes. The messenger of God then descended on Sinai. Solitary he stood, while to him the heavens and the earth seemed to dissolve and pass away.

The Eternal, who upholds all things by the word of his power, then preserved him from sinking, and from him terror withdrew her iron gripe: yet was he filled with amazement and dejection. His right hand sunk, while he, trembling, held his flaming sword, no longer shining in pale splendor, but glowing with fiery blaze, like the red lightning sent by the Almighty, as the messenger of destruction. Seized with reverence and awful love at a gracious look from the Redeemer, he approached nearer, and, alighting on mount Calvary, sunk prostrate. His voice of thunder now melted into softest accents, yet was heard by the angelic circle, while he thus addressed the dying Messiah. I, a finite being, am sent by the Soverign Judge, to fulfil his great command. O thou, the radiant Image of his grace! thou Saviour of men, who now diest that man may live for ever! strengthen me, a spirit of yesterday, united to a body formed of a midnight cloud and liquid flame. Awe and terror compass me around; yet must I execute the behests of thine Almighty Father.

He then returned to Sinai's lofty summit; where Jehovah again arrayed him in all his terrors. Dreadful he stood, pointing his sword down towards Golgotha. Behind him arose a storm, the vehicle of the immortals voice, which shook the palm groves, shook Jordan and Genesareth. Now the smoaking blood of the evening sacrifice streamed on the altar, and the immortal cried, Thou, O holy Saviour of men, who condemned by that cruel city, hast freely consented to suffer death for sinners, thine enemies, the work of mercy and of love accepted. The cry of thy blood is ascended to t Almighty, proclaiming grace to man : and in a f moments thou wilt become the prey of deal 'Thus spake the angel of death, and turned aw his face.

Meanwhile the holy, the all-gracious Savio raising his drooping eyes towards heaven, cri in a loud and pathetic voice, not like that of t dying, My God ! my God ! why hast thou fo saken me ?—The celestial spirits, filled with asl nishment, instantly veiled their faces. Now, the painful sensations of the holy, the divine Jesu were redoubled, and with parched tongue cried, I thirst. He thirsted, called, and dr then trembled, bled, and became still more pal Then again lifting up his benevolent eyes, he sai Father, into thy hands I commend my spirit ! al adding, It is finished, bowed his gracious he and died.

THE END OF THE TENTH BOOK.

THE

MESSIAH.

BOOK XI.

THE ARGUMENT.

The glory of the Messiah soars from Calvary to the Holy of Holies in the temple. The earth shakes, and the veil of the temple is rent. Gabriel tells the souls of the patriarchs that they must retire to their graves. The Messiah leaves the temple, and raises the bodies of the saints. The resurrection of Adam, Eve, Abel, Seth, Enos, Mehaleel, Jared, Kenan, Lamech, Methuselah, Noah, Japheth, Shem, Abraham, Isaac, Sarah, Rebecca, Jacob, Rachel, Lea, Benjamin, Joseph, Melchisedec, Azariah, Mishael, Hananiah, Habakkuk, Isaiah, Daniel, Jeremiah, Amos, and Job! The converted thief on the cross dies. The resurrection of Moses, David, Asa, Jehoshaphat, Uzziah, Jotham Josiah, Hezekiah, Jonathan, Gideon, Elisha, Deborah, Miriam, Ezekiel, Asnath, Jeptha's daughter, the mother and her seven martyred sons, Heman, Chalcol; Durda and Ethan, Anna, the prophetess, Benoni, Simeon, and John the Baptist.

IF in my religious flight I have not sunk too low ; but have poured sublime sensations into the hearts of the redeemed ; guided by the Almighty, I have been borne on eagles' wings ! O Religion ! I have learned from revelation a sense of thy diguity ! He who waits not, with devout awe, by the pure crystal stream that from the throne flows among the trees of life, may his applause, dispersed by the winds, not reach mine ear, or if undisper-

sed not pollute my heart ! Ah among the dust I
lain my song, had not yon living stream poured fr
the New Jerusalem, the city of God, and thit
turned back its course. Lead me still father, t
Guide invisible, and direct my trembling ste
The Son's humiliation already have I sung, and
me now rise to sing his glory. May I attempt
sing the Victor's triumph, the hills and vall
yielding forth their dead, and his exaltation to
heaven of heavens, the throne of the Eternal Fath
O ˙thou to heaven raised, hear me and hel
O help me to support the terrors of thy glory !

The eternal Redeemer, now cast his eyes on
bodies of the reconciled dead : then looked
to the Father ; but what creature can ever f
the divine transport, the delight, the love, w
which they viewed each other. Then flew ni
from the eternal throne ; and from the sun fl
the covering star. The poles of every terrestr
globe trembled, and hasted to pursue the cou
marked out by God. In haste the sun revolv
and the earth followed till they again entered t
track of their first orbit. Christ, the Redee
of the world, hovers over the cross, looking do
on his pale, bloody and pendant corpse, T
conqueror of death turns, the earth trembles ;
moves to the temple, the rocks burst, and falli
spread noise and dust through the wide expan
Instantly the sacred rays of his glory fill the H
of holies, and the mystery-concealing veil is fr
its lofty height, to its lowest border rent. H
Jesus conferred with the Father, God with G
on the complete accomplishment of the great rede
tion. But of their thoughts the soul has no id
language no words. The subject only, th
sacred muse of Sion, canst unfold. Behold h
night brightens into eternal day ! Salvation sh

be revealed to the nations, the forsaken temple shall perish, and the favorite people of the Most High be dispersed among the nations. The issue of things passed before the eyes of the Father and the Son. Religion, through a course of ages spreading among innumerable nations, and often obscured by the crimes and follies of man, becomes involved in the clouds of night, but is never totally extinguished. The resurrection of the redeemed from spiritual death, the conflicts of the church militant, her victories, and the distant antipast of heaven.

While the Father and the Son thus conferred, a voice like the noise of many waters rolled through the listening heavens, saying, By the Eternal Father, and by him who will rise from the dead, and seat himself at the Father's right hand, ye who are now mortals shall enjoy salvation! Bliss and rapture through a joyful eternity shall be yours. The Eternal High Priest has redeemed you from sin. On the altar of his death is suspended his sacred form, who has completed the sacrifice for sin, and soon will ye see the Conqueror surrounded with the effulgence of the godhead on the throne of the Eternal, covered with radiant wounds. Thus through the heavens resounded Eloa's voice. From the earth, with joyful tremor, rose the voice of the first offender, saying, the Promise of God, Christ Jesus the Faithful, the Long-suffering, the Abundant in mercy, full of Loving-kindness; has died for sinful man! O thou Shoot of Adam's stem, blossom, and rise to eternal life! Rejoice O heavens, and be glad O earth! the All-gracious has given his only begotten Son for you! Triumph, O my sons, in your Redeemer's love, his sufferings are ended, and a better, a more glorious life, awaits you above.

Jesus was still in the sanctuary. To no angel, to no patriarch had he yet revealed himself; but as he soared from gloomy Golgotha to the temple, the rustling ear and trembling earth to them announced his presence: they saw not his glory, and still adored from the heights of Moriah. The idea of the Mediator's death filled the souls of the patriarchs, and no angelic being felt their sensations. Joy mixed with the tender thoughts of thy death, heaven's most delightful solace, O thou divine Redeemer! overflowed their souls. Soft repose, the peace of God, and the love of Jesus illumined all their thoughts, and inflamed every sensation.

While the souls of the saints absorbed in these exquisite raptures, their effulgent lustre gradually returned, and the celestial love they felt for each other raised them still higher to the beatitude of loving the Redeemer! they had all one soul, which in all was the temple of their Saviour.

Gabriel, now hasting from the mount of death, appeared amongst them: His speech was at first obstructed by his joy at beholding the eternally redeemed, and their voices were to him as sweet and melodious as the sound of the celestial harps. Brethren! immortals! he at length cried; Scarce can I presume to call ye brethren; for your father is the father of Christ! I brought ye from the sun to this earth. Another command I have received, Repair ye redeemed to your graves.

The heavenly bands now dispersed, each hasting to his tomb. By the altar near which the earth had imbibed Abel's blood, was still remaining a mossy rock, in which were interred Adam and many of his descendants. There the father of men with the devout of his race assembled. On approaching their sepulchres each saw the blessed spirit who, while he was on earth had been his guardian angel, hovering round the ruins of his mouldered tomb: but on the nearer approach of these holy souls, they upwards took their triumphant flight, while the souls of the dead were at a loss to conceive the cause of their thus soaring with hymns of triumph.

Enoch and Elijah still remained on the hill of death, looking with amazement at the saints who were descending to the receptacles of their mortal frames.

Noah with Japheth and Shem, ascended to their graves on that mount where rested the ark, which, preserved by divine mercy, triumphed over all the rage of the deluge.

Abraham, with his beloved, retired to his sepulchre, near which he saw the heavenly traveller, in human form, whom, while unknown, he entertained in the friendly shade.

Moses repaired to his solitary grave on Nebo's lofty summit, where God himself made the rock his tomb. He died in the immediate presence of the Almighty; who, before he closed his eyes, gave him a view of Canaan's then fertile land. The rocks at the presence of the Omnipotent, rent under the lifeless body; it sunk down: the trembling rock closed, and thus he lay interred by the hand of God.

Nearer to Golgotha came to their graves those disciples of Moses who, armed with the thunder of eloquence, and psalms prophetic of future salvation, rescued Abraham's race from idolatry's iron chains.

Horror encompassed the fields of the sacred graves, and affrighted back every mortal foot that presumed to approach; but the angels, as if only destined to converse with spirits of the saints, returned from the clouds. Adam had entered

his grave, with his beloved, and addressing her,
thus gave vent to his amazement.   Thou, I saw
didst observe the devout awe, which I felt at the
divine command, but now, O Eve, rejoice with
me, that we are esteemed worthy, while the sacred
body of the Lord of Life sleeps in death, to be
with him, humbled in the grave.   How transport-
ing the thought of being humbled with the Eternal
Son of the Father!   Let me also exult that in the
day of judgment, he will descend to Eden, and I
shall here awake, and ye, my children with me!
Here from death we shall awake! all that now
sleep in the silent grave, for all eternity shall awake!
All my numberless devout children shall receive
bodies that are glorified—spiritualized !   O the
unutterable beatitude which the great Jehovah
has graciously allotted for us !   How hast thou,
O death of the Redeemer exalted us ! what bliss
has it procured ! ' Thou Enoch, and thou Elijab,
see how worthy a resurrection from death is of the
longing desires of an immortal.   Delay not then,
thou last of days, that for this bliss we may long
no more !—Yet, rather delay, that multitudes may
be added to the multitudes that shall then rise from
the grave to eternal life ! · Thus spake Adam, in
blissful raptures, while his listening associate also
dwelt on the gladdening thought of their joint
humiliation with the gracious Redeemer, and on the
earth's final day.

Now from the foot of the mount to the temple's
lofty pinnacles, Moriah trembled.   Clouds issuing
from the sanctuary, rolled through the court of the
temple, then rose towards heaven.   Wherever the
awful clouds turned, the earth shook, the rocks
rent, and the rivers swelled.   The clouds becoming
resplendent spread over the graves, and a loud
wind rushed from under the tombs ; but the power

of the Eternal Son was not in the storm : the earth around the graves shook ; but the omnipotence of the Redeemer was not in the trembling earth : flashes issued from the clouds ; but the Lord was not in the flashes : then from the heavens descended a soft and gentle breeze, and in this gentle breeze was the omnipotence of the Son. Behold at his command, sweet insensibility came like slumber in the cooling shade. The patriarchs knew not what was to happen ; but their sensations though dimmed, perceived the present Deity in the ambient breeze. Meanwhile, transported with fraternal joy, the angels looked down viewing the fields of the resurrection.

Adam now cried, I shall be again created ! created anew ! and strove to rise, yet still he kneeled in the dust, while the cherubim and seraphim, striking their harps, thus sang, Be thou anew and for ever created. Behold on the darkest of thy days thou diedst. Oh hail the first ! awake and live a life, O Adam, more sweet than that thou enjoyedst at thy first creation ! and now no more to die ! Adam with dimmed sight, still kneeled in the dust. The ethereal form in which since his death, his never-dying soul had been clothed, became mixed with his risen glorified body, and swiftly rising, he stood erect, with his arms stretched towards heaven, crying, O joy unutterable ! thou hast called me out of the dust, and I know of a truth, that thou, O my Redeemer ! hast created me more glorious than in Eden ! O that I could find thee, my Redeemer ! that I could find the Almighty ! How would I prostrate myself before him, and pour out my adorations ! But thou art ever near, though unseen ! This celestial murmur is the voice of thy presence ! Even those around me now awake ! Look down, ye angels, and see around the father of men, his holy children rise.

Eve now arose, and looking round, cried, Where have I been? 'Where am I? Am I in Eden? I again dwell in my original mansion, once dissolved! There, O there is Adam! how effulgent!—How effulgent I! O thou whose wounds I have seen! where art thou, O thou Restorer of Innocence, that I may pour out my praises before thee? Adam hasted to her and she to him. In transport they embraced, joy stopped their voice, and they could only stammer forth the name of him who had raised them from the dead.

Abel! my son Abel! cried Adam; for Abel hovered there like the vernal morn, clothed in radiant purple. O my son, added he, with what grace and glory has the Redeemer blessed us! These bodies were earthy when we laid them down in our kindred dust; but what are they now?

Above all that we could think or ask, said Abel; O father, has he done for us, who has put away our sins, and the sins of the world! O celestial repose! all shall like us, at the last day, awake!

Enos found himself by Seth, Mehaleel, Jared, Cainan and Noah's father, and with them was Methuselah. He found them encompassed with glory, on their trembling graves, filled with new life, in celestial bodies, more fit companions of their immortal souls. These shining frames seemed almost endued with thought, and full of the presence of God. As after the creation the morning stars sang together, so the sons of Adam hovered, uttering effusions of grateful praise and joy, and the field of the resurrection resounded with the transports of the reviving dead.

Noah, the second father of mankind, felt his new creation, and was awaked in the soft breeze of the evening twilight. A rosy cloud flowed from the shoulders of the immortal, as he rose. Ye angels, he cried, O tell me, has a body like that of Adam in Paradise been formed for me? Ah, where are we? Say, where is he who has thus created me? that I may prostrate myself with you, and join your adorations? Then seeing Japheth and Shem rise from their graves, he added, O my sons! where is he who has raised our bodies from the dead, that we may haste to prostrate ourselves before him, and pour forth our devout thanksgivings? Tell me, ye other sons of the resurrection, where, O where is he who has filled you with celestial fire, that we may kneel, and with our feeble lips pour forth our imperfect praise.

As the pious man who in all things seeks and finds God his Creator, on beholding through the breathing grove, the sun rising in his beauty, is filled with soft rapture, from its being a testimony of the glory of God ; so Abraham's guardian angel beheld the father of the faithful arise from his tomb, blessed, glorified, and immortal. Abraham laying his hand on his mouth, and looking towards heaven, wrapped in astonishment and self consideration at length thus gave vent to his amazement :. Am I again created ? How wonderful, how gracious, O my Saviour, are the consequences of thy death ! This new life to which thou hast raised us from dust, O blessed Redeemer ! flows from thy sufferings. This incorruptible body, the nobler consort of my soul, thou hast given me before the dissolution of nature. Oh who am I ? who am I ? that thou conferrest on me such felicity ! Thus he exclaimed and wept, filled with gratitude and joy.

Isaac came. Him Abraham thought a young
seraph adorned with etherial radiance, and those
smiling blushes of the morning that cover the bright
inhabitants of heaven, and cried, Didst thou see
me, O resplendent angel! raised from the dead,
and at the divine command, my consumed bones re-
vive?

O Abraham, my father! he returned, once didst
thou believe, that had I been consumed by the al-
tar, my ashes would revive, and I should again
be restored to life. My body, O best of fathers!
is now restored. How amazing is the Redeemer's
goodness! His sacred body is still suspended on
the cross, yet ours rise, and we enjoy these raptures.
I sunk as in sleep, a celestial breeze blowed around
me, and I found myself wrapped in a resplendant
cloud.

Enraptured came Sarah and Bethuel's daughter
to their beloved. With eyes lift up to them, and
then to heaven, stood the father and the son.
Long stood they speechless, while their souls
glowed with everlasting gratitude and, triumphant
praise.

Israel came exulting, and while his full soul
poured forth grateful tears from his now immortal
eyes, he cried, Hallelujah to the Mediator, the
Conqueror of Death! Oh thou hast bled—thou
hast completed our redemption—thou hast called us
out of the valley of death!

Meanwhile the seraphs were not silent: their
hymns accompanying the joyful acclamations o
the righteous patriarchs: Praise and glory, sai
they, be to him that revives the dead, to the divin
Giver of this eternal life, which now blossoms fro
the tombs. Rejoice O heaven! at thy future inha
bitants!

Israel now turning his eyes from them to Golgo

tha cried, I will join my thanksgivings with those of all the celestial choirs, when thou shalt soar from thy tomb ; when the beloved shall see thee their Redeemer on the throne of glory, in the lustre that was thine ere the earth was formed. Are you, ye angels, like me? Ye are not. You have not, like me, died, believing in him. You have not felt the joys of the resurrection. The Redeemer laid down his life for man ; and, like man, will revive. Ye blessed spirits join with us in adoring him ; but we will love him more !

, He then casting his eyes from heaven to the earth saw his beloved Joseph. An angel was at the tomb of Rachel, standing aloft on the pendant rock. She looked up to him with cordial affection, while he smiling looked down on her, with a countenance of the sweetest friendship. My tomb, O seraph, said she, is solitary—Rachel, he answered, the sepulchre in which the divine Redeemer will soon be laid is also solitary—Alas ! she returned, how has he suffered, whose earthly form a tomb in Golgotha will soon inclose ! Oh what has his condescension and death obtained for us ! The time will come when my body shall awake from sleep, when my bones, long mouldered in the dust, shall rise. Even for me has the Saviour obtained a resurrection.

While she was yet speaking a vapour arose round her feet in the tomb, fine as the breath of the rose, or of the vernal leaf dropping silver. Rachel's radiance tinges the rising vapour with gold, as the sun gilds the skirts of an evening cloud, while her eye follows the undulating vapour which in various forms waves around her, rising, falling, and drawing still nearer and more lucid. She admires the deep wisdom shewn in the ever-varying creation, equally unfathomable in what is great and what is small, without knowing the near affinity between her and the bright curling cloud, or to what thing almighty voice, O thou Redeémer ! would soon reduce it. She then leaning in the midst of the radiant dust stood musing with joyful look.

With folded hands stood her angel, viewing what passed with transport too exquisite for speech. Now was heard the omnipotent voice, and Rachel sinking down, seemed to herself as if dissolving in tears of joy, in some shady vale by a fountain side ; then appeared as if lightly rising to a flowery plain refreshed by a gentle breeze, and then as if new created amidst the fragrance-breathing flowers. Awaking from her short trance, she suddenly rises, she feels, she sees, she knows that she has a new immortal body. Enraptured she raises her eyes to heaven, and thanks him who called her forth from death. O Jesus, my brother, my Lord, and my Saviour, she cries, ever shall thy name be first on my lips, then yours Israel, Joseph, Benjamin !—My Lord and my God ! Where am I ? Lead me, O seraph lead me, that I may see the Adorable, that I may see Israel and my children. My soul pants after them ; with them will I rejoice in the glories of the resurrection.

Israel beheld her, and also Leah, with her son, who came from the banks of the Nile. Benjamin was likewise there ; but Joseph was still absent. The heavenly Joseph still hovered over his sepulchre at Sichem. Samid, one of the children whom the Mediator had kissed and blessed, was with him ; he was lately dead, and just knew himself to be an heir of eternal Life. His guardian angel had conducted him to Haman's pastures, where he perceived Joseph hovering over his grave, and thus addressed the angel, Who, my heavenly guide, is that

radiant form with looks so sweet and mild, and yet
so full of dignity?

Joseph with a smile of benignity and tempered
effulgence, thus began an endearing conversation
Thou flower that now wilt grow in the shade of the
tree of life, and near the crystal stream that flows
from the throne, know that I was once, like thee,
a happy child, till injuries involved me in miseries
that were succeeded by great prosperity, and I
became the father of nations. Knowest thou,
happy child, the son of Israel and Rachel?

O thou immortal, the son of Jacob and Rachel!
oft have I wept with joy while I have heard my fa-
ther tell me the wonderful story of Joseph. Yet
allay thy splendor, O Joseph! allay thy lustre,
then will I venture to talk with thee. The joy of
seeing thee is worth all the pangs of death, and I
would again bear those painful struggles, from
which I am but just delivered, to see and converse
with thee. I seemed awhile ago to sink into no-
thing; but from this dream of endless night, my
angel awaked me, by telling me I lived, and should
live for ever.

O early blessed soul, how little hast thou suffered
of the calamities of life! What a recompence hast
thou received, in being so soon a companion of the
heirs of bliss, and of those that stand higher than I
in the steps of salvation.

O Joseph! O son of Israel! scarce can I bear
the radiance thou hast so sweetly softened.

Soon wilt thou learn, O Samed, soon wilt thou
see Abraham! The blessed disencumbered from their
house of clay soon learn.

Gladly will I learn, O teach me, thou son of Is-
rael. Even the earthly life I have just left is not
without some heavenly intervals. How was it with

thee, in that delightful moment when no longer abl
to conceal thine affection, thou calledst out, s
loud that the distant Egyptians heard thee,
am Joseph! is my father still living? The
thy brothers—then the eyes of thy younger brothe
Benjamin gazed upon thee, and thou saidst, Mak
known to my father all the glory I enjoy in **Egypt**
and throwing thine affectionate arms about th
dear Benjamin's neck, thou shedst a flood of tears
and in thine embrace, Benjamin's tears expresse
his joy! Oh in that honr what didst thou feel
When thy father received the news, the heart o
the good old man strdggled with different thoughts
and he doubted the truth, till he heard thy word
aud saw the wagons of Pharaoh. Then his trou-
bled soul revived : It is enough, he cried, Joseph
my son, still lives! I will haste and see him befor
I die! When he came near, how didst thou run
to him, and long continue in his embraces! O let
me now die, said he, I have seen thy face, and thou
art yet alive! What O Joseph, didst thou feel in
those heavenly hours ?

Come thou, who art also Israel's son, and my bro-
ther, younger still than was my Benjamin, come and
embrace me.—Samed trembling embraced him, and
they long wept celestial tears. How it was with
me, Samed, thou thyself felt, when thou recalledst
to me the joyful history of those tears I shed on
earth. By this remembrance thou hast enhanced
the joys of heaven, and I shall offer the giver of
those blessings new thanks, and more ardent praise
than while confined to this earth.

I will also, O Joseph, learn of thee to offer up my
ardent thanksgivings. But why dost thou remain
at this tomb ?

Knowest thou, O immortal! that the divine Je-
sus is dead! He commanded us who were round

the cross, to repair to our graves. This is mine. We are to humble ourselves with the gracious, the deceased Messiah, and in silent thought, amidst the spoils of mortality, meditate on the redemption he has procured; for by his death and resurrection, we shall be freed from death, and at the last day our bodies will awake.

Here then will Joseph awake. O that my friends would bring here my remains, then should I awake near thee! Let us descend into the tomb, and see the vesture that once covered thine immortal spirit, the dust that will at length arise,

Come then Samed, said Joseph, taking him by the hand, and leading him to the darkest part of the tomb, where they found Joseph's angel, in whose countenance were blended expectation, joy, and solicitude.

I see, O seraph, that thou rejoicest that he will soon awake.

I rejoice at his exaltation, O Joseph! who will ever increase in glory, and who rewards the expectations with new and never-ceasing raptures. If thou hast been pleased with a field covered with the vivid products of the spring, and with the flowers continually rising under thy feet, amidst those with which thou hast been most delighted, one still sleeps in the gladsome field, which thou wilt expect with solicitous joy.

What new felicity, O seraph, dost thou mean? O thou immortal and still mortal, behold the favour that awaits thee!—The earth now spontaneously rose in clouds, and sunk on the side of the sepulchral rock; where Joseph's guardian angel hovered, remained a gentle waving dust, which rose and sunk in swift succession, the pregnant dust shining resplendent. Draw near and behold in the

earth said Joseph's angel, how gloriously the fu
sparks of light begin.

A soft murmur now rose in the cloud-filled grav
Samed's golden locks waved, and Israel's son, at tl
near approach of the radiant dust which on
formed his bones, returned the murmuring soun
Hastily proceeded the new creation. The ang
aud Samed saw what was done; but while it w
doing the dust changed, and Joseph, with his ris
body, stood before them, and lifting up his voic
said : O thou angel of the covenant, who in a flau
by night and in a cloud by day led the Israelit
from Egyptian bondage through the Red Sea to C
naan, while the tyrant perished, now perishes dea
a greater tyrant. But Israel is in the field
Ephron, and Rachel with him ; Abraham is al
there. Thus he spake, and darted with redoubl
radiance from the tomb, while the angel and Same
speechless through joy, followed his rapid fligl
Soon he passed by Mamre's sacred grove, and join
his father and brethren. Oh who is so skilled in t
sounds of the celestial harps, as to express the j
of this second meeting of the father and the so
in which the brothers knew the brother ? or tl
sweet sensations of the mother, at beholding h
first-born ? His dream reached even into the ete
nal life, and his brethren, now free from envy, bov
ed before his superior splendor, adoring the Giv
of more exalted favours.

A traveller had found Melchisedek, Salem
priest and king, lying on his face near the founta
of Phiala, and with respectful awe had buried hi
in the earth. Over his grave now hovered Me
chisedek. While the springs soft melodious mu
murs overflowed his soul with pleasing melod
and he seemed to hear the voice of the Almigh

jointly with the crystal stream that runs through
the heavenly Jerusalem, and passes by the tree of
life.   He sunk deep in the raptures of soft repose:
the heavens and the earth appeared to pass away;
but God and himself remained. At length he rais-
ed himself from the earth, but again sunk down
in silence, yet his eyes were filled with quivering
tears and with folded hands he invoked Jesus the
Mediator.

On a plain appeared, O sight terrific and execra-
ble, those who at the sound of the loud cornet, the
soft flute, the sweet sackbut, the melodious harp,
and the rattling cymbal, had fallen prostrate before
the shining image. In a rock on this plain the
devout Azariah, Mishael, and Hananiah had hewn
their tombs, and near the sepulchres of these
pious and heroic believers lay the vestiges of the
splendid image a mass of ruins. Once had that
king whom the Lord cast down from the palaces of
Babylon to feed among the beasts of the field,
erected it in height reaching to the clouds, as he had
seen it in his dream, and near it realms overthrown
lay in awful ruins. Mishael and Hananiah interred
Azariah rejoicing. Thee, Hananiah, the lonely
Mishael placed in his tomb, pleased with the
thought of his own approaching death. His eye
now seeks in their sepulchre the dust of the de-
ceased; yet there, though immortal, he sought in
vain. Then animated with the most joyful hopes,
he darted upwards, and poured forth the joy
of his soul, while the melody of his voice de-
scended to his beloved friends, and rose up to
heaven.

We shall at length, he sang, come forth from
these graves! How wide soever, O corruption!
thou scatterest our dust, whether it floats, O Ocean,
in thy roaring abyss, or it hovers, O Sun, in thy

x

rays ! The Omnipotent will assemble the du
once inhabited by immortal souls. Over it will l
stand, and order it to be informed with new lif
The Almighty took the dust of the ground, and t
the trembling earth said, Become thou the bod
of man. He spake, and it obeyed : thus he wi
take the dust of corruption, and again comman
it to form a body. Hallelujah ! Then will o
dust awake. The streams will roar, the stor
rise, the sea boil, the earth tremble, the heave
thunder, and night be involved in ten-fold darknes
but louder than the noise of all will the trump
sound to awake the dead !

He who saw thy steeds, O Chaldea, swift as th
leopard, or as the eagle in quest of prey : he wl
beheld thy horsemen assemble captives as the san
while they laughed at princes, and made a moc
of kings : their leader drunk with his own rag
which was as insatiable as the grave : He who sa
the avenger in the terrible glory with whic
he came from Paran, when before him walke
the pestilence, and burning coals went forth
his feet ; when he stood and measured the eartl
how far the destroying angel should pass : th
hills then sunk before him, the mountains wei
scattered, and the rivers hastily fled : the deel
sunk down, and the heights lifted up their hand
Ye sun and moon then stood still ; his arrows fle
glittering, and his spears as the blaze of lightnin
Habakkuk, who thus saw the great Helper
Judah, the Rewarder in his glory, now raised fro
the grave, touched his harp with the softest melod
while he sang, The fig-tree blossoms ! there
fruit in the vine ! the gladdening labour of th
olive fills the valleys ! the immortal seed shoo
up on high, an eternal harvest, ripening radia
in he smiling field ! Heaven, O Lord, is full of th

praise, the earth of thy glory!   Thou didst think
on us, O thou who art most merciful, when we
drank the cup of death, and had seen corruption :
therefore will I rejoice in thee my Deliverer,
and through eternity, joy in the God of my salva-
tion.

As when the whole expanse of the heavens is
shrouded in clouds, and the intent eye of encrea-
sing expectation is fixed upward, when the flame of
the Lord darts at once from the heavens, and storms
of thunder proclaim the glory of the Almighty,
thus Isaiah threw aside the night of death, shone
radiant over his grave, and poured forth his thanks
to his all-gracious Creator, who had raised him
from the dust.

Amidst the ruins of great Babylon, built by
Nebuchadnezzar in ostentation of his grandeur,
where the holy watchman with tremendous voice
denounced, Thy kindom is departed from thee, and
thy dwelling shall be among the beasts of the field:
among these solitary ruins lay the remains of Da-
niel, whom God had irradiated with his illumina-
tions, and who now sought his grave, calling to a
seraph to assist his search.   He hovered above,
amidst the cry of night birds, the hiss of serpents,
and the ruins of palaces, where the Arab had no
cottage, nor his slave a dwelling.   Instantly the an-
gel found the grave encompassed with water and
slime, and a mossy tomb-stone rose among the wa-
ving reeds.   The soul of Daniel here recollected
the fate of many who had long slept in death ; of him
whose front, like a lofty wide-spreading tree, rose
high towards heaven, an extensive shade to the
weary; but fell at the divine command, Hew it
down.   He learned wisdom from this chastisement;
but not so his son ; he, of more obdurate pride,
considered not that God has power over the nations

therefore was the hand seen near the golden branch, writing the sentence of death, Know, O king ! the years of thy power are numbered and accomplished : thou art weighed in the balance, and art found wanting : thy kingdom is divided and given to the Medes and Persians.—Then the proud mountain and its confederate hills sunk in the day of desolation. The resplendent form of the holy Daniel quick descended into his grave ; but soon arose, and as the morning star beams through the heavens, darted his rays on Babylon's solitary ruins.

, Hilkiah's gentle son had sowed in tears ; but now reaped elevated joy. He stood on his grave sensible of his new life, filled with rapturous thoughts of his complete and perfect immortality.

The herdsman of Tekoa, who among the cottages of simplicity, knew him who placed Arcturus and Orion high in the heavens, had seen the plains a scene of calamity, and the top of Carmel withered ; the palaces of Kirioth devoured by fire ; Moab and Kirioth die with tumult, shouting, and the sound of a trumpet. In the fields of Judah he had beheld confusion and death ; the altar of Bethel, and the palaces of the mighty fall : the rage of famine ; the heavens yielding no rain ; the sword devour the youth, and pestilence prey on the dead. Amos, filled with sympathy, had removed from the sights of these miseries to the peaceful grave ; but now awaked in an immortal body to behold the salvation accomplished by the Redeemer, the heavens no longer iron, nor thirst known to those who ha panted after the knowledge of the Holy One of Israel.

Job's tomb was encompassed with cool shades and his soul hovered in the waving grove. Now the rock in which it was hewn sunk down befor him, and from it rose clouds of undulating dus that flashed radiance : a dust and radiance he had never before seen.   While fixed in deep attention and rejoicing at this new appearance, he sunk in raptures amidst the splendid dust.   His angel then beholding him under the Almighty's forming hand, poured forth the fulness of his joy with a lofty voice that shook the grove and the neighbouring rocks. This Job himself perceived, who being now created a new, extatic tears of rapturous joy flowed from his eyes, and he cried with a voice that also shook the grove and rocks.   Holy, holy, holy, is He that is, and was, and is to come !

The sky about Golgotha was still covered with gloom, and round the cross the clouds of night shrouded the eminences and vales, through the whole seen of the divine sacrifice, as far as the human eye could reach.   The sacred corpse was now stiff, the head sunk, and the temples pressed with the crown of insult, stained with clotted blood, which ceased to call on the Judge for pardon and grace, and to raise its voice to the heaven of heavens, crying to the Father for mercy !   The body hung lifeless on the lofty cross, without a tear, without its trembling voice.   Around the cross the softest whisper of the air was silent, and the hill became a solitude almost forsaken by man. · So lies a field of battle, left by the souls of the dead.

The repentant thief now looked with fixed, though dim eyes, on the body of the breathless Redeemer : Thou art dead ! cried he, with a low tremulous voice, thou art dead !   I am left alone in this tormenting death.   Gladly will I suffer, gladly will I suffer all with patience ; but do not Thou forsake me !—Yet God forsook thee !   O mystery profound !   I saw thee with thy face lift up to heaven, when with a loud voice thou criedst, My God my God, why hast thou forsaken me ? and while I heard,

Heaven and .Earth vanished from my sight, an
fresh stream of warm blood issued from my ve
I thought myself dying   O my God look down
on me with pity !   Such were his thoughts wl
a divine illumination poured into his soul.

The high priest had prevailed on Pilate not
defer putting Jesus to death till the malefact
expired, lest the passover should be defiled by tl
hanging on the cross. Accordingly a slave ca
in haste with orders from Pilate to the centuri
who having given the word, the next to him l
hold of a club stained with the blood of many
the crucified dead and approached the cross,
lowed by his companions.   Then with nervous
he swung it over his head, and crying with a t
rific voice, Die villain, struck the blow, wh
broke the malefactors bones, while the cross sho
and sent forth a jarring sound.   This the repent
criminal heard, and joyfully predicted his own
proaching death.   The Roman then turned,
stood opposite the middle cross, when looking
he trembled, and fancied he saw the vengeful g
hovering round.   Terrified he stepped to the c
vert, who looked down upon him with pleased e
To put a speedy end to his torture, the executi
er exerted all his strength, striking his legs w
such force that the bones were shattered and G
gotha trembled.   He now, once more, but w
slow step advanced to the middle cross, and, sta
ing still, viewed the pendant body, then called
to the centurion, This man is already dead.   I kn
it, he answered, but take a spear and pierce
heart, then turned aside with his eyes fixed on
ground.   Soon the executioner raised the glitter
spear; and drawing back pushed it with redoub
force into the sacred corpse, and from the wou
issued blood and water.

Now as through a mist, the languishing eyes of the dying convert beheld the blood and water trickling from the body of the Most Holy. His soul struggling to free itself from his body, raised to heaven thoughts inarticulate and impassioned—Ah, now, now, be merciful even to me!—O by thy blood—by thy death, which now for all—By thy death on that cross, be merciful!—Thou Golgotha my grave, wast his altar!—Ah crushed bones, exult in your corruption, here shall ye moulder.

Abdiel now drawing near, viewed him as he hovered round with gentle flight, and the countenance of the immortal shone with brighter lustre; while he thus uttered his final benediction : Source of life, Giver of Mercies more exalted than the tongues of men or of angels are able to express, Oh be with him, and in this dark valley of death pour into his mind the joys of the celestial life, a delightful foretaste of the consummation of blessedness.

The departing soul then uttered these impassioned thoughts : Thou Love! thou eternal Love!—O my freed soul, cease thine efforts! in vain thou strivest to express thy thanks! O Lord God merciful and gracious, who forgivest iniquity, transgression, and sin, into thine hands—Ah, ye bands of Paradise, how ye wave your palms!—O Lord merciful and gracious, into thine hand I commend—Ah now no longer delay, no longer delay! This reconciled, justified, highly favoured soul, O my Saviour! into thine hands I commend.

He then expired. Together with the soul, the finest parts of the body left the corpse to become the vesture of the immortal spirit : Is this death? said the transported soul. O happy separation!

what shall I call thee ? Not death, no more shall thou be called by that dreadful name ! and thou corruption, so fearful thought, how soon art thou become my joy ! Slumber then, thou my companion in the past life : fall to dust, as seed sown by the hand of God, to ripen for the general harvest ! O corruption what a different life do I now enjoy ! this has no death ! this can know no end !

Now no longer did Abdiel conceal his radiant form. He saw the soul of the new immortal cloathed like himself in celestial splendor, and advanced towards him, irradiated with the joy of the most intimate love, brightened by his seeing him now delivered. The repentant, pardoned soul hasted to meet him, crying, servant of the Most High, for that thou art one of the blessed of God, thy dignity and unsullied brightness declared to me, when my fixed eyes saw thee from afar : then the melodious sound of thy wings filled me with transport, and chased away dread and pain. Yet still do I tremble before thee ; but this trembling is ecstatic rapture. Abdiel answered, Come thou first of the dead, the first reconciled by the sacrifice of the blest Redeemer ; thou who turnedst late to God, and first poured out thy soul to him when confined in prison ; thou the hope of future sinners, come, oh come ; for now will be accomplished the Mediator's glorious promise : come, I will conduct thee to the joys of Paradise ! He then winged his rapid flight, followed by the transported soul.

He whose face shone, when he descended from the presence of the Eternal, with such lustre that the people were unable to view him till he covered it with a veil : he who doubting that the rock would not instantly pour forth a spring of water, was permitted only to see Canaan from Nebo's lofty summit, now hovered alone, absorbed in thought, over his solitary grave, no angel present ; for none had he, in the life of probation, who, without dying, saw the glory of God pass by : but before him a resplendent cloud hovered over the dust in which he had lived. O Pharaoh, said he, long is it since thy bones, and those of thy drowned host whitened the sedgy shore. Oh how the walls of the sea fell ! How the storm rushed from the fiery column ! How Egypt sunk in death ! Even there, on this side, beyond the hills, did the cloud and fiery pillar lead us. There did God strike thee, O Amalek, while my arms were extended towards heaven, and on their sinking Israel 'suffered. There the hush burnt, the place to me was holy.—Oh rock ! why didst thou delay thy refreshing stream ?—That is Sinai the mount of thunder, and the sound of a trumpet !—Great art thou, O wilderness, the spacious grave of all whom the Almighty conducted through the Red Sea !—Nebo is mine—but lofty Gerizim and Golgotha's altar are not there !

Golgotha's bloody altar, pregnant with salvation, now sang the angels by whom the Eternal sent the covenant of the law. They sang on Nebo's summit, which was irradiated by their presence. They hovered round the grave of Moses, and touching their golden harps chanted with sweetest harmony : We immortals have not the blessings of Gerizim ; but those of Calvary are ours ! Moses, thou God to Aaron, why delays thy body ; O dust shake off thy rest, and at the Redeemer's call rise into life. Amidst the soothing sounds of the celestial harps, the dust of Moses continued sleeping ! but at the trumpet's death-awakening clangor, Nebo and the opening grave shook. The glorified Moses then arose, but instantly sunk down,

and worshipped kneeling. Long ascended
thanksgivings, long his praise, no angel now s
porting his up-lift arms.

. Even the sepulchres of the kings trembled,
dust of David awaked, as if satiated with bliss,
the glorious image of the Incorruptible, whose
surrection waited for a more exalted triumph,
the first fruits among the dead. The bright sp
of Jesse's son descended into the dark vault,
perceived near his remains the soul of Solom
The son was astonished, and the awakened w
dered at the risen. Then hasted the angels
he risen to the sepulchre crying, They rise fr
the dead!—Yes, we rise from the dead, said Ab
ham in a transport of joy. Our dry bones hear
voice of the Lord. We awake immortal, so
himself shall awake. O David, the father of
holy Jesus, thou art chosen to flourish round
cedar of God, an ever-verdant tree in the h
venly Paradise, and thy branches to wave ami
celestial breezes, with thy top piercing the clou

Mourn not, thou soul of Solomon, said Gabri
mourn not, thou highly favoured, thou shalt no
clothed with thy dust when the Cedars of
shed the first fruits of the spring.

Shall I mourn, he returned, I whom hea
crowns with such exalted favours? I who h
committed such errors, while I am permitted to
the glories of redeeming love. Rest my cruml
bones till the great day, when this vault shall
longer be able to contain you. Rise as a vap
in the mild coolness of the evening, under the
ning moon, till the instant before it shall ceas
give light to mortals.

Gabriel and the risen now leaving the sepulc
of the kings soared to Mamre's groves and to
risen within its shades.

Asa, who by the terrors of the Lord, conquered
the innumerable host of Zerah, rose.—He likewise
who preaching to the people travelled through
Judea, attended by his princes and the priests of
Lord : to him the Almighty gave unparalleled
prosperity : for Jehoshaphat led his army against
the enemy in sacred attire, with psalms and hymns
and shouts of exultation : not to battle ; but to
adore their Almighty protector, who destroyed
their enemies, and covered the plain with the dead.
Uzziah also awaked in his solitary tomb, and in
the royal sepulchre, his son, with Josiah, devout
youth, ever mild and gracious, and the destroyer of
idols ; him the men and women singers bewailed !
the Benjamites, whose tears, like wine, flowed over
Salem's ruins, bewailed him in plaintive song.
They lamented him fallen by Necho's shafts.
These all rose at once, and like resplendent rays
darted through the heavens.

ᵤ Hezekiah was not yet risen. Nisroch an angel
of the abyss that once animated an idol, now slowly
moved with the ghost of Sennacherib, from the
summit of Lebanon. Nisroch had been ordered to
bring the conqueror from hell to the sepulchres of
the kings of Judah. Who compels me, cried Sen-
nacherib, with impetuous voice, to visit the hated
earth ?

O Sennacherib, said the infernal spirit, had not
the order been given by an angel of death, I would
have disobeyed. Thou heardest him speak with
the voice of thunder. Who can support the ter-
rors of these irresistible spirits ? Thou weak and
pusillanimous, on whose altar victims have bled,
must appear as a bleeding victim before this ter-
rible angel of death. Thou pusillanimous must fly
at his command ! Thou pride-swelled conqueror,
haste and bow thyself in the dust of the kings of

Judah ! Fly thou reviler of the Mighty One;
he put a bit in thy mouth, and drag thee throi
the countries thou hast ravaged.

Sennacherib hasted, and the two spectres of
abyss soon entered the tomb where the soul of
zekiah and his g a an angel continued hover
—Wherefore, O umdel, said the blessed spirit,
these accursed come to profane my tomb ?—T
will soon know, replied the angel. This is Sei
cherib with his idol deity.—Sennacherib knoi
thou this resplendent spirit ?—How shoul
wretched that I am, know all the sons of felic
—Wretched indeed, resumed the angel, and n
wretched for thine impieties. This is he
humbly prostrated himself in the dust before:
whom thou blasphemedst, who made God his
fuge and his confidence, when thine hosts,
mighty torrent advanced against him. What ju
ments smote thee on earth thou knowest, and
this follows : he, O Sennacherib, whom t
thoughtest almost beneath thy contempt, and
insult the Omnipotent, on whose protection
magnanimous prince relied, thou shalt behol
new glory.

Does his glory then increase ? cried Senna
rib. O let me fly to my abyss ! What is H
kiah or everlasting light to me, the compa
of the darkest gloom ? Let me, O tyrant of
ven, fly.

Thou canst not escape the judgments of
Here rests his dust, thine lies under the ruin
Ninevah. It shall also awake, but dark
wretched. How different wilt thou appear
him thou wilt now behold !

Terror and dismay siezed the bloody conqu
of nations, at seeing the grave of the exalted H
kiah tremble, and at his being speedily arraye

new glory. Now, curse, thou blasphemer, curse, thou scorner, the great Awakener of the dead, cried Hezekiah, shining with effulgent lustre. Why dost thou delay? Curse him in thine infernal abyss. Sennacherib stood rooted in the rocks of the tomb, rage itself impeding his flight. Hezekiah then rising in the air, called from above: behold another kind of scorn than thy flight into the temple of Nisroth, where thy sons waited for thee, with swords prepared for unnatural murder; Sion's celestial daughter shews thee the golden crown of salvation, and the heavenly Jerusalem shakes her head at thee, thou humbled destroyer. Ah whom hast thine impious presumption despised? Against whom hast thou lifted up thine arrogant eyes and blasphemous voice? Here Sennacherib fled, with his demon to the infernal abyss.

David hasted to Kish, where was the tomb of Jonathan, who viewing him with pleasure cried, Is it thee, my David? With such splendor none have appeared but Enoch and Elijah. O thou father of the great Redeemer, how gloriously art thou changed!—The dust in my sepulchre moved, and behold I arose! Thou likewise, my Jonathan, shalt arise. Even I have risen from the dead, and hast thou sinned like me!—No: but though I had been as pious as David, I was not the father of the Messiah. Alas! how little do I deserve, and what thanks do I owe to the Giver of all good, for being thought worthy to descend from heaven to behold the blessed Jesus! O David! I have seen him die, and mine eyes shall also behold his exaltation and triumph! I am blessed also, O my David, in seeing thee! Sadness had hovered round me on this grave, where none of my fathers, nor my brothers were with me. Do not Saul's remains rest here?—Yet do not thou, O my Jona-

than complain.—No, David, rather would I c
to he! Has not God made me an heir of li
Yet on my father's dust, let me, without comp
ing, drop one tear. Jonathan's angel then ca
Dry up that tear, which too late thou sh
Dry it up and weep no more. Scarce had
called, with a voice like the sound of the cele
Hallelujah, when Jonathan sunk into a sweet
rapturous slumber, and soon awaking, stood be
David in absolute immortality, He who
heard David's and Jonathan's lofty hymns asc
to the throne, then heard their sublime discou
and knew the thoughts that surpassed their
terance.

Gideon, who refused the crown offered
by Judah, soared up in the lustre of immortal
Not so, when the loud trump shall call the
of God to judgment, shall they shine, who
their blood-stained diadems to direful conqu
or those who wantonly pollute their reigns v
slaughter, in which innocence and virtue bl
The cry of their blood will reach the ear of
mighty Judge, and when he comes he will li
to the sound.

Now awaked the dead bones of Elisha, him
the awakener of the dead, and quitting his gr
in crimson radiance, issued forth like a ve
morn.

At Deborah's tomb the palms waved th
rustling tops, above which suddenly rose the p
phetess, pouring forth praise to the Author
life. There Miriam came forth from the dus
the earth triumphant, then lift up her eyes, beam
joy, towards heaven; and then eagerly cast th
over the spacious field; but found not the i
mortal who had raised her terrestrial frame fr
death to life. Thou angel of the resurrecti

cried she here shall I find thee? What sacred
shades cover thy radiant head? In what moun-
tain does that trumpet sound, with which thou hast
awaked me from the sleep of death? Ah 'where
restedst thou after thy glorious work, lost in asto-
nishment that God should employ thee in perform-
ing such wonders?

Ezekiel now stood near his dust, and remembered
the vision in which, filled with inspiration, at his
voice the dry bones that covered the field moved,
bone joined to bone, and over them grew sinews,
flesh, and the covering skin; and again speaking
they arose a numerous-host. Thus Ezekiel stood
with a vernal lustre shining round him. His angel
then cried, I hear a distant sound as of the divine
presence; instantly the prophet's dust is in motion;
he sinks down; but soon reanimated with the
breath of eternal life, he rises erect, filled with un-
utterable joy; raises his grateful eyes to heaven,
and rushes into the embraces of the angel. Then
guided by the sound of the divine presence, they
move to the other dead, to be spectators of their re-
surrection.

Asnath seemed as if sinking into a gentle slumber
and with dubious motion, hovering, touched the
dust of her grave. So in the humid meads floats
a vapour which, enlightened by the moon, moves
in silver lustre. O my guardian angel, said she,
with what am I environed? what appearances
glide before me? What new, what nameless
sensations do I feel? Tell me, thou angel of
God; shall I again die? Methinks my voice
trembles, I faint, am weak, I sink like the soft dy-
ing sounds of the lute. I expire, O seraph, amidst
the gentle murmurs of Eden's rills, amidst the
sweet breezes in the shades of Paradise. Thus
Asnath sunk down, but encompassed with pleasing

thoughts and thrilling sensations of joy, soon aros
the heiress of immortality.

As expands the first flowers of the spring, s
awaked to life Jeptha's daughter, but never mor
to fade. Her tremulous lips in silver sounds sen
up her praises, accompanied by her angel's golde
harp, which on the wings of grateful harmony rais
ed her adorations to heaven.

Thirza, the mother of the seven sous had bee
interred with those glorious martyrs near Jerusalem
In their sepulchre the weary traveller had ofte
sought repose, and oft poured forth tears. Withi
this spacious receptacle of the dead kneeled th
soul of the happy mother, with those of her sons
offering grateful thanksgivings. While their ori
sons ascended to heaven, there came across a st ear
which ran near the sepulchre, Semida and Jethro
a man of Bethlehem, who, guided by angels, ha
seen thee, O thou adorable Redeemer! in the sta
ble where thy first infant cries were heard, an
now, spent with fatigue and sorrow he and Semida
sat down at the entrance of the sepulchre, and thu
gave vent to their thoughts.

O Semida, how shall I describe what I felt a
the death of the Friend of Man!—But tell me
O tell me, what sensation is this, which since on
approaching the sepulchre of the martyrs, has seiz
ed my mind? so it was at the approach of the an
gels who proclaimed his nativity.

Holy, O Jethro, is this tomb! What thou feel
est, I also feel. Let us retire ; some angel or de
parted spirit, now sanctifies by his presence thi
sacred sepulchre, and the sensations we feel are in
timations that we should depart.

They now arose, when Semida advancing int
the gloomy cavern, cried, O ye immortals, lamen
with us the death of our Lord! Holy he lived

holy he died ! Jesus his name on earth—Jesus his
name proclaimed by angels, cannot be to you un-
known ! .Though alarmed at your presence, we
are also the children of God, and our souls, like
you, immortal ! Permit us then to call you by an
endearing human name—to call you brethren. Be
this sepulchre of the martrys a witness, when here-
after we come to you, that even on this unhallowed
earth, and while in the veil of flesh, we termed you
our brethren-! Let us remind you, ye angels, on
our ascending to your bright mansions, to receive
us as your brethren ! Semida thenturned, and
leaving the tomb, followed Jethro.

Thirza and her sons observed them, and while
Semida spoke, viewed them unseen with surprize
and pleasure. Then turning to her sons, she said,
I could have wished their longer stay : for candour
and innocence are seated on their amiable aspects.
Depart ye in peace, The Lord be your God, and
bring you to our everlasting life.—Yes, at your
falling asleep, joyfully shall we descend from hea-
ven to meet you, our brethren.

The idea of the two mortals was still present to
Thirza's mind, when it was suddenly impressed
with a more astonishing view. Her sons, though
blessed with celestial life, sunk as into a sweet
slumber ; but two of them appeared rather in-
tranced than asleep, for their countenances became
more resplendent. Their minds overflowed with
joy, and their voices were sweet as the celestial
harps. Dost thou rise already, O most beautiful
of mornings, thou blest morning of his resurrection?
cried Benoni. Yes, joyful morning, thou art
risen ! The sepulchre shakes—Calvary and the
cross shakes ! Hail morning pregnant with bliss.
He then sunk like his brothers into rapturous
slumber. Instantly Jedidoth, the youngest of his

brothers, poured forth his joy.   O ye angels, cried
he, has the Lord already ascended to the Father's
throne? Here he sunk down, and lay like his
brothers.

Thirza's astonishment continued : before her
lay seven immortals, like mortals wrapped in sleep;
while she with a look of maternal fondness, hung
over them. But soon her eyes closed; she no
longer saw them; she sunk ; but soon she awaked,
when perceiving her risen body ; Praise, praise
be to thee ! said she with tremulous voice ; eternal
praises be to thee !   Thou hast given me joys
surpassing all conception !   They, O thou Giver
of ineffable joys, also awake.   She then kneeled,
and with folded hands, and cordial angelic tears
saw her sons awake around her : saw them rise
from their moving dust, swift as ascending flames.
The blessed mother beheld their bright transfigura-
tion ; their first smiles ; their joy-beaming eyes
raised towards heaven, and heard their new voices
burst forth in praise and thanksgiving.

Within another cave, hewn out of the rock, lay
four friends.   Their bright spirits were there, and
these seeing their mouldered dust, longed for the
resurrection.   Darda, who last survived, and had
attended the bodies of his beloved associates Ethan
Chalcol, and Heman to their rest, thus addressed
them : How happy, my friends, are we ! united
in life, united in the tomb, and we shall be united
during the endless ages of eternity ! We saw
Ethan expire, and lamented his death.   White
are now thy bones, O Ethan ! I saw also Heman
and Chalcol enter the vale of death. Chalcol
fell asleep in mine arms, and I remained less ripe
for immortality. O Chalcol ! what was mine
anguish, when I, forlorn, attended thee to thy
grave ! but God by his gracious consolations

enabled me to look up to heaven! After a few nights the sleep of death fell on me! Behold, there lie our bones waiting till they are called forth by the resurrection.—To rise from the dead, how transporting the thought; how ravishing will be the reality! O extacy, cried Heman with a voice of celestial harmony, we shall awake to life! awake to days without end! Permit me, O Thou Saviour of men! to utter a wish, which my ardent soul almost ripens into hope, that my body may awake with thine! with thine, O Jesus! for corruption has no part with thee, O grant that this sleeping dust may arise under thy shade, to glory and immortality? Ah! the blessed time is arrived! exclaimed Chalcol. See the dead

then silent. He awaked with those that revived. No time was left to thee, O Darda, for astonishment! nor for thee, O Ethan! the dead bones moved; they arose vested in redoubled splendor, and these happy friends soared hand in hand, with intermingled radiance, praising the Redeemer.

Near Jerusalem slept Anna the prophetess, who had seen the babe of Bethlehem in the temple, and knew him to be the promised shoot of Judah's stem. He was carried into Egypt, and she to her grave, whence she now awoke to glory; issued forth from her tomb, and opening her immortal eyes, saw Jesus hanging lifeless on the cross. Though thou art dead, said she, by thee am I

me a new
body before the great day of consum-
sacred blood has flowed, and loudly
ace! Here joy stopped her voice.

ly son, had left
wandering with
flow steps into the valley of mount Olivet, towards

his brother's tomb. The stone was already' cover-
ed with moss, and near it be sunk down, his eyes
stiff and red with weeping for Jesus and Benoni
—The mouths of babes and sucklings, said he,
shall speak thy praise. My grief for Benoni began
to abate, when now—But I should not mention the
divine name with that of death. I will no longer
stifle my grief for poor Benoni, who is still dead
to me. How can I presume to lament the great
Prophet ! he is the brother of angels, and surely
none but angels should dare to weep for him : but
for thee I dare—for thee I will ever grieve. ʼ) t
. He then leaned his drooping head on a stone, his
eyes languid and his visage wan. His brother's
guardian angel, and his brother himself viewed him
with intermingled joy and compassion : for the
soul of Benoni, and his angel, had descended to the
sacred silence of the tomb ; but this was unknown
to Joel. So the pious man resigned amidst his
sufferings, knows not the hand which supports him,
though it is as near as the sweet whispering breeze.
O seraph ! said Benoni, I love him more than he
loves himself : but why does he lament my death,
and not think of my more exalted life ?

Thou art gone, my Benoni, resumed Joel, and
hast left me alone, like a flower in Sharon's vale,
whose stalk is broken in its early bloom...

If I am gone, my Joel, my dearest brother, it is
to grow high in heaven, and spread a friendly shade
near the tree of life.

Our father is old. Thy death, O Benoni, will
take him from me, and sorrow bring his grey hairs
to the grave ! I fatherless, and without a brother,
shall pant for the cup of death, which though to
others bitter, to me will be sweet,

O seraph, how am I pierced by his anguish !
Dry up his tears : ! ah dry up his affecting tears !

—Ah the tomb shakes, and from the moving stones around me rises a faint light in gentle fluctuations! O my God, where am I? O thou Giver of eternal life support me! Sure thou wilt not dissolve this spiritual substance! Thus he spake in a voice soft as the dying echo. Now glorified with the resurrection body, he cried, Thou not only supportest me, O thou most gracious; but cloathest me with everlasting bliss! All praise, blessing, and honour be ascribed to thee, my Creator, who hast loaded me with thy benefits, and given me this immortal life! Rejoice, O my brother, and exult, for when thy body shall be dissolved, it shall be raised by thy Redeemer, who shall thus load thee with his benefits! Here the blessed Benoni seeing his father, added, O tender parent, lament not over my tomb, I am in a state of bliss, and it no longer contains my body!

Samma, now approaching the tomb, cried, O Joel! long have I sought thee. Let us hasten from these gloomy sepulchres. Is not that my dear Benoni's? Come, Joel, let us flee from hence. God bless thee, my child! God will speedily bless thee, returned Benoni, he will bless thee, thou tender father, with eternal life.

Simeon, after pouring forth the joy of his heart, on his seeing the Saviour, whom God had appointed the Light of the nations, the Glory of his people Israel, laid his hoary head in the grave. His spirit then arose with resplendent lustre, and his corruptible part mouldered into dust. The radient soul of the prophet now hovered over his grave, unknowing that his dust was soon to rise in celestial beauty, to enjoy eternal life. In the path which extends by the brook of Cedron from Jerusalem to the foot of mount Olivet, slowly

moved towards Simeon's sepulchre, one laden with
years, and with him a boy. These were Simeon's
brother and grandson. The eyes of the old man
were involved in darkness, the too early night of
death, ere we enter that gloomy vale. Boaz, the
youth, guided his uncertain steps, and offering
child-like comfort, they thus discoursed.

Dear father, wipe thine eyes and weep no more.
Long it is since mine eyes have seen, they are
only fit to weep. I must lament the slow ap-
proach of death, and from this darksome earth,
look up to fairer, brighter prospects. But! tell
me, Boaz, are we far from my holy brother's
bones?

No, not far. The moss on the tomb, like ivy
among those lonely ruins, says, he has been long at
rest.

Ah child, he returned, my heart is filled with
secret pleasure at recollecting those antient, those
venerable sepulchres. Has Simeon already lain so
long in the tomb? Long has mine been hewn in
the rock, yet still wants its inhabitant.

Thus spake Simeon's brother, leaning on Boaz,
and at length resumed, Tell me, child, for to thee
the sun is not extinguished, nor the mild light of
the summer's eve; tell me are the heavens se-
rene? I feel a gentle breeze refreshing my weary
limbs.

The air, said Boaz, is clear, and the wide fields
look like spring.

Ah Boaz, were it involved in blackest clouds,
and deformed by tempests, yet shall the day on
which I die be to me serene.—He thirsts for death,
said Simeon's soul to the angel; and is unable to
bear the thought that Jesus is dead. Thou dost
not know then, said the angel, that the dreadful

news has been concealed from him, lest it should shorten his days.

In the mean while Simeon's brother and Boaz sat down in the tomb. The angel now separated from the common dust, that of Simeon's bones. It moved, visible only to the angels, and arose about his soul, forming a resplendent body. His mental powers were borne on the wings of extatic melody; but returned at the completion of his new created frame, and the idea of his resurrection filled him with the sublimest transports.

At this instant one who had come to the passover, with quick step, walked by in his way back to Bethlehem, and Simeon's brother asking the meaning of his haste, Should I not haste, he answered, to carry the news of his death to my family? Whose death? called the brother of the risen. Art thou, he returned, the only one, who has not heard of the crucifixion of the divine Jesus? The old man sunk down speechless; but being at length brought to himself, was with difficulty led back by the traveller and Boaz to the gate of Jerusalem.—Shall we, O seraph! said Simeon, shall we meet his spirit, when it quits its present encumbering abode? for the ensuing morn will surely set it free No, my beloved Simeon, the angel returned, he is not dying: even in this abject life much joy awaits him; for thou art to appear to his enraptured mind, and to converse with him on the Lord's resurrection.

Here lie and rest, said John, who stood by his corrupted frame, till the great decisive day. My continuance here will be only while the Redeemer's body is wrapped in the shades of death. Then wilt thou, O Lamb of God! arise as Victor! and gather us around thee, that we may behold

thy glory.. At length, at the trumpet's joyful sound,
the body with which I now willingly remain shall
rise. O the transports of the resurrection ! How
transcendent must they be, when only the hopes of
them are so ravishing ! How delightful the wish
that my body may soon revive ! Such were his
thoughts when he beheld the blessed Benoni ad-
vancing radient through the evening twilight. O
seraph, said he to his celestial guardian, what
angel is that which issues from those pendant rocks.
Every charm of vernal beauty environs the hea-
venly youth. He resembles Benoni. Is it not
his guardian angel ?. No it is no angel, it is no
soul cloathed in a vesture of light ; yet it re-
sembles Benoni. Is he risen ? O heavenly youth,
art thou risen from the dead ? Come, whoever
thou art, wing thy way and animate thine harp.
Perhaps Benoni, lately deceased, is risen, and sent
hither to declare some new wonder of the Divine
goodness.

Here Benoni, striking his melodious harp, came
with graceful flight to John, and said, Greatest of
those born of women, the Father of all eternally
bless thee ! I bring thee heavenly tidings.. Behold
the sacred dust awakes ! Thou baptizer of the
great Emanuel, the whole plain is in motion, and
the dead in the Lord awake !

Who, O celestial youth, said John, Oh who hast
thou seen ?—I have seen, returned Benoni, the
father of men ! Enoch and Elijah stood astonish-
ed ! Abraham shone like the host of heaven ! and
Isaac came in a crimson cloud ! I saw Moses and
Job, with grateful eyes lift up in devout adoration !
I saw the seven martyrs absorbed in extacy ! May
God eternally bless thee—thee one of the race of
Adam ! thou art now to prepare for thy resurrection.

John, with amazement, beheld his body rise :

his sublime soul, animated the lucid form, and he stood erect transfigured. Now was the beatific miracle complete, and to the Redeemer the glorified saint poured forth his rapturous praise.

These names of the risen distinctly reached mine ear : others the waving palms dispersed, till Sion's heavenly muse visiting my contemplative hours, conveyed them to my thoughts.

THE END OF THE ELEVENTH BOOK.

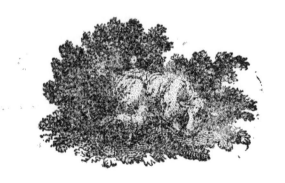

THE

MESSIAH.

BOOK XII.

• THE ARGUMENT.

Joseph obtains Pilate's permission to bury the body of
Jesus. He and Nicodemus having wrapped it in spices,
perform the interment, which is solemnized by choirs
of risen saints and angels. The disciples, many of the
seventy, and Mary, with some devout women, meet in
John's house, and are joined by Joseph and Nicodemus;
the latter bringing the crown of thorns, which he had
taken from the body at its interment. The death of
Mary the sister of Lazarus, who, with Nathaniel and
Martha, sees her die: Lazarus returns to the company
of believers at Jerusalem, and endeavours to comfort
them. Salem, John's angel, strengthens him with a
vision.

DISTRESSED and deeply plunged in bitterest
anguish, is the soul that fears her not being
admitted to her divine inheritance : bewildered in
thought, she is struck with the curses of Sinai
and of Ebal, and with the terrors of ensanguined
Golgotha: She no longer hopes to wear the white
robe and the victors crown : but afflicted, lies in
the dust, till a ray of comfort intermingled with
the blessed idea that the divine Redeemer will be
the Deliverer, breaks in upon her mind, and fills
her with hope and joy, and humble submission :
thus dejected, thus of every hope bereft, were they
who knew the Saviour, when they saw his eyes

closed, his body dead, and all around silence and solitude. Joseph of Arimathea alone bore up against this depression : To inter thee, O sacred corpse, said he, shall be his task who filled with pusillanimity, did not dare to oppose thy murderers. I will, added he, calling aloud, so that the Roman officer, and those involved in silent grief, heard his voice—I will inter the divine Jesus in my own sepulchre. Here, Nicodemus, stay for me at the cross, while I haste to the Roman governor. I will bring the funeral linen.

He hasted away : so hastes he who firmly resolved to lead a new life, despises the threats of man, the allurements of vice, and all its vain seducing charms. He soon reached the palace, where he beheld Pilate discomposed, and Portia, whose sorrowful look, and humid eyes expressed the anguish of her heart. Joseph having asked for the body, Pilate bid him send for the commanding officer at the cross, and on his arrival being assured that Jesus was really dead, ordered him to deliver the body to Joseph, who, returning him thanks, withdrew, and having fetched the linen and spices, hasted back to the hill of death.

The disconsolate mother of Jesus first saw the faithful disciple bringing the funeral linen for her son's interment ; but filled with inward grief, stood silent, while John in vain strove to give her consolation. As Joseph was hasting to the cross, he was met by Nicodemus; and to those of the faithful who drew near, they cheerfully said, We are not afraid to inter the Holy Jesus. The pious mourners then retreated, and stood at a distance, not so the celestial witnesses, the risen and the angels. These removed nearer, and now the harp, to the human ear unheard, began to sound : but had a mortal, however immersed in

sorrow, heard its rapture-breathing notes, ecstacy
would have raised him to the joys of heaven,
or the lugubrious sounds have extinguished life.

Joseph and Nicodemus having spread out the
linen and aromatics, drew the nails; took the corpse
from the cross, and gently lowered it to the ground.

They then wrapped the body in the spices and
linen, to preserve that from putrifaction, which
was soon to rise from the dead.

Eve now hovering, over the body, bowed down
her face to that of the breathless Messiah. Her
golden tresses waved over his wounds, and a ce-
lestial tear dropped on his tranquil breast. How
lovely, O my Son and my Lord said she, appear
these wounds, the testimonials of thy love! from
each vein flows salvation! Though the colour of
death has tinged thy face, yet thy closed lips and
fixed eyes speak eternal life! thou still smilest be-
nign, and every lineament of thy divine counte-
nance indicates love to man.

Thus spake the mother of the human race, while
Joseph and Nicodemus were swathing the extend-
ed body. The burial clothes being stained with
blood by the trembling hands of the disciples who
performed this tender office, the fore-fathers of
the Mediator began a plaintive song, a celestial thre-
nody. One of the choirs began; and the tears of
the blessed flowed.

Who is he coming from Calvary cloathed in red?
Who with blood-stained garments comes from the
altar? Whose divine power is concealed, and whose
salvation is everlasting?

To them answered another choir, while their
tears also flowed, and to their voices was joined
the sound of the trumpet: I am he who teacheth
righteousness; a master, who bringeth salvation
and counsel.

The first choir resumed, Why is thy raiment stained with red, and thy vesture like that of one who treads the grapes?

Did not I tread the grapes alone? and were any with me? Those who arose have I crushed in mine anger. In my indignation I trod them under foot, and my garments have been sprinkled with their blood. The day of wrath, the year of the great redemption is come! When I undertook to redeem mankind, I looked 'round, but no helper was near, none in heaven or on earth! Mine anger prevailed against the ground, I bruised the head of the serpent! Mine adversaries have I crushed in my wrath, and have trampled their power in the dust!

Thus sang the choir, joining with sadness triumphant songs. Joseph taking off the crown of insult, covered the Redeemer's sacred head. The celestial spectators that hovered over Golgotha were not silent, like Mary and the disciples; but renewed their funeral hymns, which were accompanied with celestial tears. Hadst thou, O favourite disciple of the deceased son of the most afflicted of mothers, now heard those harps, which though still a mortal, thou heardest in Patmos, how raised would have been thine extacy! The choir of the risen with their eyes fixed on the corpse, continued.

Listen, ye angels, the brook of Cedron murmurs! Listen to the murmuring of the brook of Cedron! Tread upon the proud—tread, O my soul, on the vanquished serpent! The palms groaned on Gethsemane; for there he began to die.

From another choir issued sounds hoarse as thunder: Heard he not below the roarings of the infernal floods, the bellowings of the tortured? Did not Tabor's summit shake amidst the clouds? Then

Eloa issuing from the darkness that encompasses
the Father's judgment seat, sang triumphant! He

They were silent, and then was heard in a soft
voice of complaint, He is dead! ye angels, he is
dead!

Joseph and Nicodemus now raised the sacred
body from the ground, and with slow steps carried
it down the hill.   When one of the choirs sang,
Ah he thought it no robbery to be like God! yet
Jesus, fairest among men and angels, condescend-
ed to die the death of the cross!   The servants of
sin for his vesture cast lots!   When parched with
thirst, gall and vinegar they gave him to drink,
and his afflicted soul drank of the bitter cup of
insult!

Here a fervent choir lifted up their voices to hea-
ven : Ah Jerusalem!—Woe to thee, Jerusalem!
Woe to thy sons, O Jerusalem!   Thy dreadful
voice ; thy cry for the Redeemer's blood has
reached the highest heavens!

The harps of the fathers now failed ; even in
the hand of Moses, failed the melodious strings ;
Eloa's high sounding trumpet proclaiming woe,
he withdrew from the weeping choirs, and advanc-
ing near the bloody corpse, sang accompanied by
the seraph's trump :   Long will the eternal chastise
you who have murdered this Abel.   Thou Cain I
well know.   Thy brother's blood cried for mercy,
not for revenge, and its ardent voice penetrated to
the darkness which encompasses the Holy of Holies!
but ye spurned at mercy !—Therefore from lofty
Golgotha to the lowest hell, shall the avenger's
voice resound through successive ages!   Eloa's
trumpet now ceased, and silence broke off the
glowing prophet's song.

Their looks followed the body, while the faithful

disciples carried it down to the sepulchre, which was hewn in a lonely rock bordering on the mount, and over-hung with aged trees. The disciples having rolled away the ponderous stone, which closed the entrance, Joseph, with his eyes filled with tears, choose the spot where the sacred corpse should lie, saying, He whose life and death were filled with distress and pain, has at length a place to lay his head! They then gently laid the body down, and having hung over it with streaming eyes, at length moved back the massy stone, and left the corpse of the Mediator in sepulchral darkness.

Now the celestial choirs, perceiving through the sepulchral gloom the resurrection's lucid dawn, renewed their hymns, Thou, Lord, shall not see corruption. No sooner art thou involved in the shades of death, than new life breaks forth around; for the trumpet of the chief of angels will soon proclaim the revival of the greatest among the dead! Ye harps in soft sounds shall hail the most resplendent morn, when the Conqueror of Death shall rise!! Lament him—lament; ye his beloved, who yet mortal walk in the dust! Soon will ye shed other tears; tears unknown to us, who never felt your woes!

Around the sepulchre, all were now silent, for the angels and men were with-drawn. John then turning towards the dejected Mary, said, with sympathetic tenderness, O mother, thy precious son being concealed from our view, let us retire from this hill, and let me lead thee to my dwelling. Her soul was now elevated above itself, and she answered, with her eyes red with weeping, My being thy mother, O Jesus, may be one day the source of heavenly raptures, and I rejoice that thou, his beloved disciple, art given to me as my son; but

grief and death and the grave, dwell in the thought
that He, my son, is no more !—Here again sinking
                                    face and was
slowly led by her son with sympathizing sadness
down the solitary hill.

'Amidst thick-set palms, and within the temple's
shade, adjoining to the city wall, stood the house
of the beloved disciple.   Hither was he leading the
disconsolate Mary, himself weakened and oppressed
by grief, when meeting with some of the twelve,
of the seventy, and several of the devout women,
he entreated them to go with him, and join their
endeavours to heal her wounded mind.

Sing, O muse, the tears of the lovers for the
beloved, and the complaints of mourning friend-
ship.

In this house they soon assembled. ! Mary,
with weeping eyes, entered the hall where she had
often seen the Holy Jesus, and heard him speak

empty, where he used to open divine truths, and
pronounce his affectionate benedictions, she burst
into an agony of grief, and sunk down leaning her
head on the seat.   While she was in this attitude
of grief, Mary Magdalen, the mother of the sons
of Zebedee, and Nathaniel went up to her; and at
their entreaties, she permitted the women to raise
her up ; but sat veiled, and all the company con-
formed to her silence, till Peter entering, wept
aloud, exclaiming, He is buried !—I hope, ear-
nestly hope, that we shall all be soon buried near
him !   Joseph shall promise to lay my body close
to the rock which holds my dear Lord !—And me
within the rock ! said Mary.

Arm in arm came Simon the Canaanite and
Matthew, with Philip and James the son of Al-
pheus. Lebbeus came by himself ; concern sup-

z

pressed his speech, and covering his face, he sat
in the darkest place in the hall. Next came James,
from his ardent zeal stiled the Son of Thunder,
who with uplift hands and eyes raised towards
heaven, cried, He is dead ! he is dead ! O what
is all human excellence, even the most exalted and
sublime ! for over him have the wicked triumphed !
So saying he withdrew, and walked among the
shady palms.

Hither came Bartholomew, and with him An-
drew the brother of Peter, with Cleophas, Matthias,
and Semida, all sad and disconsolate, the affliction
of each increased by that of his associates. Silence
now reigned in the hall, and nothing was heard but
the dull murmurs of grief. Mary Magdalen
lighted the funeral lamp ; after which devout
women brought linen and spices for the sacred
corpse. Even the guardian angels of the apostles
and other mourners entered the hall, and the all-
seeing eye of him whose death they bewailed, cast
a compassionate look on the assembly. Mary
Magdalen's angel, then raising her from her depth
of affliction, enabled her thus to give vent to her
grief.

Alas ! how are all things changed since he—O
mother ! do not thou also die, for then what will
become of us ?—Now I first feel now I join in
his lamentation over Jerusalem, the solitary widow,
the queen among the nations ! We lived in
obscurity, yet were happy, for he whose death we
mourn was divine : but now in what misery are we
involved ! What nights of sorrow await us ! Oh
may our nights of sorrow be few, and our last
sleep soon come ! Our enemies triumph, and
insult those that love their Lord.—To him they
offered the basest insults—to him, when athirst,
they gave gall and vinegar, doubly imbittered with

contumely—contumely cast upon him in the midst
hou Judge ! thou just A-
venger ! pour out to them 'the full cup of thy
wrath.

She ceased, and the mother of Jesus, in a faint
voice and broken accents, said, Learn, O Magda-
len ! like my Son to forgive !! Did he not, when
bleeding on the cross, filled with divine philan-
thropy, cry out, Father, forgive them, they know
not what they do !

Devout astonishment and inexpressible sorrow
here seized every heart, and all felt a conflict be-
tween the most elevated joy, and bitterest grief;
but grief prevailed, and their souls were again in-
volved in gloom. Yes, have mercy on them, O
thou Judge and Father ! said Lebbeus, have
mercy on us, and suffer us to die ! What have we
to do on earth ? He is dead ! In his Father's
house he told us are many mansions ! Ah let us
rather lie at the threshold of thine house than re-
main in the dwellings of misery ! No other com-
fort can I receive but death ; for this I long : its
name I love to utter, it is more pleasing than the
spring, it is to me as the hymns of the temple !
Be it our most delightful employment to converse
on the change those have felt who have entered
into the state of bliss, and, like active travellers,
let us stand ready with our staff in our hand ! I
love you, my beloved, as myself, I therefore wish
you the bliss of dying !—Yes, said Peter, death
is most desirable, and O thou Most Merciful !
permit us to make sepulchres for each other.

Scarce had he uttered these words, when Thomas,
with dejected look stopped at the entrance of the
room. How awful appeared the objects that
struck his convulsed mind ! to him the glimmer-
ing hall was a tomb, and the silent mourners as

the images of the dead! If ye be they, said he, entering the room, who heard the loud hosanna's, when the blessed Jesus entered into life, how can ye avoid accompanying him in death? I feel mine approach, and thought I should have found among you some who had arrived at happiness, to whom we might have paid the funeral rites. He is buried, who, when living, walked on the waves of the sea, and restored the dead to life!

Now with mournful look Joseph of Arimathea, entering, I joined the sighing assembly, saying, Your brother in Christ, and mine, my friend Nicodemus, is come with me, and trembling waits your permission to enter. He brings—Ah Joseph, thou best of men, said the mother of the Lord; what does he bring?—What, O Joseph! does he bring? Oh I see ye suffer too much, returned he, alas! what will ye suffer! Let him return, let him fly from hence, and not add to your affliction! What does he bring? ..nat, O Joseph! has he brought?—I will go, and prevail on him to fly from thence! He brings —the bloody crown!—The bloody crown! the Saviour's mother exclaimed, with cry that pierced the hearts of the whole assembly. Instantly Nicodemus entered with the crown of thorns in his hand; when breaking from those who had supported her, she took off her veil, threw it over the murderous wreath, and wringing her hands, sunk with it on the floor. They raised her up, and she stretched out her suppliant arms for divine support.—Her Son overflowing with tenderness, looked down from above, and prepared for her sublime felicity: but this being yet concealed, she, pale and languid, continued her lamentations, and crying, Why, O why was it brought! Too long did I see it encompass his bleeding head!—He that dwelleth in the heaven of heavens, though all-wise and all-gracious, hath bent his bow against me, and pierced me with his fiery arrows! Ah never, never did mother bear a son like him I saw expire on the cross!

Meanwhile the devout Mary, the sister of Lazarus, lay at the point of death. Cold sweats and the conflict of her heart, denounced her approaching dissolution. She already tasted the leaden slumber, the harbinger of sleep in the bosom of

nance sought Martha's sympathising eyes, which exhausted by continual grief, shed no tears. She then began the following discourse, in which Martha answered and she replied: I can no longer, my dear sister, continue silent. All now forsake me, even Lazarus and Nathaniel! and see I die! Ah I lived with them, but without them shall die!

Accuse not the faithful. Perhaps the divine Teacher has led them into the wilderness, that they may learn by experience how he feeds the hungry, and refreshes the weary soul.

I do not accuse them, Martha. Those whom I love never have I accused. If I have, O my dearest friends, forgive me.—Forgive all my offences. Alas! what now rises in my soul, covers it with sadness.—Shake off the solicitude with which thou art oppressed. Does that gloom which sometimes clouded the felicity of thy life, return in death.— O call not the divine disposition gloom! I conjure thee by him who judgeth us, and is now gathering me to my fathers, call not his disposition gloom. If I have suffered, have I not also had much joy, and friends like thee? have not I, in my pilgrimage to the grave, seen Jesus the delight of angels, seen his miracles, and heard his wisdom? O let me be thankful for all my afflictions! for all the supports, all the reviving cordials I have received! And above all I give thee thanks, O thou all-gracious Disposer of my life, that I have seen Jesus the friend of man, the Awakener of the dead! Leave me, Martha, go and make ready my sepulchre, where Lazarus slept, there will I sleep.

Sleep, O Mary, where Lazarus slept, and rise at the voice of him who raises the dead!—Happy Martha, what sweet hopes flow into my soul! Withdraw that I may be alone with God.—How shall I leave thee in thy last moments! I cannot leave thee. Compose thyself, dear sister, thou art alone with God, and may the God of Abraham, Isaac, and Jacob, be with thee!—Stay then. May he be with me who fills the heavens, and whose almighty voice calls the children of men to return to life. With me be the God of Abraham, Isaac, and Jacob!

Having thus spoke, she from her inmost soul thus supplicated the Forgiver of sins: Hear, O hear me and enter not into judgment with a poor sinner! What mortal can stand before thee? O God give rest to my dying heart, and rejoice my soul with the assurance of thy salvation! Thou Lord of death, cast me not off from thy presence! Give me again, O Father, thy consolations, and restore to me the joys of thy spirit! Thou who heardest Job amidst the most piercing afflictions, regard my supplications, and be my support.

Thus she prayed. Then turning to Martha, said, Dost thou, my dear sister, think that Jesus now prays for me? He shed tears on his coming to the grave of Lazarus; will he not also pity me? Oh what hope dawns into my soul! The omnipresent Lord of life and death is with me!

Mary now sunk into a deep slumber, on which Martha rose and stood by the bed to view her,

sleeping sister, scarce breathing for fear she should
awake her who had now enterd far into the gloomy
vale, while she was left alone. Sadness pervaded
her heart, and some tears flowed down her pallid
cheek, till her agonies and palpitations gradually
subsided.   Thus silent she stood, in the gloomy
chamber, enlightened only by a dim half-extinguished
lamp.   A traveller who considers death as a sub-
ject of joy, after passing through a parched and
lonely wilderness, enters the cavity of a hollow
rock, where little of the lowering day finds en-
trance, and where is presented to his astonished
sight a tomb, on which is placed recumbent, a
statue of the dead, with another of marble, the
friend of the deceased, who stands weeping. The
traveller views the tomb, is struck at the image
of the deceased, and sympathises in the grief of the
mournful surviver. So, Mary, did thine angel, on
approaching thy bed, find Martha with thee, and
at thy feet stood the celestial youth.

Of those angels who in the scale of spirits are
near to the human soul, beauty is the portion, and
those distinguished by the title of thrones are
supereminent in glory ; yet how dim their splendor
when compared with that of Him who ascended
to the right hand of the Father ! O thou who
hast triumphantly risen to the heaven of heavens,
my Intercessor ! my Brother ! grant that innumer-
able hosts of the redeemed may die the death of
the righteous.   Whether our lives be closed amidst
sufferings, or whether we enjoy a fore-taste of
heaven, O thou Redeemer ! thou Lamb of God !
let the death of the righteous be our portion !

While Chebar stood at the feet of Mary, he
found his resplendent beauty fade : from his face
fled the rosy blush of the morning, and the radient
lustre of his eyes : his wings flagged : no harmony,

no fragrant exhalations accompanied their languid motion ; no longer they glowed with celestial azure be-dropped with gold. From his head he took his radient crown, and held it in his drooping hand. He knew that though her heart strings were ready to break, he could not assist her, before Lebbeus, Martha, and Nathaniel joined their lamentations, and Lazarus poured forth his prayers.

Lazarus was still at Jerusalem, in the dejected company of the faithful, and going to the mother of Jesus, said, Behold, O Mary ! midnight is now at hand, and when I left Bethany, my sister seemed near her dissolution. I will go to see her. Perhaps if the dreadful news of what has passed at Calvary has not reached her ears, she may be still alive. Lebbeus instantly rising, said, I will accompany thee ; at which Nathaniel, embracing him, answered; Come, thou most beloved among the living, how my heart thanks thee ! They were now standing ready to go, when Lazarus addressing the mother of Jesus, said, O thou mother of him whose name the angels proclaimed ! may he who sees and counts thy tears, even the father of him who is interred, be with thee. Thou heardest. thy blessed Son pray, Father, into thy hands I commend my spirit ! I commend thy soul and mine to his and our Almighty Father.

Thus saying, they hasted towards Bethany, and amidst the silence of the night reached the house where the devout Mary lay, and stood by her sister near the bed. At length Mary awaking from her lethargic slumber, cried, Thanks be to thee, O thou Almighty Author of life and death, they are come, and with them Lebbeus. O Mary, said Lazarus, how has the Giver of every mercy supported thee ? Whatever he does, said she, how painful soever it may appear, is the effect of mercy. Ah! what has my heart endured! Now behold I die.. But where, oh where is Jesus? He knows—he knows what I suffer. Has he prayed for me?—What, O Mary! said Lazarus, dost thou now suffer?

Mary answered, My sufferings spring not from the dread of corruption, or from afflictive thoughts of being taken from these my dear friends, but from doubts which wound my bleeding soul. Ah brother how was it with thee?—But does Jesus pray for me? With the prayers of the holy Jesus will I compose myself for the sleep of death. Will not this earthly life soon be over? O say, is it not near its end?—They are silent, Martha, Nathaniel is also silent. Jesus has not yet prayed for me! this pierces my soul. Here am I, O Lord, thy will be done! Thy will is best!

Here Lazarus lifting high his folded hands, said, As a mother pities her child, so, O Lord, is thy pity towards us : but though a mother may forget to pity her child, yet thy mercy never fails.

Lazarus then weeping, Mary raised her languid head, and said, Tell me, my heavenly brother, which now belongs to me, the curse from Sinai, or the mother's love? Oh if he loves me, what triumph! What extacy! the most lofty and noble praises be offered to the Giver of eternal grace! to him whose mercy is not like that of man! to the God of all grace! But how can I know that he pities me with a mother's pity? Oh speak ; has the prayer of the Most Righteous softened my Judge, and does he look on me with the pitying eye of parental love?—O Thou who art most merciful, cried Nathaniel, look down with an eye of compassion, and no longer hide thy cheering smiles from the afflicted.—Here he ceased, and

Lazarus added, Thine afflictions, O sister, will soon end in complete felicity. Thou knowest not what a pattern we have had of patience and resignation to God, and to whom we look up in the heaven of heavens! I have been raised to life, yet wish, O Mary, to fall asleep with thee. The voice of death would to me be more melodious than the hallelujahs of the crowded temple. O Mary, our divine friend, our help in time of trouble, the blessed Jesus, who remitted sins, who raised the dead—died—on the cross.

He crucified!—He dead on the cross! cried she, with faultering accents. Ye angels! He crucified and dead!—O thou who hast permitted this, I bless and praise thee for all my sufferings, and follow my deceased Lord! Here her tongue failed, and the colour of death overspread her placid countenance. Lazarus laying his hand on her icy forehead said, O thou who art perfected in thy Redeemer's love, may this sleep convey thee among those who die in the Lord! Be thou now born to the day of light! to eternal life! My heart cleaves to thine, yet gladly do I see the dissolution of this tabernacle, and thy departure to the heavenly Canaan. O thou preserver of Israel! support her through the dreary valley, and bring her to the land of felicity, where thou driest up every tear, where no complaint, no lamentation, interrupts the grateful song of praise. To her be the sun of this earth extinguished. Thou death shed on her thy last slumber, and may her mortal frame rest in peace! Receive her, O corruption, that her body may grow up to life; a seed sown by the Lord for the great day of the harvest, when the reapers shall shout, and the trumpets sound, when the earth and the sea shall with a mighty noise bring forth their dead ; when the whole expanse of the heavens shall resound with the praises of the supreme Lord and Judge.

Chehar seeing the triumph of death over Mary, was so transported with joy, that gentle murmurs, as at a remote distance, issued from his tremulous wings. They who were present knew not what it was they heard. Soon the seraph, touching his soul-animating harp, from its enlivening strings struck such sounds of celestial harmony, that Mary raised herself and listened in an extasy, while Lazarus and Nathaniel supported her feeble frame. The seraph now no longer trembled, but from the soft thrilling strings, in sounds of inexpressible melody, poured the peace of God which passeth knowledge. The attentive soul of Mary was swelled with sensations before unknown : thoughts new and sublime, in a soul ready to leave its corruptible dust, and to enter into eternal life. Thus was it with thee, holy Ezekiel, in thy vision of the resurrection, when all around, the convulsed earth teemed with the awakening dead. The angelic harp still continued its powerful sounds, diffusing into the almost disembodied soul a repose never tasted by any that returned to life. Now the celestial herald burst into louder and still louder strains, and tempests and earthquakes seemed to accompany the notes ; while the immortal, in the transports of inspiration sang to the resounding harp. Holy ! holy ! holy ! is He who bled on Calvary !

Mary, sinking under the raptures which the celestial voice poured into her labouring heart, expired. . Her brother sunk down by her, then grasping her clay-cold hand, and wiping away his tears, said, Praise be to Him who has made death the way to life ! Glory be to the Giver of immortality ! Behold thou art now in the tents of peace, yet thy soul shall not, for ever remain alone ; for even' this corruptible shall put on incorruption; the fair flower broken by the rude storm, shall, on the·solemn morn·of the resurrection rise) in celestial lustre. ·Let us now·commit the sacred dust to its kindred earth—No, we .will for a moment forbear, and devoutly view this dear body that has just been crushed by the thunder of death, and will ise at the sound of the last trumpet. It will lie ripening through successive ages ! How mysterious are the ways of the Eternal !. Thought is lost in astonishment ! When I would consider His ways I .cannot pierce the darkness. that surrounds them : yet if a glimpse of twilight breaks out, I weep with joy, while conducted by the dawn, the harbinger of the joyful morn. With her it is now morning ! Oh receive my dear sister ! my last salutation, May he who now rests in his sepulchre, bless thee !

, The divine Jesus had already blessed her. A celestial body of radient lustre, hovered round Mary's soul, guided by the powerful hand: of creation. Environed with streams of felicity, she first cast a thought on the corpse she had left, exulting in her being freed from her encumbering clay ; and then in complete glorification, was filled with a lively sense of her beatitude. With extended arms she cried, O thou sleep of death ! thou summit of blessings ! Thou—is it possible, ye angels : is it possible, ye heirs of heaven, that I am blessed like you ? She was then silent. But soon closing her hands, she resumed, O·thou firstborn of felicity ! thou Son of Eternal light, thou Holy One of God, is it possible that I am thus blessed ?—O .sweet forgetfulness of all my sufferings, come and .infuse sensations of thy delightful repose !—No, forbear ; for to compare the

suffering's of the past life with everlasting joys,
this plenitude of bliss is extasy. Ye who never fell,
however happy in your persevering obedience and
purity unstained, know not the felicity of comparing
the wretchedness of sin with the joys of this eternal
life. Ye never wept such tears as Jesus the God
of loving-kindness now wipes from our eyes! Ye
prophetic sensations with which I have oft been
seized, I now with grateful thanks acknowledge,
ye pointed out to me, hope in the heaven of hea-
vens! Oh I will rejoice in my past misery! I will
thank thee for all my sufferings! Now my hopes
are fulfilled! In the days of my mortal life eve-
ning succeeded evening till the last, when came the
night of death. How swiftly they passed away,
and now I awake in the morning of life. The
dream which began with weeping, ended with the
tears of death! the dream of life is now over, and
I am awaked! Once more shall I awake when
my mouldering clay shall become incorruptible,
and a more worthy habitation of its spiritual inha-
bitant, and be resplendent even as the body of him
by whom it shall be raised, who also died, was bu-
ried, and will rise from the dead! Mary then as-
cended like the brightness of the morning, light as
air, swift as thought, and as she passed, saw the
wide creation opening to her view without end.

Lazarus, filled with the most elevated ideas of
death, hasted back, in order to return to the mourn-
ing disciples. On his approaching the house, one
of the seventy ardently embracing him, related with
    sy the wonders of the Lord which he himself
had seen.

On Lazarus's entering the gloomy hall, he found
it still filled with sighs, on which bursting into
tears and raising his eyes and hands to heaven, he

cried, O God of gods, reward him still farther who
in obedience to thy will, humbled himself, and
submitted to the death of the cross ! Where is
the crown of the Conqueror of death concealed ?
Let me see it, bloody as it is ! It is more dear to
me than the angels' shining crowns which I have
seen from afar ! O thou mother of the divine
Jesus ! hear and raise thyself from this abyss of
grief ; at his death the earth trembled ! Night
covered the earth, and thou hast seen its terrors !
but thou knowest not how the heavens bore testi-
mony to him. Behold in the court of the temple,
the evening sacrifice awfully blazed in the midst of
the gloom : the sacrificers who stood at the altar
trembled at the terrors of the too early night :
the priests kneeled facing the door of the sanc-
tuary, and looking towards the holy of holies,
thanked the Avenger that Jesus had been put to
death, when presuming to direct their wrathful
eyes to the most holy place they beheld the veil of
the temple instantly rent from the lofty roof to its
lowest border ; the suppliants were overwhelmed
with the terrors of the grave, which arrested all
their powers, till fear and horror dispelling their
lethargy, induced them to fly from death. Oh
what heavenly consolation flows from the thought
of the dear deceased, who while he was expiring
on the cross, wrapped the earth in darkness, had
the rocks shake, and unveiled to the eyes of mortals
his tremendous glory.

While he spake, the hearers sat in silent amaze-
ment, yet little comfort penetrated their dejected
hearts. Thus the traveller in descending a steep
and lofty precipice, beholds not the beauties of
the clear smiling day in the flowery vale. In vain
does its radiency spread through the illumined

groves, in vain it moves in the meandering stream, :
for his fears extend a cloud over all the beauties of
spring.

Lazarus still observing their fixed sadness, thus
affectionately resumed, Is it no consolation to you
that God bears testimony to our dear deceased
Lord with such signs and wonders? O let this be
a powerful consolation ! Rejoice too, that Mary,
the taught of God, and whom you loved will weep
no more !

Magdalen now with tearless eyes hastily stepped
up to him, and said, Thy words, like the voice
of an angel, bring us comfort, and we will receive
consolation from them ; for they are as refreshing
as the breeze in parching heat. Thy celestial sister
is then gone to Christ ! Hast thou no more
angelic words, no predictions of our death ? Thou
wert once in the state of the dead, O hadst thou
then no intimations whether thy friends would
soon be discharged from this world of sorrow,
soon be admitted to celestial joy ? O speak, if
thou knowest, and no longer conceal from us, whe-
ther this will soon be our blissful lot. He continu-
ing silent, she resumed, Since our lives are to be
lengthened, O thou heavenly Judge, whose judg-
ments are a great deep, may we live to see judg-
ments accumulated on those who slew thine inno-
cent, thy blameless Son !

Midnight had for some time spread its sable cur-
tain. This when spent in prayer with Christ had
been as gladdening to his followers as the vernal
day ; but under their present distress was fraught
with images of terror ; and now the more terrible,
as the voice of the divine Intercessor was silenced
by death. Their lamentations gradually subsided,
and alleviating tears no longer wetting their now
dry eyes ; the weight of cold affliction immoveably

oppressed their souls, while sympathy for their
sufferings dimmed the eyes of the attending angels.
Meanwhile Salem and Selith, John and Mary's
angels, thus conversed :

Though we, O Salem, know the glorious con-
clusion of what appears so sorrowful, yet are we
little less afflicted than they. They are mortal, and
cannot, my celestial brother, know the joys that
await them; but wert thou to reveal thyself ar-
rayed in splendor, and to shew them the happy
issue of this maze of affliction, they would esteem
it an illusive dream : their minds would be still
fixed on the gloomy labyrinth, which even over-
comes me.

I with serenity, O Selith, contemplate the divine
plan, and thou art too deeply affected by compas-
sion.—I now acknowledge that thou sufferest like
man ; 'for when we are solely penetrated with hu-
man sufferings, our thoughts resemble those that
are human. The Most High afflicts in order to
improve them, and to render them more happy
than they could have been without drinking of the
cup of sorrow, when at the time of rejoicing, the
blessed shall be admitted to drink of the river of
life.

Celestial Friend, returned Selith, the griefs which
rend the heart of the tender mother, too much
overcloud me ; but Salem will forgive me. I saw
her extreme anguish at the cross. Do thou kindly
spread over her a healing sleep ; I will hover round
her with reviving visions, and prevent the approach
of new sufferings. Rest from pain has not yet been
bestowed on her. O the raptures she will feel,
when instead of still contemplating on death, she
will awake to the joys which flow from God's right
hand !

While they were thus conversing, a short sleep

alighted on John's tearful eye, which Salem perceiving, by a dream, pregnant with bliss, filled his heart with extasy. He seemed to remove him to Lebanon, whose cedars waved their tops at his approach. The morning more beautifully arrayed in gold and purple than ever he had seen, shone through the branches of the dewy grove, while the purling of the brook in the vale below was as sweet as the music of the temple. Soon in louder strains resounded the ravishing harmony of the celestial harps and voices, chanting Happy son of the heavenly mother, dry up thy tears! Dry up thy tears, thou happy son of the heavenly mother!

The disciple seemed not to dry up his tears! these the vision, brought by the seraph, could not yet suppress; for even in sleep the briny stream ceased not to flow. The radient morn now appeared overcast, and the joint melody of the celestial harps and voices died away. Meanwhile the immortal seemed to convey him swiftly to the grove, where the astonished disciple saw men, with rage flaming in their eyes, hew down a cedar so large that Lebanon shook at its fall. The cedar was formed into a cross, awful sight! but with pleased astonishment he saw it shoot forth palms. The scene of the disciple's vision was now removed from Lebanon to Eden, where he beheld a celestial glory that infinitely exceeded the splendor of gold and purple. He now heard more sublime choirs, and his heart was filled with the sweetest sensations of joy.

THE END OF THE TWELFTH BOOK.

THE

MESSIAH.

BOOK XIII.

THE ARGUMENT.

Gabriel assembles the angels and the risen about the sepul-
chre, where they wait the Messiah's resurrection. The
emotions of Cneus, the Roman officer on guard. The
soul of Mary, Lazarus's sister, comes into the assembly
of the saints. Obaddon, the angel of death, calls Satan
and Adramelech, and orders them to leave the Dead Sea,
and either to repair to Hell, or to the sepulchre. Satan
determines on the latter, and Adramelech on the. former,
but after changing his resolution, dares not to put it in
execution. The angel of death leaves it to Abbadona
either to come to the sepulchre or not, as he pleases.
The glory of the Messiah descends from heaven. Adam
and Eve pay their adorations. The Messiah rises from
the dead. The acclamations of the angels and the risen.
The seven martyrs, the sons of Thirza, sing a hymn of
triumph. Some of the saints come down to him from
the clouds, and at last Abraham and Adam. The soul
of a Pagan brought before him, on which he judges
the soul and disappears. Gabriel orders Satan to fly
to hell. Some of the soldiers of the guard, and also
Cneus, enter the assembly of the priests. Philo puts an
end to his life, and Obaddon meeting his soul in Ge-
henna, conducts it to hell.

THE ancestors of the divine Jesus rejoicing in
their being raised from the dead, remained
near the tombs in which they had slept, while the
angels sought for those who had been sanctified

by the Redeemer : but often was their joy damped
by grief, and oft they shook their purple wings, de-
filed by the terrestrial air, as by the dust which
rises from the foot of the traveller.

Gabriel still continued at the sepulchre, and
Eloa on one of the suns that revolve round in the
heavens, waiting the descent of Christ's glory.
But now the angel of the sepulchre soared up-
ward through the creation, to behold the celestial
signs of the resurrection. Long had he fixed his
eye on an effulgent star which in its circular
course shot by another ; at this sight the expect-
ing seraph's eyes beamed a brighter fire ; he turn-
ed ; his motion was as a storm ; his descent as
lightning, and returning to the sepulchre, he
called with a voice as loud as that of the forest-
bending tempest, Come, ye celestials to the grave !
Thither the angels and patriarchs soon hasted, and
soon was the sepulchre of the Chief among the
dead, environed by an august company of celestial
beings. Over the sepulchre, as in the center of the
circle; sat Gabriel, on a golden cloud, introducing
the souls of the redeemed into eternal life. But
the angel of death, who in Jehovah's name had
announced to Jesus the separation of his immortal
essence from the body, now slowly moved to the
sepulchre, and sunk into Gabriel's arms, saying,
All around me is night. The earth trembles, and
the darkness of the hill of death is deeper than the
blackness of the midnight gloom. Never have my
immortal powers failed in performing the com-
mands of the great Jehovah, except in the last,
under which I still faint. Renew my strength,
thou ray of the Omnipotent, that soon issuing
from the grave, will rise to the right hand of the
Father ! The immortal then leaned on the rock,
where rested the sacred body of Jesus.

Ah, what sweet longings do I experience ! cried
Abraham. How blissful the thought ! I shall see
him ! I shall see the Conqueror of Death, rise to
immortal life ! Hallelujah ! hallelujah ! hallelu-
jah ! I shall see him as he is ! I shall see his body
rise from the dead. Hallelujah !

My soul shall rejoice in the Lord ! cried David.
I shall rejoice on his ascending from the sepulchre !
Ye pious, whose bodies still are dust, and ye who
can never know corruption, your joy cannot equal
ours ! O what will Jesus experience ! He, the Son
of the Eternal Father ! He, who has felt more than
the sufferings of mortality, and the terrors of death !
O Asaph, added he, embracing him, the Saviour
who suffered the painful death of the cross, will
soon awake !

He then with inward joy fixed his longing eyes
on his Redeemer's sepulchre : so a dying saint
looks up to heaven, and from thence receives the
rapturous assurance of the endless felicity that
awaits him. Asaph steadily looking at the
psalmist, caught his holy transports. David's
countenance beamed encreased radiance : his breath
was harmony : he soared aloft, the air resounded,
and now he animates the harp, and the speaking
instrument, though yet unaccompanied with
words, diffused triumph : then fired with inspi-
ration, both his voice, and strings poured forth a
stream of rapture. So the highly favoured apos-
tle to whom the glories of the apocalypse were dis-
played, beheld standing, on the heavenly Sion a
lamb covered with radient wounds, and the rich
blood of salvation ; round him was a great mul-
titude rejoicing with the Father's name written
on their forehead.   ng hands the
harps resounded like the voice of thunder ; for they,

sang the Son whose radiant wounds beamed eternal
life into the souls below.

Joseph clothed with light, and bearing in his
hand the triumphant palm, sang to his brother, who
in his embraces had once poured forth a flood of
joyful tears, O dearest Benjamin! what raptures
do I feel in recalling the hour when the Almighty
Disposer of all events, permitted me, in my former
state, to make myself known to thee! But how
infinitely superior is the celestial joy and pleasure
and triumph for which we now with eager expec-
tation wait! O thou Brother of the redeemed!
thou first among the heirs of light! throw off the
veil of blood and dust that covers thy face, and
again shew thyself in glory! We thirst, we pant
to behold thee with all thy radiant wounds, the
Conqueror of Death. The reconciliation planned
by the Father, and which thou hast accomplished,
is of perpetual efficacy, and at length will arrive
the joyful hour concealed from the earth, con-
cealed even from the blessed host of heaven—that
hour when the fullness of the Gentiles shall come,
and the children of Abraham, Isaac, and Jacob,
shall be brought to the gracious Redeemer cru-
cified for them; when the Saviour, impatient of
any farther restraint, will exclaim, I am Jesus!—
The beloved weeping, will hang about his neck,
and He distribute to them crowns and the festal
robe of innocence. How will then the celestial
messengers proclaim from star to star the resplen-
dent lights that have issued from the depths of
wisdom! How will the adoring angels then bow
before the Eternal Father! O Primordeal Source
of being! O King who alone hast immortality!
praise, worship, and honour be to thy name for ever
and ever!

The soft harp and sounding trumpet accompanied the joyful song, and soft modulations audible to the ears of the blessed alone. Not unanimated flow the heavenly hymns : these are the rapturous products of original inspiration, the first fruits of bliss and grateful triumph, to us unknown : yet they are sometimes heard by the dying, and accompany them into eternal life. Isaiah the prophet of the silent Lamb heard the seraphs, when far from the opening grave, they, covering their faces, sang Holy, holy, holy, is the Lord of Hosts, the whole earth is full of his glory ! while their fervent voices shook the gates of the temple.

Filled with the ravishing expectation of the Mediator's resurrection, the blessed continued expressing their sensations in vocal and instrumental harmony, sometimes in separate, and sometimes in united melody : for as yet they felt not the silence of joy, nor the raptures of mute felicity.

Ezekiel descended from the clouds to a tomb on mount Olivet, and sang, I once saw in a vision dry bones scattered over the plain : at the command of the Lord of Life and Death, I bad them revive, they came together ; a rapid wind diffused life into the dead, and a host innumerable rose on their feet ! Still is my heart filled with transport at the idea of that wonderful sight. I myself have just been raised from the dead ! blessed, blessed be he by whom I am raised ! His body is not, as ours was, subject to corruption, and it will soon rise triumphant, the Conqueror of death. Hail Thou who art the Resurrection and the Life ! Under thy shadow shall all in the heaven of heavens assemble ! Death, the last of enemies, shall be destroyed, and Thou wilt resign up the sovereignty to the Father, that God may be all in all. Hallelujah ! Joy glowed in the countenance of the enraptured prophet, and Gabriel turning as swift as thought from the grave to the transported Ezekiel, cried, with a voice like the roaring of the sea, Hallelujah! God shall be all in all!

The sublime Isaiah then leaving the assembly of the blessed, descended to Golgotha and stood at the cross of the sacred dead. Daniel the favourite of the Most High, also quitted the assembly of the blessed, and stood at the cross, where with a psaltery in their hands they alternately sang:

Here! Here he was wounded for our transgressions, and with his stripes are we healed!

Ah, for our sakes was He wounded! for our sakes was He bruised! He submitted to chastisement that we might have pardon, and by His stripes are we healed!

He was oppressed and afflicted, yea He opened not his mouth! As a lamb was He led to the slaughter!

From anguish and from judgment is He taken; but soon will He awake to life, and who on earth or in heaven is able to make known the duration of his felicity.

He was cut off for the transgressions of his people, and as a criminal was he put to death!

Now is finished the sacrifice for sin. His seed shall be numerous as the drops of the morning dew, and shall live for ever!

By his heavenly wisdom shall the righteous servants of God make many righteous, and the heirs of glory; for the sins of the world hath he done away!

Who is he that came up from Cedron? In the power of the divine strength he came to bear the sins of man!

It was Christ, a teacher of righteousness! Christ mighty to save! whose wounds trickled on this hill

of death ! Whose blood, O heaven of beavens !
ran down on the altar of atonement ! His precious,
his sacred blood, before whom every knee shall
bow, and every tongue confess that He is Lord to
the glory of God the Father !

Now, now is transgression finished ! Righteous-
ness and salvation shall flourish ! Praise him the

ed ! Hallelujah !

Transported with these ideas of the rising Vic-
tim, the saints repeated, with a sound like that of
breezes whispering through the tree of life, Yes,
on this hill of death was the Holy One anointed !
Hallelujah !

The guard at the sepulchre was now relieved
by another party who had seen Christ expire, the
hills shake, and the rocks split. At the stone
which closed the entrance stood the Roman band,
with Cneus their commander, who soon became
absorbed in thought. The silent night and silver
moon led him to bewilder himself in an intricate
maze of doubts, while he had no guide to direct
his way. Leaning against the rock he said to him-
self. Is he a Son of God ?—Of what God ? Of
the God of the Israelites ? Oh why do I doubt
the greatness of Jupiter ?—Why am I unwilling to
believe that he whom this weak people call Je-
hovah is worthy to be known ? How pusillani-
mous is this fear of conviction ! How despicable
does Jupiter appear ! How great Jehovah who
                        and by his actions

Jehovah was mortal ! but if he was no more than
man, how could he be so great ?

While he was thus absorbed in thought, a mes-
senger thus addressed him ; Portia sends me to

know from thee, whether all be quiet at the sepulchre, and whether any have assembled near the corpse: she at first thought to have come herself, but changed her mind. Cneus desired him to tell Portia that all was quiet, and that nobody had offered to come near the corpse. The messenger was then going, when Cneus calling after him, desired him to inform Portia, that whether Jesus would, or would not, rise again to life, was a subject that filled him with the greatest perplexity.

Cneus again giving way to thought, said to himself, This lady is no less uneasy than I, about the issue of the mysterious history of this intombed sage. If he was not the Son of the Supreme God, it must be acknowledged that he was a pious man, —The Supreme God, did I say? that is denying Jupiter, and shall I place him beneath Jehovah, whom I know not. Jehovah's miracles seem to bear a far greater stamp of truth than those attributed to Jupiter, or rather have all the evidence of certainty. Had the conqueror of Israel invoked Jupiter, the image of that God, like that of Dagon, would perhaps have fallen to the ground, and from his impotent hand would have dropped the useless thunder! Ah, what thoughts are these! What constrains me to renounce him I have worshipped, and to sacrifice him to this tremendous, this unknown God, whose voice I feel speaking irresistibly in the most secret recesses of my heart? O thou whom I ardently pant to know, make thyself known to me!

Thus he mused with uplift eyes, till his head sunk down on his breast. Ah why, added he, did not I see this pious man perform his miracles? Why did I neglect hearing his instructions? He is now dead, and incapable of conveying them. O thou unknown! my soul bewilders itself in quest

of thee ! Oh that I could understand the instruc-
tions of thy prophets ! Oh that the veil that hides
them from mine eyes was removed ! At the very
cross I might have asked him some important
questions : but now he is silent. But will he
continue so for ever ? Can the dead revive ?—The
holy man himself assured his followers that he
would. This his enemies say, and hence we are
placed to guard his body. Should he not return
to life, his history, instead of rewarding my enqui-
ries with divine knowledge, will be all inexplicable
darkness. Thus Cneus bewildered himself in the
dark path to the Deity, no helping hand yet leading
him to the heights of wisdom.

Now into the exalted assembly of the risen the
angel Chebar brought the lovely soul of Mary,
who slid with a silver sound from an etherial cloud.

Benoni received her, saying, O Mary, thou didst
not see the Redeemer die, but thou shalt see him
rise from the dead. By the blood of the Lamb
hast thou overcome, take therefore the psaltery,
and be thou one of the celestial choir. May I pre-
sume, said she, to mingle with the glorious host,
on whom, for ages past, crowns and palms have
been conferred ? O Benoni, how happy am I !
What mercy has the gracious Author of Life and
Death shewn in chusing the hour of my decease !
I shall in this blessed assembly see the Redeemer
rise from the dead ! Admit me among you, ye saints
of God ! Ye brethren of Christ ! my brethren
and my beloved, for ever receive me ! for the Fa-
ther of Mercies, who has shewn favour both to you
and me, bath sent me ! O ye celestial community,
the triumphant bridegroom's bride, we here feel a
repose hitherto unknown, joys of which we had
not before the least distant idea ! How freely do
we here drink of the river of Life ! Oh with what

transcendent faculties, fitted for tasting the bliss of salvation, hast thou enriched the souls whom Thou hast called to inherit 'Thy glory ! A bliss of perpetual duration ! 'We shall be ever with Thee the object of our love ! What joyful thanks, what rapturous praise should we offer Thee, for this extatic prospect? I am lost in wonder, love, and grateful transports ! Thy bounty knows no end ! it is infinite and everlasting like thyself ! ·

· Trembling she ceased, filled with unutterable joy. The enraptured circle of the heirs of life, then sang to their accompanying harps, He is infinite ! Infinite is the Father of existence and love ! Sooner will the New Earth be involved in night, and the New Heavens in gloom, than the overflowing stream of thy mercies fail to refresh the thirsty soul ! Behold its spring rises at the foot of the throne, and falls from the empyrean heaven, from earth to earth into regions luminous and obscure. The blessed hear the sound, the sons of light hear it round the worlds, and flock to feed on raptures ! O ye redeemed, ye brethren of the deceased, delay not, but haste to the stream of felicity ! Ye who come with trembling feet have a Helper to support you, even he who with broken heartstrings, loudly cried, It is finished. As the spent labourer after a toilsome day, resigns himself to sleep, so the mighty One slumbers in the sepulchre ; the Lion of Juda slumbers in the shade ! Hadst thou, O hell, drank less of the cup of vengeance thou wouldest be silent, lest the Mighty One who sleeps should awake, and rise from the concealing tomb : but he will rise even to the right hand of the Father, and the incensed Lamb shall tread thee under his feet. · Thy deserts shall become more dreary, and thine abysses sink deeper under the terrible steps of the incensed Lamb.

At these . words Ohaddon, the angel of death,
rose from the sepulchre, and left the holy assembly,
in order to fulfil the orders he had received, which
were, that when the assembly of the saints should
denounce the judgments of hell to be at hand, he
should haste to Satan and Adramelech, who were
confined in the Dead Sea.   He wrapped himself in
thick darkness, and standing on the shore called
up the accursed.   With the noise of a storm. they
stood before him.   The angel of death then threw
aside the darkness with which he was encompassed,
except that on his front, which still retained the
gloom of a thunder-cloud, spreading before him to
the Dead Sea.   Satan now summoning up his en-
feebled powers, thus addressed Obaddon : Happy,
almost almighty slave, what tidings hast thou
brought ?   To thy foul slanders, for ages past,
said the angel of death, no answer have I returned.
·He who was dead and is alive orders ye instantly
to fly into the abyss, or to attend me to the hill
where he was crucified.   Near that hill of death he
rises.   No longer than I brandish this flaming
sword shall ye see him !   Then he shall wound thy
head !   Abhorred sinner he demands not thy wor-
ship !   Thou art unworthy ! if ye follow not . me,
remain here, or fly to hell, where hissing, mockery,
and the roar of loud laughter await ye ! for many
of your followers saw how at Eloa's first command
ye fled.

Satan cast at him a furious look, yet stood aloof ;
for from Obaddon's sword streamed expanding
flames., The foe both to God and Satan tore up
the fragment of a rock, and dashing it against his
own forehead, stamped on the fallen shivers, and
began to blaspheme the Eternal ; but soon his. im-
pious tongue was made to cease.   Choose, I say,
exclaimed the angel of death, sheathing his flam-

.ing sword in clouds of smoke : but they still
hesitated.

Now Abbadona drew near, and as he passed
along, cast his eyes on Adramelech and Satan,
fearless of their rage and vindictive pride.   Then
approaching nearer to the angel, thus spake :
Thou thou art a messenger of vengeance, yet, O
angel of God ! thou art not insensible to pity.
May not I, since it is permitted to these rebellious,
see the divine Messiah rise ?   How can I presume
that I shall be allowed the honour of worshipping
him ? . No, welcome, welcome shall be the invisi-
ble, the omnipotent hand, that shall strike both me
and them to the dust, might I but see the Redeemer,
the Conqueror rise.

Satan indignant heard, and with stammering
rage, cried, Thou slave of hell and not of God !
thou of slaves the most wretched—Him the angel
of death, with rapid speech, instantly interrupted.
Satan, in my presence, be thou silent.   For thee,
Abbadona, I have no orders.   How long thou art
permitted to remain on earth, I know not ; nor
whether thou wilt be allowed to see the resurrec-
tion of the Lord of Life and Glory.   I can only
inform thee, that his sepulchre is encompassed by
hosts of angels, and by the righteous, by his power,
called forth from the grave.   As to these accursed,
they are allowed to see him, that his triumph
over them may begin with punishing their impious
guilt and obdurate pride.   In this, Abbadona,
thou hast no concern : but deceive not thyself,
thou canst not view him with the joy of the re-
deemed.—No, not with transport, Abbadona ;
not with joy : yet let me see him, let me see
him.

Abject slave as thou art, cried Adramelech to
the angel of death, thou mentionedst the name of

Eloa.   Yes, I go to hell, but woe be to him who there presumptuously dares to mock at me ! I'll bury him under rocks heaped on rocks. Then turning to Abbadona, added, Why dost thou not follow me, thou most abject of angels ? now no longer an angel but a servile spirit. Thou fearest and art not deceived, that I will bind thee with adamantine chains to the lowest step of my throne, on which I will sit resting my foot on thy neck. But first thou shalt fall a sacrifice on that hill to thine abject servility.

Abbadona trembling with indignation, answered, with a look of sadness, It is not thy storming words, thou apostate, that terrify me ! but that the righteous spirits, the angels, and the great Jehovah are my foes, and them I fear. He then turned aside, and Adramelech fled. I follow thee, said Satan to the angel of death, stammering with rage, while the gloom on his forehead, marked with the scars of thunder, encreased as he followed. They spread their wings, while Abbadona stood wrapped in perplexity and suspense. Adramelech now suddenly turned, revolving in his obdurate heart a blasphemy as black as hell, which he resolved to pour forth with a loud voice, in the midst of the holy assembly, and called out, I follow thee, angel. Turn back, called the destroyer, with the voice of thunder, thou shalt not see the resurrection. Blindness shall strike thine eyes, blindness prompt thy speed ; and a hideous howling shall follow thee. Already blindness seized his eyes, and behind him swelled the howling storm, impelling him reluctant. Convulsed with tremulous agonies, he fled. Quick, irresistible, and nameless terrors pursued him, while the incessant howl, like the judicial trumpet called, Woe to thee ! woe; woe to thee ! The mountains in the nearest stars seemed to him to shake, and torn from their roots, to fall on him with destructive crush

. Meanwhile the patriarchs and the seraphims heard far in the heavens Jehovah proceeding along the solar way. The harmony of the revolving worlds was silent at the voice of thunder. Already had a star hasted from its orbit to the sun. Already the whole creation stood still. The patriarchs heard the flying storm proceeding from the heaven of heavens, and resounding from star to star, as from hill to hill. It advanced to the earth with glowing front, and the flame of the Lord approached, like the suns, when sent forth from God's creative hand, to rule each earthly globe. Eloa then shot like a ray of light into the assembly of the risen, proclaiming, The hour is come ! the hour of glory is at hand ! With the day-spring will the body of the Redeemer of sinners awake from the dead ! Ye hear the footsteps of the Almighty !

He then moved down to the sepulchre. The mighty tempest, a witness throughout the heavens of Him who liveth forever, now abated its violence, lest the earth should fly before it. The thunder was restrained, and only the roaring winds were heard, before which the forests of Judea bowed to the sepulchre. The earth shook : mount Seir, Pisga, Arnon, and Hermon, with cloud-capped Lebanon trembled ; the tops of Carmel and Lebanon were afraid : the waters of Egypt and meandring Jordan fled back to their source, yet the sepulchre continued unmoved, and the ponderous stone still lay before the open sepulchre. The inhabitants of heaven sank down together with the risen, on their faces before the present Deity. Adam then sang aloud a triumphant hymn : so will sound throughout the earth the angelic trumpet, to celebrate the mighty deeds of the Most Holy. O

Increate ! once a weeping babe ! a child endowed
with wisdom ! the delight of God ! the joy of sinners ! then a heavenly teacher ! a compassionate
benevolent worker of miracles ! then a high-priest,
who offered himself and went into the sanctuary
in behalf of sinners ! then, ah ! then was crucified
and died !   O Thou incomprehensible !   Thou
God of Love ! how can we sufficiently praise thee
for what thou hast done for us !   Under thy feet
thou hast brought death and sin, and received us to
salvation. With transport we shall see thee rise.
Ah we have seen thee die !   Awake, awake, death
can no longer hold the Son of God !   Behold thou
comest in the divine effulgence, as when thou
calledst forth the sun from darkness, then thou
camest encircled with thousands of thousands of
ministering spirits preceded by the inspiring storm !
Soon will the heavenly breeze separating itself
from the storm awaken thy body. Behold the outskirts of the glory of the Lord beams down among
the stars, while before it the ruddy morn tempers
the effulgence of the divinity !   Before him let all
creatures bow the knee.   Ye princes lay down
your crowns before him !   He comes to lead captivity captive, and to give eternal life to those he has
redeemed !   Breathe thou divine breath, and awaken the corpse, whose wounds when he is raised to
the right hand of the Father, will outshine the sun,
and even the lights which illumine the heaven of
heavens.   But let me with silent joy lay my hand
on my mouth.—O my children who are still the
sons of dust, especially ye few whom he has chosen to be the witnesses of his resurrection : ye
whose eyes still shed tears of sorrow, from your
knowing him in his humiliation and death, but not
in his glory, nor the glories with which he rewards
his followers, to all the divine, the ineffable bles-

sings of his resurrection, do I consecrate you, my
children ! Blessed be your conflicts ! every victory
of the strengthened !   All your labours in the work
of the Lord !   In heaven be they blessed ! Earthly
blessings which pass away shall not be yours ; but
when your souls quit their houses of clay, ye shall
receive the victor's crown, and shall be set on the
thrones of the elders,, to judge the generations of
men..   .

Eve, who, like Adam, became more radiant,
while looking on the resplendent glory, as it de-
scended through the heavens, hearing the blessing
delivered by the father of men, extended her arms
towards the holy sepulchre, and thus gave vent to
her emotions : Flow, flow, eternal source of bliss !
rend asunder the rock, gush forth, and comfort the
souls of all that thirst after thee ! O stream that
flows into the world of joy, receive into the re-
freshing breezes of thy shore, and to thy cooling
shades the spiritual pilgrim, that he may be
strengthened in his course, and animated by the
blissful expectation of his own resurrection ! Hope,
celestial light, brighten the eyes of the dying !
thou hope of awaking and living with Christ, pour
thy joys on those who are prepared to sleep in him !
then they shall not fear the horrors of corruption !
Blessed hour soon to break forth, pregnant with
bliss ! O hour of his awaking, on which depend a
numberless number of never-dying lives ! O what
blessings are prepared for you my children ! Rend
the rock, and stream forth, thou source of eternal,
life, thou shalt be enlarged to mighty rivers, even
to the ocean of God !

The angel of the sepulchre now winged his flight
through the clouds towards Christ's resplendent
glory.

As a thousand times a thousand of those who

died in God, had lamented the fall, which was to extend to the judgment day, but is no longer to be deplored, let now the cry of the new-born, and the groan' of expiring age, ascend to heaven, amidst the rapturous hymns of those who are purified by death. They too shall be purified by death, and at the dawn of the last day, for ever will cease the babes mournful cries, and the groans of conflicting age. Overpowered by amazement, joy, and felicity, tears of gratitude will then flow from their uplifted eyes, their triumphant hymns will contend

mighty sound ; for the righteous then will be a thousand times a thousand. Not less was the host which, at the sepulchre of the Lord, panted with longing expectation of what was to come, when Gabriel descended with the divine glory. Then the earth shook, Satan like a mountain, and the guards of the sacred body like little hills, were thrown down. Then from the sepulchre the immortal rolled the stone, Jehovah himself rejoiced, and Jesus arose.

How shall I utter what was now seen ! how at a distance faintly mention the joy of those that saw the Redeemer's resplendent face ! Too presumptuous is the ardent wish, and fruitless the effort to ascend with these to heaven !

At first a short silence reigned around the forsaken sepulchre : but soon the favoured assembly, radiant with salvation, sang with triumphant joy, like the morning stars at the birth of the creation. They sang thee the Son, after thy conquest over death, not as on the cross, with drooping head ! but gloriously ascending over the rock of the open sepulchre, ineffably divine, adorned with victory, with victory ! hallelujah ! with victory, gloriously triumphant over eternal death ! Thou who art

mighty ! thou whose name is holy ! thou to whom
all knees shall bow, all in heaven, in earth, and
under the earth ! thou whose birth Bethlehem saw,
at whose death Calvary shook, and whom the grave
has delivered up !—Sink down ye depths before the
Conqueror, and ye hills rise before him and clap
your hands ! To his honour, ye archangels, strike
your harps ! ye first of thrones in the heaven of
heavens arise ! and ye human voices proclaim from
the dust your joy that he lives ! Before the eter-
nal throne join to sing the inexpressible honours of
the great Messiah ! To him, ye angels, to him,
our brother, who was flesh and bone of Adam, be
everlasting praise !

. O thou who art most mighty ! cried the triumph-
phant spirits : thou to whom our knees lowly bend,
and all our powers bow with awful adoration !
Thou great Beginner and great Accomplisher of
our salvation, art now awaked from death ! Short
was thy slumber, and thy awaking was sudden as
the creation, when called into existence by thine
almighty voice ; when, at thy command, the suns
rolled, and round them the obedient worlds ! O
thou Alpha and Omega, the most gracious First
and Last, in thee we live, and in thee are immor-
tal !

They ceased. The risen Messiah favoured them
with the sight of his divine countenance, when
overcome by their extatic bliss, they fell down in
silence.

The seven martyred sons with their mother, now
hasted to the celestial assembly, singing with holy
triumph, Arise, and shout, O earth ! for thou hast
been esteemed worthy to receive into thy bosom,
as into a mother's arms, the sacred body of Christ,
the Redeemer ! The first-born of the dead is risen,
and all the heavens saw him rise ! Earthquakes

from Golgotha to lofty Moriah, attended the Conqueror ; with the mountain trembled the cross, and the pinnacles of the temple. Arise, O earth, in thy beauty ! the glory of Christ ariseth on thee ! Less celebrated wert thou in the heavens, when after thy birth, thy first morning rose on thee. Many are thy sons, and many righteous shall be among them. As the mother of immortal children, thou shalt translate them into the heavens, that in the lucid robes of purity they may rise victorious, singing the praises of the Redeemer. Shout thou hill of death louder than all the other hills of the earth ! Rejoice, thou sepulchre, before the mountain of God ! At the last day, O earth ! shalt thou, at the call of the omnipotent Son, deliver up the dead confined in thy bosom ! Then shall be formed a new earth. Then shall the sun rule no longer over thee, nor the moon, thy companion, accompany thee : on thee as the dwelling place of the righteous will the divine glory shine, and he whose precious blood dropped on Golgotha will be thy light.

Thus sang the early martyrs, who already bore

with Benoni and Mary, leaving the assembly of the blessed, and each holding palms, descended from the clouds, and kneeled on the stone which now no longer shut up the sepulchre. There, with a love above what can can feel or express, Mary said to the partakers of her bliss, Were I still

yet would my most affectionate love be death, when compared with this exalted fervor. Benoni, Jedidoth, see the King of Glory, how is his lustre

venly Sharon ! attempered for us ! he likewise attempers himself for that cedar Eloa, whom he

also created ! He is another self of all the glorious
elect !—Another, cried Eloa, joyfully approaching
them with downward flight: to every one is he
another self ! To you, Daniel ! Moses ! Abra-
ham ! likewise to thee, thou chief angel of death !
to thee Salem ! for these had descended to them:
to thee, Mary, and to me ! to you, Benoni and
Jedidoth ! to every one according to his desire,
the overflowing, the inexhaustible source of good !
to each the most bounteous ! to all the most de-
serving of their love ! This elevated, this trans-
porting idea, too exalted for human penetration,
bears your souls aloft, and the only, the beloved
Son—through all eternity beloved, and to all
eternity the loving Son of the Eternal Father, ab-
sorbs all our thoughts, and our faculties are lost
in the immensity of the divine goodness !

While the spirits and angels conversed, the
blessed in greater numbers descending to the rock,
surrounded their Mediator and brother, rejoicing
with other joy than this world can give, or which
they who walk in its gloom can conceive.

Abraham, with his hands lift up towards heaven,
said, O thou Son of Jehovah ! (accompany me, ye
jubilant harps of my children, in joyful notes : my
harp shall lead the consecrated sounds :) Thou
quittedst thy throne ! from heaven didst thou
descend to this earth, and die ! In all the worlds
before or since created no events like these were
ever seen ! We behold the actions of the divine
Redeemer irradiated by surrounding hosts ! He
fellow worshippers, join the seraphs exalted joys,
which, O Eloa, beam down from heaven !

Adam at length immerging from a sea of rap-
tures, and from the luminous streams in which
he had been immersed, thousands of thoughts,
swift as the lighning's rapid flash, rushed into

his agitated soul.   With eager eyes he flew from
the clouds to the hill of death, and alighting at
the cross, stretched out his arms to Jesus the con-
queror, crying, I swear by thee, who livest for
ever, that on the great day of the completion of all
things, those who sleep shall awake, and death shall
be no more !

The exaltation of the Messiah began with his
awaking from the death of the cross, whence he
ascended to the throne, and sat down at the right
hand of the Father, where honour and praise
awaited him, who willingly humbled himself, and
descended from the mansions of glory to the dust
of Golgotha. In vain did Eloa himself then
strike the festive harp : in vain the blessed spirits
poured themselves forth in psalms to his praise,
too inadequate were their efforts to the sublime, the
sacred theme : how much then is it too for me !
Teach me, thou sacred muse of Sion, something
of that glorious triumph, which, from its com-
mencement in the abode of mortal sinners, rose in
continual gradations to infinitude. O enable me
with intent eye to follow him, who in the lucid
path soared to the throne !.

The Mediator affectionately looked down on
Adam, then gave a sign to an angel, who brought
a soul that thus discoursed with his conductor,
Who, thou resplendent being, is that awful and
sublime figure over that rocky hill ?—Perceivest
thou not, O soul, said the angel, the radiant bands
around him ?—Ah, I cannot turn my eyes from
him to whom thou art leading me ! He is the
chief of this divine assembly. Join thy worship,
returned the angel, he is the Lord of men and
angels, and thy Judge —The soul then exclaimed,
O Jove, who rulest in Olympus ! the greatest, the
most glorious ! O my conductor ! with what

terrors do thine eyes fill me ! Am I before the austere Minos ? Is there a passage from hence to black Cocytus ? and does the thunder of Jupiter's oaths roar along the baneful stream ? O my inflexible leader ! deignest thou not to answer the questions I trembling utter ? Now to the soul spake the Mediator, There are no such beings as Jupiter and Minos. It is me whom the oppressed invoke as their lord and judge. Then to the angel he signified the future state of the deceased. Thus in slow gradations advanced the Son's exaltation. To the witnesses Jesus said, Before I rise to my Father oft shall I be seen on Tabor ; there shall ye meet me. Jesus then disappeared, and they moved to Tabor.

Still motionless on the rock of the sepulchre, lay Satan, struck by a look of the risen Mediator. He heard Gabriel coming toward him as a storm, and having with labouring efforts, raised himself, beheld the Redeemer's messenger, who cried, Cast thyself down into thine abyss. Thou loiterest on earth. Wert thou capable of instruction thou must know that for Finite to contend with Infinite, is to be forever subdued. But thou art hardened against conviction. Avaunt ! fly, with thy plans of fresh rebellions, to the gloom of the regions of despair. But I forbear denouncing the thundering curse. Avaunt. Satan stretched his wings, yet again lingered in the wilderness, and from a towering rock fixed his eyes on the dreary prospect. Gabriel then encompassed by the terrors of God pursued him in a tempest, when spurning away the rock, he rushed through the wide creation down to hell ; but entered not, till after he had spent some irksome days at the gate.

Already had the alarmed assembly of the priests spent two nights at the house of Caiaphas, and still waking began to see the returning, morn. In silent anxiety they set waiting the issue. The stone on which they had set the seal, the Roman guard, and the safety of the body of the deceased, employed their agitated minds, which laboured under the keenest · pangs of perturbation. Now came the third day, a day of fears and apprehensions.

The Roman guard at the sepulchre began now to recover from their fright, and to discourse with each other. How was it with thee? I felt the earth shake, and was thrown to the ground. So it was with me, said his companion. Another faintly leaning on his comrade, cried, How terrible the earth shook! It threw me against the rock! At the roaring blast said another, the stone before the sepulchre split. I thought the world was at an end. No, another cried, the stone is not split, though it no longer lies at the entrance of the sepulchre.

The centurion now called, If ye are able to speak, answer to your names. They did so. Cneus then going near the sepulchre, observed that it was empty and the stone rolled away. Filled with the greatest surprize, he called one of the soldiers aside, bad him haste to the pontiff's palace and bring him word whether a council was sitting there, adding that he would follow him. The others eagerly asked the hasty · messenger whither he was going, he answered to the high-priests; and continued his way, while they followed at a distance

As a sudden thought darts into the mind of one bewildered in mazy researches, so unexpected came the messenger with panting haste, and addressed the amazed council, saying, To no purpose was your sending us to keep guard at the sepulchre. This morning the earth shook with great violence: the massy stone started from the entrance of the

tomb, and the body is not there. Then turning
his back he left them. Struck with the tidings,
they started from their seats, and stood motionless
monuments of astonishment and terror. Soon was
the messenger followed by three other Romans, who
abruptly entering the hall, exclaimed, as with one
voice, See ye to yourselves, for the great stone
spontaneously rolled away : the earth shook, and
there came a terrible whirlwind ; after which we
found the sepulchre empty. We first fell, half
dead, on the ground, and afterwards saw the empty
tomb. A rolling clap of thunder then confirmed
the report. Philo struck with madness now burst
into a hideous laughter, his speech forsook him,
and the priests sunk into a silence as profound as
that of death.

Caiaphas at length recovering his spirits, sent for
the elders, who soon came ; more of the guard
likewise resorted to the palace, and observing the
countenances, of the assembly, said, We see that
ye are no strangers to what has passed this morning.
Thanks to the gods that we are yet alive ! How
could you, ye priests, impiously put to death the
son of the God of thunder ? His sepulchre was
empty, you may go and satisfy yourselves of this
truth. Here the high priest addressing himself to
the guard, Go in to my servants, and warm your-
selves by the fire. Was your officer with you ? He
was, said they, and fell to the ground as well as
we. He likewise saw the sepulchre open. Caiaphas
then went out, and gave orders that the guard
should be liberally entertained with provisions and
wine.

Caiaphas, with unsteady steps, returned to his
seat, with his mind filled with painful agitations.
We must buy over these Romans, said he, or all
will be in a tumult. But what is life to me ? O

Saddoc ! · I almost question the truth of thy doc-.
trine ! But is not this a deception, occsioned by
their apprehensions ? There was indeed an earth-
quake, but that they actually saw the sepulchre
,empty is not so certain. Here he was interrupted
by the entrance of the officer of the guard. They
all arose, and respectfully stepped back, on which
he said, Ye are at no loss, I am sure, to know me.
I likewise saw him on the cross, and even then be-
lieved that there died the son of the gods.—Ye
have heard what passed at the sepulchre.

In the mean time came Obaddon, Philo's angel :
his piercing eyes flamed destruction : his raven
hair, in large locks, overspread his shoulders, and
he stood fixed as a rock. With fury he looked on
Philo, yet suppressed his terrific voice denouncing
death. Hail, black ensanguined hour ! said Philo
to himself, Hail hour of death, quicken thy last
advances ! Thou vale of Benhinnon, likewise hail !
While these last words passed silent through his
mind, seven-fold terrors rushed on Philo, who,
with a ghastly smile and affected composure, went
up to Cneus, and recovering his speech, stammered
forth, How ! the grave open, and no corpse in it ?
No corpse at all returned the officer. Durst thou,
O Roman, swear to it by Jupiter ? Jupiter, said
Cneus, is an empty name, when compared to the
truth of what I say. Did I mean to swear, I would
assert this truth by Jehovah himself, whom I now
worship. But will not such wretches as you cre-
dit me without an oath ? Here Philo, with roaring
voice, cried, Ah mark him ! He saw it open, and
no corpse in it ; but will not swear to it. Yet
know, O Roman, that thou hast done more than
swear. Then snatching the officers sword from
his side, and seizing it with both his hands, he
plunged it deep into his breast, and throwing it

from him, fell, weltering in his blood. With
rid rage he then tore open the wound, and th
ing the blood towards heaven, exclaimed, Be
thou Nazarene, I die! and instantly exp
When Cneus taking up his sword, walked u
the corpse, and then letting it fall, cried, To
to horror, to endless darkness and despair I d
this steel. After which he abruptly left the asse

The convulsed soul of the suicide follo
phantom which was to direct its gloomy
The angel of death was now in Benhinnon's
derous vale, and the soul of Philo, turning a
perceived him : but words are as little ab
describe his tremendous figure, as the thund
his voice, when he called out, My name is E
Obaddon, or Sevenfold Revenge. I am no
angel of destruction. It was I who destroyed
first-born of Egypt. Thou art now in Geh
and I shall conduct thee to the infernal gt
They then winged their way.

THE END OF THE THIRTEENTH BOOK. ·

THE

MESSIAH.

BOOK XIV.

THE ARGUMENT.

Jesus appears to Mary Magdalen, nine other devout
women, and Peter. This they relate to the assembly.
Thomas doubts the reality of his appearance. Jesus
discovers himself to Matthias and Cleophas at Emmaus.
Thomas goes into a sepulchre on the mount of Olives,
where he laments his incredulity, and prays. One of the
risen, whom he knows not, converses with him. Matthias
and Cleophas return. Lebbeus likewise is not yet con-
vinced. Jesus appears to the assembly.

STILL plunged in distress, and panting for
consolation, the mournful assembly continued
in the house near the temple. Thus saints on the
verge of life, insensible of their approaching feli-
city, walk lamenting by the vale which preludes
the future joys of heaven. The devout women
now mingled oil, spices, and also their tears, to
e virgins
watched to feed their lamps, and kept themselves
ready to meet the bridegroom at his first ap-
pearance ; so ye the devout attendants of your
Lord, with active sedulity, held yourselves pre-
pared by the early dawn. Scarce was the night
withdrawn when Magdalen, the wife of Cleophas,
Mary the mother of James, and Joanna, with
Salome, the sister of the mourning mother, and

Mary, the mother of the sons of Zebedee, left the disciples. At their departure, the mother of the Holy Deceased, embracing them, said, Ye, my beloved, will see him again, which I shall not. Go, in the name of the Lord, may he be with you!

They departed in silence, in the cool dawn of the rising day. On going along a difficulty arose in their minds, how they should remove the stone from the sepulchre, yet this did not retard their walk. We, said Mary Magdalen, will do all we can, and, as far as we are able, will preserve the precious body from putrefaction. Thus saying, they hasted forward with redoubled speed.

Gabriel now sat on the stone, which had been rolled away, and thus addressed Eloa and Abdiel, who were near him. See the witnesses approach. That the splendor of my seraphic glory may not overpower them, I will assume the appearance of a youth; and do ye, till they shall be more able to bear the lustre of the immortals, appear to them as men.

The Mediator now looked down from the veil by which he was concealed, on the angels and the devout women, who approached, rejoicing with that divine joy purchased by his blood. The inhabitant of Magdala, drawn by love, came first to the sepulchre, and finding it open and the body gone, turned amazed, and calling to the others, hasted back towards Jerusalem. Not so her companions : they advanced undismayed, and soon their active eyes saw on the stone which had been rolled away, a youth of a resplendent appearance, who had a garment white as snow, and with the voice of joy removed their solicitude. Fear not, said he; I know you seek the crucified Jesus. He is not here, but is risen, as he himself declared that he should. Draw near, and see the place where the divine Jesus lay. Thus saying, he led them into the sepulchre, and then added, Go, and tell his disciples that he is risen from the dead, and behold, he goeth before ye into Galilee : there ye shall see him. They still remained irresolute and trembling ; on which two angels appeared in shining vestures. The devout women, still more afraid, stood with down-cast looks, till one of the angels said, Why seek ye the living among the dead ? Jesus is not here, but is risen. Remember ye not what he said, while he was yet in Galilee ? The Son of Man must be delivered into the hands of sinners, and be crucified, and on the third day rise again. They now no longer hesitated, but, winged with animating joy, flew to the disciples, as the messengers of glad tidings.

Peter and John were now coming, and Mary Magdalen was returning with them, when John said to his companions, The lower way, by those bushes, is the shortest. As he led, the others followed. These roads were separated by a hill, which interevening, hindered the devout women and the disciples from seeing each other as they passed. Thus pilgrms to the New Jerusalem, the affinity of whose correspondent souls speaks them made for each other, are often near, yet never unite, and their first interview is in that blessed mansion, where they are mutually surprized that in this state they never met. John now hasting before Cephas asked his female companion, if the body was taken away by the priests, and she answering that she could not tell ; he observed that it was reported they had been so careful to preserve it, that they had put their seal on the stone which closed the sepulchre, and that some wretches must therefore have taken it away for the sake of the burial clothes.

John had by this time reached the sepulchre, and saw the linen lying on the ground, but, checked by timid reverence, avoided going in. Peter, soon coming up, entered the sepulchre without hesitation: the head-cloth he saw lie apart, and not folded up with the other linen. John, now prompted by Peter's example, entered the tomb, and having also examined it, the two disciples left Mary, who, being agitated with various thoughts, staid at the sepulchre, while they went away silently meditating on the important event.

Meanwhile Mary, standing by the grave, looked in, and hastily wiped away her tears, which obstructed her sight. Many an eager look she, with anxious heart, cast round the sepulchre, and though there were now angels in the tomb, she scarce perceived them ; for she only sought for Jesus. Thus the panting roe seeks only the fluid stream ; the shining sun attracts not its down-cast eyes, nor does it feel the forest's waving shade. Why, O woman, weepest thou ? said one of the messengers of joy. Ah, said she, they have taken him away whom my soul loveth, and I know not where they have laid him. Then turning aside from the sepulchre, before her stood Jesus ; but she knew him not. Why weepest thou ? said he. Whom dost thou seek ? But this he spake not with the voice with which he uttered the doctrines of eternal life ; when, supposing him to be the gardener, she answered, If thou hast taken him away, tell me, I pray, where thou hast carried him. Tell me in what gloomy recess is he laid ? that I may haste and find him. Thus near ineffable bliss mourns a soul dear to the Lord, under the last agonizing sense of the mortality of her terrestrial frame ! she lies struggling with death, and thirsting after support, lamenting before her Saviour, and so terrified at the approach of her, last trial, that instead of the merciful Redeemer, she only sees an offended Judge! but O the bliss which succeeds these tears! Mary, in the bitterness of her anguish, turned her face from him of whom she was enquiring of Jesus: from him she turned her face; but like the harps around the throne accompanying the songs of the blessed, when they sing the praises of the Lamb that was slain; but even more sweet and affectionate than harps and triumphant hymns, to the devout mourner, sounded the voice of Jesus, saying Mary! she heard and knew the voice of her Lord, and in the sudden tumult of her joy, fell trembling at his feet, and casting her fixed eyes on him, vainly strove to express her emotions, and scarce could she, with languid breath, utter Rabboui! With trembling hands she then grasped the feet of the Saviour, who with a look of benignity said, Hold me not. Some time shall I continue with thee, and thou shalt see me again. I have not yet ascended to my Father. Go to my brethren and tell them, I go to my Father and your Father! to my God and your God!

Jesus disappearing, she hasted to communicate the joyful message. Salome with her companions were near the door of the house which contained the mournful assembly, when He who had disappeared from Mary met them during the rising day. They all knew him who was now no longer among the dead, and Jesus saying to them, All hail: they trembling, fell at his feet. Be not afraid, said he, but go and tell my brethren that they go into Galilee, and there shall they see me. He then vanished from their sight.

These witnesses, filled with unutterable joy, hasted forward with the gladdening message. Peter and John had before returned, and had spread a gloom over the dejected assembly, when lo! the

witnesses of him that liveth entered.   Hear us, ye
mourners, said they.   Listen to what we have seen.
We have beheld him living, and have seen his an-
gels ; first, one at the sepulchre, and then two
others.   What, O Salome, did they say ?   for
frighted at the celestial messengers I did not per-
fectly understand them.—Here Thomas stepping
forward, interrupted them, saying, Ye were, per-
haps, too much affrighted to know what you saw
or heard.—Ah thou disciple of Jesus, said Salome,
alarm us not with thy doubts, we are amazed and
filled with joy.   He who liveth said, Be not afraid,
and yet thou, his disciple, endeavourest to renew
our fears.

No, my beloved, he returned, far be that from
me ; but allow me so ask you some questions,
while I closely search into the truth of so singular
an event.   You first saw one angel, What was his
form ?   What his appearance ?   That of a young
man, Said Salome ; but his face was radiant, and
his vesture white as snow.   That, cried the mother
of Jesus, was Gabriel.   Thomas then asked if the
sun was risen, adding, You, Salome, forget that
yesterday Pilate, at the request of the implacable
priests, ordered a Roman officer with a guard to
be placed at the sepulchre, now the armour glit-
tering in the sun might impose on you, and, de-
ceived by fear, you might imagine you saw angelic
forms.

But Didymus, it was scarce dawn, the young
man was no Roman, nor was he dressed in ar-
mour : besides it was his face that shone, and not
his attire.

Well, what did this immortal say ?

That we should not be afraid ; that he knew
we were seeking for Jesus of Nazareth ; who was
no longer there but was risen from the dead ;

adding, Come in and see the place where he lay.
Then leading us into the sepulchre, he said, Go
and make known to his disciples and to Peter, that
he goeth before you into Galilee; there shall
ye see him.   Here   eat emotion,
                                       Ah august
                                       enly consola-

tion, wert thine appearance real !   But his naming
me, and heither Mary nor John, fills me with
perplexity.

Didymus, after a long pause, asked again, What
did the angels say ?   She replied, Jesus goes
before you into Galilee, there shall ye see him—
Were the other angels of the like form ?   Their
appearance was still more heavenly, cried two of
the witnesses ; but we have also seen Jesus himself.

Was he with the angels ?—The angels had
disappeared when we saw him coming to meet us,
clothed as formerly ! but in his deportment there
was something celestial.   Such, perhaps, was his
appearance on mount Tabor.   All hail ! said he.
We instantly fell trembling at his feet, and em-
braced them. Be not afraid, continued he, but
go and inform my brethren of these things, and
that they go into Galilee, and there they shall see
me.   At these words he disappeared.—So you have
seen him ! Did all of you see him ? said Thomas,
with an anxious pensive brow—You say it was
the very form, clothing, and voice of Jesus !   He
ceased ; but being carried away by the stream of
doubts, he renewed his discourse and added, The
illusion of what ye have been relating is now too
strong upon you.   When ye are able to bear it,
I will plainly lay before you the several reasons
which move me to differ from you : but ye, the
disciples of Jesus, surely give no credit to these

fables. Thus saying, he returned to his seat.
Now to the floods of joyful tears which had
issued from the eyes of the devout women, succeeded
gentle and silent drops of pity.

Faint with joy, with pallid cheek, trembling
lips and faultering tongue, Mary Magdalen now
entered among the weeping sisters, and, with a
voice of mingled transport and terror, exclaimed,
He is risen! He is risen! She then seeming
ready to faint, John took hold of her, and she
stood leaning on him. Lebbeus soon recovering
from his amazement, said to her, Hast thou like-
wise seen the angels? I have seen, said she, not
only the angels, but himself. Here every eye was
raised towards heaven, except those of the incre-
dulous Thomas, who, with austere coldness, said.
They who can so far deceive themselves as to
think they see angels, may imagine that they see
him. Ah Didymus, answered Mary, blushing,
What have we—what has the blessed Jesus done
to thee? These eyes saw him! at his feet they
wept! James, looking at her with equal respect
and astonishment, asked if he had a celestial lustre.
He approached, said she, as a man, but with such
sweetness and dignity in his countenance as I never
saw before; no, not even in himself.

Peter, whose mind was distracted by numerous
doubts, now drew near to her; and when the
tumult of his mind allowed him to give vent to
his thoughts, he trembling said, Didst thou like-
wise hear his voice? Yes, Simon, said she, I
heard the divine voice of the risen Jesus. Ah,
what did he say? returned Peter.—I feel, but am
unable to express the grace which accompanied the
words he uttered, replied Mary. His voice was
affectionate as when, bleeding on the cross, he cried,

Father forgive them they know not what they do !
Ah Mary ! were the words he uttered.   I knew
him ! I was in heaven ! Rabboni ! was all I
could say.   I fell down before him : with trem-
bling bands I grasped his feet.   Oh, what a look
of kindness accompanied his words, when he said,
Hold me not !   Thou shalt see me again.   I have
not yet ascended to my Father.   Go to my brethren,
and tell them, I go to my Father, and your Father !
to my God and your God !

The mother of Christ, who had hitherto hung
down her head, now raised her brightening eyes,
and looking with amiable softness on Mary Mag-
dalen, arose ; then leaning on some of the assembly,
walked up to that beloved woman, and taking her
by the hand, with a benevolent look, and the soft-
est voice, thus addressed her :   Hast thou also seen
Christ, and heard his voice ? Thou hast seen and
heard my Son !—but may I, added she, casting her
eyes around with heavenly meekness, may I still
call him my Son ? Thine eyes, my dear Mary, tell
me I may : but had he still the marks of the nails ?
Here, turning aside, she wept.   Weep not, blessed
mother of the divine Jesus, said Magdalen, pressing
her hand ; he is risen from the dead.   Indeed,
I did not observe the marks of the nails ; for, dis-
ordered with my joy, I saw little put his face.
Mine eyes were fixed on the grace, the celestial
grace, which shone in his countenance, while he
stood before me amidst the cool vapours of the
morning, and the dawn's increasing light.   The
Saviour's mother ceasing to weep, now took Mag-
dalen by both her hands, and looked up to heaven,
then dropping them, stepped backward, and view-
ing her with tender admiration, said, O happy
thou ! thou hast seen Christ, and heard his voice !

The more early witnesses, who at first went with
her, filled with joy, now gathered about her, and
mentioned their being favoured first with the sight
of the angels, and then of the Lord himself.

Didymus then coming up, said, Hast thou also,
Mary Magdalen, seen angels? My sight of the an-
gels, said she, was very imperfect, mine eyes being
dimmed with weeping: but suddenly turning about,
I perceived somebody, whom I supposed to be the
gardener, and whom I did not know, till he called
me by my name.—So you scarce saw him whom
you term immortal, said he; You did not imme-
diately know him, and at first took him for the gar-
dener? The others say he was clothed as he used
to be. So then the gardener's clothes were such as
he used to wear. And how many of these angels
did you see? I saw two, she answered. The
others, he rejoined, first saw one, then two others.
Here turning from her, he walked away. Magda-
len then raising her eyes to heaven, exclaimed, O
thou tender mother, and ye the disciples of the Lord,
how great is his error! Leave me, Thomas, in
possession of my happiness. I will hereafter an-
swer thee. She then led away the mother of Je-
sus, in order to hold some joyful converse with
her.

The heart of Cephas being still torn with doubts,
and the affecting words, Tell it to the disciples, and
to Peter, sounding perpetually in his ears, he left
the assembly, and went out to indulge his melan-
choly thoughts, resolving to walk towards Galilee;
but restless and undetermined, he left the road,
and went to the sepulchre. The sight of the empty
tomb filled his mind with fresh agitations: Ex-
ecrable deed! said he, to take him from this de-
cent burial place, the gift of pious respect, and
perhaps to bury him amidst villains! What un-

worthy treatment !   Ah infernal Malice thou hast
gained thy end, and Joseph's successful petition to
Pilate has been frustrated ! The few tears of joy,
which mingled with our streams of sorrow, were
shed in vain : for how can I believe that he is
risen from the dead ?   Deceived by the illusions
of grief, these pious women imagine that they have
seen him risen ! and I have denied myself the trans-
porting joy of closing with their raptures ! Awful
cross ! added he, lifting his eyes towards that
saddening object ; too loudly dost thou bear wit-
ness to his death, and both heaven and earth have
heard thy testimony ! He died ! He died on
thee !—We are told that thou my Lord hast been
seen again ! O that this were true, and that I
might see thee raised from the dead !   I shall,
but it will not be till I see thee on the throne of
the Eternal. Why shrinkest thou back, O my
soul ! at this only rest ? Thy prayers and tears
have been heard, and thy Judge has cast a gra-
cious eye on thy heart-felt repentance ; but thou
darest not yet rejoice ! Still stands the cross, the
dreadful witness of his death ! the hill, the rock,
and the sepulchre, shaken by the divine power !
No, I cannot presume to hope that I shall again
see my Lord !

Such was his impassioned soliloquy, after which
he again surveyed the open sepulchre. Soon he
perceived at a small distance from the tomb, Mag-
dalen, prostrate on the ground, and leaning on her
right arm, Mary ! Mary Magdalen ! called the
disconsolate disciple. On hearing his voice she
arose and coming to him, they thus conversed :
Ah happy woman ! dost thou still believe that
thou hast seen him ?—O Simon, where thou sawest
me kneel, there he stood !—O Mary, lift up thine
eyes and behold the cross on which he died !—Yet

O Simon, he is risen ! he is risen from the dead !—
Mary, I conjure thee by the living God, tell me,
did those eyes which now see me standing before
thee—Whether mine eyes saw him ! cried she,
interrupting him : Yes, I protest by the Eternal
Source of Truth, that mine eyes have seen the
glory of Christ, that mine ears have heard the
voice of the Son of God, and that I felt the joys
of heaven ! Here a silent pause ensued, till Peter
said, Withdraw, thou blessed woman, and leave
me to indulge my sorrow. O that a gladdening
sight had caused such a delusion in me, as it has
in thee, and thus quieted my tortured mind ! Alas !
I cannot believe thee—Then disbelieve, said she,
thy having seen him walk on the sea, or thy having
beheld him on mount Tabor encircled with his
Father's glory !

Here they parted. O that I could believe her !
said he to himself : for she was now returning to
the sepulchre. Happy, happy woman ! she believes it from her whole soul, and it fills her with
confidence and joy ! What a composure and dignity has her fixed certainty spread around her !
unaffrighted by the grave, she would laugh at the
storms which howl through the gloomy vale of
death ! Ah ! why do I not believe her ? Cannot
he awake himself from death, who walked on
the liquid sea, and even held me up amidst the
boisterous waves ? Yes, thou Dead in God, if thou
hast really revived, forgive my sorrow, and the anguish of my soul ! When trembling I doubted,
and was sinking before the impending wave, thou
supportedst me—Oh deliver me now ! Thou
knowest, O my Lord ! that I have been under
greater terrors than these, yet thou now extendest
not thy saving right hand ! Oh by thy compassionate love ! by that gracious look thou didst cast

on me,, after I had den'ed thee ! O by thy mercy, I implore thee, pity, pity my anguish, and if thou hast appeared,. shew thyself to me !—No, presumptuous, I ask too much. The angel's words were, Go and tell it to the disciples and to Peter. Was not this inexpressible kindness ? Thou, Lord, appear to me who have repeatedly denied thee ! —to me. though thou hast neither appeared to Lebbeus. the beloved John, nor to the tenderest of mothers !

These were his thoughts, while with slow steps he ascended the hill ; and then sinking on his keees, he with down-cast looks, offered up his supplications. At length raising his eyes, he saw Christ just before him. What amazement, what joy poured into his transported soul ! The divine Redeemer graciously stretched out his right hand, when Peter unable to rise, strove to seize it, but fell prostrate in the dust : yet soon rising, he stretched out. his arms, and trembling, seized the hand of his Lord, which he easily pressed to his throbbing heart, his forehead resting on his Saviour's arm. The earth and the heavens, with all the objects round him, seemed to pass away ; but soon becoming. more composed, he lift up his eyes to the divine countenance of Jesus, and with trembling voice strove to give vent to his unutterable joy, crying, O Lord God, merciful and gracious ! Lord God, merciful and gracious ! His trembling now ceased, and he felt superabundant and ineffable consolations flow from the divine countenance.

Ithuriel, his guardian angel, with Orion, hovered round Calvary, and Ithuriel breaking silence, said, O Orion, what a transporting scene ! Oft shall we repeat our triumphs in honour of the Messiah ! Oft joyfully exalt his name ! The risen Lord shews himself to the pardoned sinner ! and Christ appears

to Peter! O come and let us mingle our joy!
How dreadful is sin! and yet the Redeemer
fills this favoured disciple with unutterable trans-
ports!

The risen Saviour then left the hill, and Peter
followed him with folded hands, till he escaped
from his sight. Then extending his arms upward,
he cried in an extatic transport, Thanks be to thee,
the Son of God, my risen Lord! O everlasting
thanks be to thee, for thou hast relieved my soul,
and filled it with consolations superior to all that
I could wish, or even conceive! Thus, O Lord
wilt thou comfort me in the gloomy hour of
death! O who am I?—What though I have
grieved for the dreadful sin of denying thee! yet,
who am I, thou Son of God? that Thou shouldst
shew such grace to me! Mine eye has seen the
glory of Christ! Mine eye has seen him risen from
the dead! O my soul break forth in perpetual effu-
sions of ardent praise! Pour forth the highest and
most noble thanksgivings! I now hope for all the
graces of heaven, for the consummation of bliss, for
the beatific plenitude of thy loving kindness!
Blessed Redeemer, thou wilt unveil to me the mys-
tery of thy death! Not the numerous host of hea-
ven! Not the powers, the thrones, the archangels,
can rejoice more, for I have seen the Son of the
Eternal God! Him who died on the cross have I
seen alive! O thought pregnant with solid bliss!
Oh tell it to the eternal thrones, proclaim it through
the heavens that he lives! Ye sons of light, let this
be the subject of your triumphant songs!

He here ceased, and for some time stood silently
looking towards heaven; then starting, cried, Ye
my brethren, shall also drink of this cup of conso-
lation, and then hasted away. Soon he reached
Salem's walls; soon he returned to the assembled

brethren, who were expecting him. With folded
hands he entered, crying, Praise, glory, honour,
worship, and thanksgiving, be ascribed to the Son
of God, who after dying a death accompanied with
many wonders, is already risen! Even to me
Christ has appeared! He stood near the cross,
and there with these eyes I saw his divine coun-
tenance.

With surprize and exultation they drew near
him, and pronounced him blessed. The Lord's
rising to life filled them with an astonishment too
great for utterance, and reverential silence for some
moments chained their tongues. At length having
all gathered round this new witness of the resur-
rection, they embraced him with overflowing joy,
pressed him to their hearts and wept. The mo-
ther of the blessed Saviour took him by the right
hand, and Magdalen by the left, saying, Now, O
Simon, thou hast also seen him! While Mary the
mother of Jesus, added, with a heavenly smile,
Thou hast seen him who is both the Son of God
and my Son! Lebbeus turning towards Mary,
cried, O thou most respectable of all mothers, it is
not now from grief; but from the extasy I feel that
I can scarce believe! O thou whom I saw with so
many dreadful wounds, and covered with blood art
thou risen? art thou revived? Here he sunk on
the breast of John, who embracing him, said, Yes,
yes, Lebbeus, he is risen! Then leaving Lebbeus,
he addressed himself to Mary, saying, Blessed mo-
ther of the divine Jesus, rejoice, rejoice! No more
shall a sword pierce thy maternal bosom!—O I
rejoice, said she, with celestial joy! Jesus is risen!
He is risen! and to me too he will appear!
Thou wilt shew thyself to me! The look thou
gavest me on the cross is a pledge of this! Bar-.

tholomew taking Peter by the hand, with com-
posed countenance said, Dear fellow disciple,
before my grey hairs go down to the grave, mine
eyes shall likewise see our divine Master raised
from the dead. Cephas took him by the hand,
and with the chearfulness of confident certainty;
answered, Yes, my dear friend, to each of us will
he be gracious.

Thomas, like a cloud that spreads darkness a-
long a serene sky, now, in gloomy agitations, ap-
proached Peter, saying, Thou too, Simon, believest
it. Were it possible, I would believe it on thine
account ; and then abruptly turned away his sor-
rowful face. Turn to us, Thomas, said Peter,
and join in our thanksgivings ; for of a truth the
Lord is risen. Yes, honour, and blessing; and praise
be to him who died, who is risen from death, and
has appeared ! He will be gracious to us all.!
At these words the mother of Christ sunk down on
her knees before Peter, and spreading her joyful
arms, with her eyes towards heaven, in the voice
of gladness exclaimed, My soul doth magnify the
Lord, My spirit rejoiceth in God my Saviour !
From thy cross thou hast looked down on thine
afflicted hand-maid, on the tears of thy mother, and
in thy mercy hast numbered them ! Succeeding
generations shall proclaim me blessed ! How won-
derful is he ! how great in all His doings ! more
mighty than death ; and sacred is His name ! Yes,
holy and eternal is he who has signalized his mercy to-
wards me ! He casteth down the pride of the blood-
thirsty, and exalteth the humble. He relieveth
the distressed ; but the proud he sendeth empty
away. Eternal is his loving-kindness. To those
who love him, he imparts the ravishing sweets of
his grace. Perpetual blessing, and praise, and ho-

nour and thanksgiving be to Jesus, who liveth, and
who is more mighty than Death !

Didymus had ascended to the lofty roof, to in-
dulge his thoughts in solitude ; and the others, in-
vited by the serene sky, and refreshing breeze, and
the extensive view of the various works of God,
went up to praise him who had rendered them so
blessed.   On their coming to Thomas, they roused
him from the pensiveness in which he had been ab-
sorbed. He at first started back, and when looking
up he saw the whole assembly about him, he has-
tily turned to go down and leave them.   Oh fly
not, thou beloved ! fly not, said Peter.   The Lord
will also have mercy on thee.   I, Thomas, doubted
too ; yet how gracious has he been to me ! But
who are they that are walking at a distance ? My
eyes deceive me, if they be not Matthias and Cleo-
phas. Stay with us, my friend, and be a partaker
of the ineffable joys that have been imparted to us.
The same transcendent joys await thee.   But who
is he that is joining them from yonder grove ? I do
not know him.   What a noble appearance has
that stranger !   Dost thou know him, Thomas?
See with what veneration they salute him. He is
now speaking. Indeed, Peter, I know him not,
said Thomas ; but I have scarce ever seen a man of
such an unaffected dignity. Peter replied, I wish
they would come to us ; the path now brings them
nearer, but those palms will soon deprive us of their
sight. Behold, with what majestic gravity, ming-
led with a manly sweetness, he seems to attend to
what they say.   Perhaps they are giving him an
account of the crucifixion of our Lord.   May not
it be one of the angels who was seen at the sepul-
chre ?

How art thou mistaken ! returned Thomas. He
is a man, yet his appearance is nobler than that of

other men.—O Thomas! said Peter, thou art a
stranger to the sweet conjectures of joy. What
thou feelest I have experienced. How little did I
hope to see Jesus, when in the deepest anguish, I
raised my languid eyes to the cross, and instantly
saw him standing alive before me. Thus, O Tho-
mas! joy did not deceive me.—But grief did, said
Thomas hastily.—Peter mildly answered, The
Lord will have mercy on thee!—God will have
mercy on me, he returned; but as for the divine
Messiah, He, like most of the prophets, has
been put to death. Here he shed tears and was
silent.

Cleophas and Matthias had now reached the
umbrageous palms. From their leaving Jerusalem,
till their being joined by the stranger, they had
conversed on the astonishing subject of Christ's
not being found in the sepulchre, and thus con-
tinued their discourse. Thou canst not conceive,
said Cleophas, the malice of the priests, or their
rage at not being able to hinder Joseph's placing
him in his tomb. They doubtless gained the
Roman officer, and prevailed on him to take out
the body, and inter it among the remains of the
wretches that lie buried on the hill.—But, O
Cleophas! what dost thou think of the angels at
the sepulchre?—Has melancholy Matthias deceived
all our friends!—Why, Cleophas, should sorrow
make them see angels? Why should it not
rather represent frightful forms, as the ghosts
of executed malefactors, or that of the unhappy
Judas?

Cleophas, starting back, answered, My beloved
fellow-disciple, satisfy me only with respect to
one doubt. How is it that our Master himself does
not appear? How should I know an angel? and
should I know him, how could I know that he

was sent by the Eternal ? Ah, my dear friend, were
he risen, would he not himself appear to us ? for
we knew him.—But, O Cleophas, consider, Did not
Mary believe Gabriel ? she consequently knew an
angel : and, what but truth can come from those
exalted spirits who attend at the throne of God ?
Do we deserve that he himself should appear to
us ? Did not we, when Gethsemane resounded
with the tumults of his outrageous enemies, 'fly
with the rest of the apostles ? and, Where were
we when his dreadful sentence was pronounced ?
We were far from him, and far from him too, when
he was bleeding on the cross.—I lament, like thee,
Matthias, our base ingratitude. Can we ever
deserve that he should appear to us ? If he is
risen, and should appear, it would be only from
compassion, and to banish our sorrow.—Yet still,
O Cleophas ! thou doubtest.—Thou knowest
Matthias, that I conceal none of my thoughts from
thee ; and when I attentively contemplate these
things, I believe : but when the anxiety of hope,
and fear, and expectation ; and when the joy, the
heavenly joy of seeing him again agitate my soul,
then indeed I doubt. Matthias here giving him
an affectionate look, said, Thou dear friend, did
we really see him, our rapturous joy would give
us a foretaste of the bliss of heaven, a joy too great
for utterance. A sight of Jesus would carry with
it a stronger conviction than the light of truth dis-
covered by speculation. O that he would appear,
said, Cleophas, and by his graceful presence heal
our torturing doubts !
    They had now passed through the shade of a
projecting precipice, and the winding road brought
them to a side view of a gentle slope, which led
up to the summit of the hill ; and there they
perceived a person of a noble and most graceful

'appearance advancing towards them,' with a slow
pace, as deeply engaged in serious thought: Let
us walk slower' said Cleophas; 'for the stranger
will perhaps accompany us. His wisdom and
knowledge may' afford us consolation under our
present perplexity. Alas! of what advantage,
said Matthias, will his wisdom be to us, if he makes
not Jesus the subject of his discourse!

The stranger now coming up, gave them a kind
salutation, which they respectfully returned. He
desired to know whither they were going; and be-
ing answered to Emmaus: he asked if they would
accept of his company; 'for he also was going
thither.' They assured him that they should re-
ceive the favour with pleasure. The stranger then
asked the subject of their discourse, observing, that
he had taken notice of their being filled with grief,
and that their thoughts seemed to be employed on
some important subject. Alas! what can we talk
of? said Cleophas. Art thou only a stranger in
Jerusalem and hast not known the things that have
come to pass there? What things? said the stran-
ger.—Oh hast thou alone not heard of Jesus of
Nazareth, a prophet mighty in deed and word before
God and all the people? Our priests inflamed by
the rage of hell, seized him and led him up to
Pilate, who, though a heathen, was unwilling to
condemn him. I scarcely dare to mention the
dreadful death he suffered—they crucified him!
Alas! we trusted that it was he who should have
redeemed Israel. . It is now the third day since
these things came to pass, and early this morning
some devout women who went to the sepulchre
found not his body; but came trembling to us,
saying that they had seen a vision of angels, who
told them that he is living. Some of those that
were with us also went to the sepulchre, and found

it open, and the body gone, even as the woman had said.

They were now come among the shady palms, when the traveller looking upon them with awful dignity, addressed them in the majestic voice of truth : Ye simple and slow of heart to believe all that the prophets have spoken ! Ought not Christ to have suffered these things, and then to enter into his glory?

With astonishment they looked at each other, and then upon him. Their eyes, before dim, now sparkled with joy and eager expectation, yet he had only begun to manifest his power and to shew them the triumph of truth. As a rising storm at first blows with restrained voilence, and sweeps not through the whole forest, the foilage still rests on the trees, and the rays of the sun penetrate through the gathering clouds. Thus began his sublime discourse, and soon he led them into the depths of revelation; in which the divine speaker explained the prophecies in relation to the Messiah with such clearness and strength of conviction, that they could no longer with-hold their assent. Thus through the forest rushes the increasing storm, the trees wave their heads, the thunders roar, the condensed clouds successively pour floods on floods down the mountains.

At length the two disciples, spent with fatigue, stood wiping the sweat from their glowing faces, and said, O Man of God, though thou art unknown to us, we behold thee with reverence ; and acknowledge thee to be divine. Let us stop here, and rest our weary limbs by the side of this cooling stream. They then seated themselves on the grass, the two disciples facing the heavenly stranger, whose speech now became more sweet ; for he discoursed of the love of the Son of God to man,

and the love of man to him. They now thought
of the good Shepherd's death, with minds more
composed, cheered with heavenly comfort. As
after the heat of the scorching sun, the cool twilight
refreshes the weary, so were they refreshed with
elevated joy. He now asked them whether they
loved 'the Messiah! They both, as with one
mouth, answered, How can we avoid loving him?
But did you always love him? Alas! we for-
sook the Lamb of God, when he was led to the
slaughter.—Now ye know that, for your sakes he
willingly died, would you die for his?—We hope,
O thou beloved stranger, we hope, that God would
enable us to die for him. But be not thou dis-
pleased with us ; it is with reverence we speak, Is
he risen from the dead? Thou knowest all that re-
lates to him : tell us then, O thou Man of God,
may we rejoice in the happiness of again seeing
Christ our Lord?—The stranger returned, Joseph's
brethren did not know him, till in the blissful hour
of joy, unable longer to conceal himself, he burst
into tears.

So saying, he arose and turned from them. They
followed him with a mixture of joy and solicitude,
imagining that he might possibly be their Lord
himself, or an angel; and coming up to him, said,
Permit us, who reverence and love thee more than
we can express, to ask, Who thou art? Oh!
who art thou, our divine teacher? We dare not
presume to embrace thee ; but tell us, Art thou
one of the angels that were seen at the sepulchre?
—Come and embrace me he kindly returned. They
long embraced him : long hung on his neck and
wept. Emmaus being now in view, he said, Bre-
thren, I go to my friends. My way lies through
Emmaus.—Oh stay with us, the day is far spent,
and the evening is at hand, said they, each holding

one of his hands. Let me go, he returned, my friends live at a distance and expect me.—With them, O Man of God ! said they, thou art always ; and thou canst not but perceive that our hearts are already thine. Oh ' remain with us, for why shouldest thou expose thyself to the perils of the night ? Tell us something more of Jesus !—O stay with us.—With a look of the sweetest benevolence, he answered, I will stay, my brethren. Cleophas thanked him, not in words, but by the joy which shone in his countenance, and hasted before to prepare for his reception.

Cleophas, for that is my companion's name, said Matthias, has a cottage at Emmaus ; before it is a clump of trees, and a limpid brook winds amidst their refreshing shade. He hastes to prepare some food that he may cheer our hearts with his slender store. What a delightful evening is this, after such days of anguish ! We return our joyful thanks, that thou wilt stay with us, and condescend to shelter thyself under the lowly roof of simplicity. Jesus when he lived, was like thee, the friend of man. He humbled himself in the dust yet was rich in wisdom ; but of Jesus I will now be silent : he was above all ; for on him the angels attended ; yet the cause of his poverty appeared to be more astonishing than his poverty itself : but thus was accomplished the purposes of infinite wisdom. O that I might live with thee, thou man of God ! that from thy lips I might be taught how best to serve the heavenly Redeemer ! For the most affectionate, and noble thanksgivings are due to our gracious Lord, who has redeemed us from sin, and loved us even to the death of the cross !

They now drew near to the dwelling of Cleophas, whom they saw fetching water for their drink from the brook, and then washing herbs in the cooling stream ; but seeing Matthias, and the beloved stranger approach, he ran up to them, Welcome, dear Man of God ! said he, may the blessings with which thou art accompanied enter with thee under my roof. On their entering the house, Cleophas speedily spread the table with all the plenty his store afforded, milk, honey, figs, bread and a little wine. They now sat down to the table, the stranger facing the two disciples, when viewing them, with a look of solemn benignity, he took the bread, and lifting up his eyes towards heaven, gave thanks. His countenance, his voice, his gesture, instantly resembled those of Jesus. They looked at him, they looked at each other trembling, while he said, We thank thee, O Father, for the gifts thou hast graciously bestowed on us. Though to many they appear small, yet are they produced by the same paternal, almighty power that created the heavens. Overcome with joy they sunk down a-doring, while he continued; Praise be to thee, thou graciously sent forth the sun to give us light, and moon and stars for our hours of rest ! and adored be thy goodness, thou hast provided our daily bread ! They now rose, and he breaking the bread, gave it to them. They took it with still stronger emot tions of joy, and looking at him endeavoured to speak ; but their hearts were too full to allow them to give utterance to their thoughts. Now again, turning his eyes towards them, he blessed them, and disappeared from their sight. They started and went out, searching for him ; but he being not to be found, they returned with their minds still filled with joy.

Now, O Cleophas, cried Matthias, we have seen him ! We have seen him !—He is risen ! I am in heaven, and no longer belong to this earth ! Oh I am in heaven !—Cleophas, sunk

Craig del.   Wallis sculp.

Christ appearing to the two Disciples.

Published by Brightly Bungay 1810.

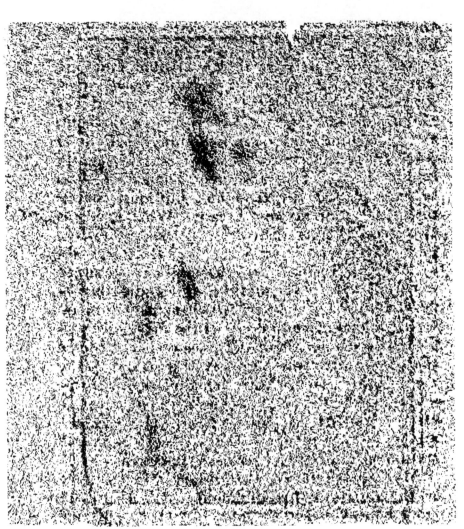

on his breast, then cried, O Matthias, did not our hearts burn within us, when, as we passed along the way, he spake of God, and revealed to us the Scriptures ?—But let us haste back. They then both took their staves and departed.

While they were on their way from Emmaus, Peter and Thomas were in close conversation. Conceal, O Thomas, said Peter, conceal thy doubts, and continue not thus to disturb our faith. Quench not the weak spark within us : they would blaze up to heaven, and thou wouldst extinguish them. Then Simon, answered Thomas, I must no more mention my thoughts ; but must conceal my grief within my own breast. What good can they receive from these dreams ? since they will be soon undeceived, and these joyful illusions will only increase their sorrow. O brother ! returned Peter, call them not illusions : I conjure thee by Him who liveth for ever, call them not illusions. Give not that name to an act of the divine omnipotence. Jesus was dead and is now alive. Sacred shall be the place where I saw him. It was to me the burning bush ; for there did I see the divine glory ! To me it was the open gate of heaven ! Here thou art encompassed with the witnesses, all the nine are present. We have each of us seen the divine Jesus, no longer dead, but risen.

My soul is grieved, said Mary Magdalen to see thy sorrow, and painful doubts. O Jesus have pity on thy distressed apostle ! He doubts not from an evil heart ; but from his anxiety and anguish of soul. Oh break not the bruised reed, nor quench the smoaking flax ! pity him, O Rabboni, as thou hast been pleased to pity me ! Ah Thomas ! be assured that not an angel from heaven proclaiming eternal life, nor choirs of angels joining in ecstatic hymns, could equal the voice of

the risen Jésus, when he relieved my panting desire
to see him; when the Risen, the Awakened from
the dead relieved my longing desire to see him, and
called me by my name.

Your intruding raptures, said Thomas, in a
low and inward voice, seem to sink me deeper in
the abyss of anguish in which I am involved.
May not the vehemence with which you speak
raise a mist before you?   Peter taking him by
the hand, with more ardent speech, returned : The
mist lies in the vehemence of thy doubts. We
have seen him, and is it strange that we should be
enraptured ?   Can we be in heaven and not feel
its transports ?   Thou hast not seen, and therefore
thou formest to thyself the images of graves and
night, and with more positiveness talkest thou of
these, than we of our risen Master, whom we have
seen and heard, and whose body our hands have
felt. He made himself known to us with his
usual compassion and loving kindness, to which
thou art no stranger. If thou art incapable of
conviction, return back to the Sadducees, and
believe with them that there are neither angels,
nor spirits, nor the resurrection of the dead.

Here Thomas could no longer refrain from tears,
and turning to Peter, said, Ah be not so cruel !
Like thee I love the divine Jesus, our dear cruci-
fied Lord !   Endeavour to assuage thy grief !
said Salome : O Didymus ! is not he whom thou
callest our crucified Lord, able to remove thine
incredulity, and to restore thy peace ? he to whom
immortality, and the life of angels, to which he is
risen, bear witness ?—Yes, the life of angels said
all the female witnesses.   His immortality was
manifest, though he had laid aside the lustre which
beamed in Gabriel, and irradiated the angels who
proclaimed his birth.

Has the Lord appeared to all here but me ? said Thomas. No, he has not appeared even to his disconsolate mother. Not to her son John. Not to him, whom when expiring on the cross, he recommended to his mother as an affectionate son ! Not to her, whom at the same awful moment, he recommended to that son, as a mother :

Thus they conversed, while the hearers were tossed amidst strong fluctuations of saddening doubt, and exulting faith. When Peter, Mary Magdalen, and the other women spoke, they walked on the sea ; but at the objections of Didymus, sank in the overwhelming waves.

The doubting apostle here withdrew, and leaving Jerusalem, retired among Olivet's most lonely tombs, to indulge his melancholy, or rather in the midst of solitude's silent retreat, to strive to allay the anguish of his mind. In solitude's right hand is a goblet, her left holds a threatening dagger. To the happy she presents the cup, and urges the wretched to use the steel. Thomas now within the gloom of a lonely sepulchre, felt the load of his griefs become more heavy, and more dark his thoughts. His soul laboured to rise above his grief ; but vain were his efforts, and had he not had recourse to the Almighty, who gives rest to the weary soul, he would have sunk under his burthen. O thou Unsearchable, said he, how dark are the depths of thy counsels ! Yet to thee alone can I have recourse in the midst of all my sorrows ! Oh look down on me, a wretched worm, writhing itself in midnight darkness ! Thou knowest, O Jehovah ! my love to him who so lately bled on the cross ! O Father ! in the overflowings of thy mercy, and in the fullness of thy grace didst thou send him ! Yet thou hast permitted him to die—to die the death of the cross ! Alas he is dead !—more dead to me

than to his other disciples ! O thou Omnipotent
Father ! where loitered Thy thunder ? where slum-
bered Thy tempests, when the lofty cross was raised ?
The earth then shook with horror ! the aërial ex-
panse resounded, and the minds of men were struck
with terror ? Yet then was he put to death, and
no rock crushed, no chasm swallowed his murder-
ers ! O thou Father Almighty ! who by a minis-
tering angel slew the first born of Egypt, yet pas-
sed over those dwellings in Ramesis that were
sprinkled with blood ! Thou who divided the sea,
and suspended the river's course to open a passage
for Israel ! Thou who being with thy Holy Son
Jesus, enabled him to calm the rage of tempests ;
to walk on the boisterous waves ; to open the eyes
of the blind, that they might see the glories of Thy
creation ; to make the cripple leap with joy, and
even to raise the dead to life ! O thou God of mer-
cy and grace, where is thy Son ? Wilt thou—will
he awaken me from this death of affliction, and
from these doubts ? Ah ! my dear Lord lies moul-
dering in the dust, and thou, O God, keepest si-
lence ! O Thou whose ways are inscrutible, all
thy floods pass over my soul !

Thus he uttered his supplications and complaints,
then in silence wrung his clasped hands. At length
resuming, he cried, Ah were I to sleep in one of these
sepulchres, he would not awake me, as he did La-
zarus and Semida ! But why should I return to a
life in which I cannot find him ? ye happy, dead
who sleep here, is Jesus known to you ? If he is,
happy are ye ! If ye knew and loved him, ah ye
are now with him ! Ye dry bones that are here
mouldering into dust, shall at the voice of God
awake, and in that glorious day thou, my Lord,
shalt also awake, and I with thee, reanimated with
the breath of life ! Happy, ye other friends of the

crucified Jesus! May ye still enjoy your happiness! Ye fancy him risen, and though it is a visionary delusion, rejoice in it no less than if it were a reality.—Blissful vision like that which filled Jacob's oppressed mind : not indeed, like his, real, but filling you with joy and praise. O thou that madest the eye, and seest the grief of my oppressed heart it is not thy will that I should rejoice with them ! Ah could I but see him, what would be life to the transport I should then feel ? With an impetuous shout of joy would I call to him, then gladly sink in silence and death ! O my Lord ! if thou hast appeared, appear to me ! What a request ! Reject, O my soul, the illusive idea ! —Yet the renewal of life is in his power. He could, if he pleased, come forth from the shades of death ! But how should he be pleased to do this ? How be pleased to die—only for a few hours ? Had he chose to live, he would have come down in triumph from the cross ! O Jesus, wert thou now living, wouldest thou not appear to me ? For who languishes like me, for conviction ? How delightfully are my friends deceived ! I pity their too easy credulity ; but O my Lord, when I see thee, when I put my finger into thy wounds, and my trembling hand into thy side, I also will believe ! Then will I joyfully grasp thy feet. But alas ! I shall never believe ! Never shall I put my finger into the wounds of thy hands ! never put my hand into thy side ! never grasp thy feet ! for thou art dead ! thou hast already had a second grave ! O thou Father of the blessed Jesus ! do not utterly forsake me.

Thus in loud and broken sentences he gave vent to the thoughts of his agitated mind, supporting himself by leaning on the fragment of a rock which had fallen from the sepulchre when the

veil of the temple was rent. The mourning
disciple was still leaning on the rock, when the
silence of the night was broke by the voice of one
gradually approaching, who called, What doleful
lamentation proceeds from the sepulchres? Art
thou wounded? Can I, O stranger, help thee?
Didymus continued silent, and the voice added,
Tell me who thou art: for hearing the voice of
thine anguish I am coming to relieve thee. I
heard thy complaints far in the valley, and if man
can give thee succour, I will. I rejoice, O stran-
ger, said Thomas, that thou hast an humane heart;
may the blessing of God be with thee: but go
whither thy nightly way calls thee. A fond wife
and tender children, perhaps, wait thy coming.
Thou canst not help me: for the wounds of which
I complain are those of the soul. Wounds of the
soul, brother! answered the voice, which now
approached nearer; stretch forth thine arm, that
I may find and embrace thee. Didymus stretched
out his arm, and the other seizing it embraced him.
Thomas then began the discourse.

Art thou, O traveller! an Israelite? Didst
thou come to Jerusalem at the late festival! What
is thy name?—I am one of the sons of Jacob. I
come from a far country, and my name is Joseph:
what brother is thine?—My name is Thomas.
—But why, O Thomas, dost thou vent thy lamen-
tations here at the sepulchres in the gloom of
night! Come let us leave this dreary place;
silence and darkness only blacken the melancholy
images which overcloud thy soul.

This silence, O Joseph! these melancholy
images which overcloud my soul, I am pleased
with. I now love nothing more than death and
the grave. If the earth would receive me into
its peaceful bed, I should no longer be the son

of misery, no longer lie in the depths of afflic-
tion.

O Thomas, my brother, raise thy head from the
dust, look up to heaven, and learn to complain
with fear and trembling ! As we should rejoice
with fear, so should we complain. Who is he
that has permitted misery ? Is it not he, who has
formed us for eternal life ? Ought thy vehement
complaints to reach the ears of the Most High
mingled with the joyful effusions of the adoring
choirs, and their rapturous hallelujahs ? Cannot
God deliver ? Will he not deliver ? Learn with
fear, I repeat it, learn with trembling to mourn.
When he, who is worthy of all praise, sends
affliction, reverence, my brother, the heavenly mes-
senger.

O Joseph ! thou art a man after my own heart.
While speaking of the Eternal, thy soul becomes
inflamed. Thou hast felt holy joy, and hast been
blessed with sorrow ; but never felt sorrow like
mine. Alas ! if thou hadst, thou wouldst have
sunk under it like me !—Speak then, O Thomas !
and mention the burthen which presses thee down.
—Yes, Joseph, it indeed presses me down. But
where shall I begin ? Oh didst thou know the di-
vine Jesus ? How long hast thou dwelt in Judea ?
—Only a few days. But messengers were conti-
nually coming from Judea to the abodes of joy
where I dwell, and have spoke much of Jesus the
Son of the Most High. At last we came down to
see Jesus die and rise from the dead.—Rise from
the dead ! Who art thou, Joseph ? Who art thou ?
—Ah, Thomas, I had a faithful friend in Judea,
from whom I was long separated. He left me in
Egypt, and him God was pleased to restore to me,
not, thou disciple, in the terrors of an earthquake,
darkness, and tempest, but coming from Cedron,

amidst the whispers of the cooling breeze ; thus
he restored to me my ever faithful, long-lost, but
everlasting friend. I must now leave thee, brother,
but will come back and see thee again.

O Joseph, stay? Where art thou, O Joseph ?
Where art thou ? Have angels the sweet name of
him who was the beloved of his father and of
God? Let me once more, O Joseph ; hear the
sound of thy celestial voice. But thou art silent.
May I call thee brother, as thou calledst me ?
Thou art still silent. Where goest thou ? Art thou
void of pity, or gone so far as not to hear me ?
He is no angel ; for no angel could ever be so cruel !
—But he lives in the abodes of joy !—The mes-
sengers from Judea speak of the divine Jesus !—
Who were the messengers from Judea ? Were they
sent from God ?—Certainly God can send angels
from Judea to heaven, He came down that is,
from heaven, to see Jesus die ! So the messengers
from Judea knew before what was to happen, And
rise from the dead ! But surely this could not be.
What could he mean ? He called me disciple !
Then Jesus came from Cedron, not in an earth-
quake, but in a gentle breeze, to restore to him
a dear friend. But when ? Before he died ? Why
then in a gentle breeze ? Yes, there was a
soft breeze that smoothed the sea. The earth-
quake was after his death. Did he then after
his death, restore to him his long lost and now eter-
nal friend, and thus, while dead, perform that
benevolent miracle ? But why dead ! Did not
Joseph see him risen ? How mysterious !—The
farther I search, the more am I perplexed.—But
was I awake ? Perhaps, while spent with sor-
row and perturbation of soul, after having rested on
the rock, I sunk down and fell asleep, and have
only seen this stranger in a dream. It must be

so." He was all benevolence, but suddenly fled:
Thus do dreams, but never a friend, whether he be
a man or an angel. Now I know, by experience,
the effects of fixed grief ; and thus the others have
deceived themselves with their seeing apparitions.
Happy illusions, which have had such effects on
them ! I will now, however, resign myself to the
will of the Almighty, and go in the way which he
directs. Thus he resolved, and listening to hear the
murmuring sound of Cedron's stream, as a guide
to direct his steps, returned, resolving to rest at
Gethsemane.

Thomas had not long left the assembly when they
were alarmed at some hasty raps at the door, on
which James hasted down, and found Matthias
and Cleophas, whom he joyfully let in. They were
out of breath and fatigued with their haste. When
they were a little recovered, James introduced them
into the assembly. The mother of Jesus, Mag-
dalen, and several others, hastily gathered round
them, and with eyes beaming joy, cried, The Lord
is risen, and has appeared to Peter. Cleophas rais-
ing his hands and voice towards heaven, exclaimed,
How blessed are we ! He is risen ! He is risen !
We also are witnesses of his resurrection. To us
Christ has likewise appeared. Peter then hastily
approached them, on which Cleophas continued,
O brother in Christ, and my brother, he called us
Brethren ! Peter answered, All about you, except
Mary, have seen him appear since his death : but
thee, his mother, he will likewise gratify by his ap-
pearance. The first who saw him was Magdalen,
and she was alone : he next shewed himself to the
nine, and appeared to me. No words can express
the raptures with which our hearts were agitated.
But behold, some of our brethren mourn while we
rejoice. They were disposed to credit us, when

Thomas, who is miserable himself, perplexed them:
they were beginning to taste of our joy, when he
drove it from them. Lord have pity on them!
Have pity on the unhappy Thomas!

John now coming up to them, said, I am not at
all perplexed by the objections of Didymus, and
am only grieved that Jesus has not appeared to me.
Why, my dear John, returned Peter, he has not yet
appeared to Mary, his and thy mother. But
brethren relate in what manner he appeared to
you.

Being filled with grief, said Cleophas, we resol-
ved to walk to Emmaus, that we might find some
alleviation to our sorrow by conversing in the open
air, and enjoying a view of the country In the
way we were joined by a stranger for whom at first
sight we conceived an extraordinary affection, which
encreased as he spake. He explained to us the
books of the prophets, shewed us that the Messiah
was to suffer, and the manner of his sufferings. All
he said to us I know, without being at present able
to relate it. Never man spake as he spake. His
speech was filled with strength and fervour. We
had now reached Emmaus. We entreated him to
stay with us, and at length, he consented. I hasted
to set water and provisions on the table. He then
—Methinks I now see him hold the bread, and hear
him beg a blessing. He had then the real voice of
Jesus, and the same divine countenance. He brake
the bread, and gave to each; then once more look-
ing kindly on us disappeared. We sought him,
but finding it in vain, without farther delay hasted
back to bring you the joyful tidings.

Lebbeus, whose faith Thomas had most shaken,
sat with down-cast eyes; and though on other
occasions he was susceptible of the tenderest im-
pressions, had listened to the joyful relation with

critical coldness ; and now gave vent to his
thoughts. I believe you, brethren, said he. Yes,
I allow that some man of eminent wisdom, or
perhaps an angel, joined you in your walk to
Emmaus. If you and the women have seen angels,
the Lord in his mercy sent them to comfort us
under our grief for the Messiah's death : a sad
addition to which is his corpse being taken away.
In pity to our anguish he sends us angels as con-
vincing evidences that the soul of Jesus is in the
bosom of eternal repose. Thus am I far from
denying that he who conversed with you, was sent
by God to comfort you. He saw farther into the
depths of divine wisdom than we, and was better
able to explain what is foretold by the prophets.
But that Jesus at last appeared in his own person,
when before he was unknown, I cannot believe.
For if it was he, how is it possible for you not to
know him at first ? Ye were certainly deceived
by your joy. While the stranger held the bread
he stood in the graceful attitude of Jesus, who,
when at our meals, used to hold up the bread to-
wards heaven, offering up his thanksgivings. After
being thus deceived, you easily amagine that you
heard the voice of Jesus, when the worthy stranger
offered up his petitions.

At Lebbeus's words trouble and gloomy doubt
flowed into the souls of those who were filled with
joy and wonder: Cleophas gave him a look of
commiseration, and Matthias embracing him, said;
O thou disciple of the risen Jesus, before we knew
him, we asked if Jesus was really raised from the
dead, and whether we might hope for the happiness
of seeing him again ; on which he said, Joseph's
brethren did not know him, till in the blissful hour
of joy, he burst into tears. O Jesus ! wert thou
living, said Lebbeus, covering his face, thou

wouldst not withstand our entreaties. Peter ob-
served him without concern ; for he was now
incapable of grief, and sedately said, As ye left the
hanging rock, we saw you from the roof. Was
it there, as ye passed near the palms, that Jesus
joined you ? Yes said they, we had scarce passed
the rock when we were joined by the divine Jesus.
Here Peter, transported with joy, exclaimed, My
dear brethren, ye have all seen the risen Jesus !
Do you hear the witnesses ? Already have ye seen
Jesus ! Thomas too has seen him ! O that he
were here ! Here the mother of Jesus, with joy-
ful amazement, cried, I too have seen my Son alive
—alive after his death !

. As a lonely surviver, just deprived by death of
his last friend, half waking amidst melancholy
dreams, in which he sees the dear person alive, but
finds himself unable to touch him, continues to seek
the illusive image, while his impassioned heart
beats strong, and joy thrills through his bones ;
such was the state of the tearful assembly.

But the seraphim, the fathers, and the rejoicing
angels now hasted to them. Simon Peter affec-
tionately looking on the assembly, perceived an
unusual lustre around them. His transport checked
a rising tear, and in a silent aspiration he said, O
thou who art unsearchable, yet ever gracious, wilt
now have pity on them !

Peter was continuing his silent devotions when
the adorable Messiah entered the assembly. Struck
with astonishment, they all stood as motionless
as a rock, with eyes fixed on him. Peace be with
you ! said the risen Jesus. They saw him, scarce
believing that he was present, and stood gazing
on him in silence. Involved in torrents of various
thoughts, they sunk in that sea of light, in which
the immortals themselves sink, and unable to un-

ravel their confused conceptions, imagined that
they saw an angel. With the voice of love, with
his own endearing voice, he then cried, Why are
ye troubled? and why do thoughts arise in your
hearts? Behold, my beloved, my hands and my
feet, angels, have neither flesh nor bones, as ye see
I have.

Here they all trembled. Mary sunk down
before him, held the feet of her risen son, and saw in
them the marks of his wounds. She then looked
up to his face, and, while she gazed upon it, her
own became like that of an angel. Here, mother,
said Jesus, pointing to the mark of the wound
from which had issued water and blood, after death
had stopped its vital course: here likewise was
I pierced. Again an angelic lustre beamed from
the mother's face. Many now kneeled about him,
looked at the marks of his wounds, and stretched
out their arms towards him; and to the risen Jesus
was uttered jubilant strains in broken accents,
which drew a tear from the eyes of him they
adored. The affectionate John long held his right
hand, long with joyful eyes looked up in his face,
desirous of expressing his deepfelt hearty thanks,
and petitions; but did it not! He began, but
stopped and was silent. Then the great Emanuel
addressing him, said, Thou stoodest by the cross
till I expired : But where is Lebbeus? Lebbeus
had lain prostrate on the floor, kissing the border
of the Redeemer's garment; but at his calling
him by name, he arose, and with a countenance
pale as death, from his over-powering joy, presented
himself before his Lord, who holding out his right
hand, said, Lebbeus, here is my hand, when the
disciple holding out his trembling hand, it sunk
down. The merciful Saviour, then stooping, took
hold of his hand, and long affectionately held it.

The joy-oppressèd disciple now with a firm voice,
cried, Of thy grace, O Lord, there is no end !
Simon the Canaanite, and James the son of Alpheus,
embraced each other, rejoicing in the Lord ; then
looked at one another, and at the Holy Jesus.
The whole assembly alternately viewed their Lord
and each other, joining in one general joy, that
he had blessed them with his presence.

Now began a second hymn of triumph to the risen
Saviour, formed of broken sentences, and the soft
voice of joyful weeping. Around him kneeled
the more early witnesses, Peter, Matthias, Cleophas,
and the favoured women, whose noble souls follow-
ed the suffering Jesus, till he expired on the cross.
Among them stood the Conqueror of Death with
his eyes lift up, and his extended arms raised to-
wards heaven. Though the fullness of his glori-
fication did not yet beam forth, yet his graceful
aspect appeared more divine, than they had ever
seen, and no longer could they keep their fixed
eyes on his face. James cast his down to the floor,
and with suppliant voice, cried, O Lord, Lord, do
not yet ascend to thy Father !—O here—I shall
still, said Jesus, remain with you my children.

A flood of the most rapturous joy now poured into
their souls. They scarcely knew what they thought
or said. O is it possible—Ye angels is it possible,
that it can be Jesus himself ? cried one. A second
exclaimed, Are we in heaven, or still on earth ?—
Is it Jesus himself ?—Ah ! art thou he whose
blood was shed on Golgotha ? Do we now behold
thee, our gracious Lord, or are we deceived by
pleasing rapturous visions ?

At this instant Jesus turned, and walking up to
the table, said, Have ye here any meat. They all
arose, and hasted to bring him food, when John
eagerly pressing through the others, set before him

a piece of an honeycomb and some broiled fish, and
then with awful silence drew back.   The Saviour
then, with mild condescension, looking at the whole
assembly said, come near, my disciples.   Ye my
beloved draw near and place yourselves at the table.
Come thou, my mother, and seat thyself by thy son.
—She came, as did the others.   He ate.   The sight
of his condescending love in suffering them to sit
at the same table with himself, while he ate with
them, at once allayed the ebullitions of their trans-
ports.   More tranquil joys, and a more settled faith
now taking possession of their more composed minds,
the Redeemer thus addressed them.   Ye believed
not the witnesses who told you that I lived, though
they had seen me when raised rom the dead.   Oh
why did ye not believe their report?   How stub-
born, my beloved, were your souls?   Did I not tell
you that I was to be crucified, and to rise on the
third day? and that all things must be fulfilled
which were written in the law of Moses, in the
Prophets, and in the Psalms, concerning me?   My
future witnesses, beginning at Jerusalem, shall
preach to all nations, repentance and remission of
sins in my name.   Ye, my brethren, are those wit-
nesses, and behold I send the promise of my Father,
aud ye shall make me known throughout the earth.
Remain ye near Jerusalem till I ascend to my Fa-
ther, and till ye are endued with power from on
high.   Then go and preach to all nations, declaring
that whoever believeth and is baptized shall be
saved ; but he that believeth not, shall be con-
demned.   Many believers shall work miracles ;
in my name they shall cast out devils ; they shall
speak with new tongues ; shall take up serpents,
and drink the most deadly potion without being
hurt: they shall lay their hand on the sick, and
they shall be healed.

The mediator then rising with a smile of compla-
cency, stepped from the table, and the assembly
joyfully thronging about him, he said, Come near,
my apostles. At this the others drew back, not
through envy, for they rejoiced at the superior bliss
of the more highly favoured, as the just made per-
fect rejoice in heaven at the superior bliss of those
whom Jesus has first chosen. Around the Saviour
stood the apostles, who were to lay down their lives
for the truth ; he in spirit saw them bleed, and
overflowing with cordial love, said, Peace be unto
you. Then as from a soul surcharged with joy,
he breathed upon them, saying, Receive the Holy
Ghost. Soon shall ye receive him more abundant-
ly. Whosoever sins ye remit, they are remitted,
and whosoever sins ye retain, they are retained.

With astonishment and submission they heard the
great decree. Now thinking that Jesus was about
to leave them they gathered round him, yet dared
not to request his longer stay ; but their looks and
gestures strongly expressed their emotions. Peter
wrapped up in thoughts, which like a flame spread
through his soul, cast himself at the feet of Jesus,
then grasping and kissing them, cried, Lord, on earth
I cannot express my thanks, in heaven I will. I
know I shall. It was said, Tell it to the disciples
and to Peter ! Thou also appearest to me !—To
me dost thou appear ! I know, O thou Most
Merciful ! thou Redeemer from sin ! thou my De-
liverer, and the deliverer of all Adam's fallen race !
that thou hast forgiven my base denial of thee !
But, O my gracious Saviour ! permit me once
more to acknowledge thee—to acknowledge thee,
my Lord, before thy face, to lament my guilt, and
before I go to those whom thou hast reconciled, and
in thy name to forgive sinners, to bear the voice of
thy forgiving goodness, and thy divine mouth pro-

nounce my pardon, with the ravishing assurance, that thou wilt receive me into eternal life.

These words he uttered with devout reverence, and with his eyes fixed on the countenance of the merciful Redeemer, who returned this gracious answer. Know, Simon, that I have prayed to my Father for thee, that thy faith fail not, and my Father has heard me. Rise, Simon, thy sins are forgiven thee. Thus spake the divine Redeemer, with a voice that pierced through the bones and marrow to the inmost soul. He then vanished from their sight. Peter transported with this favour, cried, Lord, we follow thee into Galilee. The angel of the sepulchre then said, Ye shall once more see the Lord at Jerusalem, when he will inform you, at what time ye shall see him in Galilee. The angel then vanished, his effulgence slowly disappearing.

THE END OF THE FOURTEENTH BOOK.

THE

MESSIAH.

BOOK XV.

THE ARGUMENT.

Several of those who had been raised from the dead appear:
particularly to Nepthoa, one of the children whom Christ
had placed before the people : to Dilean: to Tabitha,
whom Peter restored to life : to Cidli : to Stephen : to
Barnabas, the son of Joses: to Portia : to Beor, blind
from his birth, and brought to his sight by Jesus. Abra-
ham and Moses would appear to Saul ; but it is for-
bidden by Gabriel. Some of those raised from the dead
also appear to Samma, Joel, and Elkanan, Simeon's
brother, and to Boaz : to Mary the mother of Jesus :
to Cidli, Jairus's daughter, and to Semida, the young man
of Nain.

COME thou who oft hast filled my soul with
tranquil melancholy, and cheared it with
views of its grand expectations ! · Come contem-
plation of the future world ! For when the events
I sing were performed, the future world was on
earth : the dead appearing to the first Christians,
calling them to heaven, and consecrating them for
eternal life.

Small was now the holy society ; but from its root
rose a tree whose branches spread throughout the
heavens : the hundred and forty thousand redeemed ;
the host without number on the sea of crystal ;
the hundred and forty-four thousand who sang a

new song. which no one could learn. These will
be redeemed, from among men, and follow the
Lamb whithersoever he goeth. Behold a host
without number, composed of kindreds, tongues
and nations, assembled round the throne in white
robes, and, with palms in their hands, crying with
the voice of joy, Salvation to our God who sitteth
upon the throne, and to the Lamb ! Then the angels
and the elders shall fall on their faces, the sea shall
roar, and the conquerors wave their palms ; for
after great tribulation they shall arrive in heaven,
having washed their robes, and made them white
in the blood of the Lamb.

The smaller band, the root of the tree, had not
yet been called. They still slept under the veil
of the law ; but for the first time will awake, as if
risen from the dead : And then shall Cephas, in one
discourse, add to the community three thousand
persons. Still slumbered even those, who were to
be the first fruits, and still unknown to them was the
new everlasting hymn of joy.

Behold the work of the risen begins. From
Tabor the glorified just descend to appear to the
future Christians. Before the shining troop came
down to Salem, they gathered round the father of
men, who thus addressed them : Rejoice, my chil-
dren ! Now is arrived the hour of salvation in
which ye shall begin to thirst for the stream of
life.

Religion had penetrated the soul of the happy
child whom Jesus had placed before his hearers,
and dismissed with a blessing. Nephthoa, no
longer fond of his childish sports, was in love with
solitude, which was become the joy of his early
years. Endued with understanding, and filled with
divine grace, he bore blossoms and fruit in the
very dawn of life. Seven years had passed without

fruit, and then he longed for those precious seeds
that are unknown to those who are fond of trifling
amusements, and began to sow for the glorious har-
vest of the resurrection. Kneeling in a secret
corner of the house, he thus offered up his evening
devotions ; O Lord ! thou certainly hearest me;
though I do not always find that I am heard. Be-
fore thy bright throne, O Father ! kneel all the
children of heaven and of earth. We on earth,
whose portion is tears, kneel in the dust. They,
whose tears thou hast wiped away, kneel on shining
clouds ; these, and the angels who never wept, sup-
plicate thee for an increase of bliss ; but sweet are
the requests of those above, for they are filled with
joy. Our prayers are mixed with tears, while we
petition thee for deliverance from sin and misery,
and for the blessings of the life eternal. These peti-
tions will be granted ; for this thy great Prophet pro-
claimed, when, in the happiest hour of my life, he
placed me before the people. The blessing of this
life pass away like the whithering flower : may I
have heavenly blessing bestowed by him who was
sent not only to heal the sick, but to heal the sin-
ner. Ah ! I do not yet know him as the Guide to
eternal life : I know not yet how he will lead me in
the way of my duty ; yet on thee, O my God, will
I rely ! Thy will, not mine, be done. This poor,
short, and fleeting life, is like a flower, which blows
but to fade, and is no sooner faded than it is buried
in the dust, and hid from the sight. Thus it will
be with me. How I long to obtain knowledge and
joy ! Let me obtain them, and, O my God ! I will
wait thy time for my withering, till I sink down,
and thus become transplanted into the land of light
and repose. Here is no knowledge, no perfect de-
liverance from the gloom of that ignorance which
surrounds us : but I shall be removed to the place

where truth shines in all its brightness. Of innumerable things I am now ignorant, and shall still be so
when my soul, borne on the wings of mature years,
shall take a nobler flight. Yet, O my soul ! return
to thy rest; for he who has created thee with this
thirst after a clear knowledge of himself, will certainly gratify it. Shouldst thou who hast filled
my soul with thoughts of a future life, permit me
to return to my playful companions, I should lose
this thirst for divine knowledge, and be again in the
same state as that from which Jesus called me,
when he set me before the people and blessed me.

Thus prayed Nephthoa, while his angel, hovering round him, heard his petitions, and wrote them
in characters of flame in his book ; a book of life,
in which was written the petitions acceptable to the
infinite Giver of all grace. While the immortal's
hand was flying along the glittering scroll, Benoni
came, and drew near to the suppliant and the writer. Wilt thou, Benoni, appear to him ? said the
enraptured angel, handing him the book. The
newly-risen read, and being unable to restrain his
joy, embraced the exulting seraph, who cried, May
his petitions be granted ! An answer will instantly
descend from the eternal throne.

Benoni drew nearer to Nephthoa, who was still
kneeling, and now began this second prayer. With
joyful heart do I praise thee, O Father ! for the
favours thou hast bestowed upon me. How hast
thou overshadowed me with thy goodness ! Thou
it was, O eternal Father ! the Father of all the
children of heaven, and of all on earth, who sentest
the greatest of thy prophets to bless me ! Where
shall I, O Lord of Glory, to him I lift my tearful
eyes !—where shall I begin, where conclude thy
praise ? Even the mouths of babes and sucklings
thou hast taught to praise thee : therefore will I

Borroni appearing to Nephtou

not be silent; for the mouths of children hast thou prepared to give thee praise !

Benoni at first resolved to appear before him as one of the boys that came to the festival; but seeing the tears of joy and gratitude shed by one so young, he could not suit the character, and therefore stood before Nephthoa in his glorified form, arrayed in a vernal cloud. Nephthoa was not afraid; for oft had he seen celestial forms present themselves to him in visions and light slumbers; he therefore said, with quick voice, Tell me, O celestial youth ! has the prophet sent thee to me ? Thou art a messenger of peace, blessing, and joy; speak, sing it on thy glittering harp, and tell me why thou art come ! Relate to me, thou son of light, divine things, and tell me of my relations who have died, for thou art partaker of their felicity ! Tell me of my sister, sweet innocence ! who died among the sweet breathing roses, herself a lovely flower ! Hast thou no salutations from Dimna Kedemoth ? What did she say to thee ? Perhaps it was, Blessed be the Lord that I am here, and that my dear Nephthoa will also die, and come to me ! Pardon my presumption, thou glorified inhabitant of heaven, in daring to speak so long to thee ! Ah, divine messenger ! thou art silent.

My silence, said Benoni, is owing to my seeing thee, and my raptures at thy felicity. The Lord has sent me to thee. Jesus was dead, but is already risen from the grave, and will soon ascend to glory ! Then will his apostles bear witness in Jerusalem of his death, his resurrection, and ascension. To them attend. They will open to thee divine things, as far as it is given mortals to know. May thy sister one day receive thee in the fragrant shade of the tree of life !—Nephthoa, I must now leave thee.

C. not yet, thou inhabitant of heaven! said Neph-
thoa. Turn not away so soon, thy radiant eyes,
thy rosy blush, thy gladdening smile. But Benoni
disappeared, while Nephthoa stood as entranced,
with out stretched arms to embrace his celestial
friend, cloathed in light: But his empty arms strove
to hold a fleeting shadow. He then looking up to
heaven prayed. He was now less alone than he
imagined, for neither his angel, nor the unseen Be-
noni had left him. They still with complacency
heard him offering his tribute of praise to his gra-
cious Creator, fervently thanking him for this favour,
and for the hopes he had received of obtaining
divine knowledge.

Dilean had lost his only friend. To him was the
prophet of God known, and long had he wandered
about Jerusalem, enquiring whether Jesus was ri-
sen, or was still dead. His head was now wrapped
in night, and floods of inquietude entered his soul.
He sought repose and found it not, in a country
as luxuriant as the spring. As it was late, he re-
tired among the sepulchres on the mount of Olives,
and misleading Darkness being his guide, he walk-
ed among them with watchful eye and ear. Do
those murmurs, said he, proceed from the brook of
Cedron? Does that rustling proceed from the palms
of Gethsemane? No; the noise is in one of the
sepulchres. He now perceived a glimmering light,
which the wind had almost extinguished, and go-
ing up to it came so a sepulchre, out which were
carrying the bones; for a rich man had bought the
tomb of a poor one, whose ancestors were to be re-
moved. Dilean stood at the entrance, and saw
them with painful steps come out and return with
like tedious slowness, loaded with bags of bones;
Happy are those ye carry! said he. Give me the
torch, and I will light you. They gave him one,

on which entering the sepulchre, he held it in his hand, and leaning against the rock, thus indulged his thoughts : Ye happy, happy dead !—They who have forsaken me, are now like you. When their burial clothes are grown old like these, I shall be like them ! But now—I forsaken, have lost the great Prophet of God, my happiness here—and my future happiness !—Jesus has fallen by the rage of the wicked ; but does not the Almighty give eternal felicity to the just and provide that the best of mankind shall not forever be a prey to the worst ! Am I eternal ? Is this body to moulder in the dust ? —Is Jesus risen from the dead ? Is his body turning to corruption ? Awful questions not to be resolved. Where are ye, his departed associates ? Do ye dwell in the mansions of light and joy ?

The sepulchre was now cleared of its mortal remains, which was scarce perceived by the pensive Dilean, till he was struck by the deep silence. I am now alone, continued he ; but ye spirits that animated these bodies, where are ye ? Elisha's bones awaked the dead—the soul must then have been with the body ; for dust cannot impart life. If but one soul be here, Oh let it come, and inform me of my future lot ! Come, thou soul, I shall not be terrified at thine appearance. Come, I conjure thee, by thy last sigh, when struggling with death !—by thy hope of immortality, or thy dread of falling into nought ! Thus he called, looking into the sepulchre.

Thirza, the mother of the seven martyrs, with the souls of Dilean's friends, and that of his dear spouse, were already there. These had conducted him through the vale of the sepulchres, to the rock by which he now stood. May I venture to appear to him, said his once faithful wife ? Perhaps he would be affrighted at the sight of me. I will appear before him, answered Thirza.

Dilean 'having no hopes of seeing what he so passionately desired, endeavoured to forget his anxiety in sleep; but sought in vain the refreshment of a short balmy repose, and sadness again invaded his heart. You my friends, said he, I have lost, and thou the dear companion of my life, hast left me. I alone remain in this tumultuous world.—Ah! what's here? Who art thou that approaches me? added he, moving up to the shadowy form. Thirza suddenly became invested with the appearance of an immortal. He trembled; but instantly recovering himself viewed the radiant figure, crying, Tell me phantom, art thou an intellectual being, or an inflamed vapour of the night? Perhaps thou art only the visionary creature of my own distempered brain. Thirza now gave him the sweetest smile, and animated her eyes with such spirit, as banished every idea of an imaginary being. With the hasty voice of impatient wonder, he cried, Thou bright appearance speak! Who art thou?

Who I am, said she, thou shalt know hereafter. But happy man, think not thyself more perfect than others, from thy being favoured with my appearance. The man born blind to whom Jesus gave sight, was long involved in darkness, that he might become a witness of the glory of the Lord, and that thou mayst bear witness of the resurrection of Jesus, he has sent me. I appear not because thou calledst, for I should have appeared hadst thou been silent. Thy doubts indeed deserve forgiveness; but not a reward. The whole race of mortal sinners may have their doubts in relation to the world to come; but they will know by experience, that life dwells beyond the grave.

Dilean, who stood pale and trembling before the resplendent form, answered, I presume not to ask thee any farther questions; but, O radiant being.

I will bow myself in the dust before him who has sent thee. Then turning aside from Thirza, he kneeled, and lifting up his eyes, said, O Lord of Glory, forgive my doubts! forgive my tears! To thee my prayers are known, though they should not be understood, by the bright messenger thou hast graciously sent. O Lord! enable me to obtain the bliss pointed out to me by thy celestial messenger, then with joy and triumph, shall I, on my leaving this house of clay, ascend to thee, and to my friends in heaven.

He now arose, and before him still stood the immortal, who in melodious accents thus addressed him. Behold, as thou avoidest to ask, I will answer thee. I am Thirza, the mother of the seven martyred sons. By this rock is the happy soul of thy beloved, and some of thy friends, whom living thou knewest, and they will expect thee in the regions of joy. Know that before the Messiah's ascension to his heavenly throne, he will shew himself in Galilee to five hundred brethren at once, and there shalt thou see him.

Here the exalted Thirza, soaring upward, disappeared. With tears of joy Dilean left the sepulchres; but first poured forth his thanks to the Fountain of eternal light, from whom he had received a foretaste of heaven, and such comfort and joy as no man could bestow.

On a carpet of Tyrian purple sat the inventive Tabitha, her imitating hand employed in silken embroidery of various colours. The subject was the monument of Benjamin's mother, a flower early blighted. On the tomb rested Rachel; by her kneeled Benjamin, who with averted eyes plunged a dagger in her heart; and the fainting Rachel was supported by Tabitha. While the fair embroiderer was thus employed, an unknown person

dressed in a funeral garb entered the room with a
pale countenance, yet had not all the sufferings
of friendship been able to extinguish the charms
of the blooming Deborah, who resembled a cloudy
morning in spring. I am come, said she, to rest
myself after my weary walk. To thee, the best
beloved of all my friends, I wish everlasting joy.
Continue at thy pleasing task, while I repose
myself. She then sat down and gently leaning
against a harp, it sent forth a melancholy sound.
The skilful stranger then taking the harp, touched
it with such sweetness that it sent forth sounds
soft as the murmurs of a distant stream, when
before the howling of a storm, a dead calm reigns
through the silent grove. O God of Gods, the
stranger sang, thou hast rewarded her who is
made perfect by death. But can temporary suffer-
ings deserve the glory to which thou exaltest the
blessed? she was taken away in the bloom of life,
yet what is the flower broken by the storm, to the
Cedar of God which fell on Golgotha, which
a tempest of the Lord crushed with such vio-
lence that the rocks and the sepulchres of the dead
trembled?

Deborah ceased, and now only the strong vibra-
tions of the strings was heard, till the song was
thus renewed: They who attended his funeral were
a small company of the dejected; but the lustre
of the heavenly inhabitants was dimmed, and a
funeral hymn was sung by the invisible attendants.
Their song was not heard by the earth; but the
stars listened to the sound. It was heard by Orion
and the Judge's Balance. Then a rock rolling with
dull convulsive sound, closed his grave. There
the Saviour rested in death: but soon, ye stars of
God, be issued forth! To him, short was the
sleep of death! With glory and with hallelujahs

he awaked !—He awaked with hallelujahs and
with glory !   But a few degrees hadst thou Orion,
and thou the Balance of the Judge ascended, when
he arose.   Ye witnesses, throughout all the
heavens celebrate his resurrection ! She who bled
in the lonely grove, and he who plunged the
poinard in her heart saw the gladdening miracle !

Tabitha with silent amazement looked up to the
prophetess, who sat on the border of the carpet.
In vain she strove to rise, when Deborah resting on
the harp, thus addressed her : Learn, Tabitha ;
for greatly it imports thee to learn from the resur-
rection of the dead.   Much comfort thou needest
against death ; for twice art thou appointed to
die.   The first-born of the dead, was, and shall
hereafter be the omnipotent Awakener of those who
are fallen asleep.   First, with gentle sorrow, of re-
turning to the earth, and cheering expectations of
a second creation from the dust, must thou lie down
and die.   Neither the terrors of the open grave,
nor the idea of disfiguring corruption, appals those
who know that God will call them to the joys of
angels in his celestial kingdom.   Deborah then
taking the harp, soft sounds again issued from her
rapid fingers, and not less charming was her voice,
and her lovely countenance.

What inexpressible, what rapturous sensations,
said she, did I experience when new life raised me
from the flowery grave ! When glorification de-
scended to me from the angelic choirs, and my dust
became clothed with immortality. How I trembled !
(She trembled anew, and her splendor broke out)
What a blissful shivering pervaded the most secret
recesses of my soul !   How was my lustre brighten-
ed !   In what a light of glory was my eternal spi-
rit involved !   I turned my face, and sought the
throne of him who had created me a-new.   He was

invisible, yet gentle sounds intimating the Almighty's presence, breathed around me. Here her celestial voice softly died on the ear, and the splendid form disappeared. The thrilling harp was silent, and Tabitha continued standing pale with joy.

Gedor, a man of a tender heart, equally impressible by joy and grief, was firmly resigned in his submission to the divine dispensations, whether favourable or adverse. He lived in a happy retirement with his spouse, his companion both in this and the future life. Their love was known only to themselves and a few friends. Raised above this terrestrial state, they oft conversed about their celestial home, their approaching separation, and their journey to the world of bliss. They fondly wished, without presuming to hope, that they should depart together, and thine eye, O Lord ! was upon them, to guide them to the entrance of the dark vale. She lay at the point of death, and he seemed equally near it. Death now approached with more hasty steps. She raised her eyes from Gedor to heaven, then cast them on him, and then raised them again to heaven ; but such looks of heavenly comfort he had never seen, or heard described. I die ! I leave thee, said she, to enter into nameless bliss ! Gedor now felt himself powerfully drawn from earth, and near the entrance to that glory which his dearest Cidli was ready to enjoy. Going to her with more than calm resignation, with joy, he laid his hand on her pained forehead, and thus blessed her : Depart thou, in the name of the Lord, the God of Abraham, Isaac, and Jacob, in the name of the Great Helper in Israel, whom we have implored ! Yes, his will, his gracious will be done !

With the voice of reliance and joy, she said, Yes, let him do according to the purpose of his

will ; for all his purposes are founded in goodness.
Gedor, holding her hand, answered, As an an-
gel hast thou been resigned. God has been with
thee. Thanksgivings and praise to his glorious
name, he will succour thee ! Ah had I been so
unhappy as not to have served him, this day would
I fly to him. Be thou my guardian angel. Thou
wast mine, answered Cidli. Around this happy
pair hovered Rachel, the spouse of Jacob, with a
look of mingled pity and placid joy. As yet, O
Cidli, she was invisible to thee ; but when thine
head sunk down in death, thou perceivedst the
immortal standing, and with joyful raptures went
up to salute her.

My hand is unable to conclude the affecting sto-
ry—late tears still flowing run to waste with the
other thousands I have already shed ; but thou,
my song of the great Mediator remain, and flow
among the rocks, triumphant over time, and in thy
rapid stream, this chaplet, which with tears I
plucked from funeral cypress, convey to the lucid
regions of futurity

Under the shade of Moriah stood a house famous
for its towering height. On its silent roof was the
son of the wealthy inhabitant, a pious youth in the
bloom of life, the joy of his companions, the delight
of his mother. The moon was advancing its course
in unclouded lustre over lofty Jerusalem, and peace-
ful Moriah shed tranquil thoughts, on those whose
powers were not suppressed by sleep, the nightly
death, and chiefly on Stephen, pensive youth ! Slow-
ly he walked amidst the mazes in which the history
of Bethlehem's Prophet involved his mind. His
auburn hair hung in graceful locks, on his should-
ers ; he was wrapped in a light garment, and was
walking about musing, when a stranger, from whom
exhaled the odours of Arabia, came up to him, and

began the discourse, by observing that the serenity
of the evening had invited him to repose, and ad-
ded, Know, thou only son of thy fond parent, that
I am come from a far country, and have suffered
much—Allow me, worthy stranger, Stephen re-
turned, interrupting him; before thou relatest thy
distresses, to ask thee, if thou hast heard of the me-
lancholy death of the great prophet of Jerusalem.
Jedidoth with more hasty voice, answered, Ah,
the crucified Jesus! who died for the truth, for
more exalted truths than those which Moses taught!
Jerusalem is filled with the report that he is risen
from the dead.

Stranger, thy words fill me with astonishment;
thou sayest that he died for the truth, yet thou
art come from a far country, how then didst thou
learn his doctrines ?—How I came to know what
he taught, I shall hereafter inform thee. Didst
thou know that he not only died and rose again
as a witness of the truth, but that he died for thee
in the higher character of the Redeemer of man,
wouldst thou who art in the bloom of life, and
so rich in blessings, think it too much to lay down
thy life, in vindication of these great truths? Or
wouldst thou cleave to this life, till nature at length,
with gentle hand, bowed down thy hoary head to
the grave, rather than sooner resign it up for him
who has led the way ?—What I would do, God
alone knows; but what I most passionately wish,
is known to me.—What then, O noble youth, dost
thou wish ?

Ah pilgrim ! why dost thou ask, whether I love
the Redeemer enough to die for him ? O wish
replete with ecstacy ! how my heart beats, and all
my powers soar aloft ! Were I to die as a witness
for Jesus, with joy should my young blood flow
from all the streams of life !

Jedidoth, the pilgrim, here related the affecting
history of the heroic death of Epiphanius, the
youngest of the seven martyred sons. He ceased;
his face glowed, and a lively radiance beamed from
his eyes, while the youth trembled and shed tears
of sympathy. Precious, O youth, are thy tears!
said Jedidoth. I count them all! Precious are
the tears of the upright, sanctified by the sacrifice
of Jesus! Now the risen Saviour looking down
from the heights of Tabor, saw the mortal standing
in the light of the moon, while the immortal shone
with his native lustre. Stephen being now ready
to faint, Jedidoth cried, soaring upward, Celestial
brother, there I learned what Jesus taught me, and
pursuing his rapid flight, was concealed by the
clouds.

Barnabas, the son of Joses, a Levite from Cy-
prus's distant coast, was going down towards the
river Jordan, to view a corn field, in order to ob-
serve what promises it afforded of a future harvest.
Soon was he joined by Ananias and Sapphira, whom
their lands had likewise drawn to visit Jordan's
banks. Being come to the brook of Cedron, the
beautiful Sapphira, oft with unsteady hand placed
her staff on the smooth pebbles, washed by the
shallow stream, before she ventured to wet her feet;
and now seated herself on a stone by the brook,
Ananias sat down by her, and Barnabas stood
before them. The place they sat on was to be
their future grave. Ah little did they think, too
timorous pair, that the bearers of their bodies
would soon rest on those stones, and depart without
wishing them a joyful resurrection! But this
was known to Elisha, who, together with the vene-
rable Baptist, came hovering round them unseen.
O had some breeze wafted Elisha's warning voice,
or had John denounced to them the great apostle's

overwhelming words, Ye have lied to God, and not to man, this place might not have been their grave. Rut behold, the veil of futurity hangs down, and is not to be drawn up till the judgment day.

Sapphira; while thus resting, plucked from her grave the earliest flowers of spring, and gave them to Ananias, who was taken up with the thoughts of a gainful harvest. On their reaching their, lands, Ananias's discourse turned on the fullness of the ears, and the produce when sold. Barnabas thought with pleasure on the chearfulness of the reapers, when the long wished for evening, with its refreshing coolness came ; when the sprightly circles crowned with chaplets, the growth of the flowery field, rejoice under the olive's shade, that they have passed through the heat and burthen of the day.

I will appear, said John, to Barnabas, whose seed in the hilly ground is crushed by flints. Tell me, my beloved Elisha, returned the Baptist, is Ananias to be a Christian ? If he be let us appear to him ; for if his thoughts be too much fixed on earthly things, he stands most in need of our guidance and instruction. Let us then appear to him, said Elisha, but not as raised from the dead. They then moved towards Salem.

Ananias and his spouse returned with Barnabas to Jerusalem. There they saw them sitting as blind and lame near the temple, begging relief, with devout fervour. Barnabas gave them privately, and Ananias, though his possessions were larger, gave them less, and the value of that little was lessened by his throwing it grudgingly towards them : on which the blind and lame observed that he did not deserve their appearing before him.

Barnabas now left his company, and was hasting
home, when John meeting him, asked whence he
came. He answered, from the banks of Jordan,
where he had a piece of land. They then entered
the house, where the joyful children welcomed their
father with their embraces, which he affectionately
returned. Do you too bless my little ones, said the
fond parent to the stranger; and then ordered them
to go to that good man, who turning to the chil-
dren, with a dignity that greatly astonished the pen-
sive father, said, Ye children of Barnabas shall
likewise bear testimony to the Lord; but from this
time fewer will be the sheaves of thy ground.—
Will the Lord then forsake me and these helpless
orphans? said Barnabas. John answered, Far be
it from God, on whom we depend for more than
life. Earthly things, which last but for a mo-
ment, he gives and takes away; but the treasures
of eternity shall be thine. Thus spake the Baptist,
with increasing dignity in his look, such a dignity
in his look, such a dignity as Barnabas had never
seen; nor did he ever hear a voice which spoke of
God with such solemn fervour. He listened ab-
sorbed in wonder, and being still silent, John re-
sumed, He whom thou well knowest; he at whose
feet Mary, the sister of Lazarus, chose the better
part; he who restored to life Jairus's daughter,
the young man of Nain and Lazarus, even he is
raised from the dead. I am one of his witnesses,
and soon shalt thou be also one of them. Already
have I been his witness, when the Divine Spirit de-
scended on him in the river, and the Father's voice
from the clouds proclaimed him his beloved Son.
These words were spoke with a dignity that seem-
ed to border on glorification. Swift he turned, and
ascended, while from his vesture issued radiations

which insensibly decreased, till the prophet disappeared.

Now arose on Judah's hill the fifth morn since the resurrection. Radiant it rose, the harbinger of the brightest day. Portia awoke, but rather from unquiet dreams than refreshing sleep, and early walked in her garden; though lost to her was all its fragrance. I have lived, said she, to see another morning, yet in my sad mind still reigns perpetual night; for there, O thou Giver of life! arises no lucid day. Perplexed by continual dreams I awoke, and lay panting to know Thee, and Him whom his sepulchre no longer detains. Ah when my last sun declines, will it then also be night with me? Oh enlighten me! I shall not be dismayed by the terrors of death, when thou enlightenest me with thy light. Thy will, O thou Supreme! be done. This thought has oft composed my troubled soul, and shall be my refuge in this distress. Repose thyself on the divine will, O my soul! and dismiss thine eager desires.—But why do I delay seeking comfort, where a faint glimmering from afar seems to intimate, that at the sepulchre there may be some who lament his death, and are able to resolve my doubts?

Portia, then beckoning to a servant to attend her, set out for the sepulchre. In their way to it he was seen by Rachel and Jemima, the daughter of Job, who were holding sweet converse. She whom we expected is coming, said Jemima, and is striving to rise above the clouds in which she is involved. Let us give her our assistance. They instantly assumed the appearance of two Greek female pilgrims, who had come to the feast. They had slender staves in their hands, and their hair was bound with a purple ribbon. Portia walking

slow, immersed in thought, they passed by her;
on which the Roman lady said; Pray stay, pilgrims,
ye are hasting with melancholy looks to that sepul-
chre; did you know him who lately lay there?
Who art thou that thus questionest us? said one
of them. If thou art a Roman, leave us to our-
selves, and do not insult us. To insult innocence
and piety, said the lady, is to insult the Most High,
who dwells in the heavens. Though I am the
wife of Pilate, I should think myself base, could
I insult you, or ridicule your devotion. Has the
report reached you, that he whom the sepulchre
contained is risen from the dead? Jemima an-
swered, Thou speakest of Jesus in terms very
different from those of any idolater; hence thou
deservest to be informed, and we shall converse
with thee, with the most open simplicity and can-
dour. What we know is more than report. My
companion has seen one of the devout to whom he
has appeared since his resurrection.

Tell me, O happy woman! said Portia, what
she saw! Is she still in this world of trouble, or is
she removed to a better life?

Mary Magdalen, for that is the name of the high-
ly favoured woman, is still living, said Rachel:
She had sought him in the open sepulchre, and was
weeping till the day beginning to break, she ima-
gined that she saw the gardener. But how can I
describe her joy; then turning towards him, she
heard his well known voice, which called her by
her name! she sunk down to the earth, and trem-
bling cried, Rabboni! Weeping she lay, and kis-
sed his feet.—Oh forbear! said Portia; the joy
I feel will be too great. How hast thou relieved
my anguish! He has appeared and called Mary
by her name! Oh most transcendant joy! Who
can conceive the bliss he imparted to her? Bring

her to me, that amidst my sorrow, I may raise my
languid head, and weeping admire her. For amidst
the stream of joy with which she is overflowed, per-
haps not a drop will be my portion. I am not of
Abraham's race, but a Roman. The Conqueror
of death will only appear to the favoured daugh-
ters of Jerusalem. Oh why is not a triumph
decreed for him! A triumph with which Jerusa-
lem should resound, and Sion and the lofty temple
shake! Why are not the statutes of your ancestors
carried before him in August procession? Those
of Abraham, Daniel, Job, Moses, and that of the
intrepid David, who slew the giant, and from the
neck of the suffering people shook the yoke of Phi-
listia? Why do not the multitudes by him restored,
the lame whom he made to walk, the deaf whom he
made to hear, the blind on whose eyes he poured
the day, and the dead whom he restored to life,
march in triumph?—But how I forget myself!
His kingdom, I am told he himself said, is not of
this world.

Here Portia was silent, and laying aside her
wishes for an empty triumph, like those that were
the rewards of bloodshed and slaughter, her thoughts
were raised to the contemplation of his kingdom in
the world to come. Jemima now seeing her serene
gravity, while she continued intent on sublime
meditations, was so affected as almost to forget that
the object of her admiration was a mortal. The
beauty of the rosy evening glowed on her cheek,
and a divine smile sat on her countenance: but on
Portia's turning to her, she instantly resumed the
form of a pilgrim, and looking at her with a
gratulatory smile, said, How do I rejoice at thy
contemplations on the world to come, and on the
vain triumphs of this perishing earth being too
trifling for the Lord of Glory. Thou shalt no

more be the sport of error ; the dead is risen, and the witnesses themselves will, perhaps, assure thee, that they have seen the Lord, the Conqueror of death: Assure me ! softly breathed Portia, with joyful accent. Ye doubts vanish from her mind, resumed Jemima, laying her hand on the lady's forehead. The Eternal Sovereign, who from the beginning has been the bliss of the heavenly kingdom, be thy God ! May he who created thee be thy Redeemer ! Tears flowed from the eyes of Portia, while the immortal thus blessed her : but soon recovering her speech, she returned. Instruct me who thou art whether an highly favoured mortal, or one of the heavenly race who appear to men. Instruct me what I shall do. Oh lead me to God ! Rachel, with composed voice, said, Hast thou been informed, O Portia ! that many of the dead have risen with Jesus ? That at his resurrection they came forth from their graves, and appeared to the pious who were his disciples. O let me overcome my amazement, and recollect my thoughts ! returned the lady. Is he risen ? and are others of the dead raised from their graves ? O that I might behold such wonders !—We, Portia, will lead thee, resumed Rachel. Seek not those who have seen Christ, for when he pleases he will send them to thee. In Galilee he will appear to others besides the first witnesses ; but in Jerusalem to the first alone. In all countries are these first fruits to make known what he did and taught, and joyfully shall these first witnesses confirm their testimony with their blood. Then at the throne of the great Rewarder, shall their fidelity receive its eternal recompence. Do thou haste to Galilee, and if thou dost not there see him, he will send to thee some of those whom he particularly favours. We must now leave thee.

These words were softened by a smile of cordial
affection.

O I entreat ye, in the name of the most Gracious
God, who has also shewn favour to me, cried Por-
tia, not yet to leave me. But say, oh say, who are
ye ? A sensation such as I never felt before, elevates
my conceptions, and powerfully intimates to me
that ye are immortals ; but fain would I know it
from yourselves ; for then no cloud will darken the
dawning day which rises in my mind ; and may
God reward you with celestial knowledge !

With transport they looked at each other, and
resolved to stay, saying, We will farther teach thee
to offer up thy petitions to heaven. Then kneeling,
they repeated the Lord's prayer. No sooner had
they concluded, than, lifting up her hands to hea-
ven, she called out, and thine, O God, is the glory!
when instantly they were encompassed by a celes-
tial effulgence; and the pilgrims rose radiant in the
air among the shadowy palms, looking back with
affectionate smiles on Portia, rejoicing in her silent
joy. She remained kneeling, and, unable to rise,
stretched out her arms towards them. Jemima
soon disappeared, but Rachel awhile delayed.
Down Portia's florid cheeks streamed her lively
joy, and, light as the leaf raised by a cheerful gale,
she rose from the earth, crying, Father, thine is
the kingdom, the power, and the glory. Amen !
Thus praying, she hasted back to the gates of
Jerusalem.

Beor, a person of a gloomy mind, had retired
from society, and plunged himself in solitude. The
industrious artizan starts cheerfully from his bed at
the dawn ; but he broke off his short sleep at
unseasonable midnight, and sat in his narrow man-
sion by a glimmering light, like that of a sepulchral
lamp. There must be misery, said he, and there-

Jemima soon disapeared. &c.

Page 446.

fore some must be miserable. This is decreed by
heaven, and we are obliged to bear it. But why
are some excused from suffering this general lot, and
others, like me, ruled with a rod of iron? Was
not I born blind; and did I not long live in blind-
ness? 'Tis true, Jesus gave day to my eyes, and to
my soul imparted a glimmering of himself, yet is
this now turned to night, for he is dead—. Dread-
ful night! What avails the eye's transient day,
when the soul wanders in a gloom dark as the
valley of death? O my eyes, lose your sight! ye
can no longer enjoy a view of the creation, nor re-
joice in the radiant beams which vivify Sharon's
flowers, and the cedars of God! More dark is now
my blind soul, than before were these eyes! For,
O ye angels, he is dead.

While he was thus giving vent to his lamentations,
a man bowed down with age came in, and thus dis-
coursed with him, O Beor! hand me thy cup.
More years have passed over my head, and much
greater have been my sufferings. Greater suffer-
ings than mine! answered Beor. Thou art indeed
much older: take then my cup; for I can more
easily stoop to the brook. The stranger then asked
for food; and Beor, shewing him bread, bad him
take and eat. O Beor! said the old man, it gives
me pleasure to find thee kind to others, though thou
hardenest thy heart against thyself. I know thee,
Beor; for I was present when the creation was first
exposed to thy view.

If thou knowest me, said Beor, thou knowest
the most sorrowful of men. The most sorrowful,
as it is beyond my power to remove the cause of my
dejection. Alas! a wretchedness like mine would
dispirit the most chearful. Was not I born blind?
and did I not thus continue during the most valua-

ble part of life ? Besides, is not my mental blind-
ness still greater, with respect to the knowledge of
him whom God sent to perform the gracious mira-
cle ? and will his death enlighten me 'with new
knowledge ? Speak now, Didst thou ever know sor-
ror like mine ? Have I not reason to fear that my
being wretched from my birth is a proof that I
shall be perpetually wretched? for unremitting pain
is a presage of that to come.

Did not he, said the stranger, when thou didst
least expect it, unveil to thee the porch of the sanctu-
ary, this splendid earth ; its fulness of blessings,
with its irradiating sun ? Thus he gave thee great-
er joy than was ever felt by any who had always
enjoyed their sight; and will not He, who is the
Son of the Eternal, open to thee the future world ?
Would this, Beor, be likewise wretchedness and
the punishment of sin ? The God of Glory will
pour his beams on thee ; Jesus will display them to
thy mind ; for from thy birth thou wast chosen to
be one of his witnesses. Such have been the deter-
minations of the Eternal.

Beor exclaimed, Thou leadest me into new depths
of inquietude. Leave me as I am, sunk deep in
the abyss in which I lie ! Wert thou even an an-
gel of light, I would ask thee, how thou, though
an immmortal, knowest the hidden secrets of the
Most High ? can any thing more exceed the
verge of human enquiry, than thine assertion, that
the Almighty makes wretchedness a prelude to
felicity.

Is there then, O thou doubter, said the stranger,
no everlasting reward ? And has not this eternal re-
ward successive degrees rising to the heaven of
heavens ? Cannot God, cannot the immense Giver
of every good, amply recompense sufferings under-

gone for his sake? Thou standest on the ocean and one small drop, thou particle of dust, can satiate thee!

Venerable old man, said Beor, thou revivest my heart. But, if such are God's dispensations, how dare I so far presume as to think myself one of the blessed, whom God loads with afflictions that they may receive a glorious, an inconceivable reward?

Thou art one of those! resumed the stranger, who was the patriarch Job. This I know. Soon wilt thou know it thyself. I already see the crimson blushes of the morning, bringing on an effulgent day. Let us ere it comes, kneel, that the Lord may find us praying. They sunk down and Beor cried, O Lord God merciful and gracious! if I am chosen to be afflicted, that thy mercy to me may be more illustrious, with a thankful heart, will I raise my head—with thanks—with thanks to heaven that thou hast covered my eyes with blindness, and my soul with the gloom of night! For these mercies will I give thee eternal thanks! Then shall my soul rise with triumphant joy, that thou O God hast shewn such mercy! O thou Preserver of men! shall the darkness of my soul soon pass away?—O hope! O new and heaven taught hope! dost thou spring from the Lord? Praised, O Father! praised be thy glorious name for this bounty so full of grace! O Lord God merciful and gracious! eternally blessed be thy glorious name! thou madest me blind from my birth, thou hast sent me sufferings and tears, as divine messengers to instruct me! Thou hast sent me perplexity, doubts, and melancholy, that I might have a more inward, a more humble sense of thy help!—But shall not I also thank thee, O Jesus, the Sent of God, the Helper in Judah!

Alas ! added he, lowering his voice, he is dead.
—He lives ! He lives ! exclaimed Job, hastily
rising from his knees covered with glory, He lives !
and as a witness that he lives, I Job, am raised
from the dead !   Dost thou not believe that I have
undergone greater sufferings than thee ? and whom
did I find to pity me ?

Beor strove in vain to raise his folded hands
to heaven. As Moses on the day of battle lift
up his arms while victory prevailed, and defeat
attended their sinking, so Job kindly held up those
of Beor, then joyfully took leave of him, who
silently viewed him with a look of deep amaze-
ment, Job crying, Lo ! he was dead, but now
liveth for evermore, and soon shall he ascend into
the Heaven of heavens !   Here with solemn ges-
ture he pointed with his radiant hand to heaven,
adding, He himself has thus spoken of thee, He
was not born blind on account of his own future
sins, nor the past sins of his parents ; but to shew
forth the glory of God.   Thus he left Beor, who
could scarce support his joy.

Abraham and Moses soared to the roof of the
temple; and looking down with intent eye on those
who had resorted to the feast, to find one to whom
they should appear.   They observed Saul a young
man whose heart was filled with fervent devotion,
standing by one of the pillars.   His eyes beamed
a fire sacred to Him who liveth and reigneth for
ever.   To this young man Moses and Abraham
chose to appear, and the service of the temple being
ended, they moved to attend him, when Gabriel
hasting from Tabor's cloud capped summit, with
effulgent flight, met them, and said; Ye fathers
forbear ; for to him the Lord himself will appear.
Who, thou divine messenger, said they, is that
exalted mortal with whom we are forbid to con-

verse: Yonder lies Damascus, said Gabriel, and thither; O distressed church of God! will he, thine enraged persecutor, hasten. About him will he gather troops that will second his rage with unremitted fury; when lo! a sudden light from heaven will encompass him. He will see the Lord whom he persecuted: he will be convinced of his error, and will become a zealous disciple of the Redeemer.

Gabriel ceased, and Abraham lifting up his hands, cried, O thou Accomplisher of all things! to thy name all in heaven, on earth, and under the earth, shall bow, and every tongue confess thee to be Lord, to the glory of God the Father! Their inward extasy suppressed their farther speech; till at length Moses thus blessed the future disciple. The love of Christ and of the brethren reign in thee. Be thou enabled to cast down the powers that rise against the Lord. Be learned as man; be learned as an angel. Let love likewise dwell in thee; love like that of Christ, which is more valuable than the knowledge of mysteries dark and obstruse. The love of the brethren, which is mild, patient and kind, without envy or pride; which no longer disturbs; which seeketh not her own; is not easily provoked; thinketh no evil; rejoices in the truth: beareth all things, endureth all things, hopeth all things. This love be thine, the last born of grace among the holy messengers to whom Christ himself appears. Those who thus love shall be the members of the church above; the spotless, the irreproachable church which is the bride of the Lamb, and washed in his blood; in that blood which cries louder than that of Abel, but not for vengeance; which calls louder than the hosts of Cherubim from Sinai, and all the thunders and trumpets of the

mount of terror, but not for revenge. The patri-
archs then soared up to Tabor.

Elkanan, Simeon's brother, together with his
child-like guide, had, on the mournful evening
when they left the mossy tomb, gone to Samma, who,
though a gloomy cloud hung over his agitated
mind, received them with cordial friendship, which,
with his pressing intreaties, induced thee to stay.
As yet the report of Christ's resurrection was not
confirmed, which Elkanan, Boaz, and Joel lament-
ed. They sat in Joel's fragrant arbour, in the gar-
den which his father had given him, and imagined
that the effusions of their grief were only heard by
the moon in her nightly course ; but other hearers
had assembled in a silver cloud : these were Simeon,
Benoni, and Mary the sister of Lazarus. The la-
mentations of the afflicted being stopped by over-
powering grief, Benoni said, I can no longer forbear
making myself known to my father and my brother.
Have they not, said Simeon, drank enough of the
bitter cup of affliction ? are they not within reach
of the goal, and shall we not bring them the crown ?
—Yes, we will, Benoni. O Mary ! follow us
unseen, and thus partake of the delight of behold-
ing their joy. Do thou, Benoni, invest thyself in
a milder lustre, that they may not faint under the
transporting vision. They then moved downward.

The afflicted Samma now said, I was at my son's
sepulchre, thou at Simeon's : ah ! had we but
been at the sepulchre of Jesus, we might, perhaps,
if he be risen, have seen him rise—But, O, most
gracious God ! what lustre is that, which at a dis-
tance shines with such splendor ? O Lord God,
merciful and gracious, continued he, behold it is a
messenger from heaven !—What dost thou see ?
said Elkanan. What seest thou, Joel ? Lead

me, that I may speak to the shining appearance.
Tell me, what dost thou see? The form of a beauti-
ful youth, said Boaz, walking under the trees, and
smiling at us.—Thou bright appearance! cried
Elkanan, Who art thou? A messenger of greater
and more exalted salvation than thou canst conceive,
said the resplendent form—Ah! what voice is that?
and what face is that I see? It is Benoni! cried
Joel, sinking down. Benoni instantly stretched
forth his helping hand, and raised him up, crying,
My brother!—Joel stammered forth his joy, cry-
ing out, My brother! my heavenly brother!

Here Joel called out, O Samma, my father! and
inclining on the old man's breast, kept up the flame
of the vital lamp, and preserved him from fainting
under his tearless extasy. He then led the old man
to a mossy seat. Elkanan seated himself by him,
saying, Now shall I go down in peace to the grave;
for though mine eyes have not seen thee, O thou
blessed immortal! mine eyes have heard thy voice.
Speak, oh speak to us, thou messenger of God!—
One greater will teach thee, said Benoni, when thou
art more composed, and able to support his pre-
sence.

While they were speaking, Joel silently approach-
ed, and gathering flowers, strewed them on his bro-
ther's steps, when Benoni, looking at him with
a pleased eye, said Art thou able to support thyself
till Simeon appears? Does then Simeon's soul, cried
Elkanan, hover near me? Be strong in the Lord
Boaz, Samma, and Joel. Soon shall mine ear hear
thee, my brother. Simeon, Simeon, come! Mine
eyes, my dear brother, cannot see thee: but soon I
shall, when having passed through the night of
death, I shall awake in light!

Invested with celestial splendor came Simeon, ad-
vancing through the mild lustre of the moon. With

less terror they beheld his radiant form, than Beno-
ni's unexpected brightness, and with great astonish-
ment heard these important, words proceed from his
lips. Jesus is risen from the dead ! and by his al-
mighty power many of the righteous came forth
from their graves ! He appears, and we also ap-
pear ; but to those only whom he calls to work mi-
racles, and to obtain the first celestial crowns and
palms ! Yet the Redeemer ascends to his father's
throne in triumph, and with the sound of a trumpet,
to no less than five hundred believers will he shew
himself at once. May ye be among the number !
May the Lord bless you with this favour !

Simeon, said Elkanan, art thou risen before the
great decisive day ? Ah how my heart pants to see
thee ! But Jesus himself, O worse than blindness,
I shall not see. But my sorrow be dumb, from the
sacred hour in which Simeon sees, and converses
with me on Jesus, and his glory, be all complainings
banished. Five hundred at once ! How should
I rejoice were I present, and to hear, their trans-
ports ! Mayest thou Simeon discourse of thy heaven
and its glories !

Not to those, said Simeon, who dwell in the dust.
Such is the order of him who exalts and rewards
according to the trial : who has separated worlds
from worlds, and yet united them : who in his in-
finite plan of consummate salvation, has united all
the bounds of felicity : but compared to the bright
display of the happiness of spirits, the sensitive crea-
tion is but a shadow. The Most High builds on
wretchedness towering joys—joys to the very bless-
ed unknown. Yet learn that all eternity cannot
exhibit any thing more astonishing, more incon-
ceiveable, than that one of the heights of the Me-
diator's exaltation, has humiliation for its base !
But pry not into the important thought, which fills

the angels with wonder! Know he whole of that
happiness which God at present gives you; the
pure soul of Mary is present, and rejoices in your
joy.

Here all with one voice cried out, Is the sister
of Lazarus dead? and does she rejoice in our joy?
We, Mary, added Samma, also rejoice in thine.
How have ye, blessed messengers, dried up our
tears! O Almighty Father! thou sendest to me
my Benoni! to Elkanan his brother! and to
Joel his dear brother! added that affectionate
youth.

O God! cried Samma, what a conclusion hast
thou given to my grief! How could I ever pre-
sume to entertain such hopes! When my gloomy
melancholy, that woe of woes, began, sensible of
my wretchedness, all around me was darkness, per-
plexity, and an unfathomable abyss. Futurity
itself was a group of sable terrors! Now rouse
thyself, O reason! Thou, my dear child! I
dashed against the rock, stained with thy blood!
Till this happy morning I expected to mourn the
unnatural deed during my remaining life! Yet
this ends in celestial joy—in the most blissful
meeting ever known! O Benoni! my son Benoni!
who wast bruised by the bloody rock, how great
has been the mercy of our heavenly Father to thee!
How great his mercy to me, who, through thee,
has shewn me such favours! I know that thou
art going to leave me; yet thy going will not be
a departure; for I shall ever have thee in mine
eyes, arrayed as now, in celestial glory, an heir
of heaven. But one request I have to make
thee, O Benoni! give me thy blessing.—I, Samma,
bless thee! said Benoni, the son, the father! and
thy youngest son!—My first-born now, returned
Samma, and elder than I—elder in the days of

eternity ! For thine is real life ! This is but a sleep, to which our last awakens us !

Benoni then with uplifted hands, and his radiance increasing as he spake, said, Ah soon may thy last day come, and gentle and soft as Simeon's dying day !

Joel then added, I would likewise ask thy blessing, did I not fear that thou wouldst bless me with length of days.

That O youth, cried Benoni, is fearing a great reward. The deeper a life of goodness strikes its root here, the higher shoots its top in heaven, and the wider spreads its leafy branches. Say, shall I now, my Joel, my brother, bless thee ? Joel kneeling, Benoni laid his hand on his glowing forehead, saying, Receive the blessing of blessings, Eternal life be thine ! May God, who raised Jesus from the dead, lead thee to him ! They then disappeared ; on which Boaz cried, O Elkanan, they are vanished ! and Joel rising, thus expressed his grateful joy : O spotless spirit of Mary ! shouldst thou still remain on earth, convey to them our most lowly and most fervent thanks for their gracious appearance to us, their heavenly discourse, and inestimable blessings. Thus spake the youth and sunk into his father's arms.

The mother of Jesus was sitting on the lofty roof, with the sacred harp by her side. The sun was set, and the evening star cheered the serene firmament, When behind the brook she beheld the appearance of a female pilgrim, who soon assuming an etherial form, soared aloft, and in celestial lustre alighted on the roof, close by her. Amazement had now no longer place in the mind of the blessed Mary. She was sensible that it was either an angel, or a person raised from the dead ; for she had seen the risen body of her Son.—To thee, the mother of the Lord, said the bright appearance, I do not veil myself : for thou wilt soon shine with me before the throne ! I too, Mary, am a mother—the mother of the obedient Abraham ; of the heavenly Enoch, who was exempted from lying in the grave. I am even she who brought forth the Restorer of Innocence: I am the mother of mankind. And hither am I come to join with thee in praise of thy Son, the great Emanuel.

Mary and Eve, with alternate answers and replies, thus continued the discourse : I see, O joy unutterable ! the mother of Abel and of Cain ? But can I, O thou immortal !—Can I who have not tasted of death, sing with the mother of men ? But the Redeemer is the subject of our song. Begin then O Eve ! and teach me to of sing my exalted Son.

Twice was I created by his power ! He who was born of thee called me twice into life ! He, O mother ! was born, who created both thee and me, and who formed the heavens !

He who created the sun, the moon, and the stars, and formed even thee and me. O Eve ! was born. This was the hymn sung by the angels of God, when he was born in a stable.

When the procession chanting hymns of praise, returned to heaven, the top of the tree of life waved, and the celestial spirits bowed in reverence to the new-born babe.

He cried in a manger at Bethlehem. Yet before he wept, the angels had proclaimed his name, and called him Jesus. The cedars and the palms heard the name of Jesus ! Tabor, and thou bloody Golgotha, heard the name of Jesus !

The throne from which the Lord's anointed descended, and all the host of heaven, kneeling, heard his name !

O thou mother of men ! didst thou see my holy Son expire ! Didst thou hear him cry, It is finished ! Didst thou hear him exclaim, O Father ! into thine hands I commend my spirit !

Ah I heard the words of eternal life ! I heard the players on the harps chanting forth the praises of the exalted Redeeemer, when raising his head, he cried, it is finished ! and when lifting up his eyes to heaven, he added, Father into thine hands I commend my spirit !

Praise be to my Son who gave me to mourn ? Behold the hours of anguish are now become the subject of my joy ! Blessed am I, who brought forth the Redeemer ! Blessed art thou, the mother of those he has redeemed !

Blessed am I, formed in Paradise from a bone of Adam ! My dust has he awakened ! I am the mother of the redeemed, and thy mother, O Mary !

O thou first daughter of the creation, the risen daughter of the eternal life ! from thee is descended the Eternal, whom Mary, a mortal, brought forth in a stable ! O thou parent of his mother ! celestial joys flow in upon me ! I sink in a flood of light ! He has blessed me, and made me the heiress of heavenly felicity ! Before my hymn for my Beloved's benediction ascends to the throne, once more shall I see him in these fields of death ! I have seen the resplendent Gabriel who has told me that I shall once more behold him ! O mother of Abraham, and my mother ! sing thy Son's resurrection, when his head no longer sunk down on the lofty cross ; his eyes were no longer closed, his temples no longer pressed by the bloody crown ?

When the thunder of God's omnipotent voic-

once more proclaimed, Let there be light, and there
was light, then he arose!   Then sunk our harps :
then sunk our palms.   We shouted hallelujahs to
God the Mediator! our hallelujahs ascended like
the roaring of the sea.   Then the heavens and the
earth were silent, till the martyrs sang triumphant
hymns ; and soon Adam descending to the Media-
tor, thus addressed him with an expressive voice,
I swear by thee who liveth forever, that on the
great day of the completion of all things, those
who sleep shall awake and death shall be no more !

Ah his joyful call shall penetrate the partner in
his inheritance !   Strew my grave with the flowers
of the harvest. The seed sown by the Lord shall
shoot forth and flourish !.

. Soon, O Mary ! shalt thou lie down in the sleep
of death, that I may receive the mother of the Lord
in the vale of peace ! In that blissful vale we may
sing the Son who now from his throne dries up the
tears of Christians, and silences the soft complain-
ings of sorrow !   Behold He who bore the sins of
the world is love !   He who took on him the griefs
of Adam, and hung on Calvary, is love !   He is
love, who unknown and despised, gave himself up
to die as a sacrifice—as a sacrifice for sin, while
the archangels themselves were struck dumb with
wonder !

Thus they sang. Eve then departed, and Mary's
wondering eyes long followed her effulgent flight
towards Tabor.

The holy band now began to return to the mount
of transfiguration, there to rejoice together in the
joy they, by their appearance, had infused into the
hearts of mortals.   As when twilight gives place to
approaching night, the stars successively come forth
from the immense creation, so assembled those re-
splendent beings, and gradually over-spread the
sacred mount.

Cidli, Jarus's daughter, sat in an arbour on the
roof of the house where she lived, observing the
lustre of the rosy dawn. She had not seen her be-
loved Semida, since he left her to visit his former
grave. O guiltless love ! said she, for so I dare
call thee, when wilt thou leave me ? If I was rais-
ed from the dead, that I might solely consecrate
myself to God, O love, to me all pain, yet full of
innocence ! why dost thou stay with thine unremit-
ting softness ! But if I am not raised to consecrate
myself entirely to my Maker, how shall I know it ?
Who will deliver me from this maze of doubt ?

Cidli was then joined by one who appeared to be
a female pilgrim that came to the feast, and had
been conducted to the roof by her mother. The
pilgrim began, I have been seeking one of those
who have testified the glory of Jesus : who, while
in his state of abasement, raised to life the brother
of Mary, the young men of Nain, and thyself.
Thou hast heard of thine awakener's triumph over
death ; but has the reproach reached thine ear,
that many saints arose after his expiring on the cross,
and appeared to the righteous, who love him ? I
love him—I love him, O pilgrim ! cried Cidli, Is
this report really true ? It will not be long, returned
the pilgrim, before thou wilt be convinced by thine
own experience. 'Tis said, that the righteous who
are risen, will assemble on the mount of trans-
figuration, and I will join the sacred assembly,
with thee, who hast been raised from the dead. I,
O pilgrim ! said Cidli, have been raised from the
dead ; but am still mortal. Yet will I go with thee.
Should we see any bright apparitions, thou wilt
support my sinking spirits. The mother, Cidli,
and the pilgrim then set out for Tabor.

Semida had by his meditations and his assiduous
inquires after the Redeemer's resurrection overcome
his doubts, and his heart rested in the firm belief of

that glorious event, so rich in blessings. His love now returned, and Cidli appearing created for him, his tenderness took possession of all his powers. I am in the midst of darkness, cried he, and who will lead me through it ? How shall I be certain, that my dearest Cidli, whom I love with a celestial flame, returns my passion ? Who will lead me to the lucid summit of joy, or sink me into the vale of sorrow ?—But be still my grief. Yet how strange is my fate ! In the bloom of active life, I fell a victim to death. On my being again permitted to breathe the vital air, I imagined myself immortal ; but how was I mistaken ! I found myself unhappy in not having exerted the utmost ardour in learning wisdom from him who died and rose again, that I might render it a seed for a blessed harvest, when time shall be no more. O, thou who art raised from the dead ! before thou ascendest to the Father, call me to thee, that I may learn more of what thou hast termed the one thing necessary ?

Here a stranger hastily coming up, said, O young man ! it is in thy power to assist me. Above the foot of mount Tabor, lies a man who appears grievously wounded by robbers. In the way sits one who seems blind and perishing with thirst, while no spring is near. In the way to him lies an old man, who, spent with fatigue, has fallen, and lies groaning on the rock. Pity also my weakness and thirst.

Semida, with generous warmth, cried, Here is something for thyself, and the others. The rest of my store I'll reserve for the old man, who shall be my care. Go thou to the blind.

Semida advancing to the old man, gave him bread, and the refreshing juice of the vine. Then raising him up, went to the pilgrim, to assist him in succouring the blind, and promising to re-

turn and conduct him to Jerusalem, hasted forward
to ascend the mountain, light as the breath of the
early dawn : but had scarce passed its foot, when
he perceived Cidli between her mother and the pil-
grim. A torrent of mingled joy and timidity rushed
upon his mind, yet he proceeded with his unknown
guide, who brought him to the man who had been
wounded, and lay a dismal spectacle, pale and
covered with blood. They were binding up his
wounds ; when Semida turning, saw Cidli approach,
and she observing him employed in affording re-
lief to the wounded traveller, with a mixture of
joy and melancholy, trembling passed by. Semida
with tremulous eagerness ran after her ; but on his
overtaking her, the passions that affected their
minds obstructed their speech, and they stood
gazing at each other in silence. When the female
pilgrim bidding her not to stay, Semida cried,
Must I again so soon part with my Cidli ? She
then returning no other answer but a flood of tears,
followed her guide.

Semida, with his companion, remained comfort-
ing the wounded traveller. Meanwhile two men,
his brothers, came up, and all three expressing their
warmest thanks for Semida's humanity, he, with the
kindest wishes, took his leave.

In proceeding up the mountain, said the stranger,
we will take a shorter way than they have chosen,
and will meet them at the summit. I will accom-
pany thee, said Semida ; but wilt thou return
back with me ? The stranger answering that he
should not return, Semida desired to know where
he lived, on which the other returned that blissful
was his home, and that heavenly friends expected
him there. Talk not then of poverty, said Semida,
since thou hast valuable friends to gladden thy
life : let me know their names. The stranger

with a look of complacency, said, these are some
of my friends, and then mentioned several of the
patriarchs and worthies of Israel. Semida viewed
him with astonishment, and this was greatly in-
creased, when instantly he beheld his face glow
with celestial beauty, and become resplendent.
The more this increased, the more did a mixture
of joy and fear spread paleness on Semida's cheeks:
but his immortal friend supported his trembling
steps.

In the other path, the female pilgrim, who was
cheerfully followed by the mother of Cidli, sud-
denly stopping and turning to her, said, My worthy
friend, follow me no farther; for they only who
are raised from the dead, are allowed to appear
at the Messiah's triumph. Must I then, said
she, part from my Cidli, from whom I have never
yet been separated? Oh soon, my heavenly daugh-
ter, return, and rejoice thy mother, by relating
what thou shalt now see. God grant that the
glories thou wilt behold, may heal all thine in-
quietudes. Return towards Salem, said Megiddo
the pilgrim, to the mother; for thou wilt not soon
see again thy happy daughter. My dear mother!
said Cidli, May the Lord be thy guide. Thou
heavenly friend, let me soon return to embrace my
mother!

They tenderly embraced, and then parting, the
weeping eyes of the afflicted mother long followed
them. As they drew near the summit of the
mountain, Cidli, while absorbed in silent astonish-
ment, saw at a distance in a grove of cedars, Semida
with his companion, who now shone with all his
splendor. Semida likewise perceived her. The
two mortals stopt, walked forward, trembled and
stopped again, while on either side radiant beings
smiling, gathered round them. Oh how bright

though yet unknown, shone the old man, the blind, and the wounded traveller with his brethren ! The celestials around them increased in number and effulgence. No words can express the transports of the loving pair. They gazed around filled with wonder, then downward casting their humble eyes, strove to speak, but their trembling words stopped in the midst of their broken utterance. How great was their joy and fear when environed by the ineffable splendor, and the soft, sweet-sounding benedictions of the immortals near them ! They approached each other. Then expressed their thoughts, and, happy pair ! their glorification began and was soon complete. They then flew into each others embraces; now no longer liable to a separation. To meet again, O thou loving ! to meet again, when with the dust of one the dust of the other rests ! was Cidli's thought ; but it was only a dream of Cidli's joy. She now shed other tears ; but it was only for Semida's joy she wept.

THE END OF THE FIFTEENTH BOOK.

Lightning Source UK Ltd.
Milton Keynes UK
UKHW011935061218
333598UK00010B/595/P